JEFFREY R. PARSONS

SERIES: IDEAS, DEBATES AND PERSPECTIVES

Cotsen Institute of Archaeology
Ideas, Debates and Perspectives

Settlement, Subsistence, and Social Complexity marks the first book in our new series that focuses on cross-disciplinary themes relevant to archaeology and the study of ancient societies.

Volume 1   *Settlement, Subsistence, and Social Complexity*, edited by Richard E. Blanton

SETTLEMENT, SUBSISTENCE, AND SOCIAL COMPLEXITY:

ESSAYS HONORING THE LEGACY OF JEFFREY R. PARSONS

EDITED BY
RICHARD E. BLANTON

COTSEN INSTITUTE OF ARCHAEOLOGY
UNIVERSITY OF CALIFORNIA, LOS ANGELES
2005

THE COTSEN INSTITUTE OF ARCHAEOLOGY at UCLA is a research unit at the University of California, Los Angeles that promotes the comprehensive and interdisciplinary study of the human past. Established in 1973, the Cotsen Institute is a unique resource that provides an opportunity for faculty, staff, graduate students, research associates, volunteers and the general public to gather together in their explorations of ancient human societies.

Former President and CEO of Neutrogena Corporation Lloyd E. Cotsen has been associated with UCLA for more than 30 years as a volunteer and donor and maintains a special interest in archaeology. Lloyd E. Cotsen has been an advisor and supporter of the Institute since 1980. In 1999, The UCLA Institute of Archaeology changed its name to the Cotsen Institute of Archaeology at UCLA to honor the longtime support of Lloyd E. Cotsen.

Cotsen Institute Publications specializes in producing high-quality data monographs in several different series, including Monumenta Archaeologica, Monographs, and Perspectives in California Archaeology, as well as innovative ideas in the Cotsen Advanced Seminar Series and the Ideas, Debates and Perspectives Series. Through the generosity of Lloyd E. Cotsen, our publications are subsidized, producing superb volumes at an affordable price.

THE COTSEN INSTITUTE OF ARCHAEOLOGY AT UCLA
Charles Stanish, Director
Julia L. J. Sanchez, Assistant Director and Director of Publications
Shauna Mecartea, Publications Assistant

This book is set in 10-point Janson Text, with titles in 18-point Meridien.
Edited by NOVA Graphic Services
Designed by William Morosi
Cover photograph courtesy of Richard E. Blanton

Library of Congress Cataloging-in-Publication Data

Settlement, subsistence, and social complexity : essays honoring the legacy of Jeffrey R. Parsons / edited By Richard E. Blanton.
   p. cm. -- (Ideas, debates, and perspectives ; 1)
   Includes bibliographical references and index.
   ISBN 1-931745-23-4 (hard cover)
   ISBN 1-931745-20-X (soft cover)
   1. Human territoriality. 2. Land settlement patterns. 3. Ethnoarchaeology. 4. Landscape archaeology. 5. Demographic archaeology. 6. Subsistence economy. 7. Parsons, Jeffrey R. I. Parsons, Jeffrey R. II. Blanton, Richard E. III. Cotsen Institute of Archaeology at UCLA. IV. Series.
   GN491.7.S48 2005
   304.2'3--dc22
                        2005017645

To future generations of survey archaeologists

Acknowledgments

Richard E. Blanton would like to express his gratitude to several people whose contributions and encouragement made this book possible, including Mary Hrones Parsons, who, so far as I know, kept the project a secret from Jeff until the last minute; Richard Ford, then director of the Museum of Anthropology, University of Michigan; and Charles Stanish, Director of the Cotsen Institute of Archaeology. Julia Sanchez, Director of Publications of the Cotsen Institute, provided much assistance and good cheer. Several people have joined me in living and breathing every word of this book, including Shauna Mecartea, Publications Assistant of the Cotsen Institute, and Lane Fargher, who assembled the indexes, and, in the process, discovered errors the rest of us had missed.

Contents

Illustrations and Tables

Figures

Plates

Tables

INTRODUCTION

RICHARD E. BLANTON
Purdue University

MARY HRONES PARSONS
University of Michigan

LUIS MORETT ALATORRE
Universidad Autónoma Chapingo, Mexico

CARLA M. SINOPOLI
University of Michigan

This book honors Jeffrey R. Parsons's career. Its authors acknowledge Jeff's contribution to their discipline through their reported research, which reflects his laudable influence on both archaeological method and research on the pre-Hispanic civilizations of the New World. Here we provide a few comments that go some distance toward documenting and explaining Jeff's impact on anthropological archaeology during a period in which we were striving for a more scientific and anthropological discipline. We found the beginnings of his successful archaeological career from William Sanders's anthropological training and in a geology fieldwork experience that predates Jeff's archaeological training. We were fortunate to find a description of the latter in a tribute to an undergraduate geology professor, which Jeff wrote some years ago and recently published (Parsons 2002). Jeff's ability to learn from this early experience and to translate it into a model of sound research practice for archaeological survey provides insight about the strength of his character and intellect.

THE "GREAT DIVIDE" AND THE DEVELOPMENT OF ARCHAEOLOGICAL SURVEY METHOD

Archaeology experienced a course correction in method and theory beginning roughly a half-century ago that changed the way we do archaeology and how we understand the past. The causes and consequences of the "Great Divide" (Renfrew 1980), between an earlier cultural historical approach, and the orientation of New Archaeology, have been addressed in an abundant reflexive literature that helps us understand why change was thought necessary and how new ideas impacted field methods. One of the most important proposals of the emerging New Archaeology, one carried forward from its foundational sources (e.g., Binford 1964), is that researchers should view human behavior and socio-cultural systems from a spatial perspective. A methodological implication of this approach, as Flannery (1976) put it, is that activity areas, houses, communities, and regions became the relevant units of data collection and analysis for archaeology, replacing a research design that considered archaeological sites mere "layer cakes of discarded sherds" (Flannery 1976: 5). As a consequence, since mid-century, settlement pattern research at the regional scale is one method that has undergone extensive development in epistemology, theory, analytical methods, and field methods (e.g., Alcock and Cherry 2004; Barker and Mattingly 1999–2000; Billman and Feinman 1999; Fish and Kowalewski 1990), which changed how we view the past (e.g., Sabloff 1994: 68). Some of the most creative and productive archaeologists have turned to research that emphasizes settlement pattern method (e.g., Adams 1981; Cowgill 1997; Hole 1987; Jameson et al. 1994; Millon 1973; Willey 1953).

This is not to assert that pre-"divide" archaeology completely ignored the spatial dimensions of human social life, for example, as indicated by the tradition of British Landscape Archaeology (Stoddart 2000; Potter and Stoddart 2001), or Manuel Gamio's research in the Teotihuacan Valley that pioneered a regional approach there (Gamio 1922), among others. But the present settlement pattern archaeology more directly reflects the growing interest in sociocultural process that had its origins in the mid-twentieth-century return of evolutionist and cultural ecological theories to anthropology (e.g., Armillas 1971; Harris 1968: 683–687; Service 1975; Wolf 1976), later supplemented by theory and method originating from human geography (Haggett 1966; Kowalewski 1990; Skinner 1964, 1965; Smith 1976; cf. Nichols 1996: 79–81). Unlike the earlier landscape archaeology, recent settlement pattern research has developed in tandem with processual archaeology, exemplifying its concern to relate method, theory, data, and hypothesis (Fish and Kowalewski 1990; Parsons 1972), and to incorporate methods of cross-regional and temporal comparison for theory testing (e.g., Alcock and Cherry 2004; Blanton et al. 1993; Wright 1986).

For Americanists, Gordon Willey's (1953) famous Virú Valley settlement pattern survey in Peru exerted a strong influence on method (Billman and Feinman 1999), but Basin of Mexico researchers' more recent work provides the methodological foundation for many contemporary projects in various world areas. Urban settlement pattern research traces its origins to René Millon, George Cowgill, and others at Teotihuacan (Millon 1973). While Millon and others surveyed the urban center, William Sanders and his students pioneered a field-by-field survey method for the rural Teotihuacan

Valley that could cover larger areas, using aerial photographs as field guides and as a medium for recording both site locations and environmental and agronomic information (Sanders 1965: 12–13). This was considered the first phase of a long-term survey-based project that would expand our knowledge of demographic and social history in the "Central Mexican Symbiotic Region," an environmentally and economically complex area extending over 20,000 km^2 (Sanders 1956, 1965). Major areas surveyed to date are shown in Figure 1-1. Following up on Sanders's survey, Jeffrey Parsons finalized the development of a regional method for the Basin of Mexico now referred to as "full-coverage survey" (Fish and Kowalewski 1990), and through his synthetic publications, Jeff positioned it as key element of research design for anthropological archaeology (Parsons 1972, 1990). Full-coverage survey aims to systematically record all visible archaeological sites, other archaeological features, and selected environmental and agronomic variables, from naturally identifiable regions hundreds or thousands of square kilometers in area. Site areas and artifact densities are carefully evaluated, making possible the estimation of site populations, and by extension, regional population sizes by period and the reconstruction of long-term regional demographic changes across archaeological periods. Crews who record all sites and features of all archaeological periods laboriously examine survey areas, field by field (requiring that at least some members of each crew have a full knowledge of the ceramic sequence). Sampling methods, such as transects, that might miss key sites are avoided (Parsons 1990).

Parsons's first detailed description of the method is found in his publication of a field-by-field pedestrian survey of the Texcoco Region (1971:16–20; cf. Sanders, Parsons, and Santley 1979: 14–30 for subsequent Basin of Mexico methodology). In Chapter 3 of this volume, Thomas Charlton and Deborah Nichols detail the history of the method as it unfolded in the Teotihuacan Valley survey. As fully developed, full-coverage method uses aerial photographs, usually at a scale of 1:5,000, as field guides and as a medium for data recording. Crews usually consist of five people walking at intervals of 15 m to 100 m, depending on terrain. Since the great majority of sites are not visible on the aerial photographs, this close spacing allows for the discovery of even the smallest sites, such as isolated houses and other small features (e.g., terraces and canal fragments). Site occupational chronology is established by noting the distribution of pottery from different periods on the aerial photographs. Tape measures, compasses, and pacing are used to record mounded buildings, house remains, and other features, and crew leaders take extensive notes on each site describing soil, landscape, land use, and artifact density or other information pertinent to inferring site function. Grab-bag collections of 100 to 200 diagnostic sherds are made over whole areas of small sites, but

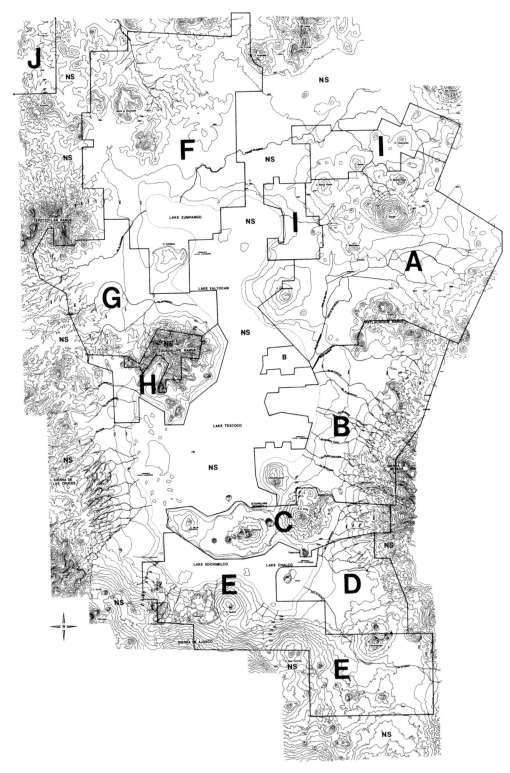

Figure 1-1. The Basin of Mexico Survey areas: (A) Teotihuacan Valley, (B) Texcoco, (C) Ixtapalapa, (D) Chalco, (E) Xochimilco, (F) Zumpango, (G) Cuauhtitlan, (H) Tenayuca, (I) Temascalapa/North Slopes of Cerro Gordo, (J) Tula. Modified from a map by Robert Santley, in Sanders, Parsons, and Santley (1979: map 4). Reprinted with permission from Academic Press and the authors.

Plate 1-1. Surface collecting and note-taking as part of the Otumba Project, Teotihuacan Valley, 1988 (see Chapter 3). Photo courtesy of Thomas Charlton and Deborah Nichols.

in multiple locations on larger sites (Plate 1-1), and are used to confirm field estimations of periodicity. They became the basis of a Basin of Mexico ceramic repository, much of which is now housed at the Museo Nacional de Agricultura, Unversidad Autónoma de Chapingo, available for distributional analyses and other purposes (e.g., Hodge and Minc 1990; cf. Nichols et al. 2002). Full-coverage survey is a highly appropriate method for studying not only many of the demographic, agronomic, scale, and social organizational properties of large complex systems, including urban form and function, rural-urban relations, settlement hierarchies, and craft specialization, among others, but also their changes over long time periods (Nichols 2004).

The success of the Basin of Mexico surveys propelled Millon, Sanders, and Parsons to the forefront of Mesoamerican settlement pattern studies, and this approach has gained recognition far beyond the Basin of Mexico confines. Jeffrey Parsons, in particular, has been a major facilitator of regional archaeology through his research in the Basin of Mexico (1971, 1974; Parsons et al. 1982, 1983), his synthetic and methodological papers (1972, 1990), and his application of similar methods in the Central Andes (Parsons, Hastings, and Matos 2000). Full-coverage method has been replicated as closely as possible by researchers elsewhere in Mesoamerica (the number of projects is too numerous to cite them all here, but see Nichols [1996] for a recent comprehensive review). A few prominent examples illustrating the diffusion of method are surveys in the Valley of Oaxaca (Blanton 1978; Blanton et al. 1982; Kowalewski et al. 1989), the Mixteca Alta and other mountainous uplands of Oaxaca (Balkansky et al. 2000; Finsten 1996), Morelos (Hirth 1980, 2000), and Veracruz (Stark 2003). Outside the semiarid highland Mesoamerica, full-coverage survey methods are typically modified somewhat to adjust to local circumstances, but they have influenced research design in several world areas, for example, in Peru (Stanish 1999; Wilson 1988), various areas of the Mediterranean (e.g., McDonald and Rapp 1972; cf. Cherry 1983), including Turkey (Blanton 2000) and Italy (Potter and Stoddart 2001: 23), in the American Southwest (Fish et al. 1990), and now a growing number of archaeologists working in China are using full-coverage survey methods (e.g., Underhill et al. 2001; cf. Shelach 1999; see Chapter 6).

IMMERSION IN LANDSCAPE, CULTURE, AND METHOD

Three of the authors who wrote this introduction have all learned archaeology from Jeffrey Parsons. For Richard E. Blanton and Mary Hrones Parsons, these experiences go back to the early days in the Teotihuacan Valley and Texcoco regions, and for Luis Morett Alatorre, from his participation in Jeff's most recent project, a survey of the Lake Texcoco lakebed, more than 30 years after Blanton's and Hrones Parsons's first field experiences. What we all gained from working with Jeff is far more than a knowledge of survey techniques. Instead, we assimilated and lived a philosophy of survey archaeology. This entailed a total immersion in the landscape, the pre-Hispanic cultures and societies, and the method. Total immersion sometimes included lengthy weekend trips visiting numerous archaeological sites and museums with Jeff as our tour guide. Some of the sites visited in 1966 and 1967 alone included Teotihuacan, Tula, Xochicalco, Cholula, Malinalco, Tepoztlan, Teoponzalco, Copilco, Cuicuilco, Tenayuca, Tlatelolco, Tlatilco, and El Tajín—what a great archaeological education!

Immersion was required because crewmembers, no matter how junior or inexperienced, were expected to develop into research colleagues who could contribute to the project's goals at a high level of competence and interest. This level of involvement and responsibility motivated crew members to contribute positively to a project's research goals, even in trying conditions, although Jeff's good cheer and self-effacing humor also helped us through the bad times. Perhaps to a greater degree than is true for other archaeological methods, survey archeology done in this way is based on a highly committed and knowledgeable crew's accurate data collection. Members identify sites, call out ceramic identifications, recognize rare objects, estimate ceramic and lithic densities, identify site boundaries, and so on, through a multiplicity of field operations requiring independent and knowledgeable decision makers. While checks and balances confirm important decisions, in order to cover meaningfully large areas, survey method is built around its cadres of highly trained and devoted workers. We are convinced that Jeff's egalitarian mode of field direction infected people with a level of enthusiasm, allowing us to endure the physical hardships and discomforts of survey and return year after year for more of the same!

As he wrote a tribute to his geology professor, Rob Scholten, Jeff began to understand how he could develop this successful model for field research (Parsons 2002). We excerpt some of his thoughts as follows:

"It was not until the mid-1980s that I began to fully realize what had happened. I had blundered into the field of anthropological archaeology precisely at the point when a radical shift was under way, but this radical shift still lacked an effective method for regional survey. From my geological fieldwork with Rob Scholten during the summer of 1960, along the continental divide between Dubois, Idaho and Lima, Montana, I came onto the scene with a good sense of how to do systematic regional survey. From this experience, I sensed what needed to be done at the tactical level, perhaps more clearly than did most archaeologists of that day. In 1960, Rob Scholten had provided me with a clear vision of how to deal systematically with regional data in the field; in 1961, Bill Sanders provided me with the chance to begin to develop appropriate archaeological tactics at the regional level in the Valley of Mexico. It all 'clicked,' one of those cases of having the great fortune to be in the right place at the right time.

"Just as important, Rob Scholten also provided me with a model of how to conduct myself in the field: attention to detail; planning out the daily campaigns; working with maps and air photos; using willpower to overcome the inevitable fatigue and lethargy; coping with tough living and working conditions; looking past present discomforts to future results; respecting the interests of local inhabitants and enlisting them to the extent they might wish as willing participants; regarding students and other assistants as younger colleagues in the research enterprise fully deserving of respect and encouragement. Plus, of course, the importance of taking a little time off to smell the roses."

The above addresses Jeffrey Parsons's contributions in archaeological field contexts, and if asked to describe his career, Jeff would undoubtedly define himself primarily as a field archaeologist. However, his archaeological life has two other important components: his roles as university professor at the University of Michigan's Department of Anthropology and as museum curator at the University of Michigan's Museum of Anthropology, where he has served as curator of Latin American archaeology. As already observed, Jeff views fieldwork as a teaching opportunity, welcoming and nurturing young scholars in their transition from students to full colleagues. He has long brought the same supportive environment to his teaching and curation roles at the University of Michigan, where he has taught since 1966. Throughout this time, Jeff has taught a range of undergraduate and graduate courses on Mexican and Andean archaeology, on regional survey methods, and on theoretical approaches to the study of state emergence and the development of social and political complexity. In addition, he served on numerous doctoral committees, including on those of many of this volume's contributors. In his typically understated way, he has provided cogent guidance and suggestions to several generations of graduate students working in diverse regions of Latin America and across the globe.

As a curator of Latin American archaeology at the University of Michigan's Museum of Anthropology, Jeff is responsible for the museum's collections from highland Mexico and Peru. The Latin American Collection, divided into Lowland and Highland regions, totals more than 155 individual collections and more than 76,000 objects, primarily pre-Columbian ceramics and lithics. Perhaps most important are the type collections of ceramics from the Basin of Mexico collected by Jeff Parsons and James B. Griffin, as well as the Mayer-Oakes collection of excavated Basin of Mexico ceramics.

Equally or more important than the collections are the extraordinary documentary resources that Parsons has accumulated on Latin American archaeology, the majority deriving from his own fieldwork. Parsons' extensive field notes, maps, drawings, photographs, and other documentation from his many field projects in Mexico and Peru are available in the museum, scrupulously organized and filed in the Latin American Division. Jeff has long been keenly aware of the rapid destruction of the archaeological record, particularly in the Basin of Mexico, and of the fact that he and his colleagues have documented thousands of sites that no longer exist. As such, he has devoted considerable effort over the last decade to assuring that this documentation is accessible and organized, so that future scholars can access it.

Considering all that Jeff has contributed to our discipline, it is a little scary to consider the fact that we almost lost him to geology, or at least we would have if the Dean of the College of Mineral Industries at Pennsylvania State University had prevailed. Upon discovering that Jeff had agreed to join Bill Sanders to do archaeology, the Dean sent the following letter to Jeff's father:

"Dear Mr. Parsons:

It is always a pleasure to report on the progress of a student when his work has been as outstanding as that of your son Jeffrey. In June he will be granted his B.S. degree in geology and mineralogy with highest distinction, the only student in the June graduating class of this College to be awarded this high honor. You and he have every right to be proud of the work he has done at Penn State.

I do regret, however, that Jeffrey has seen fit essentially to abandon the results of his successful four years here to change his field of specialization to archaeology. As you undoubtedly know, the opportunities for archaeologists who do not have independent incomes of some size are quite limited while any geologist of Jeffrey's ability, with one or more graduate degrees behind him, can choose from a wide variety of positions. Perhaps it may be that Jeffrey's further acquaintance with archaeology will place the merits of a geological career in a more favorable light."

THE CONTENTS OF THIS VOLUME, PART I: SETTLEMENT PATTERN RESEARCH AND ITS CONTRIBUTIONS

The archaeologist's desire to contribute meaningful knowledge about past human societies is always compromised by limited time and resources. The survey archaeologist's particular challenge is maximizing the area studied while simultaneously collecting high-quality data comparable between time periods and regions. In the first chapter, Carla M. Sinopoli discusses the impact of the full-coverage survey methods pioneered by Jeffrey Parsons and others on South Asian archaeology. In her project at Vijayanagara, Sinopoli and her colleagues developed a method that came remarkably close to the ideals of full-coverage survey, given their time limitations and the rugged local terrain. Their method provides the kind of fine-grained data on archaeological sites of all periods and types, providing not only valuable insights into Vijayanagara city and its metropolitan area, but also data to potentially compare with other South Asian regions and other world regions. Pioneered by William Sanders and Jeffrey Parsons, the full-coverage survey method represents the most effective resolution of the survey archaeologist's major dilemma: how to cover a large area while simultaneously maintaining high-quality data. The full-coverage method we now use endured a lengthy process of trial and error. In the second chapter, Thomas Charlton and Deborah Nichols provide a fascinating and detailed account of the various survey method experiments that occurred in the Teotihuacan Valley Project and subsequent projects that eventuated in the full-coverage method recognized today. Their discussion illustrates the varying ways researchers addressed key problems inherent in survey method, especially regarding the ideal intensity of coverage, the most effective uses of surface collections of artifacts, and making site descriptions comparable across survey crews, time periods, and even whole regional surveys. This chapter also illustrates how questions brought to light by regional survey can be further pursued by more fine-grained methods at selected sites.

Once developed and refined in the Teotihuacan Valley and other Basin of Mexico surveys, the full-coverage method proved robust, and as previously mentioned, it has been adapted to a variety of cultural settings and landscapes unimagined in the days of the original Teotihuacan Valley work. In recent decades, it has contributed more new information than any other method to our understanding of the pre-Hispanic Basin of Mexico. Elizabeth Brumfiel's chapter examines the latter by following up on some of Jeffrey Parsons's suggestions, in this case, based on his Texcoco region survey (Parsons 1968, 1971). Her chapter illustrates how survey data elucidate the nature of broad patterns of culture historical change, providing hypotheses for evaluation through more fine-grained research, including excavation. Based on her research at Xaltocan, Brumfiel evaluates Jeff's suggestion that after Teotihuacan's decline, the Basin of Mexico was marginalized due to its location at the boundaries of the spheres of influence of Tula, Hidalgo (the Toltec capital), and Cholula, in the Puebla Valley. This is an important issue for Basin of Mexico research, since the later imperial Aztec system grew out of this marginal boundary setting.

The next two chapters illustrate the value of full-coverage survey method as applied in other regions. Timothy Earle describes the results of the Upper Mantaro Archaeological Research Project that built on Jeffrey Parsons's survey of the Upper Mantaro and Tarma regions in Peru (Parsons, Hastings, and Matos 2000). In Earle's data, we see middle-range social formations, the Xauxa/Wanka chiefdoms, that illustrate few of the middle-range societies' expected features as typically described in the neoevolutionist literature on the evolution of social complexity. Theory building and theory evaluation are dependent on this kind of documentation of cross-cultural variability in types of social formations. The important question of variation in middle-range societies is also addressed in Robert D. Drennan's and Christian Peterson's comparative study of chiefdoms from three very different regional settings, in Northeast China (the Chifeng Region of Eastern Inner Mongolia), the Alto Magdalena region of the Colombian Andes, and the Valley of Oaxaca, Mexico. These chapters illustrate the value of a consistent and rigorous regional survey method for pursuing cross-cultural comparative research at a high competence level (cf. Fish and Kowalewski 1990; Alcock and Cherry 2004).

THE CONTENTS OF THIS VOLUME, PART II: RESEARCH THAT BUILDS ON REGIONAL SURVEYS

Full-coverage survey is widely recognized as one of the most productive research strategies in recent decades, in Mesoamerica and elsewhere, but the success of this approach must be measured beyond what its practitioners learned about settlement pattern and demographic change. While the central facts of survey archaeology pertain to site locations and sizes, long-term population histories, and other matters directly related to settlement patterns, a frequent outcome of survey is the serendipitous encounter of surface evidence for past behavior that stimulates new lines of research. Survey archaeologists' discovery of foreign enclaves in the ancient city of Teotihuacan, the Oaxaca and Merchants' Barrios (Millon 1973:40), is a good example of this kind of serendipity. Coupled with evidence from the regional Basin of Mexico surveys indicating that immigration fueled Teotihuacan's rapid population growth (Parsons 1968), these discoveries have prompted follow-up research on immigrants' role in Teotihuacan's economy and society. Chapter 7, by Michael Spence, Christine White, Evelyn Rattray, and Fred Longstaffe, presents the most recent methodological advance in the study of the city's foreign residents, using stable isotope analysis of excavated human remains to distinguish individuals who grew up outside the city from those who lived in Teotihuacan.

While the major rationale for surface collections in full-coverage survey method has been to refine site boundaries and the chronological placement of sites, an unexpected bonus is that surface-collected artifacts provide information about agricultural and craft production and their changes. Jeffrey Parsons and Mary Hrones Parsons have both been important contributors to research on these topics, including evidence for diachronic change in maguey and cotton fiber spinning. Their work has led researchers to reevaluate the widely accepted model of a primarily *milpa* (maize, bean, and squash) economy in highland regions of Mesoamerica (M. Parsons 1972, 1975; Parsons and Parsons 1990)(Plate 1-2). Similarly, Jeff's research has been the major source for our understanding of the pre-Hispanic Basin of Mexico salt industry (Parsons 2001). Chapters 8, 9, and 10 follow up on these discoveries. Susan Toby Evans builds on the results of the Teotihuacan Valley survey through her excavations in the Aztec Period rural community of Cihuatecpan. Her work provides new data pertinent to understanding rural household economies, especially relating to the production of maguey and its products. Gary M. Feinman and Linda M. Nicholas are similarly interested in household economies, especially the rethinking of the *milpa* model of subsistence production. Following up on the regional archaeological survey of the Valley of Oaxaca, they base their investigations on intensive surface surveys of several sites as well as excavations and

Plate 1-2. Maguey field, near Lake Tecocomulco, on Thomas Charlton's Trade Route Survey in the northeastern Basin of Mexico. Photo courtesy of Thomas Charlton.

botanical surveys at El Palmillo, in the Tlacolula region. Here, in the driest part of the Valley of Oaxaca, in a piedmont setting well above the most desirable *milpa* land, they document a diverse economy in which people extensively used xerophytic plants.

The final chapter, by Richard E. Blanton, Lane F. Fargher, and Verenice Y. Heredia Espinoza, was originally inspired by Jeff Parsons's research on the extensive Late-Postclassic salt industry fringing the saline Lake Texcoco in the Basin of Mexico, as well as by his follow-up work documenting the development of the Basin of Mexico salt industry (Parsons 2001). He concluded that at least some of this Late Postclassic salt was feeding into the dyeing industry as a mordant and that fiber dyeing might have been carried out at these sites. His conclusions are surprising because nothing comparable has been found pertaining to earlier periods. During the Late Postclassic, there must have been substantially more cloth dyeing than in earlier periods, but why? Thinking about this prompted development of a goods-based approach to understanding changes in Mesoamerican economies that could help us gain a better understanding of the Late Postclassic economy in comparative and processual perspectives.

REFERENCES CITED

Adams, Robert McC.
1981   *Heartland of Cities: Surveys of Ancient Settlement and Land Use on the Central Floodplain of the Euphrates.* The University of Chicago Press, Chicago.

Alcock, Susan E., and John F. Cherry (editors)
2004   *Side-by-Side Survey: Comparative Regional Studies in the Mediterranean World.* Oxbow Books, Oxford.

Armillas, Pedro
1971   Gardens on Swamps. *Science* 174:653–661.

Balkansky, Andrew K., Stephen A. Kowalewski, Verónica Pérez Rodríguez, Thomas J. Pluckhahn, Charlotte A. Smith, Laura R. Stiver, Dmitri Beliaev, John F. Chamblee, Verenice Y. Heredia Espinoza, and Roberto Santos Pérez
2000   Archaeological Survey in the Mixteca Alta of Oaxaca, Mexico. *Journal of Field Archaeology* 27:365–389.

Barker, Graeme, and David Mattingly (editors)
1999–2000   *The Archaeology of Mediterranean Landscapes.* 5 Vols. Oxbow Books, Oxford.

Billman, Brian R., and Gary M. Feinman (editors)
1999   *Settlement Pattern Studies in the Americas: Fifty Years Since Virú.* Smithsonian Institution Press, Washington, D.C.

Binford, Lewis R.
1964   A Consideration of Archaeological Research Design. *American Antiquity* 29: 425–441.

Blanton, Richard E.
1978   *Monte Albán: Settlement Patterns at the Ancient Zapotec Capital.* Academic Press, New York.

2000   *Hellenistic, Roman and Byzantine Settlement Patterns of the Coast Lands of Western Rough Cilicia.* BAR International Series 879, Oxford.

Blanton, Richard E., Stephen A. Kowalewski, Gary M. Feinman, and Jill Appel
1982   *Monte Albán's Hinterland, Part I: The Prehispanic Settlement Patterns of the Central and Southern Parts of the Valley of Oaxaca, Mexico.* Memoirs No. 15, Museum of Anthropology, University of Michigan, Ann Arbor.

Blanton, Richard E., Stephen A. Kowalewski, Gary M. Feinman, and Laura M. Finsten
1993   *Ancient Mesoamerica: A Comparison of Change in Three Regions.* 2nd Ed. Cambridge University Press, Cambridge.

Cherry, John F.
1983   Frogs Around the Pond: Perspectives on Current Archaeological Survey Projects in the Mediterranean Region. In *Archaeological Survey in the Mediterranean Area*, edited by Donald R. Keller and David W. Rupp, pp. 375–415, BAR International Series 155, Oxford.

Cowgill, George L.
   1997   State and Society at Teotihuacan, Mexico. *Annual Review of Anthropology* 26: 129–161.
Finsten, Laura M.
   1996   Periphery and Frontier in Southern Mexico: The Mixtec Sierra in Southern Mexico. In *Pre-Columbian World-Systems*, edited by Peter N. Peregrine and Gary M. Feinman, pp. 77–96. Prehistory Press, Madison, Wisconsin.
Fish, Suzanne K., Paul R. Fish, and John H. Madsen
   1990   Analyzing Regional Agriculture: A Hohokam Example. In *The Archaeology of Regions: A Case for Full-Coverage Survey*, pp. 189–218. Smithsonian Institution Press, Washington, D.C.
Fish, Suzanne K., and Stephen A. Kowalewski (editors)
   1990   *The Archaeology of Regions: A Case for Full-Coverage Survey*. Smithsonian Institution Press, Washington, D.C.
Flannery, Kent V.
   1976   Research Strategy and Formative Mesoamerica. In *The Early Mesoamerican Village*, edited by Kent V. Flannery, pp. 1–11. Academic Press, New York.
Gamio, Manuel
   1922   *La población del valle de Teotihuacan*. 2 Vols. Secretaría de Educación Pública, Mexico, D.F.
Haggett, Peter
   1966   *Locational Analysis in Human Geography*. St. Martin's Press, New York.
Harris, Marvin
   1968   *The Rise of Anthropological Theory: A History of Theories of Culture*. Thomas Y. Crowell, New York.
Hirth, Kenneth G.
   1980   *Eastern Morelos and Teotihuacan: A Settlement Survey*. Vanderbilt University Publications in Anthropology 25, Nashville.
   2000   *Archaeological Research at Xochicalco*. Vol. 1, *Ancient Urbanism at Xochicalco: The Evolution and Organization of a Pre-Hispanic Society*. The University of Utah Press, Salt Lake City.
Hodge, Mary G., and Leah D. Minc
   1990   The Spatial Patterning of Aztec Ceramics: Implications for Prehispanic Exchange Systems in the Valley of Mexico. *Journal of Field Archaeology* 17:415–437.
Hole, Frank (editor)
   1987   *The Archaeology of Western Iran: Settlement and Society from Prehistory to the Islamic Conquest*. Smithsonian Institution Press, Washington, D.C.
Jameson, Michael H., Curtis N. Runnels, and Tjeerd van Andel
   1994   *A Greek Countryside: The Southern Argolid from Prehistory to the Present Day*. Stanford University Press, Stanford.

Kowalewski, Stephen A.
1990   The Evolution of Complexity in the Valley of Oaxaca. *Annual Review of Anthropology* 19:39–58.
Kowalewski, Stephen A., Gary M. Feinman, Laura M. Finsten, Richard E. Blanton, and Linda M. Nicholas
1989   *Monte Albán's Hinterland, Part II: The Prehispanic Settlement Patterns in Tlacolula, Etla, and Ocotlán, the Valley of Oaxaca, Mexico.* Memoirs No. 23, Museum of Anthropology, University of Michigan, Ann Arbor.
McDonald, William A., and George R. Rapp (editors)
1972   *The Minnesota Messenia Expedition: Reconstructing a Bronze Age Regional Environment.* University of Minnesota Press, Minneapolis.
Millon, René (editor)
1973   *Urbanization at Teotihuacán, Mexico Vol. 1, The Teotihuacán Map, Part I: Text.* University of Texas Press, Austin.
Nichols, Deborah L.
1996   An Overview of Regional Settlement Pattern Survey in Mesoamerica: 1960–1995. In *Arqueología Mesoamericana: Homenaje a William T. Sanders,* edited by Alba Guadalupe Mastache, Jeffrey R. Parsons, Robert S. Santley, and Mari Carmen Serra Puche, pp. 59–96. Instituto Nacional de Antropología e Historia, Mexico, D.F.
2004   The Rural and Urban Landscapes of the Aztec State. In *Mesoamerican Archaeology: Theory and Practice,* edited by Julia A. Hendon and Rosemary Joyce, pp. 265–295. Blackwell, Oxford.
Nichols, Deborah L., Elizabeth M. Brumfiel, Hector Neff, Mary G. Hodge, Thomas H. Charlton, and Michael D. Glascock
1986   Neutrons, Markets, Cities, and Empires: A 1000-Year Perspective on Ceramic Production and Distribution in the Postclassic Basin of Mexico. *Journal of Anthropological Archaeology* 21:25–82.
Parsons, Jeffrey R.
1968   Teotihuacan, Mexico, and its Impact on Regional Demography. *Science* 162:872–877.
1971   *Prehistoric Settlement Patterns in the Texcoco Region, Mexico.* Memoirs No. 3, Museum of Anthropology, University of Michigan, Ann Arbor.
1972   Archaeological Settlement Patterns. *Annual Review of Anthropology* 1:127–150.
1974   The Development of a Prehistoric Complex Society: A Regional Perspective From the Valley of Mexico. *Journal of Field Archaeology* 1:81–108.
1990   Critical Reflections on a Decade of Full-Coverage Regional Survey in the Valley of Mexico. In *The Archaeology of Regions: A Case for Full-Coverage Survey,* edited by Suzanne K. Fish and Stephen A. Kowalewski, pp. 7–32. Smithsonian Institution Press, Washington, D.C.

2001   *The Last Saltmakers of Nexquipayac, Mexico: An Archaeological Ethnography.* Anthropological Papers No. 92, Museum of Anthropology, University of Michigan, Ann Arbor.

2002   Geological Mapping With Rob Scholten in the Beaverhead Range, SW Montana and Adjacent Idaho, Summer, 1960. *Penn State Department of Geosciences Newsletter* 1 (4): 4–11.

Parsons, Jeffrey R., Elizabeth M. Brumfiel, Mary H. Parsons, and David J. Wilson

1982   *Prehispanic Settlement Patterns in the Southern Valley of Mexico: The Chalco-Xochimilco Region.* Memoirs No. 14, Museum of Anthropology, University of Michigan, Ann Arbor.

Parsons, Jeffrey R., Charles M. Hastings, and Ramiro Matos M.

2000   *Prehispanic Settlement Patterns in the Upper Mantaro and Tarma Drainages, Junín, Peru.* 2 Vols. Memoirs 34, Museum of Anthropology, University of Michigan, Ann Arbor.

Parsons, Jeffrey R., Keith W. Kintigh, and Susan A. Gregg

1983   *Archaeological Settlement Pattern Data from the Chalco, Xochimilco, Ixtapalapa, Texcoco, and Zumpango Regions, Mexico.* Technical Reports No. 14, Museum of Anthropology, University of Michigan, Ann Arbor.

Parsons, Jeffrey R., and Mary H. Parsons

1990   *Maguey Utilization in Highland Central Mexico.* Anthropological Papers No. 82, Museum of Anthropology, University of Michigan, Ann Arbor.

Parsons, Mary H.

1972   Spindle Whorls From the Teotihuacan Valley, Mexico. In *Miscellaneous Studies in Mexican Prehistory*, edited by Michael W. Spence, Jeffrey R. Parsons, and Mary H. Parsons, pp. 45–80. Anthropological Papers No. 45, Museum of Anthropology, University of Michigan, Ann Arbor.

1975   The Distribution of Late Postclassic Spindle Whorls in the Valley of Mexico. *American Antiquity* 40:207–215.

Potter, T. W., and Simon Stoddart

2001   A Century of Prehistory and Landscape Studies at the British School at Rome. *Papers of the British School at Rome* 69:3–34.

Renfrew, Colin

1980   The Great Tradition Versus the Great Divide: Archaeology as Anthropology? *American Journal of Archaeology* 84:287–298.

Sabloff, Jeremy A.

1994   *The New Archaeology and the Ancient Maya.* Scientific American Library, New York.

Sanders, William T.

1956   The Central Mexican Symbiotic Region. In *Prehistoric Settlement Patterns in the New World*, edited by Gordon R. Willey, pp. 115–127. Viking Fund Publications in Archaeology 23, New York.

1965   *The Cultural Ecology of the Teotihuacan Valley*. Manuscript on file, Department of Anthropology, Pennsylvania State University, University Park.

Sanders, William T., Jeffrey R. Parsons, and Robert S. Santley

1979   *The Basin of Mexico: Ecological Processes in the Evolution of a Civilization*. Academic Press, New York.

Service, Elman R.

Origins of the State and Civilization: The Process of Cultural Evolution. W. W. Norton and Company, New York.

Shelach, Gideon

1999   *Leadership Strategies, Economic Activity, and Interregional Interaction: Social Complexity in Northeast China*. Kluwer Academic/Plenum, New York.

Skinner, G. William

1964   Marketing and Social Structure in Rural China: Part I. *Journal of Asian Studies* 24:3–43.

1965   Marketing and Social Structure in Rural China: Part II. *Journal of Asian Studies* 24:195–228.

Smith, Carol A. (editor)

1976   *Regional Analysis*. 2 Vols. Academic Press, New York.

Stanish, Charles

1999   Settlement Pattern Shifts and Political Ranking in the Lake Titicaca Basin, Peru. In *Settlement Pattern Studies in the Americas*, edited by Brian R. Billman and Gary M. Feinman, pp. 116–128. Smithsonian Institution Press, Washington, D.C.

Stark, Barbara L.

2003   Cerro de las Mesas: Social and Economic Perspectives on a Gulf Center. In *El urbanismo en Mesoamerica*, Vol. 1, edited by William T. Sanders, Alba Guadalupe Mastache, and Robert H. Cobean, pp. 391–426. Instituto Nacional de Antropología e Historia, Mexico, D.F.

Stoddart, Simon (editor)

2000   *Landscapes from Antiquity*. Antiquity Papers No. 1. Antiquity Publications, Cambridge.

Underhill, Anne P., Gary M. Feinman, Linda M. Nicholas, Gwen Bennett, Hui Fang, Fengshi Luan, Haiguang Yu, and Fengshu Cai

2001   Regional Survey and the Development of Complex Societies in Southeastern Shandong, China. *Antiquity* 76: 745–755.

Willey, Gordon R.

1953   *Prehistoric Settlement Patterns in the Virú Valley, Peru*. Bureau of American Ethnology Bulletin No. 155. Smithsonian Institution, Washington, D.C.

Wilson, David J.

1988   *Prehispanic Settlement Patterns in the Lower Santa Valley, Peru*. Smithsonian Institution Press, Washington, D.C.

Wolf, Eric R. (editor)
  1976   *The Valley of Mexico: Studies in Pre-Hispanic Ecology and Society*. University of New Mexico Press, Albuquerque.
Wright, Henry T.
  1986   The Evolution of Civilizations. In *American Archaeology Past and Future*, edited by David J. Meltzer, Don D. Fowler, and Jeremy A. Sabloff, pp. 323–368. Smithsonian Institution Press, Washington, D.C.

REGIONAL SURVEY AT VIJAYANAGARA, SOUTH ASIA:

NEW WORLD METHODOLOGIES IN OLD WORLD URBAN CONTEXTS

CARLA M. SINOPOLI

University of Michigan

South Asia's rich archaeological record has been the focus of scholarly research for more than two centuries, with the formal infrastructure of colonial India's archaeology (India and Pakistan) firmly established by the mid-nineteenth century (Chakrabarti 1988a, b). Throughout this period, thousands of archaeological sites have been identified, spanning from the middle Pleistocene to the colonial era. South Asian archaeologists have established broad chronological and typological frameworks for the region's past and have explored many of the classic questions addressed by scholars in other world regions: the origins of sedentism and agricultural economies, trade and exchange, social inequality, and state formation, among others (see Settar and Korisettar 2002: Volumes 1–4, for an excellent overview of the many accomplishments of South Asian archaeology).

In this paper, I wish to consider a small subset of South Asian archaeological projects—those explicitly focused on regional dynamics and processes. My goal is to explore how New World perspectives and methodologies, such as those pioneered and perfected by Jeffrey Parsons, have influenced work in the region, particularly in the development of systematic regional survey projects.

In a significant sense, regional perspectives are not new to South Asia. Early archaeologists, during both colonial and postcolonial eras, were concerned with documenting archaeological remains found within administrative districts or archaeological "circles," defined by the Archaeological Survey of India (ASI). The various annual reports of the ASI have long been replete with lists of sites identified by government and university archaeologists in specific *taluks*, or districts (Archaeological Survey of India, 1904–2004). Such lists typically provide brief information on chronology, diagnostic artifacts and architecture, and site location—all variables familiar to readers of modern survey reports. However, the mode of site discovery commonly practiced to generate such lists typically differs from what contemporary scholars would recognize as systematic survey. Instead, "village" or "village-to-village survey" has been the dominant means of site location (Shaw 2000; Chakrabarti 2001). This successful strategy, as its name suggests, is centered on existing rural communities and relies heavily on the knowledge of local residents to identify archaeological features. Thus, archaeologists travel from village to village inquiring about the presence of old temples, inscriptions, and other archaeological features in the area. Once located, summary information is recorded on these sites. Sculptures may be collected if they are not currently in worship and are deemed culturally significant, and estampages are made of any inscriptions identified.

Village survey approaches have both inherent strengths and weaknesses. Rural herders and farmers are intimately familiar with the regions they inhabit and can provide a ready source of information on a range of features. It is perhaps not coincidental, however, that many sites identified through these means are historic, with preserved architecture. These are easily recognizable as human constructions, and in many contexts, ancient temples and shrines remain in use today. In contrast, surface scatters of lithic or ceramic artifacts may not be recognized as culturally significant, or if so, may not be considered worthy of mention by individuals unaware of their antiquity or significance. Similarly, the antiquity of features such as agricultural terracing or ancient road networks is also unlikely to be recognized by local inhabitants. Finally, village survey works well in areas where modern villages are present, though even there, may dangerously presume a concordance between earlier patterns of landscape habitation and current ones. It is impossible to know what sites have been missed if scholars only travel to those locales where sites are known.

While village survey has proven invaluable for identifying numerous archaeological sites across South Asia, it is clearly not adequate for identifying the full range of archaeological features in a region or for developing systemic understandings of long-term regional histories. These require systematic techniques of site identification and documentation such as provided by regional survey methodologies. In the following sections, I briefly summarize the history of systematic regional survey in South Asia, noting major projects of the last few decades. I then address research, that I and my colleagues have been engaged in and around the fourteenth through sixteenth-century South Indian capital of Vijayanagara.

SYSTEMATIC REGIONAL SURVEY IN THE SOUTH ASIAN CONTEXT

Regional survey was introduced into South Asian archaeology not long after the methodology began gaining prevalence in the New World and Middle East. However, even today, the technique is rarely applied in South Asia, and the dominant research strategy of most archaeologists remains site-focused. One of the most significant and dramatic regional survey projects conducted in South Asia was initiated in the mid-1970s by University of Pennsylvania trained archaeologist Mohammad Rafique Mughal (1972, 1982, 1990a, 1990c, 1997). Mughal's surveys focused in the Baluchistan and Cholistan regions of Pakistan. His discoveries in Cholistan—located along the modern Indian-Pakistani border, on the course of the dry beds of the Ghaggar and Hakra rivers (also known as the Saraswati)—radically altered scholarly understandings of the third-millennium BC Indus or Harappan civilization (Mughal 1982, 1997).

This Ghaggar–Hakra system lays parallel and some 60 km to the south and east of the Indus River and its major tributaries, creating a dual river system not dissimilar to Mesopotamia's Tigris and Euphrates rivers. Hydrological and geomorphological studies reveal that the Ghaggar–Hakra rivers underwent dramatic changes from c. 2500-1500 BC, as tributaries of the Yamuna and Indus rivers successively captured their headwaters. By 1500 BC, they had largely disappeared, and today, the region is sparsely occupied and arid, dominated by expanding sand dunes and desert. Early archaeological work in the region by L.P. Tessitori (1916–1918), Sir Auriel Stein (1940–1941), and A. Ghosh (1951–1953), and postindependence studies on the Indian side of the border indicated that the area had a rich archaeological record (Mughal 1997: 26-27). But it was not until Mughal's survey along a 15 to 20-mile-wide strip following the bed of the ancient Hakra in Pakistan that scholars realized that this had been part of the core area of the misnamed "Indus" civilization. In four seasons of survey, Mughal identified more than 420 archaeological sites. The entire Harappan trajectory was documented, from preurban village communities through Early, Mature, and Late Harappan phases (Mughal 1993). Additional late prehistoric and early historic and medieval sites were also recorded.

Included among the 174 Mature Harappan sites that Mughal documented is the still unexcavated urban center of Ganweriwala, whose multiple mounds extend over 81.5 hectares, comparable in mounded area to the urban sites of Harappa and Mohenjo-daro. The large numbers of small industrial and habitation sites that Mughal documented were equally dramatic. The preservation of these features in this arid region stands in marked contrast to the much lower visible site density along the still-active Indus and its tributaries, where meters of alluvium typically conceal small sites. Thus, Mughal's research not only revealed what was then the third-largest urban center of the Indus civilization (Mughal 1990b; two more important urban sites—Rakhigarhi and Dholavira—have since been identified in India), but it also revealed a complex pattern of rural settlement and industrial features in its hinterland.

Mughal did not make explicit references to major New World survey projects in his reports on the Cholistan research. Nonetheless, his intellectual history suggests that he was well aware of contemporary surveys in other regions, and his work can be viewed as part of broader methodological innovations of 1960s and 1970s archaeology, including the systematization of regional survey efforts.

While a benchmark in South Asian archaeology, Mughal's survey was not quickly replicated, and as noted, even today, systematic survey projects remain relatively rare in South Asia. It is equally rare for published reports on those surveys that have occurred to contain explicit discussion of survey methodologies, making it impossible to assess just how systematic or comprehensive they were (however, see Chakrabarti 2001; Fogelin 2003; Shaw 2000; and Abraham 2003, for important exceptions). Nonetheless, several important survey projects conducted during the 1980s and 1990s are noteworthy. These include Makkhan Lal's (1984, 1987) survey in the area between the Ganges and Yamuna rivers (the Ganga-Yamuna Doab) in Khanpur district (Uttar Pradesh, Northern India). While his was a more traditional village-to-village survey, Lal was clearly influenced by the burgeoning New World literature on systematic survey, and his bibliography refers to Western scholars, including Jeffrey Parsons. George Erdosy (1988) conducted another survey in the Ganges region around the early historic urban center of Kausambi; his analyses explicitly focused on settlement distributions and settlement hierarchy. And a long-term village-to-village survey by Dilip Chakrabarti (2001) in the lower and middle Ganges in eastern India and Bangladesh focused on identifying major settlements and routes of movement. Chakrabarti's (2001) recently published volume on this work contains a detailed discussion of various survey methodologies and a discussion of why he felt a nonsystematic methodology was most appropriate for his ambitious project. His primary reasons lay in the small-scale, 'one-man' operation of his project, and the vast area that needed to be covered in a region where relatively little baseline archaeology had been conducted.

In peninsular India, particular mention must be made of the work of Vasant Shinde (1991, 1998) and colleagues in Maharashtra's Tapti basin, K. Paddayya (1982, 1991) in the Hunsgi and Baichbal regions of northern Karnataka, and K. Rajan (1997) in the Coimbatore District of Tamil Nadu. Two recent smaller-scale surveys in South India include Shinu Abraham's research (2003) along the Palghat Gap in Kerala and Lars Fogelin's (2003) full-coverage survey in the hinterland of the early historic Buddhist monastery of Thotlakonda, Andhra Pradesh.

This brief list provides some insights into the range and contributions of regional research in South Asia. Certainly, other surveys have been conducted and some are ongoing, but for the most part, they have not employed systematic methods, and have instead relied on village-to-village techniques (Hooja 1988). Rather than review these, in the remainder of this paper, I turn to my systematic surface archaeology projects within the urban center and hinterland of the imperial capital of Vijayanagara, South India. I address two projects—the first focused on intensive documentation and surface collection within a residential district in the city of Vijayanagara, and the second, a systematic regional survey in the capital's 650-km^2 hinterland. The history of these projects, to some extent, echoes work in the comparable urban center and peripheries of Teotihuacán. In both projects, I was directly influenced by Jeffrey Parsons's Latin American scholarship, though unlike much of his work and somewhat to his disappointment, our regional survey was not designed as a full-coverage survey.

SYSTEMATIC SURFACE ARCHAEOLOGICAL SURVEY AT VIJAYANAGARA

Since the late 1970s, several programs of systematic surface archaeology at the fourteenth to sixteenth-century South Indian imperial city of Vijayanagara have examined the city and its hinterland.[1] These projects have varied in scale and intensity. Most spatially expansive is the Vijayanagara Metropolitan Survey, directed by Kathleen D. Morrison and Carla M. Sinopoli (Morrison 1995; Morrison and Sinopoli 1992; Sinopoli and Morrison 1991, 1992, 1995, 2001; and contributions in Fritz, Raczek, and Brubaker, eds., in press), which documented archaeological remains in the c. 650 square kilometer urban hinterland of Vijayanagara. The more focused and intensive Vijayanagara Research Project, directed by John Fritz and George Michell (Fritz, Michell, and Nagaraja Rao 1985; Michell 1990; Michell et al. 2001) restricted its research to the c. 25 square kilometer Vijayanagara 'urban core.' At a finer scale, Kathleen D. Morrison (1990), Alexandra Mack (2002), and I (Sinopoli 1986) have focused intensively on specific neighborhoods or districts within the urban core.

Each of these lenses into Vijayanagara urban form provides different insights into urban organization and each raises distinct methodological and logistical challenges for surface survey—of survey intensity and design and recovery procedures. Before turning to the specifics of my work, I first provide some background on Vijayanagara history and archaeology.

Vijayanagara: City and Empire

The Vijayanagara empire was the major political force in South India from the mid-fourteenth through the mid-seventeenth centuries AD, dominating a vast area of the peninsula (Figure 2-1) with a population estimated at 25 million (Stein 1989). For much of that period, the eponymous imperial capital lay at the northern boundary of the empire along the banks of the Tungabhadra River. In the centuries prior to Vijayanagara's emergence, the central Tungabhadra region was marginal to the various competing seats of political power in the peninsula and was inhabited by small agricultural and pastoral communities. The area remained relatively isolated from the turmoil sweeping South India in the wake of the early fourteenth century expansion of the North Indian Delhi Sultanate into the region. By the mid-fourteenth century, the Sultanate and virtually all other South Indian states had collapsed. It was at this time that Vijayanagara's founders established a base near a small temple center and town along the Tungabhadra River, and a period of military expansion and consolidation began, ultimately incorporating much of the peninsula. The transformation of this small temple town in to the capital of Vijayanagara, "City of Victory" was rapid and dramatic. Populations flowed into the city from newly incorporated Tamil-, Telugu-, and Kannada-speaking regions throughout the south, and by AD 1400, Vijayanagara's essential form was established, with as many as 100,000 inhabitants in residence. This population more than doubled a century later when the city and empire reached their apogee after AD 1510.

Vijayanagara collapsed even more rapidly than it rose—in AD 1565, during a period of internal conflict and warfare with external neighbors. After suffering a major military defeat, Vijayanagara was abruptly abandoned and the imperial capital shifted south to a more secure location. Populations declined precipitously throughout the central Tungabhadra region, and indeed, in 1567, only two years after its abandonment, Italian traveler Cesare d' Federici observed: "The Citie of Bezeneger is not altogether destroyed, yet the houses stand still, but emptie, and there is dwelling in them nothing, as is reported, but Tygres and other wild beasts" (Sewell 1900:208).

Vijayanagara's abandonment had a long-term impact on settlement in the region, and it is only in the last few decades following the 1950s construction of a hydroelectric reservoir along the Tungabhadra that populations have begun to approach Vijayanagara levels, with potentially disastrous consequences for the region's well-preserved archaeological record.

The Vijayanagara capital is located in an area dominated by rugged and dramatic granitic outcropping hills. These outcrops provided effective barriers to movement, and when supplemented by constructed barriers in the form of fortification walls, the framework for the capital's extensive defensive

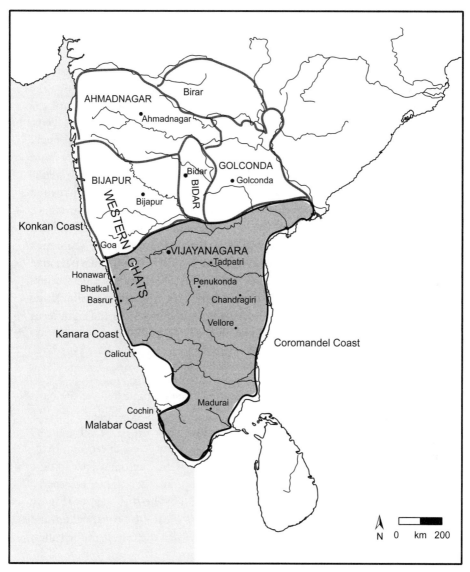

Figure 2-1. The Vijayanagara Empire.

infrastructure (Brubaker 2003). The region also has relatively low economic potential compared to the fertile river valleys of southern and northern India. Canal irrigation is only of limited potential in the dissected landscape of the southern Deccan and this is one of the driest areas of peninsular India, averaging around 15 inches of rainfall per year (Morrison 1995). Nonetheless, along with its tremendous defensive potential, the area had powerful sacred associations to the Hindu deities Shiva and Rama; both factors undoubtedly contributed to its selection and maintenance as the imperial capital for more than two centuries.

The imperial city of Vijayanagara can be divided into a core urban zone—the c. 25 km² city center mentioned above, and an outer periphery of some 650 km², defined on the basis of the locations of constructed fortifications and natural barriers. I will return to this larger 'metropolitan region' below. Here I focus on the urban core, which archaeologists John Fritz, George Michell, and M. S. Nagaraja Rao (1985) have divided into several distinct zones (Figure 2-2).]Along the southern bank of the Tungabhadra is an area dominated by four large temple complexes, designated the city's 'sacred center.' A large irrigated valley separated this zone from a walled zone of elite and nonelite residence and markets, which I will term the "residential core" (Fritz et al. 1985 call this the urban core, but I am using that phrase to refer to the entire 25 km² area). Southwest of this zone lays a smaller walled area that Fritz et al. have termed the "royal center," which contained royal temples, residences, and administrative structures. While these divisions likely do not directly parallel those held by the city's occupants, they nonetheless encompass real and significant organizational features of Vijayanagara's urban layout.

The East Valley

Other zones of Vijayanagara's urban core can be distinguished on the basis of topography and/or constructed remains. In 1984, I conducted intensive surface collections in one such area, called the "East Valley," located in the center of Vijayanagara's residential core. The valley is bordered by northeast–southwest trending outcrop ridges, which define an open area some 1 km long by 200 to 500 m wide. At its narrowest point, the valley was bisected by a north–south wall, part of the enclosure wall of the royal center (Figure 2-3). The area to the west of this wall thus lies within the royal center and the land to the east outside it. A large road ran down the center of the valley, passing through a gate in the wall, known from a nearby inscription as the "Monday Gate" (Patil and Patil 1995), possibly referring to a weekly market held nearby.

Marked architectural differences are visible among the preserved structural remains in the western and eastern portions of the valley. Features on the west royal center side include a number of small shrines and a walled architectural complex containing elaborate drains and one or more elite residences and possible administrative structures. (These have since been excavated but were not exposed when I conducted my study.) The area to the east of the Monday Gate also contains the remains of a number of structures. However, unlike

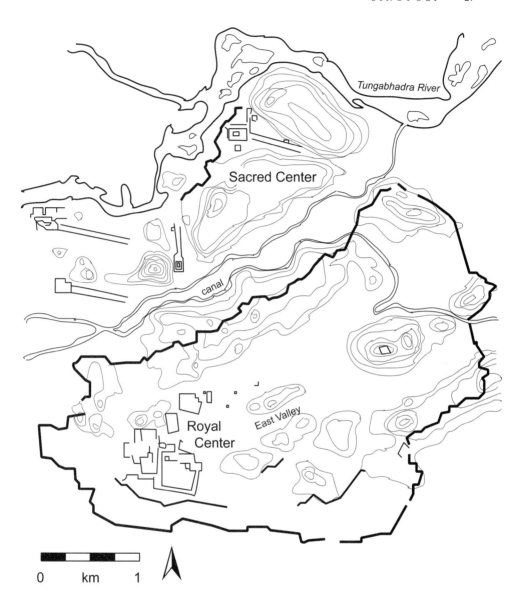

Figure 2-2. The Vijayanagara Urban Core.

the western part of the valley, no elite residences or civic structures are found outside of the walls of the royal center. Preserved stone architecture is overall less common in this area, consisting of several small Jain and Hindu shrines and carvings and columned structures. There is thus evidence for religious and functional diversity across the valley, as well, presumably, of status differences between inhabitants who dwelt inside and outside of the royal center.

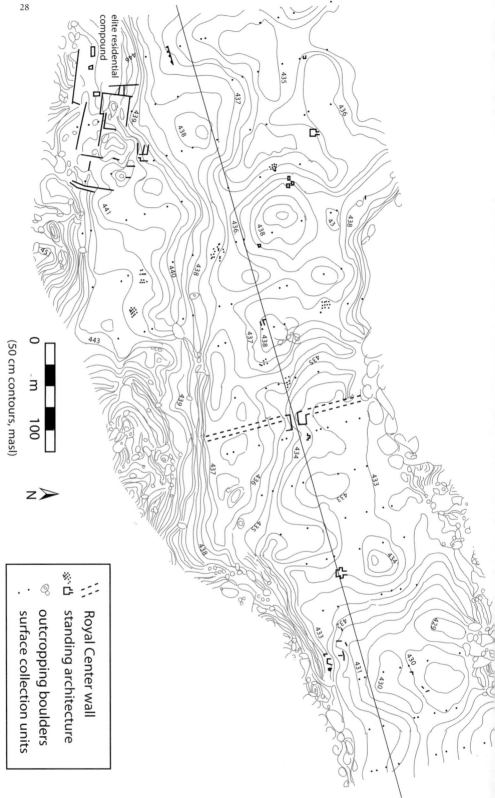

elite residential
compound

Figure 2-3. The East Valley. (Dots show the location of collection units along arbitrary axis.)

(50 cm contours, masl)

0 — m 100

N

⁝ Royal Center wall

◻ standing architecture

◯ outcropping boulders

· surface collection units

The most ubiquitous surface remains across the East Valley are earthenware ceramics. Hundreds of thousands of pottery fragments are distributed across the valley's surface, in some areas forming a literal carpet of sherds. These artifacts, virtually all dating to the Vijayanagara period, constitute the remains of a diverse range of consumption and production activities. Although various erosional and colluvial processes certainly affected their distributions, it is unlikely that these resulted in major displacement of materials. The analysis of broad distributional patterning (e.g., east–west halves of the valley, near the road or on valley edges, and the like) thus can potentially inform on the spatial and social organization of this Vijayanagara urban district.

Surface architectural features in the valley were documented by the Vijayanagara Research Project in the early 1980s (Fritz et al. 1985; Michell 1990). In 1984, we prepared a detailed topographic map of the valley and conducted a systematic surface collection. To obtain a large representative sample of surface artifacts, we employed a stratified systematic sampling strategy, using "dog-leash" collection units with a radius of 2m. Two hundred and ninety-four units were collected, resulting in a cumulative sample of 3,700 m^2 in a valley some 170,000 m^2 in area (a 2.2% sample). The collections yielded more than 90,000 sherds and a much smaller number of nonceramic objects. Ultimately, only half the units were analyzed in detail, some 38,000 body sherds and 7,000 diagnostics (Sinopoli 1986).[2]

Artifact Distributions in the East Valley

Although finer scale analyses were undertaken, in this discussion, I largely restrict my focus to the broader patterning in artifact distributions between the valley's western (Royal Center) and eastern (Residential Core) zones (Sinopoli 1986: 260–327 for a full discussion of the East Valley ceramic distribution). Marked differences existed between the two halves of the valley in overall ceramic densities, ware distributions, and distributions of specific vessel forms.

Ceramic densities were roughly twice as high in the eastern portion of the valley as in the west. These differences do not appear to be primarily a product of postoccupation taphonomic factors since both halves of the valley would have been subject to similar erosional and depositional forces. Instead, multiple cultural and behavioral factors likely play a part in the observed patterning. Contributory factors probably include differences in settlement density between the royal center area and nonelite residential districts, with more densely packed settlement occurring in nonelite areas than in areas dominated by the large, widely spaced residential complexes and nonresidential spaces of the royal center.

In addition, it is likely that residents of the royal center had greater access to metal vessels than their lower status counterparts. In this regard, it is important to note that in historic South Asian contexts, and specifically in Hindu India, earthenware ceramics were of low social and economic status. Elites and commoners alike used ceramic vessels for storage and food preparation, but they were considered inappropriate for use as dining or serving vessels. Earthenware vessels are believed to be particularly vulnerable to the absorption and transmission of corporeal pollution, which can endanger the ritual purity of individuals who come into contact with them (Sinopoli 1999). Therefore, the texts proclaim that food should be consumed from metal vessels. For those who could afford them, preferred materials, in order from least to greatest purity, were bronze, silver, and gold vessels. Those who could not afford such vessels dined off disposable banana leaves, which could be discarded after one use. In many regions of the world, ceramics attain high social value and elaboration due to their role in consumption activities such as feasting. These contexts of visible display and high social valuation of ceramic vessels were absent in Hindu South Asia.

Perhaps a result of the low social status attributed to ceramics, more than 80% of Vijayanagara-period earthenware pottery consists of undecorated or simply decorated black or dark brown plain wares. Less common were red plain and polished wares, black polished ware, and a buff-colored coarse ware used in architectural fittings and roof tiles. Black/brown plain wares predominated in both halves of the valley, comprising 82.8% of the ceramics on the west side of the gate and 77.3% on the east side. These differences, though relatively small, are nonetheless statistically significant. Overall, the eastern side of the valley contains higher diversity of wares and higher frequencies of decorated ceramics than the western half, perhaps evidence that, in lower status areas, these characteristics had a greater significance than in areas with greater access to metal or other prestige goods.

Vijayanagara vessels were classed into nine broad functional classes based on vessel size and proportions (Figure 2-4; Sinopoli 1986, 1993b, 1999). Restricted or necked vessels predominated in the assemblage and included vessels categorized as small, medium, and large low-necked, relatively open, cooking vessels (RV1-3) and high, narrow-necked, storage and transport vessels (RV4-6). Unrestricted vessels were much less common, comprising approximately 10% of the total diagnostic assemblage, and included small saucers used as oil lamps, shallow bowls, and other bowls. Interestingly, the last two unrestricted forms occur in highest frequencies in the city's Islamic residential quarter, where proscriptions against the use of ceramics in food consumption were not operative. While all morphological forms are found in both halves of the East Valley, their frequencies differ both overall and in various zones within each half. For example, ceramics recovered around the palace complexes on

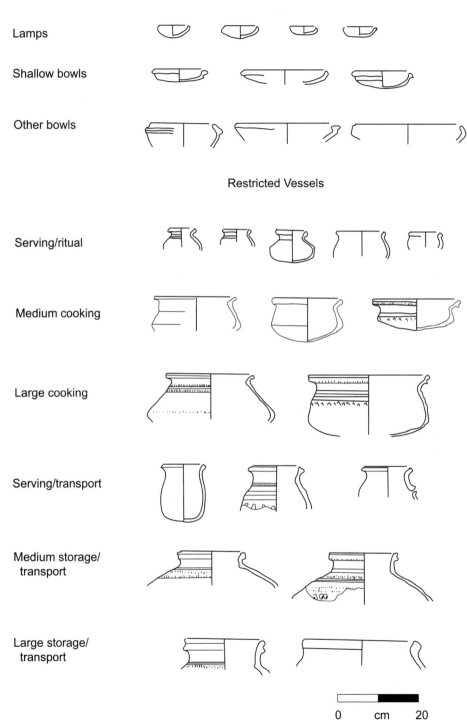

Figure 2-4. Vijayanagara Ceramics: major functional classes.

the royal center side of the valley revealed higher than expected frequencies of large water storage and transport vessels and large cooking vessels, perhaps indicating that larger households or social groups engaged in consumption and food preparation in those complexes. The highest diversity of morphological forms occurred near the gate in the center of the valley, perhaps in the area of the "Monday" market alluded to in the nearby inscription. Oil lamps tended to cluster near shrines, where they would have been used in worship.

These and similar patterns (not described here) in the distributions of the nine morphological vessel classes across the East Valley most likely result from the interplay of multiple factors. These include the functional division of space within the valley, defining areas dominated by particularly activities, such as iron working, residence, or worship and commerce. The rigidity of such boundaries is unclear. A strict reading of Hindu proscriptions concerning residential segregation of castes and occupational groups would suggest clearly defined boundaries, but patterns documented in other areas of the city suggest that reality was, not surprisingly, more flexible than texts might suggest (Sinopoli 1993b). And the patterning observed in the East Valley is neither neat nor unambiguous. Sampling errors, postabandonment factors, and the contributions of products from numerous pottery workshops may also affect distributional patterns in ways difficult to evaluate from surface evidence alone.

While the sources of variation cannot be fully assessed, it is apparent that the distributions of ceramic classes are not homogenous across the East Valley. The greatest distinctions are found between the western and eastern halves of the valley, with additional spatial divisions within each. In addition, significant variations were documented between the East Valley and other districts of Vijayanagara. All of this evidence suggests that careful analysis of the distributions and forms of surface materials across large urban sites has the potential to contribute to understandings of spatial organization and activity distributions in ancient South Asian urban sites (see also Miller 1999; Smith 2001, 2003).

The Vijayanagara Metropolitan Survey Project

In the preceding section, I considered intensive surface documentation within the urban core of Vijayanagara. Here I turn to our extensive regional work, which more closely draws upon New World methodologies of regional survey. From 1987 to 1997, the Vijayanagara Metropolitan Survey (VMS, co-directed by Kathleen D. Morrison and me) documented archaeological remains in the c. 650 km² fortified hinterland of Vijayanagara.

Unlike Jeffrey Parsons' survey projects in Meso- and South America, our project was designed as a sample survey, not a full-coverage survey. This was in part a practical decision, resulting from team size, available resources, and time and permit constraints, as well as a response to the logistical challenges posed by the region's rugged topography. I was and remain ambivalent, however, about our choice of survey strategy, and while I still believe we chose the best path given the context of our work, I am nonetheless saddened by what we did not and now cannot document. On one hand, our sampling design (approximately 50% of the 110 km² region immediately surrounding the city core) permitted us to survey a much larger portion of the metropolitan region than would have otherwise been feasible. As a result, we gained a robust understanding of site distribution patterns and regional organization, and I am confident that these would not be significantly changed by full coverage survey. In addition, we were able to cover those areas we did survey with relatively high intensity, with a survey spacing of 20 m (and indeed we had chosen a full coverage strategy with lower intensity, we would have missed numerous sites, since nearly two-thirds of the sites documented were less than 15 m in diameter). On the other hand, the rapid destruction of archaeological sites in the region, which has been occurring at an accelerating pace over the last decade, means that it is no longer possible to return to many unsurveyed areas, and that many sites that likely existed when we began our project have since been destroyed.

The South Asian archaeological community, particularly those scholars dedicated to systematic regional work, is small compared to much of Latin America or areas of the Old World such as the Mediterranean. And the archaeological record throughout South Asia is threatened by population growth, agricultural expansion, and industrialization. Areas remain where basic archaeological fundamentals must still be established, and in those techniques, extensive surveys such as that by Chakrabarti (2001) discussed above, make considerable sense. In the Vijayanagara region, we had a some-what better sense of fundamentals and chose to be more systematic, though I believe many New World survey archaeologists and perhaps all classical survey archaeologists would criticize our choices.

Turning to the survey itself, we defined the metropolitan region as that region encompassed by the outermost fortifications of the city (Figure 2-5). This proved to be somewhat of a shifting target. As we identified new features on the outskirts of the region throughout the project, we came to recognize that the area was considerably larger than we had originally thought and that it also varied over time as the city and empire's fortunes waxed and waned. For much of the Vijayanagara period, an estimate of some 450 km² is reasonable, while during the early sixteenth century period of urban expansion, 650 km² is more accurate. This did not affect our research strategy significantly, as we focused our most intensive survey efforts on areas near to the Vijayanagara urban core and conducted less intensive work in the outer zone, where efforts focused primarily on documenting defensive and agricultural sites.

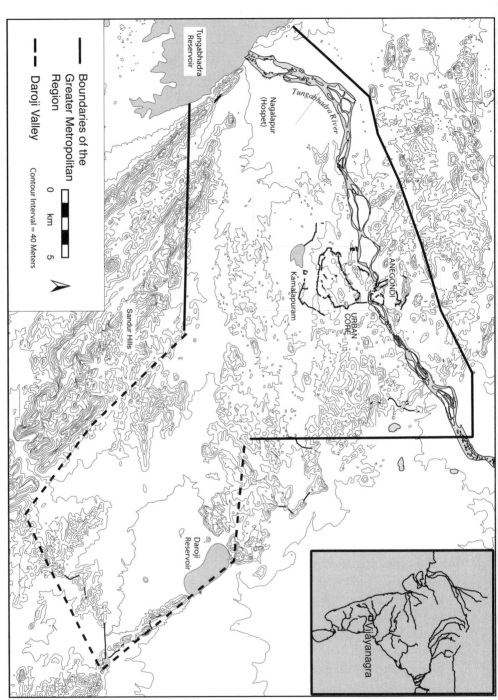

Figure 2-5. The metropolitan region of Vijayanagara.

Following the mapping system of the region created by Fritz and Michell, we divided the entire survey region into arbitrary blocks, 4.5 km on a side, and conducted a 50% transect survey in the eight square blocks immediately surrounding the urban core (Figure 2-6). Survey teams of three to five members each walked 250 m by 4.5 km north-south transects, spaced at 20-m intervals.

As sites were identified, their location was recorded on 1:25,000 base maps of the region. All sites were mapped and photographed, and information on environmental and topographic setting, site layout, architectural remains, surface artifacts and current land use or disturbances were recorded on standardized field forms. Systematic surface collections were conducted, and preliminary interpretations of site function and chronology were also recorded. Sites in the extensive survey area were similarly documented.

Over eight seasons of survey, we documented 659 sites in the intensive survey area, with an additional 79 documented in the extensive survey region. Since this was a sample survey and the entire region was not covered, this is indeed an impressive site density. Also impressive was the array of different kinds of sites identified, which provide evidence for a rich and varied use of Vijayanagara's metropolitan region during the period of the city's major occupation, as well as in earlier and later periods.

We have grouped the sites into broad general categories based on their primary function (Figure 2-6). Major site categories include (1) defensive sites, including fortifications, bastions, and other features ($n=97$); (2) transport sites, such as roads, bridges, and gateways ($n=77$); (3) sacred sites, including large and small temples and shrines and isolated images ($n=144$); (4) craft production sites, such as smelting or quarrying sites ($n=8$); (5) agricultural sites, including canals, wells, reservoirs (or tanks), and terraces ($n=161$); and (6) settlements, including towns, villages, isolated houses, and inhabited rock shelters ($n=74$). Thirty-three prehistoric or early historic sites were also documented. Many sites, of course, had multiple functions, and others ($n=86$) were classified either as "unknown" or "other." Thus, settlements often contained multiple shrines and temples as well as evidence for craft production activities, roads, defensive features, and the like. In our GIS and master site database, we have divided each site into multiple features or components (totalling approximately 3,350). This allows us to examine each of these diverse functions separately.

Together, the sites documented by the VMS point to a complex, densely settled urban landscape, whose chronology roughly paralleled the fortunes of the dynasties that ruled from the capital and known from historical sources—with a burst of growth in the late fourteenth and early fifteenth centuries, a period of decline or stagnation in the late fifteenth century, and an explosive burst of growth under the Tuluva dynasty in the early sixteenth century, followed by cataclysmic collapse and abandonment in AD 1565.

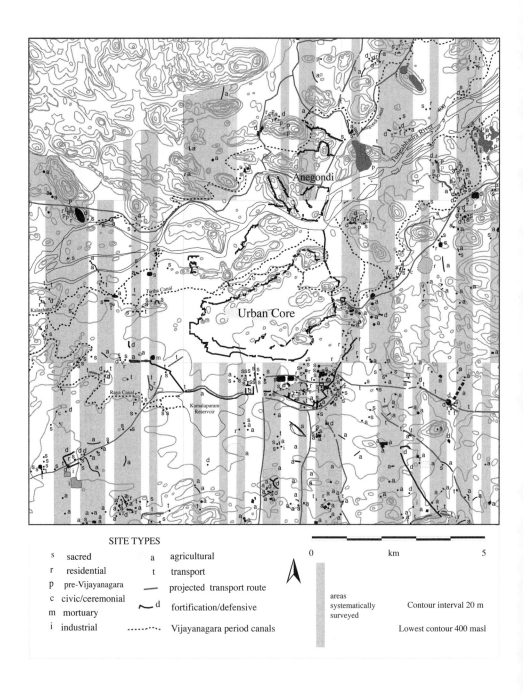

SITE TYPES

s   sacred   a   agricultural
r   residential   t   transport
p   pre-Vijayanagara   —   projected transport route
c   civic/ceremonial
m   mortuary   ⌐d   fortification/defensive
i   industrial   ·······   Vijayanagara period canals

0   km   5

areas
systematically   Contour interval 20 m
surveyed
                            Lowest contour 400 masl

Figure 2-6. Vijayanagara Metropolitan Survey: intensive survey area.

Considerable investment was made in the city's defensive infrastructure (Brubaker 2000, 2003), not surprising for an imperial capital located on the northern boundary of the empire it ruled. Massive fortification walls spanned strategic passes into the metropolitan region, and routes of movements and settlements were protected by bastions, outposts, and stone enclosures.

The region's rulers and inhabitants sought to insure some degree of economic security by investing in a rich variety of agricultural features, ranging from river-fed canals, to complex networks of large and small run-off fed irrigation reservoirs, to small-scale terracing and check-dams (Morrison 1993, 1995, 1997, in prep.). Virtually all potentially arable areas contained evidence of Vijayanagara-period use.

After agricultural features, sacred sites—temples, shrines, sculptures, Muslim tombs—constituted the next most numerous site category documented. These features, dedicated to numerous Hindu deities, as well as to local goddesses, Jaina and Muslim saints, and Allah, attest to a complex sacred landscape, produced through imperial investment in major temple centers and by large and small communities (Sinopoli 1993a).

Vijayanagara period settlement was largely restricted to fortified nucleated settlements located along major routes into and out of the city, but also included smaller settlements and isolated households located near agricultural fields (Sinopoli 2004). Craft production sites, my main interest in beginning the survey, were surprisingly scarce; though, an examination of evidence for production activities in sites classed into other primary function categories revealed evidence for production activities, particularly stone and metal-working, in more than 80 sites (Sinopoli 2003).

CONCLUSIONS

As I have tried to demonstrate, regional survey has considerable potential for contributing to the study of South Asia's historic and prehistoric past. In our new project, focused on late prehistoric/early historic sites found in a 35 km^2 region on the northeast edge of the Vijayanagara intensive survey area, we plan to fill in our sample survey to achieve 100% coverage in that area, where prior work has already identified 22 sites dating from the South Indian Neolithic (c. 2800–1100 BC) and Iron Age/Early Historic periods (c. 1100 BC–AD 500). And a number of new projects that will apply similar methodologies in several areas of northern Karnataka are currently being developed. Nonetheless, the rapid destruction of the region's archaeological record increases its urgency in the Vijayanagara region and throughout the subcontinent, and in many regions, I fear that the window of opportunity for such work has already closed.

In this contribution, I have provided a broad overview of regional survey efforts in South Asia and described my work within the Vijayanagara urban core and in its metropolitan region. In both of these projects, as well as in my new work on late prehistoric/early historic developments in the Tungabhadra region, I have been influenced by Jeffrey Parsons, first as my professor and member of my doctoral committee, and more recently, as a colleague. His gentle and insightful critiques have profoundly influenced my work, as have his intellectual openness, integrity, decency, and commitment to working with colleagues and students from multiple institutions in the United States and Latin America. Latin Americanists are very fortunate to have had such a scholar working in their research area; perhaps you can now loan him (or clone him) to mine.

Acknowledgments

Thanks to Rich Blanton and Mary Parsons for allowing me to be a part of this volume. I also extend my gratitude to the Government of India, The Karnataka Department of Archaeology and Museums, The American Institute of Indian Studies, and my many collaborators in Vijayanagara research. Finally, I acknowledge Jeff Parsons—teacher, colleague, friend, and role model.

NOTES

1. In addition, teams of the Archaeological Survey of India (Narasimhaiah 1988) and Karnataka Department of Archaeology and Museums (Nagaraja Rao ed. 1983, 1985; Devaraj and Patil, eds., 1991a, 1991b) have had ongoing excavation projects at Vijayanagara, which are not discussed here.

2. I also examined ceramics from two other districts of the city—the main Islamic residential quarter and an area termed by local archaeologists "the Nobleman's Quarter" dominated by a large number of elite residential compounds. Those have been published elsewhere (Sinopoli 1986, 1993b, 1999) and are not discussed here.

REFERENCES CITED

Abraham, Shinu
   2003   Chera, Chola, Pandya: Using Archaeological Evidence to Identify the Tamil
           Kingdoms of Early Historic South India. *Asian Perspectives* 42:207–223.
Archaeological Survey of India
   1904–1919   *Annual Report of the Archaeological Survey of India*. Government Printing
           Office, Calcutta.
   1920–1996   *Memoirs of the Archaeological Survey of India*, Volumes 18–95. Government
           Printing Office, Calcutta and New Delhi.

1960–2004   *Indian Archaeology: A Review*. Annual Report of the Archaeological Survey of India, New Delhi.

Brubaker, Robert P.

2000   The Infrastructure of Imperial Security at a Pre- Colonial South Indian Capital: Recent Research at Vijayanagara. In *South Asian Archaeology 1997*, edited by Maurizio Taddei and Guiseppe de Marco, pp. 1471– 1488. Istituto Italiano per L'Africa eL'Oriente, Rome.

2003   Cornerstones of Control: The Infrastructure of Imperial Security at Vijayanagara, South India. Unpublished Ph.D. dissertation, Department of Anthropology, University of Michigan, Ann Arbor.

Chakrabarti, D. K.

1988a   *A History of Indian Archaeology from the Beginning to 1947*. Munshiram Manoharlal, New Delhi.

1988b   *Theoretical Issues in Indian Archaeology*. Munshiram Manoharlal, New Delhi.

2001   *Archaeological Geography of the Ganga Plain: The Lower and Middle Ganga*. Permanent Black, Delhi.

Devaraj, D. V., and C. S. Patil (editors)

1991a   *Vijayanagara: Progress of Research, 1984–87*. Directorate of Archaeology and Museums, Mysore.

1991b   *Vijayanagara: Progress of Research, 1987–88*. Directorate of Archaeology and Museums, Mysore.

Erdosy, George

1988   *Urbanisation in Early Historic India*. British Archaeological Reports, International Series, No. 430, Oxford.

Fogelin, Lars

2003   Beyond the Monastery Walls: The Archaeology of Early Buddhism in North Coastal Andhra Pradesh, India. Unpublished Ph.D. dissertation, Department of Anthropology, University of Michigan, Ann Arbor.

Fritz, John M., George Michell, and M. S. Nagaraja Rao

1985   *Where Kings and Gods Meet: The Royal Center at Vijayanagara*. University of Arizona Press, Tucson.

Fritz, John A., Teresa Raczek, and Robert P. Brubaker (editors)

In press   *Vijayanagara: Archaeological Exploration, 1990–2000. Papers in Memory of Channabasappa S. Patil*. Manohar, New Delhi.

Hooja, Rima

1988   *The Ahar Culture and Beyond: Settlements and Frontiers of 'Mesolithic' and Early Agricultural Sites in South-Eastern Rajasthan, C.3rd–2nd Millennia B.C.* British Archaeological Reports, International Series, No. 412, Oxford.

Lal, Makkhan

1984   *Settlement History and Rise of Civilisation in Ganga-Yamuna Doab from 1500 B.C. to 300 A.D.* B.R. Publishing Corporation, Delhi.

1987   Populations Distribution and its Movement During the Second and First Millennia B.C. in the Indo Gangetic Divide and Upper Ganga Plain. *Puratattva* 11:1–10.

Mack, Alexandra
2002   *Spiritual Journey, Imperial City: Pilgrimage to the Temples of Vijayanagara.* Vedams, New Delhi.

Michell, George A.
1990   *Vijayanagara: Architectural Inventory of the Urban Core.* Directorate of Archaeology and Museums, Mysore.

Michell, George A., and Phillip B. Wagoner, with the assistance of Jayaram Poduval
2001   *Vijayanagara: Architectural Inventory of the Sacred Centre.* Manohar and American Institute of Indian Studies, New Delhi.

Miller, Heather
1999   Pyrotechnology and Society in the Cities of the Indus Valley. Unpublished Ph.D. dissertation, Department of Anthropology, University of Wisconsin, Madison.

Morrison, Kathleen D.
1990   Patterns of Urban Occupation: Surface Collections at Vijayanagara. In *South Asian Archaeology 1987*, edited by M. Taddei, pp. 1111–1126. Istituto Italiano per il Medio ed Estremo Oriente, Rome.

1993   Supplying the City: The Role of Reservoirs in an Indian Agricultural Landscape. *Asian Perspectives* 32:133–152.

1995   *Fields of Victory: Vijayanagara and the Course of Intensification.* Contributions to the Archaeological Research Facility, No. 52, University of California, Berkeley.

1997   Agriculture at the Edges: Archaeology and History in the Vijayanagara Hinterland. In *South Asian Archaeology 1995*, edited by B. Allchin, pp. 783–791. Oxford and IBH, New Delhi.

in prep *Oceans of Dharma: A Political Ecology of Place.* Unpublished manuscript in possession of author.

Morrison, Kathleen D., and Carla M. Sinopoli
1992   Economic Diversity and Integration in a Pre-Colonial Indian Empire. *World Archaeology* 23:335–352.

Mughal, Mohammad Rafique
1972   Explorations in Northern Baluchistan. *Pakistan Archaeology* 8:137–150.

1982   Recent Archaeological Research in the Cholistan Desert. In *Harappan Civilization*, edited by G. L. Possehl, pp. 85–96. Oxford and IBH, New Delhi.

1990a   The Harappan Settlement Systems and Patterns in the Greater Indus Valley (circa 3500–1500 BC). *Pakistan Archaeology* 25:1–72.

1990b   The Harappan "Twin Capitals" and Reality. *Journal of Central Asia* 13:155–162.

1990c   The Protohistoric Settlement Patterns in the Cholistan Desert. In *South Asian Archaeology, 1987*, edited by M. Taddei, pp. 143–156. Instituto Universitario Orientale, Naples.

1993   The Geographical Extent of the Indus Civilization During the Early, Mature, and Late Harappan Times. In *South Asian Archaeology Studies*, edited by G. L. Possehl, pp. 123–143. International Science Publisher, New York.

1997   *Ancient Cholistan: Archaeology and Architecture.* Ferozsons, LTd., Rawalpindi, Pakistan.

Nagaraja Rao, M. S. (editor)

1983   *Vijayanagara: Progress of Research, 1979–83.* Directorate of Archaeology and Museums, Mysore.

1985   *Vijayanagara: Progress of Research, 1983–84.* Directorate of Archaeology and Museums, Mysore.

Narasimhaiah, B.

1988   A Decade of Excavation at Vijayanagara (Hampi). In *Early Vijayanagara: Studies in its History and Culture*, edited by G. S. Dikshit, pp. 191–222. B. M. S. Memorial Foundation, Bangalore.

Paddayya, K.

1982   *The Acheulian Culture of the Hunsgi Valley (Peninsular India): A Settlement System Perspective.* Deccan College Postgraduate and Research Institute, Poona.

1991   The Acheulian Culture of the Hunsgi–Baichbal Valleys, Peninsular India: A Processual Study. *Quartär* 41/42: 111–138.

Patil, Chanabasappa, and Vinoda C. Patil

1995   *Inscriptions of Karnataka, Vol. I, Inscriptions at Vijayanagara (Hampi).* Vijayanagara Research Centre Series No. 8. Department of Archaeology and Museums, Mysore.

Rajan, K.

1997   *Archaeological Gazetteer of Tamil Nadu.* Manoo Pathippakam, Thanjavur.

Settar, S., and Ravi Korisettar

2002   *Indian Archaeology in Retrospect*, 4 Vols. Indian Council of Historical Research and Manohar, New Delhi.

Sewell, Robert

1900   *A Forgotten Empire (Vijayanagar).* Swann Sonneschein, London.

Shaw, Julia

2000   Sanchi and its Archaeological Landscape: Buddhist Monasteries, Settlements, and Irrigation Works in Central India. *Antiquity* 74:775–776.

Shinde, Vasant

1991   The Late Harappan Culture in Maharashtra, India: A Study of Settlement and Subsistence Patterns. *South Asian Studies* 7:91–96.

1998   *Early Settlements in the Central Tapi Basin.* Munshiram Manoharlal, Delhi.

Sinopoli, Carla M.

1986   *Material Patterning and Social Organization: A Study of Ceramics from Vijayanagara, South India*. Ph.D. dissertation, Department of Anthropology, University of Michigan. University Microfilms, Ann Arbor.

1993a   Defining a Sacred Landscape: Temple Architecture and Divine Images in the Vijayanagara Suburbs. In *South Asian Archaeology 1991*, edited by A. J. Gail and G. J. R. Mevissen, pp. 625–635. Franz Steiner Verlag, Stuttgart.

1993b   *Pots and Palaces: The Earthenware Ceramics of the Noblemen's Quarter of Vijayanagara*. American Institute of Indian Studies and Manohar Press, New Delhi.

1996   The Archaeological Ceramics of the Islamic Quarter of Vijayanagara. In *Vijayanagara Progress of Research 1988–91*, edited by D. V. Devaraj and C. S. Patil, pp. 105–123. Directorate of Archaeology and Museums, Mysore.

1999   Levels of Complexity: Ceramic Variability at Vijayanagara. In *Pottery and People: A Dynamic Interaction*, edited by James Skibo and Gary M. Feinman, pp. 115–136. University of Utah Press, Salt Lake City.

2003   *The Political Economy of Craft Production: Crafting Empire in South India, AD 1350–1650*. Cambridge University Press, Cambridge.

2004   Beyond Vijayanagara's City Walls: Regional Survey and the Inhabitants of the Metropolitan Region. In *Archaeology as History: South Asia*, edited by Himanshu P. Ray and Carla M. Sinopoli, pp. 257–279. Indian Council for Historical Research and Aryan Books, New Delhi.

Sinopoli, Carla M., and Kathleen D. Morrison

1991   The Vijayanagara Metropolitan Survey: The 1988 Season. In *Vijayanagara: Progress of Research, 1987–88*, edited by D. V. Devaraj and C. S. Patil, pp. 55–69. Directorate of Archaeology and Museums, Mysore.

1992   Archaeological Survey at Vijayanagara. *Research and Exploration* 8(2):237–239.

1995   Dimensions of Imperial Control: The Vijayanagara Capital. *American Anthropologist* 97:83–96.

2001   The Vijayanagara Metropolitan Survey Project. In *New Light on Hampi*, edited by John M. Fritz and George Michell, pp. 100–111. Marg Publications, Bombay.

Smith, Monica L.

2001   *The Archaeology of an Early Historic Town in Central India*. Archaeopress, Oxford.

2003   Early Walled Cities of the Indian Subcontinent as 'Small Worlds.' In *The Social Construction of Ancient Cities*, edited by Monica L. Smith, pp. 269–289. Smithsonian Institution Press, Washington, D.C.

Stein, Burton

1989   *Vijayanagara*. Cambridge University Press, Cambridge.

SETTLEMENT PATTERN ARCHAEOLOGY IN THE TEOTIHUACAN VALLEY

AND THE ADJACENT NORTHEASTERN BASIN OF MEXICO

A.P. (AFTER PARSONS)

THOMAS H. CHARLTON
University of Iowa

DEBORAH L. NICHOLS
Dartmouth College

William T. Sanders's Teotihuacan Valley Project (TVP) in the early 1960s (1960–1964) was the context for a seminal event in Central Mexican archaeology, the introduction of the regional settlement pattern research strategy and the development of effective surface survey tactics to implement it. The project yielded significant new details on both the settlement and population history of the Teotihuacan Valley and the development of pre-Hispanic states and cities; it was also important for its explicit statement of cultural ecological and evolutionary theory and the development of methods and techniques of systematic regional settlement pattern survey (Charlton 1965, 1972, 1973; Nichols 1996, 2004; Parsons 1971, 1989; Parsons and Sanders 2000; Sanders 1965, 1999, 2000; Sanders et al. 1979). Among those students who first learned and applied settlement pattern surface surveys within Sanders's TVP were Jeffrey R. Parsons and Thomas H. Charlton. Deborah L. Nichols, a later graduate student of Sanders, benefited from the influence of the TVP within the context of surface surveys directed by Sanders in 1974 in the Cuauhtitlan–Tenayuca area of the Basin of Mexico.

It was within the forge of the TVP that many details of modern settlement pattern survey methodologies were hammered out. Many of the students involved in Sanders's project later applied the settlement pattern strategy in their own research, on other problems, in other areas, and for other time periods (e.g., Charlton 1973; Diehl 1983; Parsons 1971; Parsons et al. 1982). Jeffrey Parsons, who joined the TVP in 1961, was an active contributor to these developments from the beginning. Later he applied and refined many of the TVP methodologies in his surveys of the Texcoco, Chalco, Xochimilco, and Zumpango areas of the Basin (Nichols 1996:70–71; Sanders et al. 1979:23) (Figure 1-1). One of his students, Richard Blanton, employed those same methodologies to survey the picturesque Ixtapalapa Peninsula (Blanton 1972). The Basin of Mexico survey methodology subsequently has been applied to other regions of Mesoamerica (Kowaleski et al. 1989; Nichols 1996; Sanders 1999) and other parts of the world (Underhill et al. 1998).

THE LEGACY OF THE TEOTIHUACAN VALLEY PROJECT

When the Teotihuacan Valley Project began, systematic archaeological surveys were in their infancy (Willey 1956). The survey methodology, which developed over the course of the project, became its core methodological legacy (Charlton 1994:227–228; Mather 1968:46–56; Nichols 1996:69–71; 2004:268–69; Parsons 2004:1–3; Parsons and Sanders 2000:502; Sanders 1965:12–13,1999:12–16,2000:60–65; and Sanders et al.1979:11–30). The methodology revolves around a field-by-field intensive survey and recording of archaeological, environmental, and present-day land use data on aerial photographs and on a standardized form for each agricultural field. Sanders shelved this procedure at the end of the first field season because he considered it too time consuming relative to the results achieved (Sanders 1999:14).

During 1961 and 1962, Sanders replaced the 1960 intensive survey methodology (2000:60). With the help of Charles Fletcher and Joseph Marino, he implemented a general survey method designed to locate archaeological sites more rapidly by walking transects in the valley and recording sites encountered on a 1:25,000 composite aerial photograph.

In 1963, Sanders reintroduced the intensive survey—this time, focusing on each site located during the general survey. The 1960 field forms were converted into site forms. Although the least expensive and most readily available commercial composite aerial photographs, printed at scales of 1:10,000 and 1:25,000, were useful for the general survey; the scales were impractical for the intensive survey. With some ingenuity, William G. Mather systematically photographed, in small sections, the entire 1959 1:25,000 aerial photographic coverage of the Teotihuacan Valley (Mather 1968:48–50). In turn, he could print each negative to a scale from 1:3,500 to 1:4,500, yielding an 8.5" x 11" print, a size suitable both for carrying in the field and on which to record survey data (Parsons and Sanders 2000:502; Sanders 2000:60).

Initially, in 1963, different graduate students, each with expertise in the ceramics of the appropriate period, surveyed multicomponent sites several times. At the same time, all students were instructed in the complete ceramic sequence to be able to recognize occupations other than their period specialty. Survey teams were generally composed of one to two students and a Mexican laborer.

Thus the 1963 survey was a site-centered intensive survey designed to determine site size, presence of architecture, and period(s) of occupation. It was not, at least at the onset, the 1960 field-by-field intensive survey method, focusing on the field as the survey unit.

Procedures actually used in survey, collection, and recording varied to some extent between investigators. They were generally comparable, involving intensive surveys of fields, and occasionally house-lots, until the edge of the site, as defined through a drop-off of artifact density, was reached. In 1963, Parsons found that his previous experience in using aerial photographs in geological surveys proved useful (Parsons 2004). He told Charlton, at the time, that aerial photographs were more useful than topographic maps on which to locate archaeological surface data. At that time topographic maps for Mexico at scales appropriate for archaeology were, like the commercially available aerial photographs, not widely available. An examination of Parson's 1963 site reports reveals that as the summer field season progressed he gradually instituted a field-by-field survey. This covered contiguous fields within and between Aztec sites where several closely spaced sites had been reported by the general survey. Such reports included notations of earlier occupations with occasional astute forays into early colonial period ceramics. The survey data from adjacent 8.5" x 11" enlarged aerial photographs would be traced onto a single map, and site and intersite data were noted. Such survey techniques required the small crew to repeatedly walk back and forth across the fields (Parsons and Sanders 2000:502; Sanders 2000:60–61).

One goal of the TVP surveys was to reconstruct population history and this required developing a method to estimate population size from the archaeological survey data. These figures were generated using estimates of surface artifact densities (Parsons 1971:16–17). Determination of occupation density—through collecting and counting ceramic rims within a 1 x 1 m square—was initially tried in 1960, briefly reinstated in 1963, and is present on the site recording form. Charlton recalls at least one such collection being made near Tepexpan when the intensive surveys began in July 1963. It was abandoned in favor of more subjective criteria to speed up the intensive survey. Surface collections became purposively selected noncomprehensive "grab" samples of rims and chronologically diagnostic body sherds. With collections made and surveys conducted at the same time, considerable weight was carried during the rest of the day (see Sanders et al. 1979:22).

By late summer 1963, Parsons had modified the site-based intensive survey methodology into a field-by-field survey when clusters of Aztec period sites were being recorded. When he returned to the Teotihuacan Valley in late spring 1964, Parsons applied this methodology in the eastern Teotihuacan Valley, where there was a highly dispersed Aztec settlement pattern (Parsons

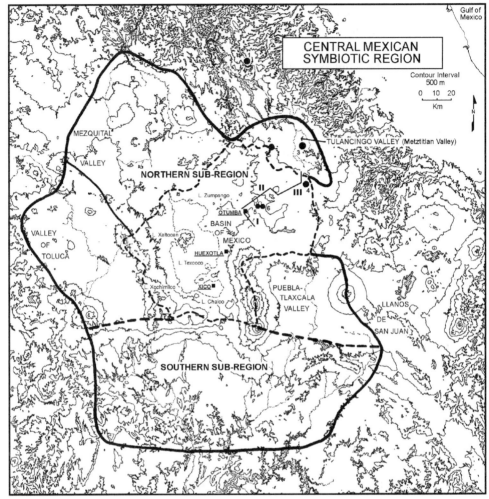

Figure 3-1. Central Mexican Symbiotic Region with sites, surveys, and obsidian sources mentioned. Obsidian source areas: 1, Zacualtipan; 2, Pachuca; 3, Tulancingo; 4, Tecocomulco; 5, Otumba; 6, Malpaís. Trade Routes I, II, and III. Base map was derived from the Detenal 1:250,000 series maps NE 14–1 to NE 14–3 (1970), NE 14–4 to NE 14–6 (1976), and NF 14–10 to NE 14–12 (1970). Contour Interval = 500 m. Map prepared by Cynthia Otis Charlton.

and Sanders 2000:502; Sanders 2000:60–61). Charlton used *this* methodology in his 1963 and 1964 TVP surveys near San Cristobal Colhuacan, on the northern slopes of Cerro Gordo, and in the eastern Teotihuacan Valley near the Haciendas Soapayuca and Tlaltehuacan (Figure 3-1).

In the late summer and continuing through the fall of 1963, Sanders on the north slopes of Cerro Gordo, faced with extensive or dense concentrations of settlement and multi-component occupations, also began to survey field by field and to record environmental data, as well as archaeological and modern occupations, with the field as the survey unit. Data were recorded on aerial photographs and/or in notebooks and sites were later defined using the ceramic distributions for different periods as traced from the aerial photographs. The same surveyor(s) (Sanders 2000:60–61) recorded occupations from all time periods.

As previously mentioned, until fall 1963, survey teams had been composed of only one or two archaeologists and a Mexican worker. This kind of intensive field-by-field survey meant substantial walking back and forth for the small survey teams to cover each unit. In fall 1963, however, in conjunction with the field-by-field survey, Sanders reduced the amount of walking by initiating the now familiar team approach with more survey crewmembers. All would move in evenly spaced lines across each field and provide information on architecture during the survey and on occupational phase and density once the field survey was completed (Charlton 1996:461). Sanders also began to take the purposive "grab" samples once the sites were defined. Charlton remembers doing this for Sanders, with one Mexican worker, on a miserable, cloudy, cold, windy November day in 1963. The collections focused on questions of chronology, function, and class structure and were neither structured by sampling procedures nor inclusive of all materials encountered—either ceramic or obsidian.

These procedures, implemented by individual archaeologists or by survey teams, reflect the basic core methodological legacy of the TVP for later intensive surveys in the eastern Teotihuacan Valley and other areas of the Basin of Mexico (Parsons and Sanders 2000:502; Sanders 1999:16, 2000:61; Sanders et al. 1979:20–26) (Figure 1-1).

TEOTIHUACAN VALLEY SURFACE SURVEY PROJECTS: 1966–2002

In this section, we examine the changes in settlement pattern survey and collection methodologies developed and applied between 1966 and the present in the Teotihuacan Valley. We conclude our general overview with a more detailed presentation of the settlement pattern survey and collection methodology used in our Otumba Project.

Projects involving settlement pattern surveys in the Teotihuacan Valley from 1966 to 2002 are listed in Table 3-1. All these projects began with prior knowledge of the field methods and results of the earlier surface surveys carried out in conjunction with the TVP. Each of these projects addressed specific questions and issues raised by the TVP. Further, they were influenced by theoretical developments and debates on early state formation, including urbanism, and the roles of craft specialization, agricultural intensification, trade, and demography in early state development. Urban–rural interrelationships during the Teotihuacan period and the Late Aztec period also form part of these studies.

Table 3-1. Teotihuacan Valley Projects with Surface Survey and Collection Components: 1966-2002

Project	Fieldwork	Directors/Authors
1. Teotihuacan Valley	1966	J.R. Parsons and W.T. Sanders 2000
2. Post-Conquest Developments	1966-1969	T.H. Charlton 1973
3. Trade Routes	1975	T.H. Charlton 1978
Plate 1-2		
4. Floodwater Irrigation	1977	T.H. Charlton
5. Rural Aztec Life: Cihuatecpan	1984	S.T. Evans 1988
6. Otumba Project	1987-1989	T.H. Charlton, D.L. Nichols, and
Plate 1-1		C.L. Otis Charlton 2000a, 2000b
7. Malpaís Obsidian Source Area 1998		T.H. Charlton and C.L. Otis Charlton
Plate 3-1		
8. Teotihuacan Hinterlands 1	1998-1999	T.H. Charlton, C.L. Otis Charlton, and
		W.T. Sanders 2002
9. Teotihuacan Hinterlands 2	2001-2002	T.H. Charlton, C.L. Otis Charlton, and
		R. García Chávez

The problem foci of these projects prompted adjustments in survey methodology and in collection procedures. These included statistical sampling and technical analyses of collected materials, thus paralleling disciplinary trends in archaeology (Sabloff and Ashmore 2001).

Beginning with the methodological inheritance of the TVP, the surveys from 1966 to 2002 in the eastern Teotihuacan Valley:

(1) continued the intensive field-by-field survey technique by individuals or by survey teams for discovery or to resurvey previously known sites;

(2) developed standardized forms to record cultural and environmental data for each numbered field survey unit and each bucket auger test;

(3) developed standardized forms to record environmental and contextual data for each surface collection;

(4) took surface collections from standardized surface areas within field-based survey units;

(5) initiated the use of sampling designs procedures to locate standard sized surface collections; and

(6) used modified collection procedures to ensure the recovery of materials from previously ignored time periods, including the post-conquest occupations, and from archaeologically ephemeral activities such as various types of craft production and carrying sites as noted below.

Substantively, the post-TVP projects:

(1) linked previously intensively surveyed areas by surveying the spatial gaps in survey coverage between them (TVP 1966, Post-Conquest Developments, Trade Routes, Otumba);

(2) extended the surveys to include immediately adjacent areas to the north and northeast- and southeast of the Teotihuacan Valley using intensively surveyed transects, which reached the Metztitlan Valley (northeast) and the border of the State of Tlaxcala (southeast) (Trade Routes);

(3) included the Otumba and the Malpaís Obsidian Source Areas within zones to be surveyed intensively (Trade Routes, Otumba Project);

(4) searched for traces of ephemeral activities such as carrying sites, and debris from manufacturing activities such as obsidian and ground stone tool production, as well as from maguey processing (Trade Routes, Otumba Project);

(5) resurveyed five Teotihuacan-period rural sites, systematically made surface collections at each, and excavated at three sites (Teotihuacan Hinterlands 1 and 2); and

(6) surveyed and excavated floodwater irrigation canals within Otumba (Floodwater Irrigation, Otumba Project).

THE EVOLUTION OF SURFACE SURVEY METHODOLOGIES IN THE TEOTIHUACAN VALLEY, 1966–2002

During this period, survey and collection methodologies continued to be refined within the contexts of the several previously mentioned sequential projects in the Teotihuacan Valley. Charlton (1994:227–231) and Nichols (1996:69–71, 75–77) have discussed some of these changes.

Survey Units

The arbitrary and pragmatic use of agricultural fields as survey units was continued in the 1966 field season of the TVP directed by Parsons for Sanders to survey intensively two areas, the southern piedmont with alluvium and the eastern slopes of Cerro Gordo (Parsons and Sanders 2000:502). Similarly the Post-Conquest Developments Project, the Trade Routes Project, the Otumba Project, and the Teotihuacan Hinterlands Project continued this practice. Although field boundaries on the ground, in many instances, had changed, there were usually sufficient markers available to delineate the most recent field boundaries on the photographs.

Since the 1980s, such changes have, unfortunately, become increasingly problematic as population pressure and more readily available heavy earth-moving equipment have combined in most rural areas of the Basin of Mexico to rework field boundaries and field surfaces. The use of such equipment was intended to increase agricultural production by creating more arable land, and hence to slow the migration of rural people to the Mexico City megalopolis (Parsons 1989). Unfortunately, many sites discovered during the TVP have suffered serious damage and such archaeology that can be conducted at them is frequently salvage (Charlton, Otis Charlton, and Sanders 2002; Charlton et al. in press).

Plate 3-1. Malpaís obsidian source survey, 1998, from Cerro de la Calera facing northeast to Ciudad Sahagún, Tepeapulco, and the northern Llanos de Apan.

However, as the Rural Aztec Life, Otumba, and Hinterlands Projects have demonstrated, the remnant sites in the Teotihuacan Valley, although greatly modified and subjected to various destructive forces, warrant further investigations. When accompanied by modern technology for site and collection location, including GPS as used by Parsons in his recent Lake Bed Survey, and compositional analyses of artifacts and osteological specimens from both old and new collections, the continuing archaeology of the Teotihuacan Valley can address, through a growing number of collections, cultural processes involved in the origin and functioning of early urban states.

The use of fields as survey units obviously only works when there are or have been field boundaries on the ground. The Malpaís Obsidian Source Area Survey had lacked such well-defined units (Plate 3-1) (cf. Finsten and Kowalewski 1999 in forested areas of Oaxaca). The presence of heavy vegetation in much of the area made a close reliance on aerial photographs difficult, at best, since details were obscured. In these surveys, topographic features such as hills and drainages were used as the survey units since they could be readily identified on both the 1:25,000 aerial photographs as well as on the 1:50,000 topographic maps.

During 1964, when Charlton was conducting ethnographic settlement pattern research (1966), he used larger aerial photographs, of varying scales (1:25,000, 1:10,000, 1:2,000), covering more area than a single 8.5" x 11" survey print. These larger aerial photographs were attached to a map board made of plywood (64 cm x 70 cm), carried by the surveyor. When incorporated into archaeological survey projects (Trade Routes, Otumba Project), this map board worked better than multiple 8.5" x 11" prints. Parsons and Sanders (2000:502) noted that Parsons developed a similar solution by the end of the TVP surveys in 1966 and incorporated it into his Texcoco Project in 1967.

Survey Methodology
As in the 1963 to 1964 TVP surveys, the size of the survey team since 1966 varied by project and by phase within a particular project. Usually, the size was budget-related, a factor often overlooked in discussions of archaeological methods. However, the intensive survey procedure—developed by Parsons and Sanders, with crewmembers knowledgeable about the complete ceramic sequence—was the norm for all projects even when it meant that a lone archaeologist would have a lot of ground to cover. The procedures of intensive surveys with a team of archaeologists systematically walking the surface of a survey unit separated by distances related to the density of archaeological remains were modified only during the Malpaís Obsidian Source Survey. The goal of this project was to locate and sample all obsidian outcrops within the source area. Hills, with evidence of obsidian in the drainages around their bases, were surveyed by three archaeologists walking in a series of concentric circles increasing in elevation until the summit was reached.

Except for the Malpaís Obsidian Source Survey, all collections were made after the surveys were completed and the site(s) defined. In the Malpaís survey, geological collections of obsidian, being small, were taken as the survey proceeded. These attempted to recover obsidian samples evenly throughout the surveyed area where there were outcrops of obsidian. No one wanted to walk up the vegetation-covered steep slopes a second time to take samples. The outer edges of the exposed and exploited obsidian outcrops were defined. Few residential sites were located in the area and those were Aztec period.

Survey Data Recording
The Post-Conquest Developments Project collected ethnographic as well as archaeological settlement data along with some environmental observations such as slope. Initially these data were recorded on the 1:4,000 8" x 10" aerial photograph enlargements from the TVP.

Additional environmental data were recorded in a notebook by numbered field. The archaeological data were traced off the aerial photographs and sites defined.

Beginning with the Trade Routes Project (Plate 1-2; Figure 3-1) and forming part of a general trend in archaeology (with an emphasis on methodological rigor and standardization in data recording), a standardized form was developed to record all archaeological, ethnographic, and environmental data from a survey unit as defined on a 1:5,000 or 1:6,000 aerial photograph enlarged from the original flight negatives. Color and black-and-white photographs were taken to supplement these data. The same standardized form was used in all subsequent projects except the Malpaís Obsidian Source Survey Project, where such data were recorded on the standardized obsidian sample form developed in the Otumba Project.

Collection Methodology

Again, with the exception of the Malpaís Obsidian Source Area Survey Project, all surface collections were made after surveys had been completed for large areas and sites had been defined in the laboratory. Obviously, this would include sites defined by previous projects, such as the TVP, as well as sites defined by ongoing surveys. Initially, in the Post-Conquest Developments Project, some TVP collection procedures were also followed. The collections were purposive, but standardized for duration of collection time, although not for size of the area from which the collections were made. For the Post-Conquest Developments Project—the first modern historical archaeology project in the Teotihuacan Valley involving survey—the collection strategy was expanded to include a greater range of materials, such as glazed ceramics. However, the collections continued to be biased against the recovery of undecorated Aztec Plain Orange bodies and handles, and against the systematic collection of obsidian (Charlton 1994:229–230). Only comprehensive and intensive pre-excavation surface collections included all materials. These collections were controlled neither for surface area nor for time spent making the collections (Brodkey 1978).

Although the Trade Routes Project continued making purposive collections after sites had been defined, innovations—such as the systematic collection of all types of artifacts (not just diagnostic pottery types) from a constant area of 20 square meters, by a knowledgeable collection crew within a period of 20 minutes—were instituted to ensure comparability of collections. This procedure was also instituted because, after reviewing the collections from the Post-Conquest Developments Project, it became obvious that some important colonial ceramics were present only in the comprehensive collections or in the excavated materials. It was also decided that any decision to eliminate materials from a collection would be best undertaken in the laboratory, not during the field collection. No statistical sampling techniques were applied.

Within the Otumba Project, we undertook further refinements and used a stratified random sampling program at a one percent level for the entire Otumba site of c. 200 ha and at a one plus four percent level for the southeastern sector where craft manufacturing areas were concentrated. To address debates about the role of craft specialization in Aztec city-state development and in Aztec economic organization by Brumfiel, as well as concerns about the archaeological identification of craft specialization raised by Clark, we needed comparable quantitative data on artifact types and densities (Charlton et al. 1991, 2000a, 2000b). These collections were supplemented by nonrandomly chosen collection units within Otumba and within several zones of the badly destroyed rural dependent sites. All artifacts larger than a thumbnail were collected. The collection unit was a standard 25 square meters (5 x 5 m), no time limits were enforced, and a standardized form was completed for each collection detailing environmental and cultural data relevant to the collection (Plate 1-1) (Charlton 1994:230; Charlton et al. 2000a, 2000b).

In addition intensive nonrandom surface collections (2 x 2 m or 5 x 5 m) were also made either before or in lieu of excavations. Such collections can be used to evaluate the representativeness of surface artifacts. A standardized collection form was used. Otumba is one of the most intensively surveyed and collected Aztec city-state capitals. Excavations confirmed identifications of craft specialization and workshops determined from survey data. Each survey and collection program at the site has yielded additional identifications of manufacturing loci in a range of industries.

Collection procedures in the recent Teotihuacan Hinterlands Project involved the use of the standardized collection form developed at Otumba and the 5 x 5 m collection area, but not the random sampling procedure. Intensive collections were made in a grid of 5 x 5 m squares based on the Otumba Project intensive collection procedures. A bucket auger (and related standardized form) at the corners of each 5 x 5 m square was introduced but with mixed results given the heavy stone deposits. The bucket auger was used to test for depth of archaeological deposit and for the presence of architectural remains. These data would help define where to excavate. Similar results were obtained from the use of a bucket auger at Oztoyahualco (Manzanilla 1993). The Teotihuacan Hinterlands Project collections were similar to those of the Otumba Project made prior to or in lieu of excavations.

An important finding of the TVP was the high density of Late Aztec period sites, both rural and urban. Evans initiated investigations involving the relocating of extant mounds, the excavation of some of these, and a surface collection program of fourteen unexcavated mounds at At Cihuatecpan (TA-81), a village site initially intensively surveyed and collected by Charles Fletcher in 1963 in the TVP, Evans (1988:228) used a standardized 10 x 10 m square for the fourteen purposive surface collections. She does not mention the use of a collection form to record data and notes that undecorated utilitarian wares such as Plain Orange are virtually non-existent in the surface collections a situation she atributes to differential artifact visibility (Evans and Abrams 1988:228).

SURFACE SURVEY AND COLLECTION METHODOLOGY OF THE OTUMBA PROJECT

The substantive contributions of the TVP to our later research in the Otumba city-state, located in the eastern Teotihuacan Valley, included the site reports and survey maps prepared by TVP personnel in 1963 and 1964 (Thomas Charlton, Charles Fletcher, Charles Kolb, William Mather, John McCullough, and Jeffrey Parsons), and by the TVP 1966 final survey personnel, students of Parsons (Robert Bettarel, Richard Blanton, William Engelbrecht, Mary Hrones, Lembi Kongas, and John Speth).

Supplemented by similar data from the Post-Conquest Developments Project and the Trade Routes Project, both of which investigated areas of the Otumba city-state where post-conquest occupation had been documented in archival sources and where documentary and ethnographic sources, as well as preliminary archaeological surveys, attested to the presence of trade routes. The settlement data were updated and augmented by resurveys and new surveys of additional areas by the Otumba Project from 1987 to 1989. Of particular importance as baseline data were the reports and maps prepared in 1963 by Mather (TA–80), in 1964 by Parsons (TA–36–39, 56–59, 71, 85 and 86), and in 1966 by Parsons's students (TA–236).

Just as the TVP provided substantive survey contributions essential for later research in the Otumba city-state, it also provided a basic methodology for surveys and collections as modified through intervening projects. Parsons's methodological contributions to the Otumba Project came through his maps and site reports and those 1963 intensive site surveys where Charlton accompanied him, primarily in the Lower Teotihuacan Valley.

Survey Methodologies

At the onset of the Otumba Project, Charlton, Otis Charlton, and Tenorio Coronel carried out a complete new intensive survey of the Otumba city-state center, Otumba (TA–80), without taking collections (Charlton 1988). Mather previously surveyed Otumba in 1963 (Mather 1968). The survey methods involved the survey team walking in line across each numbered field—Survey Unit—with one archaeologist carrying a map board with a 1:5,000 aerial photograph, on which archaeological data and field boundary changes from Mather's 1963 survey were noted. Once a field was surveyed, field data from each survey unit were also recorded on the standardized form introduced during the Trade Route Project. Using the same procedures, we surveyed additional areas around Otumba to link the site with areas to the east surveyed by Parsons and to incorporate additional areas not previously surveyed to the west, north, and east around and in modern Otumba.

In the case of the dependent sites around Otumba, most had been intensively surveyed by Parsons and had been the subject of surface collections during Charlton's Post-Conquest Developments Project, which had also surveyed areas between groups of sites recorded by Parsons (Charlton 1972, 1973). In 1988, during the Otumba Project, we conducted brief, rapid, reconnaissance surveys at the dependent sites with photocopies of the survey maps as traced from the original 1:4,000 or 1:5,000 aerial photographs to determine the status of their preservation. No collections were taken during these reconnaissance surveys.

Collection Methodologies

In our studies of the Otumba city-state, the surface collection program involved a combination of probabilistic and purposive sampling accompanied by a standardized surface collection form to record environmental conditions, land use, artifact types and densities, and the presence of mounds or any other special features. The institution of these strategies—combined with a standardized surface area and the inclusion of all materials on the surface(both developed in the Trade Routes Project)—would provide us with representative and comparable artifact samples from different, previously identified parts of Otumba and from rural dependencies so that we could consider questions about economic and political structure. Although Elizabeth Brumfiel, a student of Parsons, used probabilistic sampling strategies at Huexotla in the Texcoco Region (Brumfiel 1976) and at Xico in the Chalco Region (Brumfiel 1986), none, to the best of our knowledge, had been used in the Teotihuacan Valley prior to the Otumba Project.

At Otumba, TA–80, where most collections were made we employed a stratified, systematic, unaligned sampling design, supplemented by purposive, nonrandomly chosen samples where appropriate. The aim of the sampling program was to ensure an even distribution of samples from all parts of the site. This also controlled for differences in ground conditions.

We divided the site map based on the 1987 resurvey into 972 50 x 50 m sampling strata. This was convenient for the scale of the site map traced from the 1:5,000 aerial photograph, yet small enough to control for different field conditions. One 5 x 5 m square, a one percent sampling fraction, was randomly selected from each stratum using a table of random numbers. A total of 798 collections were made in 794 different strata. Excluding four duplicate and additional collections, 1.985 km2 of the site area was sampled at the one percent sampling level, and a total surface area of 19,850 m2 was collected at the one percent level. A variety of circumstances, such as landowner recalcitrance, dense, spiny vegetation, roads, and *barrancas*, precluded our making random collections in some parts of the site. No alternative units were chosen in those cases.

We had noted heavy concentrations of artifacts from craft activities in the southeastern section of the site in 1987, so we increased our sampling fraction from one to five percent with an additional four percent sample, for an additional 296 collections. Although most strata sampled at an additional four percent level coincided with those sampled at the one percent level, the additional four percent sample did add 10 strata, which fell outside the one percent sampled area. Occasionally mounds, workshops, or other unusual artifact concentrations were inadequately sampled by the randomly chosen squares. Using the same size squares and collection procedures, we made nonrandom collections when these were encountered.

In addition to this surface collection program, we also took collections from each unit to be excavated or under consideration for excavation. In two instances, we expanded the surface collections to include a larger area around the excavated zones, and in the case of a maguey-fiber workshop, we substituted the surface collections for excavations (Nichols et al. 2000).

Although we had intended to apply random sampling to three outlying dependent sites, our rapid reconnaissance in those sites indicated that it would not be possible due to partial or complete destruction from chisel plowing and reforestation. Instead, we used the same collection procedures as at Otumba but in a purposive sampling strategy. One hundred and eighty-nine collections were made in site remnants located in three zones at various distances and directions outside of Otumba.

Field Applications

In the field, we used site maps, a compass, and 50-m tapes to locate one corner of each randomly selected square (Plate 1-1). The other three corners were set out with a compass and four ropes, each cut to a 5 m length. Temporary stakes were placed in each corner and recovered after the collection was made. All squares, random and nonrandom, were oriented to true north. All artifacts within the square were collected (ceramics including vessel fragments, figurines, and spindle whorls and their molds, obsidian, ground stone, glass, and metal). Crews were instructed to collect only those sherds larger than a thumbnail, but not everyone adhered strictly to this rule. When some squares contained large quantities of recent garbage, not all of this was collected.

The standard form completed for each collection unit served to identify and describe each square. Included in the description were type of vegetation, soil depth and condition (wet versus dry), degree of erosion, current land use, type and density of artifacts, size of mound, if present, and any other special features. Photographs were taken of mounds and general site conditions. The environmental information is relevant for analyses of artifact densities since ground conditions at the time of collection, along with collector experience, affect artifact visibility.

Collection crews usually consisted of five to seven people and included at least one experienced archaeologist. The crews were composed of one to three students and three to four Mexican workers. Two people located and laid out each square while one person completed the collection form, filled in the bag tags, and supervised the collection in general. Depending on accessibility of fields due to agricultural conditions, one or two crews would make the collections.

The Otumba Project surveys, surface collections, and excavations confirmed and expanded our previous knowledge of craft specialization and details of occupational history in the Otumba city-state. The Late Postclassic urban center of Otumba included household-based craft production, some of which was organized into barrios of households with the same productive activities. Clay-based industries, including figurine, spindle whorl, and local pottery production, occurred in a barrio setting, as did maguey fiber processing, spinning, and weaving. Jewelry production from obsidian and more exotic stones occurred both in a loose barrio setting and in individual households (Otis Charlton 1993). Clay incense burner production appears to be associated partly with the clay artifact producers' barrio and partly with a central area of the site where elite priests may have been involved in incense burner production. Similarly, obsidian core-blade production is associated with dispersed individual households, some of which are in the nucleated core of the city. Basalt grinding tools were manufactured in three widely separated areas outside of the site's core.

Both in the urban center and throughout the city-state, cotton was spun in individual households as was maguey fiber. However, in the dependent sites, the only other craft activity practiced was obsidian biface manufacture (Charlton et al. 1991, 2000a, 2000b).

EPILOGUE

The TVP fieldwork ended with the 1966 season's intensive surveys of the eastern slopes of Cerro Gordo and the southern piedmonts of the Middle Teotihuacan Valley by students of Parsons. Its influence continued as Sanders, Parsons, and Diehl developed and modified the TVP intensive survey and collection methodologies in their settlement pattern surveys in other regions of the Basin of Mexico and Central Mexico. Yet, archaeological research also continued in the Teotihuacan Valley. Just as research in other areas was energized by the TVP substantive and methodological contributions, these also energized a series of continuing survey and excavation projects in, or setting out from, the eastern Teotihuacan Valley. Those projects used survey data from the TVP generated by Mather, Parsons, and Parsons's students.

They also continued the evolution of the survey and collection methodologies developed in the TVP by Sanders, Parsons, and others. In a series of projects, the survey methods, developed in 1966 in the TVP by Sanders and Parsons, underwent minor modifications that consisted primarily of the addition of standardized survey unit forms and the observation of materials marking ephemeral activities and post-conquest occupations. These survey methods remain highly productive to this day.

Collection methodologies, on the other hand, related to additional survey goals, underwent major changes, retaining nonrandom or purposive collections, but adding statistical sampling strategies. The areas of surface collections were standardized. Introducing an arbitrarily defined size limit, above which all collected materials must fall to be included in the collection, ensured standardization in size of materials to be collected. A standardized data collection form was instituted for each surface collection and extended to bucket augers when used. Similar changes occurred in the Texcoco region and elsewhere when research goals beyond surface survey discovery were included (Brumfiel 1976, 1986).

In sum, the post-1966 archaeological projects in the Teotihuacan Valley represent continuity and change from the methodologies of the TVP. We are indebted to Jeff Parsons and Bill Sanders for their pioneering efforts in implementing the Settlement Pattern approach in the Teotihuacan Valley of the Basin of Mexico. Their development of survey, collection, and data recording methods in the TVP forms the foundation upon which all later Teotihuacan Valley surveys rest and more generally upon which the regional approach to archaeology in Central Mexico rests.

Acknowledgments

Thomas H. Charlton's research in the Otumba Area of the eastern Teotihuacan Valley has been supported since 1963 by research grants and fellowships from different agencies including the following: Social Science Research Council 1963–1964; Canada Council 1966; Associated Colleges of the Midwest 1967; University of Iowa Off-Campus Assignment 1969, Research Assignment 1975, Developmental Assignments 1975, 1982, 1988, 1993; Career Development Awards 1998–1999, 2005; Old Gold Summer Faculty Research Fellowships 1968, 1970, 1980, 1985; Arts and Humanities Initiative Research Grant 2003–2004; International Travel Grants 1992, 1996, 2002, 2004; Foundation for the Advancement of Mesoamerican Studies, Inc., Research Grant; National Science Foundation Research Grants GS–2080, 1968–1972, BNS–871–9665, 1988–1990, SBR–97–14583, 1997–2001—the latter two for collaborative research with Deborah L. Nichols as PI on Research Grants BNS–871–8140 and SBR–97–07462; National Endowment for the Humanities Research Grants RO–20173–81–2231 1981–1983, RO–21705–88 1988–1989, and RO–22268–91 1992–1995—the latter two for collaborative research with Deborah L. Nichols. We both received support from the Archaeometry Program of the Missouri University Research Reactor Facility in the analyses of the materials recovered.

Deborah L. Nichols received additional support from the Dartmouth Class of 1962, the Reiss Senior Faculty Grant, Nelson A. Rockefeller Center for the Social Sciences at Dartmouth College, the Claire Garber Goodman Fund, and the Dartmouth Faculty Research Fund.

All field and laboratory research was done under the authorization of permits issued by the Instituto Nacional de Antropología e Historia, with the active support of the Departamento de Monumentos Prehispánicos, the Dirección de Arqueología, and the Consejo de Arqueología.

REFERENCES CITED

Blanton, Richard E.
  1972   *Prehispanic Settlement Patterns of the Ixtapalapa Peninsula Region, Mexico.* Occasional Papers in Anthropology No. 6, Department of Anthropology, Pennsylvania State University, University Park, Pennsylvania.
Brodkey, Dale D.
  1978   Postconquest Settlement Patterns of the Otumba Area, Mexico. Manuscript on file, Department of Anthropology, University of Iowa, Iowa City.
Brumfiel, Elizabeth M.
  1976   *Specialization and Exchange at the Late Postclassic (Aztec) Community of Huexotla, Mexico.* Ph.D. dissertation, Department of Anthropology, University of Michigan. University Microfilms, Ann Arbor.
  1986   The Division of Labor at Xico: The Chipped Stone Industry. In *Economic Aspects of Prehispanic Highland Mexico*, edited by Barry L. Isaacs, pp. 245–279. *Research in Economic Anthropology*, Supplement 2, JAI Press, Greenwich.
Charlton, Thomas H.
  1965   Archaeological Settlement Patterns: An Interpretation. Ph.D. dissertation, Department of Anthropology, Tulane University, New Orleans.
  1972   Population Trends in the Teotihuacán Valley, A.D. 1400–1969. *World Archaeology* 4:106–123.
  1973   *Post-Conquest Developments in the Teotihuacán Valley, Mexico. Part I: Excavations.* Report No. 5, Office of the State Archaeologist, Iowa City.
  1978   Teotihuacan, Tepeapulco, and Obsidian Exploitation. *Science* 2000:1227–1236.
  1988   *Otumba, México: Reconocimientos de superficie del sitio de TA–80, Otumba: Informe técnico final.* Report submitted to the Instituto Nacional de Antropología e

Historia, Mexico City. Manuscript on file, Department of Anthropology, University of Iowa, Iowa City.

1994   Economic Heterogeneity and State Expansion: The Northeastern Basin of Mexico During the Late Postclassic Period. In *Economies and Polities in the Aztec Realm*, edited by Mary G. Hodge and Michael E. Smith, pp. 221–256. Studies on Culture and Society, Vol. 6. Institute for Mesoamerican Studies, State University of New York, Albany.

1996   Early Colonial Period Ceramics: Decorated Red Ware and Orange Ware Types of the Rural Otumba Aztec Ceramic Complex. In *Arqueología Mesoamericana: Homenaje a William T. Sanders*, 2 vols., edited by Guadalupe Mastache, Jeffrey R. Parsons, Mari Carmen Serra Puche, and Robert S. Santley, pp. 461–479. Instituto Nacional de Antropología e Historia, México, D.F.

Charlton, Thomas H, Deborah L. Nichols, and Cynthia L. Otis Charlton

1991   Aztec Craft Production and Specialization: Archaeological evidence from the City-State of Otumba, Mexico. *World Archaeology* 23:98–114.

2000a   Otumba and its Neighbors: Ex Oriente Lux. *Ancient Mesoamerica* 11(2): 247–265.

2000b   The Otumba Project: A Review and Status Report. In *The Teotihuacan Valley Project Final Report, Vol. 5: The Aztec Period Occupation of the Valley*, Part 2, *Excavations at T.A. 40 and Related Projects*, edited by William T. Sanders and Susan T. Evans, pp. 841–847. Occasional Papers in Anthropology No. 26, Department of Anthropology, Pennsylvania State University, University Park, Pennsylvania.

Charlton, Thomas H., Cynthia Otis Charlton, and William T. Sanders

2002   Influencias urbanas dentro de comunidades rurales: Teotihuacan y sus dependencias cercanas 100 a.C.–650 d.C. In *Ideología y política a través de materiales, imágenes y símbolos*, edited by María Elena Ruíz Gallut, pp. 487–499. Memoria de la Primera Mesa Redonda Sobre Teotihuacan, Conaculta–INAH, Mexico, D.F.

Charlton, Thomas H., Raul García Chávez, Cynthia Otis Charlton, Verónica Ortega Cabrera, David Andrade Olvera, and Teresa Palomares Rodríguez

In press   Salvamento arqueológico reciente en el valle de Teotihuacan, Sitio TC–83, San Bartolomé el Alto. In *Memorias de la Tercera Mesa Redonda de Teotihuacan*. Conaculta INAH, Mexico, D.F.

Diehl, Richard A.

1983   *Tula, The Toltec Capital of Ancient Mexico*. Thames and Hudson, London.

Evans, Susan T. (editor)

1988   *Excavations at Cihuatecpan: an Aztec Village in the Teotihuacan Valley*. Vanderbilt University Publications in Anthropology No. 36, Nashville.

Evans, Susan T., and Elliot M. Abrams

Archaeology at the Aztec Period Village of Cihuatecpan, Mexico: Methods and Results of The 1984 Field Season, In *Excavations at Cihuatecpan: an Aztec Village in the Teotihuacan Valley*, edited by Susan T. Evans, pp. 50-234, Vanderbilt University Publications in Anthropology No. 36, Nashville.

Finsten, Laura, and Stephen Kowalewski

1999   Spatial Scales and Process: In and around the Valley of Oaxaca. In *Settlement Pattern Studies in the Americas, Fifty Years since Virú*, edited by Brian R. Billman and Gary M. Feinman, pp. 22–35, Smithsonian Institution Press, Washington, D.C.

Kowaleski, Stephen A., Gary M. Feinman, Laura Finsten, Richard E. Blanton, and Linda M. Nicholas

1989   *Monte Albán's Hinterland, Part II: Prehispanic Settlement Patterns in Tlacolula, Etla, and Ocotlán, The Valley of Oaxaca, Mexico*. Memoirs No. 23, Museum of Anthropology, University of Michigan, Ann Arbor.

Manzanilla, Linda

1993   Introducción. In *Anatomía de un conjunto residencial Teotihuacano en Oztoyahualco*. Vol. 1, *Las excavaciones*, edited by Linda Manzanilla, pp. 15–30. Instituto de Investigaciones Antropológicas, U.N.A.M., Mexico, D.F.

Mather, William G., III

1968   The Aztec State of Otumba, Mexico: An Ethno–Historical Settlement Pattern Study. Master's thesis, Department of Anthropology, Pennsylvania State University, University Park, Pennsylvania.

Nichols, Deborah L.

1996   An Overview of Regional Settlement Pattern Survey in Mesoamerica: 1960–1995. In *Arqueología Mesoamericana: Homenaje a William T. Sanders*, 2 vols., edited by Guadalupe Mastache, Jeffery R. Parsons, Mari Carmen Serra Puche, and Robert S. Santley, pp. 59–95. Instituto Nacional de Antropología e Historia, Mexico, D.F.

2004   The Rural and Urban Landscapes of the Aztec State. In *Mesoamerican Archaeology Theory and Practice*, edited by Julia A. Hendon and Rosemary A. Joyce, pp. 265–295. Blackwell, Oxford.

Nichols, Deborah L., Mary Jane McLaughlin, and Maura Benton

2000   Production Intensification and Regional Specialization: Maguey Fibers and Textiles in the Aztec City-State of Otumba. *Ancient Mesoamerica* 11:267–291.

Otis Charlton, Cynthia L.

1993   Obsidian as Jewelry: Lapidary Production in Aztec Otumba, Mexico. *Ancient Mesoamerica* 4:231–243.

Parsons, Jeffrey R.

1971   *Prehistoric Settlement Patterns in the Texcoco Region, Mexico*. Memoirs No. 3, Museum of Anthropology, University of Michigan, Ann Arbor.

1989   Arqueología regional en la cuenca de México: Una estrategía para la investigación futura. *Anales de Antropología* 26:157–257.

2004   Critical Reflections on Forty Years of 'Systematic Regional Survey'. Paper presented at the 69th Annual Meeting of the Society for American Archaeology, Montreal.

Parsons, Jeffrey R., and William T. Sanders

2000   The 1966 Survey of Zones 10 and 17 of the Teotihuacan Valley. In *The Teotihuacan Valley Project Final Report, Vol. 5: The Aztec Occupation of the Valley, Part 2, Excavations at T.A. 40 and Related Projects*, edited by William T. Sanders and Susan T. Evans, pp. 501–563. Occasional Papers in Anthropology No. 26, Department of Anthropology, Pennsylvania State University, University Park, Pennsylvania.

Parsons, Jeffrey R., Elizabeth Brumfiel, Mary H. Parsons, and David J. Wilson

1982   *Prehispanic Settlement Patterns in the Southern Valley of Mexico: The Chalco–Xochimilco Region*. Memoirs No. 14, Museum of Anthropology, University of Michigan, Ann Arbor.

Sabloff, Jeremy A., and Wendy Ashmore

2001   An Aspect of Archaeology's Recent Past and its Relevance in The New Millennium. In *Archaeology at the Millennium: A Source Book*, edited by Gary M. Feinman and T. Douglas Price, pp. 11– 32. Kluwer Academic/Plenum, New York.

Sanders, William T.

1965   *Cultural Ecology of the Teotihuacan Valley*. Department of Anthropology, Pennsylvania State University, University Park. Pennsylvania.

1999   Three Valleys: Twenty-Five Years of Settlement Archaeology in Mesoamerica. In *Settlement Pattern Studies in the Americas: Fifty Years Since Virú*, edited by Brian R. Billman and Gary M. Feinman, pp. 12–21. Smithsonian Institution Press, Washington, D.C.

2000   Methodology. In *The Teotihuacan Valley Project Final Report, Vol. 5: The Aztec Period Occupation of the Valley, Part 1, Natural Environment, 20th Century Occupation, Survey Methodology, and Site Descriptions*, edited by Susan T. Evans and William T. Sanders, pp. 59–84. Occasional Papers in Anthropology No. 25, Department of Anthropology, Pennsylvania State University, University Park, Pennsylvania.

Sanders, William T., Jeffery R. Parsons, and Robert S. Santley

1979   *The Basin of Mexico: Ecological Process in the Evolution of a Civilization*. Academic Press, New York.

Underhill, Anne G., Gary Feinman, Linda Nicholas, Gwen Bennett, Fengshu Cai, Haiguang Yu, Fengshi Luan, and Hui Fang

1998   Systematic Regional Survey in SE Shandong Province, China. *Journal of Field Archaeology* 25:453–474.

Willey, Gordon R. (editor)

1956   *Prehistoric Settlement Patterns in the New World*. Viking Fund Publications in Anthropology No. 23, New York.

OPTING IN AND OPTING OUT:
TULA, CHOLULA, AND XALTOCAN

ELIZABETH M. BRUMFIEL
Northwestern University

SHERDS AND "SPHERES OF INFLUENCE"

Analyzing prehistoric settlement patterns in the Texcoco Region, Mexico, Jeffrey Parsons (1971:203–208) suggested that the distributions of Mazapan and Aztec I ceramics in the Basin of Mexico demarcated the "spheres of influence" of two Early Postclassic capitals: Tula, 70 km to the northwest of Texcoco, and Cholula, 75 km to the southeast. Specifically, Parsons noted:

(1) Red-on-Buff (Mazapan) ceramics in the Texcoco and Tula regions are very similar, suggesting that Early Postclassic Texcoco lay within Tula's sphere of influence.

(2) Mazapan and Aztec I ceramics rarely occur at the same sites in the Basin of Mexico. Mazapan pottery generally occurs in the central and northern Basin, and Aztec I pottery is most common in the southeastern quarter. This mutually exclusive distribution suggests that the Basin of Mexico lay on the frontier between Tula to the northwest and Cholula to the southeast during the Early Postclassic period.

(3) Early Postclassic settlement in the Texcoco region is highly dispersed, possibly explained by the region's location on the edge of Tula's sphere of influence and its proximity to potentially hostile settlements to the south, which were aligned with Cholula.

Settlement surveys in other parts of the Basin added both clarity and complexity to this picture. The northern Basin survey (Zumpango Region) revealed a dense Early Postclassic population with sizable provincial centers. This was consistent with the idea that the northern Basin had been integrated into a state system centered on Tula. The southern Basin surveys (Ixtapalapa, Chalco, and

Xochimilco Regions, see Blanton 1972; Parsons et al. 1982) revealed that the distributions of Aztec I pottery and Chalco Polychrome pottery were practically isomorphic. Chalco Polychrome is a regional variant of the well-known Mixteca-Puebla ceramic sphere centered on Cholula (Vaillant 1938; Noguera 1954; Müller 1970); thus, its presence in the southern Basin supported the idea that the southern Basin lay within Cholula's sphere of influence.

Later research questioned the relationship between Mazapan pottery and Tula's sphere of influence. Significant amounts of Mazapan pottery were found in the southern Basin, usually at small, rural sites. These contrast with major centers in the southern Basin such as Culhuacan, Mixquic, and Chalco, which yielded heavy concentrations of Aztec I pottery. Either Mazapan settlement in the southern Basin preceded Aztec I settlement (Parsons et al. 1982), or two cultural traditions coexisted in the southern Basin, with Aztec I settlement representing an urbanized way of life, and Mazapan, a more rural population (Blanton 1972:188). In addition, excavations in the Teotihuacan Valley suggest that Mazapan pottery is most common in the Teotihuacan Valley and the eastern Basin of Mexico rather than at Tula (Koehler 1986; Sanders 1986).

Still, recent research at Xaltocan, an Early through Late Postclassic site in the northern Basin of Mexico, confirms Parsons's original suggestion that the Basin of Mexico lay between Tula's and Cholula's "spheres of influence." This research also indicates that Xaltocan experienced a dramatic reorientation of interregional ties at the beginning of the Early Postclassic, ca. AD 900. Prior to this date, ceramics from the Xaltocan region more closely resembled the ceramics of Tula rather than Cholula. After this date, Xaltocan fell within Cholula's ceramic sphere. This sudden, seemingly deliberate realignment of ceramic ties poses interesting questions. What social, economic, or political relationships are implied by ceramic differences and similarities between Tula, Cholula, and Basin of Mexico communities during the Early Postclassic? How were these ties forged? How and why were they altered? Using an agency-centered approach to interregional interaction, I suggest that people in the central and southern Basin of Mexico sought ties to Cholula to increase their access to Gulf Coast trade goods and to resist political and economic domination by Tula.

AGENCY-CENTERED APPROACHES TO REGIONAL STYLE

Agency-centered approaches to regional style have developed gradually over the past twenty years, providing an alternative to models that regard the spread of artifact styles across broad geographic areas as a mechanical process that does not require consideration of human decision-making. Mechanical models of regional style include both the cultural historians' models of cultural contact and diffusion (Rogers and Wilson 1993) and the evolutionary archeologists' models of human adaptation through random variation and differential selection (Dunnell 1980:62). In both approaches, human decision-making is regarded as a constant, taken-for-granted process, unworthy of detailed analysis. In contrast, agency-centered approaches to regional style postulate that people purposefully adopt items of material culture for reasons of their own choosing, frequently relating to their specific economic, social, or political goals. These choices and purposes can be inferred through the analysis of material culture in archaeological context.

Archaeologists first used agency-centered approaches to regional style to explore the role of elite exchange in articulating geographically distant areas (Caldwell 1964; Flannery 1968; Brown 1976; Meachan 1977; Friedel 1979; Renfrew 1979; Smith and Heath-Smith 1980; Blanton and Feinman 1984; Renfrew and Cherry 1986; Helms 1993). These early discussions featured elites as agents who actively promoted the spread of regional styles: local rulers exchanged goods and information with nearby and distant elites to enhance their social status at home and to gain prestige in the eyes of their peers in other polities. These elite exchange models provided the first alternatives to discussions of "contacts" between undifferentiated "cultures" that eschewed intentionality. Elite exchange models explicitly posed questions of agency: *which* specific social groups were engaged in interaction, and *why* did they find it in their interests to do so (Renfrew 1986:8, following Cowgill 1975:507)?

Schortman (1989) amplified these models in useful ways. First, he suggested that the exchange of exotic goods accompanied the spread of translocal affiliations or identities, i.e., culturally defined categories of people that guided interpersonal behaviors and were signaled by specific material symbols (i.e., items of dress, repertoires of behavior, etc.). Following Barth (1969), Schortman suggested that individuals adopted status goods and their linked affiliations and identities for instrumental reasons: to gain access to valued resources controlled by others such as productive sites, status goods, social labor, and military alliances. Second, Schortman observed that such identities always developed in opposition to a perceived group of "others," who could be excluded from access to the valued resources. Finally, Schortman and Nakamura (1991) proposed that this model could explain both the spread of cultural styles through interregional interaction and the failure of styles to spread. For example, elite Maya culture did not diffuse beyond certain limits on the southeast Maya periphery because non-Maya leaders beyond these limits were trying to develop their own trade links with eastern Honduras free of Maya interference.

More recently, agency-centered approaches have been modified to recognize the ways that groups besides elites (e.g., merchants, commoners) and other identities other than status (e.g., gender, ethnicity) could affect interregional interaction (Minc 1994; Lightfoot and Martínez 1995; Stein

1998, 2003; Smith and Berdan 2003). In addition, the boundaries between regional systems are no longer regarded as solid barriers. Boundaries are seen as breakpoints in the social, political, and economic rules that channel interactions between individuals but not absolute barriers to interaction (Green and Perlman 1985:4; Heyman 1994; Lightfoot and Martínez 1995; Berdan 2003). Finally, archaeologists have explored not just the spread of existing styles, but also interaction processes such as creolization and ethnogenesis that sometimes generate entirely new categories of identity and regional style (Deagan 1990, 1998; Lightfoot and Martínez 1995; Stein 2003). Stein (2003) combines these ideas in an elegant model of interregional interaction that, above all, emphasizes the agency exercised by all participants in creating and crossing regions and frontiers.

An agency-centered approach seems particularly appropriate for interregional interaction in the Xaltocan area because this area's ceramics suggest a dramatic reorientation of interregional ties at the Epiclassic-to-Early Postclassic transition, c. AD 900. The ceramic data are described below, followed by a discussion of what these data might imply about the influence of regional centers on the Basin of Mexico during the Early Postclassic.

XALTOCAN: AN EARLY-THROUGH-LATE POSTCLASSIC CENTER IN THE NORTHERN BASIN OF MEXICO

Xaltocan is a low island rising 5 to 6 m above the bed of Lake Xaltocan in the northern Basin of Mexico (Figure 4-1). It is oval shaped with an east–west length of 800 m and a north–south width of 400 m. The pre-Hispanic site lies under the modern town, and in some places, extends beyond its borders, covering an area of about 68 ha. The extent of the site is defined by substantial concentrations of surface pottery, lithic debris, and extensive mounding that rises as much as 6 m above the level of the surrounding lakebed. In pre-Hispanic times, Xaltocan was completely surrounded by shallow lake and marsh, although a causeway linked the island to the western shore at the time of Spanish conquest (Díaz del Castillo 1956:356). Excavations suggest that the "island" of Xaltocan results entirely from human activity; it consists of fill, structural remains, and occupational debris lying directly upon the sterile lakebed clay.

The political history of Xaltocan is outlined in native histories dating to Mexico's early colonial period. According to these accounts, Xaltocan was settled in the mid-eleventh century AD, immediately after the fall of Tollan (Alva Ixtlilxóchitl 1975–1977 I:293; *Anales de Cuauhtitlan* 1945:14). During the twelfth and thirteenth centuries, Xaltocan became an important regional center, the capital of Otomí-speaking peoples in southern Hidalgo and the

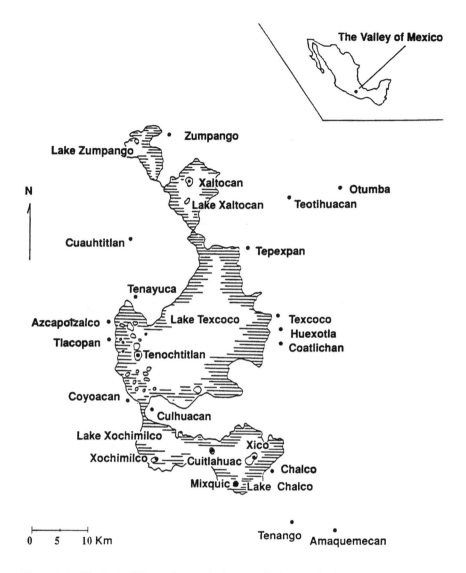

Figure 4-1. The Basin of Mexico showing the location of Xaltocan and other important Postclassic settlements.

northern Basin of Mexico (Alva Ixtlilxóchitl 1975–1977 I:423, II:299; see Carrasco 1950). Xaltocan interacted with other Postclassic centers in the Basin of Mexico such as Tollan, Azcapotzalco, Tenayuca, Huexotla, Culhuacan, and Chalco, but the histories never mention interactions with Cholula (Carrasco 1950:260–1; see also Davies 1980:144–5, Nazareo 1940:124; Alva Ixtlilxóchitl 1975–1977 II:17, 18, 51; *Anales de Tlatelolco* 1948:28).

In 1395, Xaltocan lost a war to the neighboring town of Cuauhtitlan and its Tepanec allies. In the wake of Xaltocan's defeat, the town was deserted and lay empty for more than thirty years (*Anales de Cuauhtitlan* 1945:50). In 1428, it fell subject to the Aztec Triple Alliance, and the rulers of Tenochtitlan and Tlatelolco settled a new population of tribute-payers in Xaltocan (Hicks 1994). A military ruler (*cuauhtlatoani*) sent from Tenochtitlan governed this population. In 1521, Hernán Cortés attacked and burned Xaltocan, ending the pre-Hispanic era (Nazareo 1940:120; Cortés 1971:118).

Archaeological survey and excavation at Xaltocan supplement, and to some extent contradict, the information provided by ethnohistory, particularly for the earliest phases of Xaltocan's history. Although the documents state that Xaltocan was settled in the mid-eleventh century, archaeological evidence suggests that the site was first occupied at the beginning of the tenth century, and possibly earlier. Although the histories do not indicate links between Xaltocan and Cholula, archaeological evidence reveals both direct and indirect ties between the two sites. Although the histories extol the brilliance of the Toltec capital Tollan, archaeological evidence suggests that the extent of the Toltec influence was limited.

Archaeological investigations at Xaltocan began in 1987. The research was focused on the interaction of politics, economics, and demography during the six centuries of Xaltocan's pre-Hispanic occupation (Brumfiel in press). Investigations at Xaltocan included an intensive surface survey and systematic surface collection of most of the site, followed by the excavation of twenty-four 2 m x 2 m test pits, three of which were expanded into broader excavations (Figure 4-2). During the 1997 field season, we also completed a systematic surface collection at a small (1 ha.), heavily looted, Epiclassic site lying on the lakebed 1 km north of Xaltocan. We first called this site the ET site and later named it Michpilco.

The survey and excavation data provide the basis for several observations:

(1) During the Epiclassic period (c. AD 650–900), ceramics from the Xaltocan region more closely resembled the ceramics of Tula than Cholula.

(2) Continuity existed between the Epiclassic population of the northern Basin of Mexico lakebed and the Early Postclassic (c. AD 900–1200) inhabitants of Xaltocan.

(3) The Early Postclassic ceramics of Xaltocan share many stylistic attributes with those of Cholula.

(4) Although the Early Postclassic pottery at Xaltocan was contemporaneous with the Corral and Tollán phases at Tula, Corral and Tollán-phase diagnostics are rare at Xaltocan.

The evidence for these observations is presented below, together with a discussion of their implications for patterns of interregional interaction.

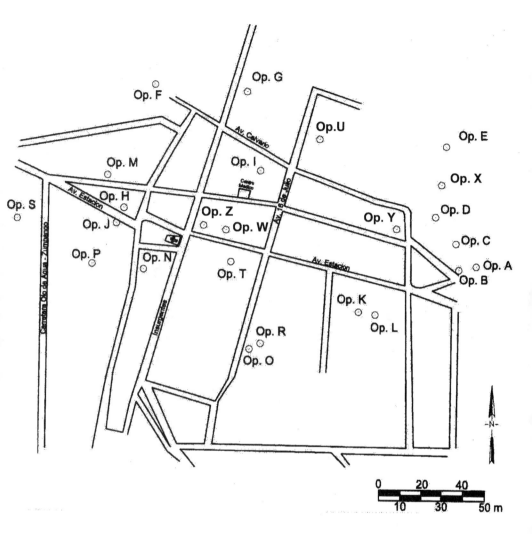

Figure 4-2. Xaltocan showing the locations of 24 test pits ("Operations").

EPICLASSIC CERAMICS IN THE XALTOCAN AREA

In the Xaltocan region, the Epiclassic is represented by the ET site, a small (1 ha) lakebed site lying 1 km north of Xaltocan. A systematic surface collection of this heavily looted site yielded a representative 11% sample of pottery from the site. Brumfiel and Rodríguez-Alegría (1998) provide a provisional typology of the ET ceramics. This pottery closely resembles the Epiclassic ceramics of Tula, but not Cholula.

Many of the decorated vessels at the ET site have parallels in the Epiclassic Prado and Corral phases at Tula. For example, the most common decorated

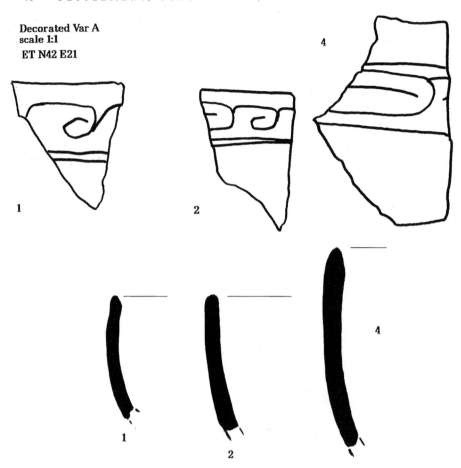

Decorated Var A
scale 1:1
ET N42 E21

Figure 4-3. Variant A ceramics from ET (Mixpilco).

type at ET is Variant A, an upright rim light grayish brown hemispherical bowl with a band of incised spirals on its exterior wall (Figure 4-3). Such bowls constitute 64% of all decorated bowls and 11% of the entire ET assemblage. Variant A has a counterpart at Tula, Artesia Café Inciso, but at Tula, this is a rare Corral-phase decorated type (Cobean 1990:189–94). The second most common decorated type at ET is Variant D, which resembles Classic Thin Orange pottery in surface color, wall thickness, and vessel form. Variant D constitutes 18% of all decorated bowls and 3% of the entire ET assemblage. Tula also has ceramic type that resembles Thin Orange, Animas Anaranjado Pulido, an important component of the Prado-phase ceramic assemblage (Cobean 1990:118–26). Variants B and J at ET are painted bowls with motifs that place them generally within Coyotlatelco Red-on-Buff and Coyotlatelco Red-on-Cream wares, common at Corral-Phase Tula (Cobean 1990:130–73,

181–89). However, Coyotlatelco from ET has its own peculiarities (Figure 4-4). Perhaps because of the high salt content of the northern lakebed soils, a grayish yellow paint replaces the red paint on "Coyotlatelco" sherds from ET. In addition, the Coyotlatelco designs occur on the interiors of hemispherical bowls at ET, while at Tula, they occur on the exteriors of upright rim bowls. In this regard, "Coyotlatelco" sherds from ET more closely resemble Coyotlatelco Red-on-Buff bowls from Xometla, in the Teotihuacan Valley, where 63% of the Coyotlateloco bowls had interior decoration (Nichols and McCullough 1986:87).

An Instrumental Neutron Activation Analysis (INAA) of "Coyotlatelco" bowls from ET revealed that they originated in an unidentified production center that was definitely not Tula (Johnson 2000). This is consistent with INAA analysis of Coyotlatelco sherds from other parts of the Basin of Mexico, which suggest the existence of many production centers, each with a relatively limited area of distribution (Nichols et al. 2002).

It is difficult to compare the Epiclassic ceramics of ET with those of Cholula, primarily because little consensus exists as to what Epiclassic ceramics from Cholula might look like. Many archaeologists, influenced by the conclusions of the Proyecto Cholula, believe that Cholula was almost abandoned in Epiclassic times, so that a hiatus exists in Cholula's ceramic sequence (Dumond and Müller 1972; Müller 1978; Mountjoy 1987). In contrast, McCafferty and Suárez (1996) argue that Cholula maintained its status as an important regional center throughout the Epiclassic and Postclassic periods. McCafferty (1996b:309–312, 2001) assigns an Epiclassic date to ceramics excavated from the Patio of the Carved Skulls at Cholula. These ceramics are quite unlike those from Epiclassic ET.

At the Patio of the Carved Skulls, Tepontla Burnished Grey/Brown is a dominant type. A few Tepontla Burnished vessels are hemispherical bowls with "shallow geometric and curvilinear incising on the exterior" (McCafferty 2001:40), and these may be analogous to Variant A from ET. But most Tepontla Burnished bowls have flat bottoms with nubbin supports, and thus are quite unlike ET's Variant A. The Patio of the Carved Skulls yielded neither Thin Orange nor Coyotlatelco, in clear contrast with the ceramics from ET or Prado- and Corral-phase Tula. The Patio of the Carved Skulls did yield ample amounts of Cocoyotla Black-on-Natural ceramics (McCafferty 1996b:309–312). This is analogous to Aztec I Black-on-Orange, which is well represented at Xaltocan, but only during the succeeding Early Postclassic period (see below). If we accept the materials from the Patio of the Carved Skulls as dating to the Epiclassic, then the ceramics from ET much more closely resemble those of Prado- and Corral-phase Tula than those of Epiclassic Cholula.

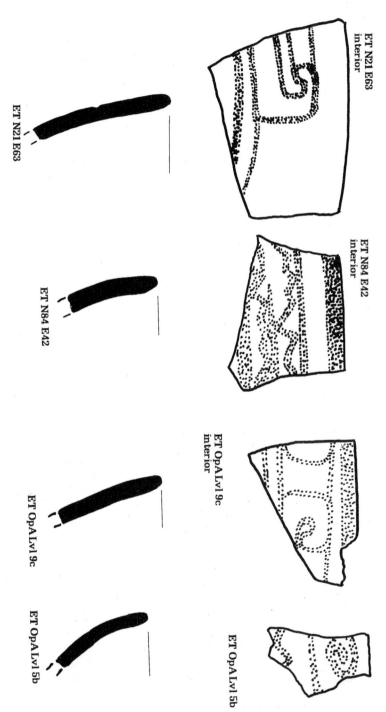

Figure 4-4. "Coyotlatelco" ceramics from ET (Mixpilco).

THE EPICLASSIC TO EARLY POSTCLASSIC TRANSITION AT XALTOCAN

Operation Z at Xaltocan yielded evidence of continuity between the Epiclassic population of ET and the Early Postclassic inhabitants of Xaltocan. Excavated in 2003, Operation Z was a 2 m x 2 m test pit located in a mound just northeast of Xaltocan's central plaza (Figure 4-2). The top of this mound had been leveled to facilitate modern construction; nevertheless, the disturbed remains of two burials were found near the surface of the excavation unit, and a well preserved room was found beneath. This room had adobe walls (1 m in height) and two superimposed plaster floors. The room yielded a mix of Aztec I Black-on-Orange and polychrome serving vessels that define the Early Postclassic period at Xaltocan (see below). This room was underlain by a foundation of dense, black mud; beneath this black mud foundation, an earlier midden was found at a depth of 3 m. This midden yielded Aztec I and polychrome sherds in association with brownish-black incised bowls that closely resemble Variant A bowls from ET. The five "Variant A" rims from these strata constituted 12.5% of the total rims from these strata, comparable to the 12.5% polychrome rims and the 17.5% Aztec I Black-on-Orange rims from these same strata.

Since this midden yielded only one of the ET decorated types in association with Aztec I and polychrome ceramics, it does not seem likely that this stratum was created through a mixing of Epiclassic and Early Postclassic deposits. Rather, this association seems to indicate the survival of one Epiclassic decorated type into Early Postclassic times, suggesting the continuity between the Epiclassic population of the northern Basin of Mexico lakebed and the Early Postclassic inhabitants of Xaltocan. But this continuity was marked by a startling reversal of ceramic affiliation in Xaltocan. During the Early Postclassic, ceramic ties to Cholula became very strong while ceramic ties to Tula diminished to the point of insignificance.

EARLY POSTCLASSIC LINKS BETWEEN CHOLULA AND XALTOCAN

Survey and excavation revealed strong stylistic linkages between Xaltocan and Cholula near the beginning of the Early Postclassic, c. AD 900, or perhaps a century earlier. The first link is the ample presence of Aztec I Black-on-Orange pottery in Xaltocan. Aztec I most commonly occurs as hemispherical bowls with interior decoration, but common vessel forms also include bowls with exterior decoration and interior-decorated dishes with tripod supports. Aztec I pottery is defined by its painted designs, drawn in a bold black line on the brownish-orange base color of the vessel (Figure 4-5). Complex decorative bands with curvilinear or glyphlike motifs occur on the vessel walls, and large floral or zoomorphic motifs cover the interior bases (Brenner 1931; Séjourné

Figure 4-5.   Aztec I Black-on-Orange ceramics from Xaltocan, Operations D, G, and L.

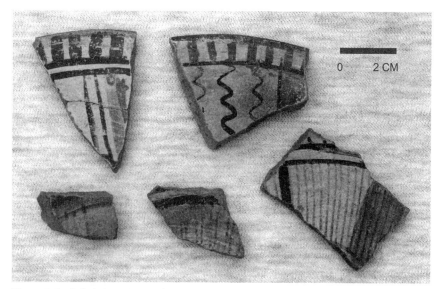

Figure 4-6. Polychrome ceramics from Xaltocan, Operations G and X.

1970; Minc 1991). Some dishes have raised molded designs on their interior bases; these vessels probably served as chili graters (*molcajetes*).

At Xaltocan, Aztec I sherds are well represented in the surface collections. In addition, unmixed Aztec I-phase deposits were found in six test pits (Operations G, I, M, T, Y, and Z), distributed over the full length and breadth of the site (Figure 4-2). These Aztec I layers were impressively thick, offering up to 5 m of stratified deposits. In unmixed deposits, Aztec I Black-on-Orange was a major type: It comprised 24% of all rim sherds and 78% of all decorated sherds. Four radiocarbon dates from the excavations at Xaltocan date the unmixed Aztec I deposits between AD 880 and 990 (Parsons et al. 1996:225).

The general resemblance of Aztec I Black-on-Orange ceramics from the Basin of Mexico to Black-on-Natural ceramics from Cholula is well recognized (Noguera 1937, 1954; Vaillant 1938:545; McCafferty 2001). Black-on-Natural vessels from Cholula include hemispherical bowls decorated on the interior base with geometric, floral, and zoomorphic motifs in broad black lines on the natural light-brown to orange surface of the vessel (Noguera 1954; Müller 1978:187, McCafferty 2001:55–58). Tripod bowls with mold-impressed decoration on their interiors occur in Cholula as they do in the southern Basin of Mexico (McCafferty 2001:42).

Although these similarities are unmistakable, they seem to be indirect. For example, McCafferty (1996b:310) observes that "Cocoyotla pottery [from Cholula] resembles 'Aztec I' Black-on-Orange pottery from the Valley of Mexico in both form and decoration, although it does not fit neatly into any of the categories defined by Hodge and Minc (1991)." Furthermore, INAA of 33 Aztec I sherds from Xaltocan reveals that none were imported from Cholula. Instead, about half were produced at Xaltocan, and the others were manufactured at various other Early Postclassic centers in the Basin of Mexico: Cuauhtitlan, Culhuacan, Chalco, and an unidentified source in the southern Basin (Nichols et al. 2002:64). Rather than representing a pottery type produced at a single source, Black-on-Orange/Black-on-Natural seems to define a sphere of cultural interaction that extended from Cholula, to the southern Basin of Mexico, Xaltocan, and eastern Morelos (Smith and Heath-Smith 1980; Norr 1987).

Polychrome ceramics are also found at both Xaltocan and Cholula. At Xaltocan, polychromes are consistently associated with Aztec I sherds: They comprise about 4% of all rim sherds and about 12% of all decorated pottery in unmixed Aztec I deposits. At least some of the polychrome styles from Aztec I contexts at Xaltocan closely resemble those found at Cholula. For example, some polychrome sherds from Operation G at Xaltocan are nearly identical to McCafferty's (2001) Torre and Aquiahuac polychrome types from Cholula (Lind's [1994] Albina Polychrome), and others resemble McCafferty's Cuaxiloa Matte Polychrome (Lind's Christina Polychrome) (Figure 4-6). Some of these vessels were probably imported from Cholula. INAA indicates that some Torre and Aquiahuac polychrome vessels manufactured in Cholula were exported to the southern basin (Neff et al. 1994:124), and from there, they could have been carried to Xaltocan.

Effigy braziers recovered at Xaltocan and Cholula are a third tie between the two sites. At Xaltocan, the braziers are thick, tan, biconical vessels from 18 to 20 cm tall (Figure 4-7)—roughly finished, with a thick white paint on their rough surfaces. Anthropomorphic clay figures are attached to the front of the vessels, also covered with thick white paint, with details added to the figure's surface in black and blue paint. Each of the three complete effigy braziers recovered from Xaltocan is unique, and none bears the obvious insignia of a Postclassic deity. Perhaps they are portraits of honored ancestors or lineage founders. Only one effigy vessel has been found in context at Xaltocan: It was discovered lying face-down in the adobe-walled room in Operation Z, suggesting that effigy vessels were used in domestic rituals in Xaltocan. The Xaltocan effigy braziers were apparently manufactured locally; at least, this is suggested by a mold for a large figurine head, of the appropriate size for an effigy vessel found in Operation G, another adobe-walled house dating to the Early Postclassic.

Müller (1978:204) illustrates three similar effigy braziers from Cholula. The braziers from Cholula appear technically similar to those from Xaltocan, but according to Müller, they bear the insignia of Late Postclassic gods such as Tlaloc, Xochiquetzal, and Macuilxochitl (Müller 1978:199–200). This might suggest that Cholula's effigies were more closely tied to state religion than

Figure 4-7. Effigy vessel from Xaltocan, Operation Z.

Xaltocan's. Thus, effigy vessels at Cholula and Xaltocan suggest a similarity of ritual form but a difference in religious beliefs between the two sites.

CONNECTIONS BETWEEN XALTOCAN AND TULA

In contrast to the robust stylistic ties between Xaltocan and Cholula, Xaltocan's links to Tula are very attenuated. The links consist of occasional Macana (Wide-Band) Red-on-Buff sherds, and even fewer Mazapan Red-on-Buff sherds, present in Aztec I contexts at Xaltocan. Together, these styles constitute less than 1% of the Aztec I-phase ceramic assemblages. Macana and Mazapan Red-on-Buff date to the Terminal Corral and Tollan phases at Tula, c. AD 900 to 1050 (Cobean 1990:302); thus they confirm the Early Postclassic date of Aztec I deposits at Xaltocan. But their very low frequencies suggest that Xaltocan fell outside the sphere of Tula's dominance. This supports Smith and Heath-Smith's (1980:26) assertion that Tula's empire was "much smaller in geographical extension…than either the earlier Teotihuacan or the late Aztec empires" (see also Smith and Montiel 2001).

DISCUSSION

The ceramic data from Xaltocan indicate a striking reorientation of inter-regional ties at the Epiclassic-to-Early Postclassic transition, which might be interpreted as the result of a simple shift in the frontiers of two expanding regional states. But the reorientation of ceramic styles was accompanied by continuity between the Epiclassic and the Early Postclassic populations of the Xaltocan area. This suggests that at the end of the Epiclassic, the residents of Xaltocan abandoned styles associated with Tula in favor of those associated with Cholula and allied groups in the southern Basin of Mexico. This reorientation of ceramic styles poses agency questions with some urgency: Which specific social groups at Xaltocan were interacting with the southern Basin of Mexico and Cholula, and why did they find it in their interests to do so?

It is apparent that Xaltocan's interaction with the southern Basin was *not* a classic case of elite interaction. As noted above, substantial amounts of Aztec I Black-on-Orange and smaller quantities of Cholula polychromes were found in all six test pits with unmixed Aztec I-phase deposits, distributed over the full length and the breadth of the site. This suggests that both elite and commoner households at Xaltocan adopted Aztec I Black-on-Orange and the less common polychrome and effigy vessels. Market exchange appears to have provided at least one medium for Xaltocan's interaction with the southern Basin: The INAA of the Aztec I vessels from Xaltocan show that the ceramics in any single household came from a number of different production centers, which indicates the existence of consumer choice of the type provided by market systems (Hirth 1998; Nichols et al. 2002).

What drew populations into Cholula's market sphere? A conclusive answer requires a detailed examination of Xaltocan's Early Postclassic household economy, which I am not yet prepared to make. However, Cholula's advantage over Tula might have been its superior access to lowland products, especially cotton and cotton textiles. On the eve of Spanish conquest, Cholula's merchants are said to have traveled to the Gulf Coast, Oaxaca, and the Maya lowlands, bringing back such widely used commodities such as raw cotton and cotton textiles, copal, cacao, and polychrome ceramics (Durán 1971:278). Commoner households incorporated many of these items into consumption rituals during the Postclassic (Smith 1987; Brumfiel 2004). In particular, cotton and cotton textiles were items of both commercial and social exchange in Postclassic Mesoamerica (Berdan 1987; Brumfiel 1987; Smith 2003:124). Once Teotihuacan's grip over Gulf Coast trade declined at the end of the Classic period, the availability of cotton textiles may have been the primary force drawing communities such as Xaltocan into Cholula's trade sphere.

Sahagún (1961:75) names four source regions for cotton textiles entering the Basin of Mexico at the time of Spanish conquest. The first was irrigated land, probably concentrated in the current state of Morelos, where cotton production was underway by the Classic period (Hirth 1978). In the sixteenth century, this region paid a heavy tribute in cotton to both the Aztec and Spanish states

(Brumfiel 1997:58; Smith and Hirth 1988). The second source area for cotton textiles was the Gulf lowlands, where cloth was produced for export as early as the fourth century AD and increased through the Postclassic era, stimulated by growing commercial trade and increased tribute extraction (Stark et al. 1998). By the sixteenth century, this region was a major production area for cotton and cotton textiles (Berdan 1987; Sullivan 1982). The third source area for cotton was the lowland of west Mexico, extending down the Pacific coast, at least as far as Río Viejo, Oaxaca. The fourth source area for cotton textiles was the northern desert.

Several lines of evidence suggest intensive interaction between Cholula and Gulf Coast Veracruz during the Early Postclassic (McCafferty 1989). Stylistic influence from the Gulf is evident in Cholula's elite architecture (Acosta 1970; Marquina 1970:41) and its ceramics (McCafferty 2001:123). Many Early Postclassic spindle whorls at Cholula are coated with bitumen (McCafferty and McCafferty 2000:48), a decorative treatment common on spindle whorls from the Gulf Coast regions of Mixtequilla (Stark et al. 1998) and Matacapan (Hall 1997). According to native histories, Cholula was conquered by the Olmeca-Xicallanca, a group with Gulf Coast roots, around AD 800; Cholula is said to have subsequently extended its sphere of influence to central Veracruz (Jiménez Moreno 1942). These Cholula-Gulf Coast linkages were facilitated by Cholula's location on the southeast corner of Mexico's central highlands: Trade routes linking Cholula to Oaxaca and the Gulf Coast were shorter and more easily negotiated than those available to Tula (McCafferty 1996a:2).

In contrast, Tula appears to have maintained links with western and northern Mesoamerica. Ceramics suggest that Tula controlled settlements in the Bajío region to the west of Tula, and the prevalence of Zinapecuaro obsidian at Tula suggests exchange with west Mexico (Smith and Montiel 2001:263). Cacao, Plumbate ceramics, and marine shells were obtained from the Pacific coast of Chiapas and Guatemala (Diehl 1983:116). Malachite, azurite, cinnabar, pyrite, lead, specular iron, opal, quartz crystals, and peyote were imported from north Mexico (Williams and Weigand 1996; Schaafsma and Riley 1999). Although Tula apparently acquired a wide range of luxury goods from west and north Mexico, probably including some cotton textiles, Tula appears to have been cut off from the prime cotton-growing and textile-producing areas of the Gulf Coast lowlands. Although Huastec ceramics at Tula suggest contact with the northern Gulf lowlands, Huastec ceramics are not very abundant. Fine Orange ware is absent at Tula suggesting infrequent contact with southern Veracruz, Tabasco, and Campeche (Diehl 1983:115).

The obsidian exchange spheres defined by Braswell (2003:145–146) provide a rough gauge of the extent of Cholula's and Tula's trade networks. Tula's network, coinciding with Braswell's Central Mexican Early Postclassic exchange sphere, would have covered most of the modern Mexican states of western Hidalgo, Mexico, western Morelos, Guerrero and western Oaxaca. Cholula's trade network, coinciding with Braswell's Peripheral Gulf Coast Early Postclassic exchange sphere, would have encompassed Puebla, Veracruz, and eastern Oaxaca. These data suggest that Tula would have had access to cotton and cotton textiles from western Morelos and the Pacific Coast, but the quantity and quality of these textiles may not have equaled those from the Gulf Coast and Oaxaca, whose trade was dominated by Cholula.

Tula may have embarked on a campaign of imperial expansion to seize, by force, what it could not effectively acquire through commerce. The *Anales de Cuauhtitlan* (1945:14) relates that Toltecs from Tula fought a battle at Nextlapan, on the western shore of Lake Xaltocan, which suggests that Tula tried to expand further south into the Basin of Mexico. Tula's aggression may have hardened the boundaries between Tula and Cholula, causing hinterland sites such as Xaltocan to affiliate with one or the other, but not both. This might also explain Xaltocan's location. Shortly after the battle of Nextlapan, Xaltocan was founded 5 km to the east, in the middle of the shallow lake (*Anales de Cuauhtitlan* 1945:14). The location was inconvenient, but it offered an effective defense against attack by outsiders. The *Anales* say refuges from Tula settled the town, but ceramics suggest that it was founded by local people who, looking to defend their access to Gulf Coast goods, placed themselves within Cholula's economic and political sphere.

CONCLUSIONS

Together, these data confirm Parsons' suggestion that competition between Tula and Cholula defined the climate for Early Postclassic settlement in the Basin of Mexico. Further, they enhance our understanding of the Epiclassic-Early Postclassic transition in the Basin of Mexico. The ties between Xaltocan, the southern Basin, and Cholula were forged only at the beginning of the Early Postclassic, perhaps as Cholula replaced Teotihuacan as the major importer of goods from the Gulf Coast and Oaxaca, and as the demand for these goods increased with the growth of commoner household consumption rituals in the Basin of Mexico. The boundaries between Cholula's and Tula's "spheres of influence" may have hardened as settlements in the Basin of Mexico resisted Tula's efforts to usurp Cholula's trade.

The agency-centered perspective on region style has been useful in this paper because it has focused our attention on *which* social groups were engaged in contacts with other regions, *which* items of material culture were involved in these contacts, and *what* might have motivated these contacts. These more focused questions encourage archaeologists to consider the shifting array of economic, political, and cultural circumstances that establish the context for human decision-making and behavior. An agency-centered perspective on region style leads us beyond the classical equation of artifact styles with ethnic groups, an equation that has been increasingly called into question (Hodder 1982; Dongoske et al. 1997; Sanders 2002), and it invites us to consider the economic, political, and social interactions that stylistic boundaries might imply.

REFERENCES CITED

Acosta, Jorge R.
   1970   Sección 3. In *Proyecto Cholula*, edited by I. Marquina, pp. 47–56. Instituto Nacional de Antropología e Historia, Mexico, D.F.
Alva Ixtlilxóchitl, Fernando de
   1975–1977   *Obras Históricas*, edited by E. O'Gorman, 2 vols. Universidad Nacional Autónoma de México, Mexico, D.F.
Anales de Cuauhtitlan
   1945   *Anales de Cuauhtitlan* in *Códice Chimalpopoca*, translated by P.F. Velázquez, pp.1–118. Universidad Nacional Autónoma de México, Mexico, D.F.
Anales de Tlatelolco
   1948   *Anales de Tlatelolco*, edited by S. Toscano, H. Berlin, and R.H. Barlow. Antigua Librería de José Porrúa e Hijos, Mexico, D.F.
Barth, Fredrik
   1969   Introduction. In *Ethnic Groups and Boundaries*, edited by F. Barth, pp. 9–38. Little, Brown, Boston.
Berdan, Frances F.
   1987   Cotton in Aztec Mexico: Production, Distribution and Uses. *Mexican Studies/ Estudios Mexicanos* 3(2):235–262.
   2003   Borders in the Eastern Aztec Empire. In *The Postclassic Mesoamerican World*, edited by Michael E. Smith and Frances F. Berdan, pp. 73–77. University of Utah Press, Salt Lake City.
Blanton, Richard E.
   1992   *Prehispanic Settlement Patterns of the Ixtapalapa Peninsula Region, Mexico*. Occasional Papers in Anthropology No. 6, Department of Anthropology, The Pennsylvania State University, University Park, Pennsylvania.
Blanton, Richard E., and Gary M. Feinman
   1984   The Mesoamerican World System. *American Anthropologist* 86:673–682.
Braswell, Geoffrey E.
   2003   Obsidian Exchange Spheres. In *The Postclassic Mesoamerican World*, edited by Michael E. Smith and Frances F. Berdan, pp.131–158. University of Utah Press, Salt Lake City.

Brenner, Anita
   1931   *The Influence of Technique on the Decorative Style in the Domestic Pottery of Culhuacan*. La Escuela Internacional de Arqueología y Ethnología Americanas, Mexico, D.F.
Brown, James A.
   1976   The Southern Cult Reconsidered. *Midcontinental Journal of Archaeology* 1:115–136.
Brumfiel, Elizabeth M.
   1987   Elite and Utilitarian Crafts in the Aztec State. In *Specialization, Exchange and Complex Societies*, edited by Elizabeth M. Brumfiel and Timothy K. Earle, pp. 102–118. Cambridge University Press, Cambridge.
   1997   Tribute Cloth Production and Compliance in Aztec and Colonial Mexico. *Museum Anthropology* 21:55–71.
   2004   Meaning by Design: Ceramics, Feasts, and Figured Worlds. In *Ancient Mesoamerica*, edited by Rosemary A. Joyce and J.A. Hendon, pp. 239–264. Blackwell, Oxford.
Brumfiel, Elizabeth M. (editor)
   In press   *Production and Power at Postclassic Xaltocan*. Memoirs in Latin American Archaeology. Department of Anthropology, University of Pittsburgh and Instituto Nacional de Antropología e Historia, Pittsburgh and Mexico City.
Brumfiel, Elizabeth M. and Enrique Rodríguez-Alegría
   1998   Descripción preliminar de los tipos cerámicos del Sitio ET. In *Unidades domésticas en Xaltocan Postclásico*, edited by Elizabeth M. Brumfiel, pp. 97–148. Report on file at the Instituto Nacional de Antropología e Historia, Mexico City, and Department of Anthropology, Northwestern University.
Caldwell, Joseph R.
   1964   Interaction Spheres in Prehistory. In *Hopewellian Studies*, edited by Joseph R. Caldwell and Robert L. Hall, pp. 134–143. Illinois State Museum, Scientific Papers 12, No. 6, Springfield, Illinois.
Carrasco, Pedro
   1950   *Los Otomíes: Culture e historia Prehispánica de los pueblos Mesoamericanos de habla Otomiana*. Biblioteca Enciclopédica del Estado de México, Mexico, D.F.
Cobean, Robert H.
   1990   *La cerámica de Tula, Hidalgo*. Instituto Nacional de Antropología e Historia, Mexico, D.F.
Cortés, Hernán
   1970   *Cartas de relación*. Porrúa, Mexico.
Cowgill, George L.
   1975   On Causes and Consequences of Ancient and Modern Population Changes. *American Anthropologist* 77:505–525.

Davies, Nigel
1977   *The Toltecs Until the Fall of Tula*. University of Oklahoma Press, Norman.
1980   *Toltec Heritage: From the Fall of Tula to the Rise of Tenochtitlan*. University of Oklahoma Press, Norman.

Deagan, Kathleen A.
1990   Accommodation and Resistance: The Process and Impact of Spanish Colonization in the Southeast. In *Columbian Consequences, Volume 2: Archaeological and Historical Perspectives on the Spanish Borderlands East*, edited by David H. Thomas, pp. 297–314. Smithsonian Institution, Washington, D.C.
1998   Transculturation and Spanish–American Ethnogenesis: The Archaeological Legacy of the Quincentennary. In *Studies in Culture Contact*, edited by James Cusick pp. 23–43. Southern Illinois University Press, Carbondale.

Díaz del Castillo, Bernal
1956   *The Discovery and Conquest of Mexico*. Translated by A.P. Maudslay. Noonday Press, New York.

Diehl, Richard A.
1983   *Tula: The Toltec Capital of Ancient Mexico*. Thames and Hudson, London.

Dongoske, Kurt E., Michael Yeatts, Roger Anyon, and T.J. Ferguson
1997   Archaeological Cultures and Cultural Affiliation: Hopi and Zuni Perspectives in the American Southwest. *American Antiquity* 62:600–608.

Dumond, Don, and Florencia Müller
1971   Classic to Post-Classic in Highland Central Mexico. *Science* 175:1208–1215.

Dunnell, Robert C.
1980   Evolutionary Theory and Archaeology. *Advances in Archaeological Method and Theory* 3:35–99.

Durán, Diego
1967   *Historia de las Indias de Nueva España*. 2 vols. Porrúa, Mexico.
1972   *Book of the Gods and Rites and The Ancient Calendar*, translated by F. Horcasitas and D. Heyden. University of Oklahoma Press, Norman.

Flannery, Kent V.
1968   The Olmec and the Valley of Oaxaca: A Model for Inter-Regional Interaction in Formative Times. In *Dumbarton Oaks Conference on the Olmec*, edited by Elizabeth P. Benson, pp. 79–110. Dumbarton Oaks, Washington, D.C.

Friedel, David A.
1978   Culture Areas and Interaction Spheres: Contrasting Approaches to the Emergence of Civilization in the Maya Lowlands. *American Antiquity* 44:43–54.

Green, Stanton W., and Stephen M. Perlman
1985   Frontiers, Boundaries, and Open Social Systems. In *The Archaeology of Frontiers and Boundaries*, edited by Stanton W. Green and Stephen M. Perlman, pp. 3–13. Academic Press, Orlando.

Hall, Barbara Ann
  1997   Spindle Whorls and Cotton Production at Middle Classic Matacapan and in the Gulf Lowlands. In *Olmec to Aztec: Settlement Patterns in the Ancient Gulf Lowlands*, edited by Barbara L. Stark and Philip J. Arnold III, pp. 115–135. University of Arizona Press, Tucson.

Helms, Mary W.
  1993   *Craft and the Kingly Ideal*. University of Texas Press, Austin.

Heyman, Josiah McC.
  1994   The Mexico–United States Border in Anthropology. *Journal of Political Ecology* 1:43–65.

Hicks, Frederic
  1995   Xaltocan Under Mexica Domination, 1435–1520. In *Caciques and Their People: A Volume in Honor of Ronald Spores*, edited by Joyce Marcus and Judith F. Zeitlin, pp. 67–85. Anthropological Papers No. 89, Museum of Anthropology, University of Michigan, Ann Arbor.

Hirth, Kenneth
  1979   Teotihuacan Regional Population Administration in Eastern Morelos. *World Archaeology* 9:320–333.
  1998   The Distributional Approach: A New Way to Identify Marketplace Exchange in the Archaeological Record. *Current Anthropology* 39:451-76.

Hodder, Ian
  1981   *Symbols in Action*. Cambridge University Press, Cambridge.

Hodge, Mary G.
  1991   Aztec II, III, and IV Black/Orange Type Descriptions. Appendix 3. In *Aztec-Period Ceramic Distribution and Exchange Systems*, edited by Mary G. Hodge and Leah D. Minc, pp. 109–155. Final report submitted to the National Science Foundation for Grant BSM–8704177.

Hodge, Mary G., and Leah D. Minc
  1990   The Spatial Patterning of Aztec Ceramics: Implications for Prehispanic Exchange in the Valley of Mexico. *Journal of Field Archaeology* 17:415–437.

Jiménez Moreno, Wigberto
  1942   El enigma de los Olmecas. *Cuadernos Americanos I* (5):113–145.

Johnson, Andrea
  2000   Compositional Analysis of Ceramics from Lake Xaltocan, Mexico: The Influence of Epiclassic Regional Centers on Small Satellite Sites in the Basin of Mexico. Paper Presented at the Annual Meeting of the Midwestern Mesoamericanists, Champaign–Urbana.

Koehler, Thomas
  1986   Excavations at Maquixco Bajo (TT25A). In *The Teotihuacan Valley Project, Final Report Vol. IV: The Toltec Period Occupation of the Valley*, edited by William T. Sanders, pp. 7–51. Occasional Papers in Anthropology No. 13,

Pennsylvania State University, Department of Anthropology, University Park, Pennsylvania.

Lightfoot, Kent G., and Antoinette Martínez

1995   Frontiers and Boundaries in Archaeological Perspective. *Annual Review of Anthropology* 24:471–492.

Lind, Michael D.

1994   Cholula and Mixteca Polychromes: Two Mixteca-Puebla Regional Sub-Styles. In *Mixteca-Puebla*, edited H.B. Nicholson and Eloise Quiñones Keber, pp. 79–99. Labyrinthos, Culver City, California.

Marquina, Ignacio

1969   Pirámide de Cholula. In *Proyecto Cholula*, edited by Ignacio Marquina, pp. 31–46. Instituto Nacional de Antropología e Historia, Mexico, D.F.

McCafferty, Geoffrey G.

1989   Ethnic Identity in the Material Culture of Postclassic Cholula. Paper presented at the Annual Meeting of the Society for Historical Archaeology, Baltimore.

1996a   Reinterpreting the Great Pyramid of Cholula, Mexico. *Ancient Mesoamerica* 7:1–17.

1996b   The Ceramics and Chronology of Cholula, Mexico. *Ancient Mesoamerica* 7:299–323.

2001   *Ceramics of Postclassic Cholula, Mexico*. Monograph 43, Cotsen Institute of Archaeology, University of California, Los Angeles.

McCafferty, Geoffrey G., and Sergio Suárez C.

1996   The Classic/Postclassic Transition at Cholula: Recent Investigations at the Great Pyramid. Paper presented at the 60th Annual Meeting, Society for American Archaeology, Minneapolis.

McCafferty, Sharisse D., and Geoffrey G. McCafferty

2001   Textile Production in Postclassic Cholula, Mexico. *Ancient Mesoamerica* 11:39–54.

Meacham, William

1976   Continuity and Local Evolution in the Neolithic of South China: A Non-nuclear Approach. *Current Anthropology* 18:419–440.

Minc, Leah D.

1991   Black/Red Type Descriptions. Black/Red Incised Type Descriptions, Black-and-White/Red Type Descriptions. In *Aztec-Period Ceramic Distribution and Exchange Systems*, edited by Mary G. Hodge and Leah D. Minc, pp. 156–222. Final report submitted to the National Science Foundation for Grant BSM–8704177.

1994   *Political Economy and Market Economy Under Aztec Rule*. Ph.D. dissertation, The University of Michigan, UMI Dissertaion Services, Ann Arbor.

Mountjoy, Joseph

1986   The Collapse of the Classic at Cholula as Seen From Cerro Zapotecas. *Notas Mesoamericanas* 10:119–151.

Müller, Florencia
  1978   *La Alfarería de Cholula*. Instituto Nacional de Antropología e Historia, Mexico, D.F.
Nazareo de Xaltocan, Don Pablo
  1940   Carta al Rey Don Felipe II. In *Epistolario de Nueva España*, Vol. 10, edited by F. del Paso y Troncoso, pp. 109–129. Antigua Librería Robredo, Mexico, D.F.
Neff, Hector, Ronald L. Bishop, Edward B. Sisson, Michael D. Glascock, and Penny R. Sisson
  1994   Neutron Activation Analysis of Late Postclassic Polychrome Pottery from Central Mexico. In *Mixteca-Puebla*, edited by H.B. Nicholson and Eloise Quiñones Keber, pp. 117–141. Labyrinthos, Culver City, California.
Nichols, Deborah L., Elizabeth M. Brumfiel, Hector Neff, Mary Hodge, Thomas H. Charlton, and Michael D. Glascock
  2002   Neutrons, Markets, Cities, and Empires, A Thousand-Year Perspective on Ceramic Production and Distribution in the Postclassic Basin of Mexico. *Journal of Anthropological Archaeology* 21:25–82.
Nichols, Deborah, and John McCullough
  1986   Excavations at Xometla (TT21). In *The Teotihuacan Valley Project, Final Report Vol. IV: The Toltec Period Occupation of the Valley*, edited by William T. Sanders, pp. 53–194. Occasional Papers in Anthropology No. 13, Pennsylvania State University, Department of Anthropology, University Park, Pennsylvania.
Noguera, Eduardo
  1954   *La Cerámica Arqueológica de Cholula*. Editorial Guaranía, Mexico, D.F.
Norr, Lynette
  1987   Postclassic Artifacts from Tetla. In *Ancient Chalcatzingo*, edited by David C. Grove, pp. 525–546. University of Texas Press, Austin.
Parsons, Jeffrey R.
  1970   *Prehistoric Settlement Patterns in the Texcoco Region, Mexico*. Memoirs No. 3, Museum of Anthropology, University of Michigan, Ann Arbor.
Parsons, Jeffrey R., Elizabeth Brumfiel, and Mary Hodge
  1996   Developmental Implications of Earlier Dates for Early Aztec in the Basin of Mexico. *Ancient Mesoamerica*. 7:217–230.
Parsons, Jeffrey R., Elizabeth Brumfiel, Mary H. Parsons, and David J. Wilson
  1982   *Prehispanic Settlement Patterns in the Southern Valley of Mexico: The Chalco-Xochimilco Region*. Memoirs No. 14, Museum of Anthropology, University of Michigan, Ann Arbor.
Price, Barbara J.
  1977   Shifts in Production and Organization: A Cluster Interaction Model. *Current Anthropology* 18:209–234.
Renfrew, Colin
  1977   *Problems in European Prehistory*. Cambridge University Press, Cambridge.

1986   Introduction: Peer Polity Interaction and Socio-Political Change. In *Peer Polity Interaction and Socio-Political Change*, edited by Colin Renfrew and John F. Cherry, pp. 1–18. Cambridge University Press, Cambridge.

Renfrew, Colin, and John F. Cherry (editors)
1986   *Peer Polity Interaction and Socio-Political Change*. Cambridge University Press, Cambridge.

Rogers, J. Daniel, and Samuel M. Wilson
1993   Theoretical Orientations on Culture Contact. In *Ethnohistory and Archaeology: Approaches to Postcontact Change in the Americas*, edited by J. Daniel Rogers and Samuel M. Wilson, pp.17–18. Plenum, New York.

Sahagún, Fray Bernardino de
1961   *Florentine Codex: General History of the Things of New Spain, Book 10: The People*, translated by Charles Dibble and Arthur J. O. Anderson. The School of American Research and the University of Utah Press, Salt Lake City.

Sanders, William T.
1986   Ceramic Chronology. In *The Teotihuacan Valley Project, Final Report Vol. IV: The Toltec Period Occupation of the Valley*, edited by William T. Sanders, pp. 367–373. Occasional Papers in Anthropology No. 13, Department of Anthropology, Pennsylvania State University, University Park, Pennsylvania.
2002   Late Xolalpan-Metepec/Oxtotipac, Ethnic Succession or Changing Patterns of Political Economy: A Reevaluation. Paper presented at the 67th Annual Meeting of the Society for American Archaeology, Denver.

Sanders, William T., Jeffrey R. Parsons, and Robert S. Santley
1978   *The Basin of Mexico: Ecological Processes in the Evolution of a Civilization*. Academic Press, New York.

Schaafsma, Curtis F., and Carroll L. Riley (editors)
1997   *The Casas Grandes World*. University of Utah Press, Salt Lake City.

Schortman, Edward M.
1989   Interregional Interaction in Prehistory: The Need for a New Perspective. *American Antiquity* 54:52–65.

Schortman, Edward M., and Seiichi Nakamura
1990   A Crisis of Identity: Late Classic Competition and Interaction on the Southeast Maya Periphery. *Latin American Antiquity* 2:311–336.

Séjourné, Laurette
1970   *Arqueología del valle de México I: Culhuacan*. Instituto Nacional de Antropología e Historia, Mexico, D.F.

Smith, Michael E.
1987   Household Possessions and Wealth in Agrarian States: Implications for Archaeology. *Journal of Anthropological Archaeology* 6:297–335.
2004   Key commodities. In *The Postclassic Mesoamerican World*, edited by Michael E. Smith and Frances F. Berdan, pp. 117–125. University of Utah Press, Salt Lake City.

Smith, Michael E. and Frances F. Berdan (editors)

2003   *The Postclassic Mesoamerican World*. University of Utah Press, Salt Lake City.

Smith, Michael E., and Cynthia M. Heath-Smith

1979   Waves of Influence in Postclassic Mesoamerica? A Critique of the Mixteca-Puebla Concept. *Anthropology* 4(2):15–50.

Smith, Michael E., and Kenneth G. Hirth

1988   The Development of Prehispanic Cotton-Spinning Technology in Western Morelos, Mexico. *Journal of Field Archaeology* 15:349–358.

Smith, Michael E., and Lisa Montiel

2001   The Archaeological Study of Empires and Imperialism in Pre-Hispanic Central Mexico. *Journal of Anthropological Archaeology* 20:245–284.

Stark, Barbara, Lynette Hiller, and Michael A. Ohnersorgen

1998   People With Cloth: Mesoamerican Economic Change from the Perspective of Cotton in South-Central Veracruz. *Latin American Antiquity* 9:1–30.

Stein, Gil J.

1997   Heterogeneity, Power, and Political Economy: Some Current Research Issues in the Archaeology of Old World Complex Societies. *Journal of Archaeological Research* 6:1–44.

2002   From Passive Periphery to Active Agents: Emerging Perspectives in the Archaeology of Interregional Interaction. *American Anthropologist* 104:903–916.

Sullivan, Thelma D.

1983   Tlazolteotl-Ixcuina: The Great Spinner and Weaver. In *The Art and Iconography of Late Post-Classic Central Mexico*, edited by Elizabeth H. Boone, pp. 7–35. Dumbarton Oaks, Washington, D.C.

Vaillant, George C.

1938   Correlation of Archaeological and Historical Sequences in the Valley of Mexico. *American Anthropologist* 40:535–573.

Williams, Eduardo, and Phil C. Weigand

1995   *Las cuencas del occidente de México: Época prehispánica*. El Colegio de Michoacán, Zamora, Mexico.

THE TUNANMARCA POLITY OF HIGHLAND PERU AND ITS SETTLEMENT SYSTEM (AD 1350–1450)

TIMOTHY EARLE

Northwestern University

INTRODUCTION

Jeff Parsons has been a leading exponent of settlement pattern studies, an innovator in systematic and total site survey of large regions, and a professor to generations of processual archaeologists at the University of Michigan, where, in the early 1970s, I was one of his students. Among Jeff's substantial achievements was his comprehensive survey of three regions in Peru's Junin Province (Parsons, Hastings, and Matos 2000). These surveys were the first systematic, large-scale, and comprehensive settlement studies undertaken in the Andes, setting a standard for all subsequent work. The Upper Mantaro Archaeological Research Project (UMARP), which I codirected from 1977 to 1986 with Terry D'Altroy, Christine Hastorf, and Cathy Scott, was built upon the results of Jeff's careful survey of the Upper Mantaro region.

The Upper Mantaro region is one of the largest and richest intermontane valleys in highland Peru (Figure 5-1). At 3,200 to 3,400 m above sea level, the broad alluvial plain produces maize and in modern times, wheat. Bordering the plain are hill slopes and rolling uplands on which quinoa, potatoes, and other Andean tubers are grown. Higher still, above 3,700 m, is the grassland *puna*, pastures for llama, alpaca, and now sheep. The ragged Andes and glaciers stand above 4,400 m. Community lands cut vertically across these different zones allowing for a diversified local economy, and this pattern of economic integration appears to have existed in the past.

UMARP focused on the Yanamarca Valley, a small, side basin of the Mantaro drainage. Cut off by a glacial moraine, its tributary river flows into a limestone sink near the town of Tragadero (the swallower), through which it eventually joins

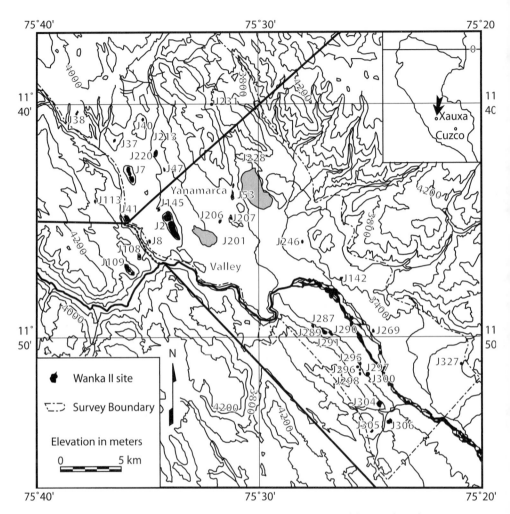

Figure 5-1. Upper Mantaro Region, showing main Late Intermediate period sites and Wanka chiefdom territorial divisions (see D'Altroy 1992: Figure 4.3)

underground the main river. The valley floor lies at 3,500 m where frosts pose a significant agricultural hazard. In prehistory, the valley's people built extensive drained and irrigated fields to increase productivity and minimize risks (Hastorf and Earle 1985). On the hills above this valley, we studied the settlements of several Late Intermediate period (LIP) polities of the Xauxa/Wanka people.

Of particular interest are three unusually large settlements, Tunanmarca (J7), Hatunmarca (J2), and Llamap Shillón (J109) (Figure 5-1). These were fortified centers placed prominently on hilltops above the valley floor. Each contained several thousand stone buildings within surrounding fortification walls, and ceremonial spaces with a few special buildings were at their hearts. These political centers and their dependent settlements formed regional polities, each with populations easily exceeding 10,000 people. For the Mantaro Valley and elsewhere in the highlands, such polities were exceptional for the Late Intermediate Period.

What were these polities, and why were they built? I propose that Tunanmarca, Hatunmarca, and Llamap Shillón were chiefdoms. Chiefdoms are regionally organized polities that organize population in the low thousands to tens of thousands, spread across many semiautonomous settlements (Beck 2003; Carneiro 1981; Johnson and Earle 2000). To organize such middle-range polities requires various institutions and cultural characteristics that can include regional ceremonial complexes, prestige goods exchanges, redistribution, and the like. The specific cultural makeup of each chiefdom is highly variable, and that variation is what researchers now try to understand (Beck 2003; Blanton et al. 1996; Earle 1991, 1997). My purpose here is to explicate the specific organizational characteristics of one Xauxa/Wanka chiefdom to illustrate a case for that variation.

Some, including Jeff Parsons (personal communication), would not classify the Xauxa/Wanka polities as chiefdoms, because they represent a political reorganization following the collapse of the Wari state. Certainly, with the variation that exists among intermediate-level societies, others propose typological categories beyond chiefdoms (McIntosh 1999). My sense, however, is that we want to look at the general class of societies with intermediate-size scale to investigate the alternative means used to organize them. Typologically, I am a "lumper," but I take this stand to define the variation explained in crosscultural perspective. Personally, I like the term "chiefdom" with its connotation of leadership based on some degree of instituted inheritance and social stratification, but as a category-like state, it should not be expected to conform to narrow specifications typical, for example, of the Polynesian chiefdoms or any other specific historic case.

This chapter presents a synthesis of UMARP data for the Late Intermediate period chiefdom that surrounded the central settlement of Tunanmarca. I use a multiscalar approach to the settlement data collected by UMARP. The scales to be considered are the regional polity (the Tunanmarca settlement hierarchy), individual settlements (sites with residential architecture), and households (distinct residential compounds). My approach envisions each scalar unit as a building block from which larger units were constructed (Johnson and Earle 2000).

In the period immediately preceding Inka conquest, intense warfare characterized the Mantaro Valley as it did elsewhere in the highlands. Many fortified LIP settlements (Hyslop 1977; Krzanowski 1977; Parsons, Hastings, and

Matos 2000) attest to the endemic nature of warfare throughout the Andean highlands. It probably resulted both from structural principles of opposition characteristic of Andean societies (Hastorf 1993; Parson and Hastings 1987) and from escalating resource competition where no overarching political system existed to mediate it (LeBlanc 1981). Warfare also became a source of power for would-be chiefs in some regions, such as the Mantaro.

In *How Chiefs Come to Power* (Earle 1997), I argue that the war chiefs of the Wanka seized on the opportunity of intense intercommunity competition to expand and consolidate political power. I see the Wanka polities as "hill-fort chiefdoms." In addition to characteristics common to all chiefdoms, hill-fort chiefdoms have heavily fortified settlements, a preponderance of population living in the central settlement, warfare to defend territory, emphasis on staple finance, and stress on warrior might as the primary source of power (Earle 1997:121). In such chiefdoms, as characterized Iron Age Britain, Maori or Fijian societies of the Pacific, and the high Andes, individual polities were sufficiently strongly defended to become secure against conquest and further political consolidation until confronted by overwhelming force, such as presented by the Roman, British, or Inka empires.

RESEARCH ON THE WANKA II

The history of archaeology in the Mantaro parallels broader trends in Peruvian archaeology. Starting in the twentieth century, the primary concern was to establish cultural histories based on ceramic chronologies. Archaeologists visited the Mantaro Valley, test-excavated sites, and established basic sequences. Lumbreras (1957), Matos (1959), Flores Espinoza (1959), and Lavallée (1967) first described the main Wanka types. By the 1960s, along the Peruvian coast, settlement pattern archaeology had become more common, and in the highlands, Ramiro Matos (1966) was early to encourage these new interests and methodologies. When visiting Mexico in 1967, he met the young Jeff Parsons, whom he encouraged to come to Peru. Ramiro then welcomed Dave Browman, a graduate student of Tom Patterson, who had been running settlement surveys on Peru's central coast, to the Mantaro. There, with his support and encouragement, Dave completed a valley-wide reconnaissance survey and synthesis for his doctoral dissertation (Browman 1970).

In 1975 and 1976, in coordination with Ramiro Matos, Jeff Parsons directed large-scale and comprehensive surveys in three environmentally contrasting regions of the Central Highlands: the Xauxa segment of the Mantaro Valley, Tarama (a network of small valleys to the east that cut down to the tropical forest), and Chichacocha (the rolling high *puna* to the north) (Parsons, Hastings, and Matos 2000; Parsons and Matos 2001). As conceived in his Basin of Mexico surveys, Parsons (1971) used systematic methods for total pedestrian survey that could recognize sites with reasonable ceramic spreads or with standing architecture. Each site's location was outlined on the aerial photographs carried in the field, site characteristics were described according to an established format, and ceramic collections were taken for dating by Ramiro. Their work produced a full inventory and general dating for Xauxa region settlements.

On Flannery and Parsons's recommendation, Matos welcomed the UMARP team to join his umbrella Junin Project, and Jeff generously provided us with full documentation of his earlier Mantaro regional survey, including copies of all site forms, aerial photography, and maps. Over six subsequent field seasons, UMARP conducted three major field campaigns. The first two, 1977 to 1979 (Earle et al. 1980) and 1982 to 1983 (Earle et al. 1987), considered the ends of the sequence (the Wanka periods), while the third, in 1986 (Hastorf et al. 1989), looked at earlier periods. A fourth campaign, scheduled to begin in 1988, was abruptly cancelled because of the growing Sendero Luminoso insurgency. Over the span of our research, a main objective was to use multiscalar approaches to document social evolution in the Mantaro Valley (D'Altroy and Hastorf 2001), focusing on the inchoate development of complex polities during the Late Intermediate Period and on Inka conquest during the Late Horizon.

The first campaign's lead objective was to refine the ceramic chronology to study societal change on a finer scale (Earle et al. 1980). Deep stratigraphic excavations and small test excavations provided the ceramic collections that Cathy Scott (LeBlanc 1981) used to define three late Xauxa/Wanka phases: Wanka I, AD 1000-1350; Wanka II, AD 1350-1450; and Wanka III, AD 1450-1533. Late-period sites in the Yanamarca area were intensively surface collected and test-excavated to refine our understanding of the changing settlement patterns and supporting economy. Research by the three coprincipal investigators of UMARP produced foundational dissertations. Emphasizing changes in social organization as related to settlement pattern, population, and warfare, Cathy Scott (LeBlanc 1981) studied the LIP Wanka I to II transition from the end of Wari influence until Inka imperial conquest. Christine Hastorf (1983, 1993) studied the same political transition, describing intensification and political uses of agricultural resources. Terry D'Altroy (1981, 1992) concentrated on the impact of Inka conquest for the Wanka III settlement and economy, looking at imperial domination, reorganization, and staple finance. This phase of work completed our initial site characterization based on intensive site probing.

The second campaign studied the Wanka II to III transition in terms of continuity and change in the household economy (D'Altroy and Hastorf 2001). At seven sites that ranged from large centers to small villages and dated both before and after imperial conquest, we excavated 74 architectural groups of both elite and commoner households. The household was our primary unit of analysis to see how economic subsistence and specializations were organized both within and between Xauxa/Wanka settlements before and after imperial conquest. Using the household data, Cathy Costin (1986) wrote her dissertation on ceramic production, exchange, and use, Glenn Russell (1988) wrote on similar topics dealing with lithics, and Elsie Sandefur (1988) wrote about faunal remains. Christine Hastorf analyzed the botanical remains, and for her doctoral research, Melissa Hagstrum (1989) prepared an ethnoarchaeological comparison between modern ceramic production and the Wanka archaeological collections. Three important masters' theses dealt with the use of metal objects (Owen 1986), with traditional crop processing (Sikkink 2001), and with household and settlement architecture (DeMarrais 1989, 2001). The results and main conclusions are presented in the volume edited by D'Altroy and Hastorf (2001).

ETHNOHISTORY

Early Spanish documents describe Wanka society in some detail, and these have been mined by ethnohistorians, including especially Espinoza Soriano (1971). Source criticisms and detailed reconstructions are available in several UMARP publications and theses (D'Altroy 1987; D'Altroy and Hastorf 2001; Hastorf 1993; LeBlanc 1981; LeVine 1979). Here I summarize the main findings of these studies relevant to Wanka social organization. Prior to Inka conquest, the Wanka fought fiercely, were lead by hereditary war chiefs, and were organized into local communities embedded within larger polities.

Two early inspections (*visitas*) by Spanish officials survive that describe Wanka society prior to Inka conquest. The 1570 *visita* by Dan Francisco de Toledo (Toledo 1940 [1570]) includes interviews with five elderly (83 to 94 years) leaders (*curacas*), who were asked standard questions; their individual answers were recorded. The 1582 *visita* (Vega 1965 [1582]) contained general summaries of new interviews. Those questioned at both times would have grown up and lived under Inka rule, and their knowledge of pre-Inka thus came from their grandparents' generation. Their accounts would be best considered somewhat romanticized, presenting a golden age of Wanka valor and independence. The responses, however, are remarkably consistent.

Before Inka conquest, warfare was said to be a constant threat and opportunity, waged locally among Wanka communities to capture land, animals, and women. They did not go outside the valley to fight, but those of one bank of the Mantaro River fought against those of the other bank. Apparently, war's major motivation was to seize land to support expanding community populations (Toledo 1940 [1570]:28). A community's wealth and survival depended on raiding, conquest, and vigilant defense against its neighbors.

When towns conquered each other, they could kill all males and take possession of the defeated town and its lands (Toledo 1940 [1570]:28). In battle, Wanka warriors sought to capture women for themselves, to increase the community's agricultural land and herds, and to build a reputation for their leader and group (*ayllu*).

War chiefs (*cinchecona*) were said to lead the Wanka community in war, and to a lesser degree, in peace (Toledo 1940 [1570]:23, 34). They had to be valiant and protect followers from attack. Leadership typically passed from father to son, but the efficacy of a new leader had to be proven in battle. The power and wealth of a leader then increased with his success in war. Although much of the conquered lands would have been held corporately by the *ayllu*, its victorious leader divided the land and evidently received substantially more. His valor in war and increased wealth in peace would thus have strengthened his leadership in all sectors of society.

As I argue from the archaeology and its strong settlement hierarchy, the Yanamarca Wanka were organized into compact regional chiefdoms, but according to the ethnohistorical sources, the institutional power and scope of leadership were problematic. Each household and each community (*pueblo*) were said to be independent and self-governing (Toledo 1940 [1570]:18), but it is also said that communities united in battle, either through alliance or conquest. When a community chose to go to war with its neighbor, the stronger force could eradicate a defeated community and take its lands, subjugate the community's population, or negotiate a peaceful subservience (Toledo 1940 [1570]:18). Whatever the means, the outcome would have been to build a regional chiefdom.

The ethnohistoric sources suggest that the Xauxa/Wanka were organized segmentally into households, communities, and unstable chiefly polities. Both scale and hierarchy of these polities are consistent with a broad definition of chiefdom—regional settlement polities with hereditary leaders. I image opposing forces of integration (constant treats of warfare and opportunities for wealth through conquest) and of fragmentation (intense cultural independence at both household and community levels). The ethnohistoric accounts suggest an elemental organization that does not prepare us for the scale and impressiveness of central settlements like Tunanmarca.

A MULTISCALAR APPROACH TO THE TUNANMARCA SETTLEMENT SYSTEM

The existing archaeological evidence of the Tunanmarca chiefdom helps us draw more detailed conclusions about its sociopolitical organization, economy, and ceremonial practices. Here I present these conclusions as they pertain to three scales of integration: the regional settlement system, the component settlements, and their constituent household groups. I emphasize the somewhat unexpected characteristics of internal disorder, ceremonial minimalism, and little institutional elaboration at the level of the regional chiefdom and its constituent settlements. As I argue elsewhere (Earle 1997), the intense warfare of the Wanka may help explain these particular characteristics of regional and settlement structure.

Organization of Regional Settlements

The Tunanmarca chiefdom had a sizeable and dense population. The settlements were organized into a clear three-level hierarchy. Internal to the chiefdom, some community specialization and intercommunity exchange existed, but largely, communities provided for their own subsistence needs. Ceremonialism of the chiefdom was partly centralized at the large central settlement. To determine the likely regional extent and organization of the Tunanmarca polity, three steps are involved: identification of the regional centers; definition of the lands and settlements located closer to Tunanmarca than other centers; and evaluation of the economic and ceremonial evidence available to evaluate the proposed political system.

The three major Wanka II regional centers in our research region (Figure 5-1) were Tunanmarca (25.4 ha), Hatunmarca (73.7 ha), and Llamap Shillón (18.6 ha). These central settlements are close to each other and fairly regularly spaced (Tunanmarca-Hatunmarca, 5.3 km; Tunanmarca-Llamap Shillón, 7.4 km; Hatunmarca-Llamap Shillón, 5.0 km). Average distance between centers is thus only 5.9 km, a 1 to 2 hour walk. Each center was positioned defensively on a high ridge, above 3800 m.

The territories associated with each center and its polity can be marked by lines of equal distance and by topographic features such as streams and ridges. The boundaries between the polities were only a few kilometers from each center's walls, but large tracts of land extended out from the centers at roughly 120° angles, respectively, to the north of Tunanmarca, east of Hatunmarca, and southwest of Llamap Shillón. The territories of each center contained lands ranging in elevation from about 3,500 m to above 4,200 m, giving access to diverse zones productive for potato and quinoa farming, some maize, and upland *puna* for herds. The proximity of these three centers suggests a clustering toward, and probable competition over, the intensively farmed uplands, hill slopes, and bottomlands of the Yanamarca and Upper Mantaro Valley.

Working with the territories thus determined, the Tunanmarca chiefdom can be postulated to contain eight settlements (Tunanmarca, Umpamalca, Chawín, J37, J38, J47, J213 and J22O; Figure 5-1). Based on measurements

Table 5-1. Settlements of the Tunanmarca Chiefdom

Settlement	Type	Ha	Population[1]	Range
Tunanmarca	regional center	25.4	10,600	7955–13259
Umpamalca	town	14.8	5,200	3889–6482
Chawín	large village	5.6	650	504–840
J37	large village	6.0	700	540–900
J38	large village	4.9	600	441–735
J47	large village	6.0	700	540–900
J220	large village	12.2	1,450	1098–1830
J213	hamlet	0.5	50	45–75
Total	chiefdom polity	75.4	19,950	15012–25021

[1]Center of estimated population range (D'Altroy 1992) rounded to nearest 50.

and calculations prepared by D'Altroy (2001:Table 4-2), sizes in hectares and estimated population for these settlements are presented in Table 5-1. The total size of the core territory is about 150 km², but it is likely that the chiefdom's territory extended into the high *puna* to the north where population densities would have been low.

Demographic statistics for the Tunanmarca chiefdom are impressive (compare Drennan 1987) and can be estimated reliably based on the well-preserved architecture and extensive excavations. For the Tunanmarca chiefdom, the total population of the polity is estimated at about 20,000 people, with a population density of 130 per km² within the core territory. More than half (53%) the polity's total population lived at Tunanmarca, and more than three-fourths (79%) lived in that center and its secondary town. The scale of the polity alone would seek comparison with complex chiefdoms as described for Polynesia or the American Bottom (Earle 1978; Steponaitis 1978).

A strong settlement hierarchy was also evident. Settlements of the Tunanmarca chiefdom were arranged in a three-tiered hierarchy: one center (10,600 people), one town (5,200), and five villages (600 to 1,450 people in each) (Table 5-1). The settlement typology described by D'Altroy (2001) follows: Centers like Tunanmarca had large residential areas with an estimated population over 7,500 people. They were placed defensively and surrounded by multiple defensive walls. Each center had a small, ceremonial zone that included an open plaza space, presumably for civic ceremonies, and some architecturally distinctive structures. Towns like Umpamalca had smaller but still substantial populations, between 2,000 to 7,500 people. In many senses, these settlements were similar to the regional centers, with sizeable populations and surrounding walls, but lacking a civic-ceremonial core. Originally, they may have been centers of independent polities incorporated through conquest into larger systems. Villages were substantially smaller, below 2,000 people, although they were typically fortified in the Wanka II phase. Two Wanka II hamlets (J113 and J213) are anomalous within the settlement hierarchy, perhaps being special use or auxiliary sites.

The territory of the Tunanmarca polity was arranged to encompass the full range of resource zones needed for subsistence. The main subsistence crops were maize, quinoa, potatoes, and legumes (Hastorf 1993, 2001a). Animals consumed by the Tunanmarca groups included the dominant camelids (especially llama) and lesser amounts of wild deer, dogs, and guinea pigs (Sandefur 2001). All plants and animals that were part of the diet likely came from the zones located within the chiefdom's territory. The dominant source of calories was certainly the agricultural crops, grown on the lands that formed the core territory of the Tunanmarca chiefdom.

The Tunanmarca territory's core contained highly intensified agricultural systems that used capital improvements, including irrigation, drained field complexes, and earth-walled terraces (lynchets) (Hastorf and Earle 1985). None of these systems required management for purposes of construction, because they were technically simple and could be expanded progressively as needed by families and communities. These systems were, however, probably embedded within an overarching political organization, which defended property rights in the highly productive agricultural facilities needed to support Tunanmarca's large and dense population; could resolve issues of coordination and risk management; and could mobilize a surplus from households caged economically by their long-term commitment to improved lands (Earle 1997).

One major capital improvement in the Tunanmarca chiefdom was the Wanka II irrigation system, linking together at least six pockets of highly productive soils associated with four high-elevation settlements of the chiefdom (Parsons 1978). Originating in the *puna* above 3,900 m, the ditch soon divided into two main forks, one channeling water west toward J38 and the other, south past J37, Chawín, and Tunanmarca (Hastorf and Earle 1985:Figure 8). Each fork had at least one additional secondary channel to irrigate separate areas. These ditches were technically simple: less than 1 m wide, clay lined, and often supported by a stone retaining wall. Three rudimentary earth and stone aqueducts were also used to cross low points in the terrain. The total length of the ditches for this system was just over 24 km, and they watered at least 100 to 200 ha of high and productive land (above 3,800 m). Productivity on such high-elevation land is limited by a short growing season, beginning with the commencement of rains. Since irrigation, however, allows for predictable early planting regardless of the first rain, it maximizes the growing season's length.

The ditches also provided a permanent water source to the hilltop settlements that were far from other reliable sources.

Other capital improvements found within the Tunanmarca territory include extensive areas of drained fields and lynchets and a small section of ridged fields (Hastorf and Earle 1985). The whole floor of the Yanamarca valley was probably cultivated by drained fields, some of which are still visible in aerial photographs (Earle et al. 1980:12). The most visible drained field complex is 6.6 ha edging Laguna Tragadero, within the territory of the Hatunmarca chiefdom. These fields formed an open checkboard pattern of raised plots demarcated by surrounding ditches that drained excess water. Similar fields were likely developed through the entire valley section located near the village site J220 and controlled by Tunanmarca. In addition, lynchets (*andenes rusticos*) were constructed on pockets of gently sloping land. "The lynchet is an earth-banked field which was constructed by leveling soil and removing rocks to make a gentler slope for short fallow agriculture" (Hastorf and Earle 1985:579). These were common throughout the core territory of the Tunanmarca chiefdom, and its limestone-based soils seem ideal for this form of intensification. Furthermore, directly below Chawín is a small area of ridged fields, apparently used to lessen crop losses to frost. Extensive areas of such ridged-field agriculture have been described elsewhere in the Junin *puna* to the north of the Yanamarca (Matos 1975) but were barely used here.

Was the economy of the Tunanmarca chiefdom further integrated by exchange between specialized production at its settlements? The answer seems to be that each community was largely self-sufficient, though some specialization existed in both food and craft goods. Each community had access to productive agricultural lands and facilities that would have supported its population, and Hastorf (1993, 2001a) has shown each community's diet was somewhat different corresponding to the productive lands immediately available to it. Only some special crops like maize may have been restricted to a few communities' lands, and the wild deer and perhaps camelids were probably best suited to the higher zones of the more northern settlements.

For several important classes of craft goods, especially chert blades, ceramic vessels, and textiles, partial community specialization can be documented for the Tunanmarca chiefdom. Although chert blades were widely used for sickles to cut plant materials, their source was limited to the Pomacancha quarry, located in the very west of the chiefdom's territory (Russell 1988:165–172). Extending over 30 to 40 ha along a limestone ridge, the quarry's surface is littered today with slabs, nodules, and chert debris. In prehistory, the slabs and nodules would have been picked up from the surface and initially struck to form blade cores. Then, in Wanka II times, these cores were taken to the nearest settlement, Umpamalca (and apparently, the neighboring chiefdom, Hatunmarca). At

Umpamalca, specialized knappers struck the blades, which in turn, were traded to other sites, such as the central settlement of Tunanmarca. Russell (1988) documents the community specialization in blade production by contrasting the producing site of Umpamalca with the consuming site of Tunanmarca. Both sites had similar densities of used blades, but differed sharply in the frequency of production debris, including blade cores and used blade. Umpamalca had 23 blade cores from 283 excavated loci contrasting Tunanmarca's only 1 blade core from 456 loci. For the production index of unused to used blade, Umpamalca was 2.26 versus only 0.50 for Tunanmarca.

The same pattern is visible for ceramics, when we look at the distribution of production debris, in this case, "wasters" that were vitrified in error when fired at a too-high temperature. Costin (1986) documents community specialization in pottery making by contrasting indices of production debris to finished goods (N wasters / N local sherds x 100): Umpamalca's production index of 0.28 with an N of 10,251 sherds versus Tunanmarca's index of 0.06 with an N of 43,931. Systematic surface collections at Chawín yielded no wasters, but one was found at J37. Umpamalca was apparently the main ceramic-producing community within the Tunanmarca chiefdom.

The pattern is less clear, however, when we consider that only some local ceramics vitrify (waste) when fired at the temperatures possible with traditional firing methods. The painted styles (Wanka Red, Blase Clara, and Cream slip) evidently waste, while the plain cooking ware (Micaceous Self-slip) does not, and so we have almost no wasters for this ware. Although undocumented by its production index for pottery, the center of Tunanmarca may well have produced the cooking ware and perhaps other forms (Costin 1988:188–194). One test excavation at the site found an extraordinarily dense ceramic dump with over 16,000 sherds in a single, small test trench (0.9 m³). These ceramics were predominantly (53.4%) cooking vessels.

To determine whether ceramics were produced within the research area and differentiated one chiefdom from the next, Costin (1986) conducted petrographic analysis of nearly 6000 sherds. For the local Wanka II decorative ceramics (Base Clara, Wanka Red, and Cream slip), the scores on the canonical paste variables show that the materials used for the ceramics of Tunanmarca and Umpamalca were similar, and together, they contrasted with the ceramics from neighboring chiefdom, Hatunmarca (Costin 2001:Figure 9-13). Ceramics produced within the Tunanmarca chiefdom were largely distributed and used within the settlements of that chiefdom. Political and exchange boundaries apparently corresponded.

For Wanka II textile production, villagers at higher elevations spun proportionately more yarn than at lower settlements (Costin 1993). Relative involvement in textile manufacture was measured by the ratio of spindle whorls

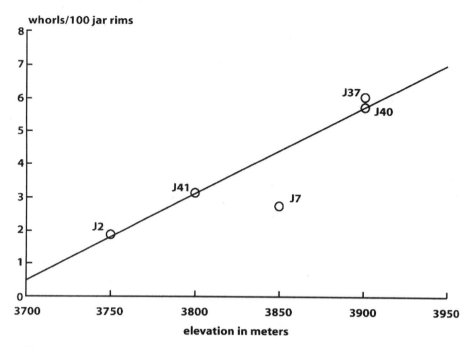

Figure 5-2. Wanka II spindle whorl frequencies at J2 (Hatunmarca), J7 (Tunanmarca), J37, J40 (Chawín), and J41 (Umpamalca), showing the regression line between elevation and relative frequency (Costin 1993: Fig. 3).

to 100 sherds, as indicative of normal household activities (Figure 5-2). At 3,800 m, Umpamalca textile production index was 3; at 3,900 m, the settlements of Chawín and J37 had indices of 5.3 and 5.8, respectively. The central site of Tunanmarca (J7) was anomalous; at 1,850 m, its ratio was only 2.1. The inference is that higher elevation sites, more closely associated with grasslands for alpaca herding, were partly specialized in cloth production. In contrast, the central settlement appears to have been barely involved in spinning, probably receiving textiles from other sites.

A number of community-level specializations are thus evident within the Tunanmarca chiefdom. Umpamalca was involved in the manufacture of chert blades and Wanka decorated ceramics. The higher sites were especially involved in textile production and probably animal-raising more generally. The central site of Tunanmarca was a consumer of products that it received in exchange or tribute. Craft goods were probably distributed person to person among the settlements of the chiefdom. As discussed in the historical documents, local leaders probably received a disproportionate amount of staple goods by holding highly productive lands through the chiefdom's territory and by owning more animals lent out to herders living at higher levels. Despite the denial in the historical records that the war chiefs received tribute, the patterns of consumption seem to suggest that chiefs likely received goods from dominated communities. The Wanka informants may have strategically denied paying tribute to lessen the obligations that the Spanish were certain to impose.

On a regional basis, ceremonial activity of the Tunanmarca chiefdom was not elaborately materialized. The association with ceremonial architecture (e.g., large, open ceremonial spaces, temple mounds, or distinguished burials of chieftains) identifies, archeologically, many chiefdoms. In contrast, the Tunanmarca chiefdom had very little ceremonial architecture. Only at the central site of Tunanmarca does clear architectural evidence exist for either chiefdom-wide or community ceremonialism. Here is located a small central plaza and building complex at the center of the settlement, and this distinctive architecture distinguished special ceremonial functions for the chiefdom's largest settlement. No civic-ceremonial spaces or architecture are recorded at other settlements in the Tunanmarca chiefdom. Only the surrounding fortification walls at settlements (the central settlement, its secondary town, and several villages) illustrate further corporate labor constructions beyond the agricultural facilities already described. These defensive walls defined the settlements spatially and symbolically as community insiders versus outsiders, so the wall may have served as defining community monuments.

Organization of Settlement

Settlements that represent the three levels in the settlement hierarchy of the chiefdom are the regional center of Tunanmarca; its secondary town, Umpamalca; and the dependent village, Chawín. These single-component sites were apparently built within a few generations during Wanka II times and abandoned at Inka conquest. They were positioned on rocky ridge tops and above most agriculture. As a result, the architecture at these sites is remarkably well preserved, allowing mapping from aerial photographs and ground inspection (DeMarrais 2001; Hastorf 1983; LeBlanc 1981).

The pattern of Wanka II settlement planning is consistent. Surrounding fortification walls defined the sector(s) of concentrated residential housing. Irregular paths allowed movement across the residential areas and gave access to informal neighborhoods with clustered patio groups. The differences, from one site to the next, were primarily in size, both of spatial extent and estimated population. Only the central site of Tunanmarca was distinctive, with its central plaza zone and unbuilt corridors that completely separated the two residential sectors (each the scale of a town-size settlement).

Tunanmarca (Figure 5-3a) was the central settlement of the chiefdom that bears its name. The settlement was built high (3,850 to 3,900 m) on a limestone

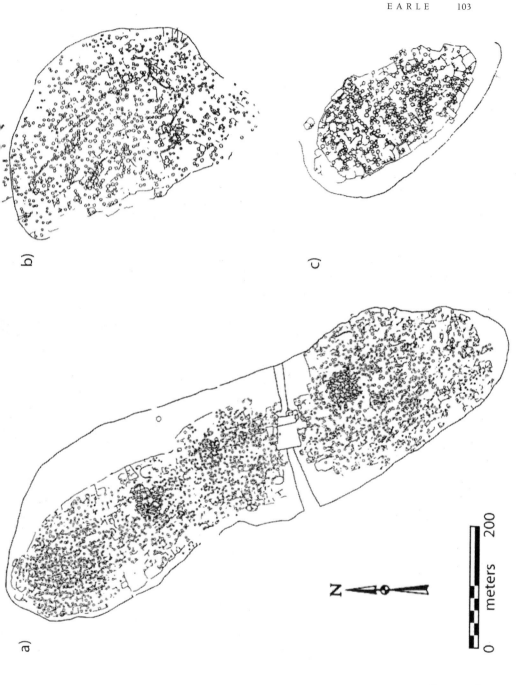

Figure 5-3. Site maps for a) Tunanmarca, b) Umpamalca, and c) Chawín all done at the same scale (D'Altroy 1992: Figure 6.5; DeMarrais 2001: Figures 6.8, 6.9). Circles are houses, and straight lines are walls.

a)

b)

c)

N

0   meters   200

ridge above the Yanamarca Valley to the east and rolling farmlands to the west. Within an area of 25.4 ha, about 4,400 circular stone houses were concentrated for an estimated 10,000 people.

Central to the site was its plaza complex, an irregular shaped open area of about 2,325 m², enclosed by a standing stone wall, not unlike those that enclosed larger patio groups (Figure 5-4; LeBlanc 1981). Leading to the central plaza from both sides of the site were two walled corridors that crossed the site, separating the residential sectors. These long (85 and 100 m) and narrow (usually less than 20 m) spaces had no entrances on the plaza. Rather, they gave a clear visual axis to the central features and separated the residential sectors. The plaza entrances were nonmonumental, obscure openings to the two residential sectors. An internal wall further subdivided the plaza space. The larger plaza (1,800 m²) was located almost exactly midway across the site, and the smaller space (525 m²) was off to the west. On the smaller space were two circular buildings and the only two rectangular stone structures on Tunanmarca. On the larger space, one circular structure sat within the plaza.

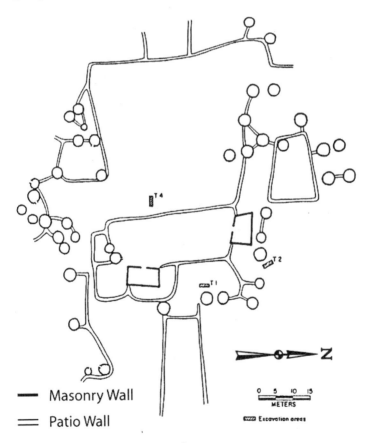

Figure 5-4. Central plaza complex at Tunanmarca with flanking walled corridor spaces (LeBlanc 1981).

What was this central plaza complex? One hypothesis is that it was a civic-ceremonial precinct where public ceremonies for the chiefdom and its central settlement could have been performed. That hypothesis would fit with a model of many chiefdoms, seen as relying heavily on ceremonial means of integration. We had planned to test that hypothesis with extensive excavations during our aborted 1988 field season.

Alternatively, as a hypothesis for future research, I propose that the central zone may have been a residential compound—a large patio group for Tunanmarca's paramount chief. This hypothesis seems reasonable. The size of the two plazas was small, and thus unsuited for large social gatherings; only a fraction of Tunanmarca's population and certainly that of its chiefdom could have gathered there. Since the plazas lacked monumental entrances and were not focal to the settlement's pathways, the plazas appear less as public space than as private space with restricted access and view. If true, the ceremonies held here would have been more personal, associated with the paramount chief rather than with a larger group identity of the chiefdom.

Beyond the central plaza complex, the settlement's elemental organization settlement is unmistakable. Two fortification walls on the west and one on the steeply sloping east encircled and defined the settlement. These substantial outer walls probably originally stood 2 m tall, constructed of limestone quarried from the ridge. They were pierced at several points by gates that allowed restricted access to the residential areas. Between the concentric fortification walls were open, unbuilt spaces that may have served to corral llamas and alpacas. Between the walls and immediately inside of a gate on the northeast was one distinctive large circular stone tower that was probably used for defense.

The settlement was divided down the middle by the central plaza complex and its open corridors. To either side were the two large residential sections of similar size (4,000 to 6,000 people) and organizational structure. Each appears, at first, as a massed jumble of circular buildings, but on closer inspection, they are seen as arranged into small residential compounds defined by stone terrace and standing walls, a common patio space, and one to six structures. These patio groups were not organized formally in any way; they did not focus, for example, on common plazas, burial monuments, or other corporate facilities. They may, however, have been grouped informally into neighborhoods defined by patterns of access. The irregular paths of residential areas had no evident axial order or other pattern. They were not oriented on plazas, entranceways, or other features. They simply provided access to some, but not all, patio groups. Many of the groups were apparently accessible only through other patios, suggesting more interaction and association in these patio clusters.

Umpamalca (Figure 5-3b) is the only town-sized settlement of the chief-dom. It was built at 3,800 m on a low limestone knoll with a sheer drop to the Quishuarcancha stream to the west and rolling farmlands to the east. The settlement is positioned strategically near the proposed boundary between the three warring chiefdoms, where it could have defended the land, animals, and women sought in war and raiding by neighbors. In an area of 14.8 ha, about 2,150 circular residential structures were concentrated that housed an estimated 5,200 people. Umpamalca was thus equivalent in size to one of the main sectors of Tunanmarca, and it was similarly organized.

The elemental organization of Umpamalca is first defined by its fortification wall. The wall enclosed the settlement, except along the western edge, where a sheer cliff drops 300 m to the valley below. Several gates then entered into the residential area. Unlike Tunanmarca, the lack of a second wall, however, meant that no enclosed common space could have served for corrals. Perhaps this relatively low settlement had few animals. Within the fortification wall was one large residential section with many circular buildings of typical size and construction. These residential buildings were clustered into small patio groups with enclosing standing walls, a common patio space, and a few struc-tures. No common plazas or burial monuments existed here (Hastorf 1983). The irregular networks of paths had no evident axial order or other pattern. They provided irregular access between the patio groups and may also have divided the site into informal neighborhoods like at Tunanmarca. Outside the wall was a small, undefended cluster of 20 or so residential structures. Unlike Tunanmarca, no central plaza complex existed here.

Chawín (Figure 5-3c) is one of five large villages that form an arch of settle-ments east and north of Tunanmarca. Population of the villages is each around 800 (600 to 1,450) persons, and combined is approximately equal to the size of a town-sized settlement. Chawín itself was built at 3,850 m on a limestone hilltop to the north of Tunanmarca and overlooking the upper section of the Yanamarca Valley. The settlement is positioned strategically above the chiefdom's irrigation system and a trail giving access to the central settlement. Within an area of 5.6 ha were concentrated about 420 circular buildings that housed an estimated 650 inhabitants.

The elemental organization of the settlement is much like a small version of the town Umpamalca. Two fortification walls enclosed the settlement, except along the eastern edge, where a sheer drop protected the settlement, and only one wall was built. At several points, gates provided restricted access. The outer wall created enclosed spaces, perhaps for animals. The inner wall had one residential area with a typical array of circular buildings clustered into small patio groups. No common plazas or burial monuments existed. Crisscrossing the residential sector were the typical paths that lacked axial order or other pattern. They provided access to many of the patio groups and may also have divided the site into neighborhoods.

Using the analyses proposed by Hillier and Hanson (1984), DeMarrais (2001:Table 6-3) provides a statistical description of Tunanmarca, Umpamalca, and Chawín settlement plans. Two important points are clear: First, the settlements do not approximate either a grid or axial arrangement. Second, the three sites, regardless of size and position in the settlement hierarchy, were organized in remarkably similar ways. The settlements' arrangement shows very little centrality, even at Tunanmarca with its central plaza complex. These settlements were agglomerations of varying size, and their haphazard internal structure suggests no central planning. This characterization applies apparently to all Wanka settlements and emphasizes the paucity of ceremonial features like central plazas, mounds, or burial monuments that could have provided a visual or ceremonial focus for community relationships. Populations of different sizes were clustered together apparently for defense, and the maintenance of the group structure within a fundamentally segmental system would have been maintained largely by threat rather than by strong inducements of economic or ceremonial integration.

The primary organization seems to be segmental, organizing large groupings that may represent *ayllu* communities of varying sizes. These are what the ethnohistorical sources refer to as *pueblos*. The groups then may have been arranged structurally according to principles of balanced opposition (*yanantin*) that can take on a strong hierarchical character (Hastorf 1993:49). Separating Tunanmarca's residential areas into two discrete sectors seems to illustrate such an organization, and a similar dual structure existed at the nearby center of Hatunmarca (D'Altroy 2001:Figure 4-2). The center of Tunanmarca contained roughly half the chiefdom's total population. The other half of the population was itself divided approximately equally into a southern population at Umpamalca and a northeastern distribution of five villages. The settlement hierarchy appears to have been organized by principles of unity in opposition.

The Household

We have associated the individual patio group with a household (D'Altroy and Hastorf 2001), and the house structures and enclosed patio space appear to materialize or objectify continuity in a minimal social and economic house unit (Gillespie 2000). This unit was involved in a broad range of production and consumption activities, coresidence, and substantial associated ritual. In Sahlins' (1972) terms, it was organized by the Domestic Mode of Production, with some amounts of social differentiation by status and part-time specialization.

The general form of the patio group follows: one, two, or more individual residential structures opened onto a patio space that was enclosed by standing walls, terrace walls, and wall of those and neighboring houses (Figure 5-5). With only one or two narrow entrances, the patio group was set off from the

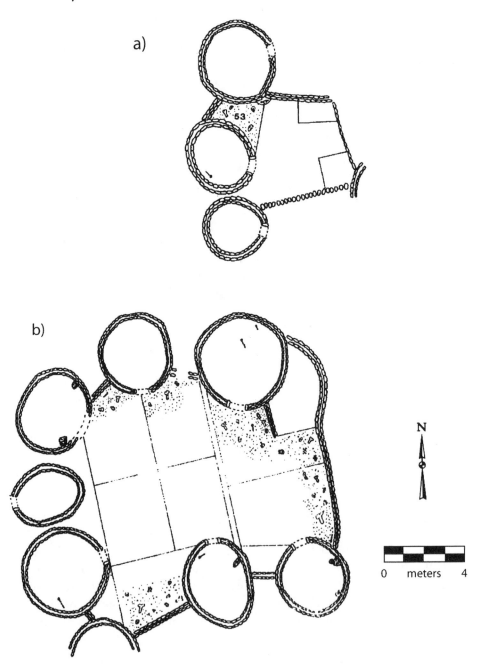

Figure 5-5. Comparison of elite and commoner patio groups at Tunanmarca: a) commoner patio group 7–9; b) elite patio group 7–2 (after Earle et al. 1987).

outside in terms of restricted movement and view. It was a private space. With the exception of two rectangular structures in Tunanmarca's central complex, all structures were circular. A single doorway provided access to each house (DeMarrais 2001). Walls were double-faced, 30 to 70 cm wide, roughly coursed, and set in mud mortar. Some were beautifully chinked on the exterior, suggesting they were built to be admired. At Tunanmarca, the average diameter of a structure was 3 to 4 m, creating an individual roofed space averaging about 9.5 m² (DeMarrais 2001:123).

Among the patio groups that we excavated, the number of structures ranged from one to six, most with only one or two houses. Structures were functionally undifferentiated; they all were similar in form and had the same basic residential uses, documented by internal hearths and by similar artifact inventories involved in cooking, eating, some work activities, and probably sleeping. Total size of patio area varied from about 30 m² to more than 200 m², and the roofed area varied according to the number of structures, often less than 10 m² to nearly 60 m² (DeMarrais 2001:145). Despite differences in total size, the overall arrangement and forms of the patio structures and space was remarkably similar, suggesting a common structural character to Wanka household groups. The main contrast was the numbers of houses that would seem to represent modular units, each probably housing a family unit. The patio group with multiple houses could therefore have been either an extended family (several generations living together) or a polygynous family (each structure housing separate wives and children).

The patio group defined the primary domestic and economic unit. Within each patio group was evidence for both production (lithic waste, grinding stones, spindle whorls, and less commonly, ceramic wasters) and consumption (animal bones and burnt plant remains, used stone tools and broken pots, and various items of dress such as silver and copper tupu pins and small disks). Debris from production and consumption was distributed across the house floors and open patios, but most was concentrated in small trash heaps in the patios' corners and aside of house doors.

Was there a difference between elite and commoner households? Although the overall arrangement of patio groups was similar across the whole sample, some visible differences helped us classify patio groups as elite or commoner social status (D'Altroy and Hastorf 2001). Within both Tunanmarca and Umpamalca, elite patios were thought to be those located in the central sector of the sites and at their higher elevations; at Tunanmarca, these locations were to either side of the settlement's central plazas. The stone architecture of these elite patio groups was noticeably finer with more careful coursing, chinking, and stone shaping (as indicated by limestone flake densities). Following excavation, when compared with commoner patio groups, Wanka II elite patio groups were substantially larger in the average number of structures per patio group (4.4 versus 1.5 structures), amount of total roofed space (41.7 versus 12.1 m^2), in the unroofed patio area (124.9 versus 74.3 m^2), and in the estimated total labor invested in stone-wall construction (2036 versus 642 hours) (DeMarrais 2001:Table 6.5). Elite households probably contained substantially more people than commoner households, as estimated by the size of the roofed area.

Were Wanka households, especially between elite and commoners, economically differentiated? In terms of consumption, household trash contained the same range of food remains, used tools, and objects of display; they were qualitatively similar (Costin and Earle 1989; D'Altroy and Hastorf 2001; Hastorf 2001a). Most food, vessels, and even display objects were broadly distributed. Quantitatively, however, some things were significantly more common in elite households. Elites ate more desirable foods such as deer meat (Sandefur 2001), used more decorative pottery including both locally made and imported styles (Costin 2001), and had more prestige objects like silver pins, disks, shell beads, and pendants for personal decoration (Owen 2001). While households shared a common pattern of household consumption, elites were higher consumers of special products.

The special consumption patterns within elite households probably reflected feasting that would have celebrated special status at life crisis ceremonies (Costin and Earle 1989; Hastorf 2001b). In the trash of elite households contained specific indicators of feasting activities, namely higher densities of cooking jars, grinding stones, decorative storage jars that might have held chicha, and burnt bone. I emphasize that this feasting took place within household contexts; the limited spaces available would suggest small and essentially private contexts for the feasting. With this perspective, I suggest that if the central plaza complex of Tunanmarca were, in fact, residential, the resident paramount chief and his family would have hosted feasts closely identified with their personal status. Among the Aztecs, Brumfiel (1987) has identified such household feasting as related to intensive internal factionalism with elite individuals vying for power and status.

In terms of specialization, most Wanka households show similar patterns of domestic production, but some households from Tunanmarca and Umpamalca apparently document part-time specialization. As discussed previously, these settlements were economically differentiated with more ceramic and chert blade production occurring in the households of Umpamalca (Costin 1986; Russell 1988). For example, within Umpamalca—with its overall ceramic waster index of 0.26—the six households' waster index varied from 0 (one case) to 1.14. Within Tunanmarca—with its index of only 0.07—the eight households varied from 0 (three cases) to 0.25. In each settlement, several households were involved in part-time pottery manufacture, but overall production was low and concentrated at the town of Umpamalca with its community-level specialization. Although households were highly generalized in a wide range of economic activities, households in certain communities appear to have concentrated activities on specific activities geared to production for exchange outside their community. This specialization was embedded within the generalized Wanka household (Costin 1991).

During Wanka II times, specialized production of wealth objects was low volume and broadly distributed with little concentration in elite households. This suggests that wealth production was not closely controlled with attached craftsmen living in elite households. Prestige goods were relatively rare, and most appear to have been imported from some distance (regionally or long distance) (Earle 2001). Decorated Wanka ceramics were certainly concentrated in elite households (Costin and Earle 1989), but their production was apparently broadly distributed and not controlled by elite households, which had low production indices ranging from 0.05 to 0.24. Textiles used as personal clothing likely served as status markers among the Wanka, but textile production, too, was broadly distributed among households as indicated by the density of spindle whorls and needles. Although the densities of both spindle whorls and needles were higher among the elite household, that pattern was not strong (Costin 1993; Owen 2001). Production debris from metal production was very low, suggesting that most objects were imported as finished objects. The manufacturing debris does concentrate weakly in elite households (Owen 2001). No convincing evidence, however, exists for attached specialization among the Wanka II chiefdom of Tunanmarca.

As a final consideration of the Wanka household, much of the society's ritual activities were apparently household (versus group) oriented. I have already discussed the remarkably limited amount of public ceremonial space in Tunanmarca's settlements, absent at all sites except the center itself, where the small central plazas may have been that of the ruling chief's household. In contrast, household-based ritual activities were common. Although concentrated in elite households, all households used decorative ceramics, often with highly elaborated symbolic materials, probably indicative of household ritual use. Individuals were buried within household compounds, typically below the floors of their houses (Owen and Norconk 1987). No specialized burial structures existed, in contrast to other places in Peru where *chulpas* were associated with *ayllu* groups. Also found within households were special ritual deposits including dog burials and small ritual offerings.

Between the households of the Tunanmarca chiefdoms, some differences existed both in terms of social status and subsistence activities. These differences were, however, subtle. Elite patio groups were larger and involved more labor for their building. They contained more decorated ceramics and metal display objects, and were apparently more involved in small-scale feasting. Differences were, however, largely of degree, and it is evident that the elite sector was neither exclusive nor highly distinctive. The Wanka informants' description of the independent households apparently had some degree of truth even within the context of a chiefly society.

SYNTHESIS

Though the Tunanmarca chiefdom was unusually large, it was surprisingly little differentiated according to the activities that occurred in the center versus dependent settlements and in elite versus common households. The central settlement was over 10,000 people, and the total polity was probably about 20,0000. Political domination of the center is demonstrated by its size alone. Economic interdependence among the chiefdom's settlements is suggested by the irrigation system that combines four of the settlements, by some economic specialization and exchange between settlements, and by the likely necessity to coordinate community responses to both natural risk and the threat of attack.

Despite the evident complexity of the chiefdom, little formal institutional order existed. The settlements were simple agglomerations of house groups without overarching structure except to be defined by surrounding fortification walls. The amount of ceremonial space and monumental elaboration was minimal. Prestige goods were relatively unelaborated and quite broadly spread. So, what was going on?

Since the particular sources of power used by chiefs affect a chiefdom's cultural characteristics (Earle 1997), the apparent unusual nature of Wanka society likely results from its reliance on military force as the means to fashion and maintain political order. In the Tunanmarca chiefdom, the creation of its exceptionally large polity was recent. Rapid population growth and increasing competition escalated warfare and must have helped force people together into their fortified hilltop settlements well away from their fertile fields (LeBlanc 1981). The primary source of power was evidently proven success in warfare and corresponding coercive threats of suppression. In such a situation, a basic form of staple finance evidently supported chiefly rule, but ideological power, although certainly a factor, was little elaborated compared to many other chiefdoms (Earle 1997). Wanka chieftains came to power to defend the community, and coercive power of the warrior chiefs served to keep them in power. The settlement of the Tunanmarca chiefdom fell to the Inka, and its population was forcefully removed. As a footnote to history, however, the Wanka came back for their revenge. They allied with the Spanish conquistadors against the Inka overlords, and thus helped change world history irrevocably.

Acknowledgments

UMARP was a joint project involving the dedicated work of many people (see Earle et al. 1983; D'Altroy and Hastorf 2001). I am particularly indebted to my former codirectors, Terry D'Altroy, Chris Hastorf, and Cathy Scott, and to my other former PhD students, Cathy Costin, Melissa Hagstrum, Glenn Russell, and Elsie Sandefur. We were full field collaborators and a close research family. While I wrote this chapter, I have enjoyed reliving those good times in Jauja together. Ramiro Matos and Jorge Silva were valuable Peruvian colleagues providing important perspective on regional archaeology and absolutely necessary logistical support for the project. Without Jeff Parsons's field survey and positive mentoring, UMARP could never even have been conceived. Among other sources, the National Science Foundation (BNS–8203723) provided the primary funding for UMARP. Terry D'Altroy, Liz DeMarrais, Eliza Earle, and Chris Hastorf read earlier drafts of my manuscript and provided valuable assistance.

REFERENCES CITED

Beck, Robin
  2003   Consolidation and Hierarchy: Chiefdom Variability in the Mississippian Southeast. *American Antiquity* 68:641–661.
Blanton, Richard, Gary Feinman, Stephen Kowalewski, and Peter Peregrine
  1996   A Dual-processual Theory for the Evolution of Mesoamerican Civilization. *Current Anthropology* 37:1–14.
Browman, David
  1970   *Early Peruvian Peasants: The Culture History of a Central Highlands Valley.* Ph.D. dissertation, Harvard University, Cambridge.
Brumfiel, Elizabeth
  1987   Consumption and Politics at Aztec Huexotla. *American Anthropologist* 89:676–686.
Carneiro, Robert
  1981   The Chiefdom as Precursor of the State. In *The Transition to Statehood in the New World*, edited by Grant Jones and Robert Kautz, pp. 39–79. Cambridge University Press, Cambridge.
Costin, Cathy
  1986   *From Chiefdom to Empire State: Ceramic Economy among the Pre Hispanic Wanka of Highland Peru.* Ph.D. dissertation, Department of Anthropology, University of California, Los Angeles.
  1991   Craft Specialization: Issues in Defining, Documenting, and Explaining the Organization of Production. *Archaeological Method and Theory* 3:1–56.
  1993   Textiles, Women, and Political Economy in Late Prehispanic Peru. *Research in Economic Anthropology* 14:3–28.

2001   Production and Exchange of Ceramics. In *Empire and Domestic Economy*, edited by Terence D'Altroy and Christine Hastorf, pp. 203–242. Kluwer Academic/Plenum Press, New York.

Costin, Cathy, and Timothy Earle
1986   Status Distinction and Legitimation of Power as Reflected in Changing Patterns of Consumption in Late Prehispanic Peru. *American Antiquity* 54:691–714.

D'Altroy, Terence
1981   Imperial Growth and Consolidation: The Xauxa Region of Peru under the Incas. Ph.D. dissertation, Department of Anthropology, University of California, Los Angeles.
1987   Transitions in Power: Centralization of Wanka Political Organization under Inka Rule. *Ethnohistory* 34:78–103.
1992   *Provincial Power in the Inka Empire*. Smithsonian Institution, Washington, D.C.
2001   The Archaeological Context. In *Empire and Domestic Economy*, edited by Terence D'Altroy and Christine Hastorf, pp. 65–96. Kluwer Academic/Plenum Press, New York.

D'Altroy, Terence N., and Christine Hastorf (editors)
2001   *Empire and Domestic Economy*. Kluwer Academic/Plenum Press, New York.

DeMarrais, Elizabeth
1989   Architecture and Prehistoric Settlement Organization among the Wanka of Highland Peru. Master's thesis, Department of Anthropology, University of California, Los Angeles.
2001   The Architecture and Organization of Xauxa Settlements. In *Empire and Domestic Economy*, edited by Terence D'Altroy and Christine Hastorf, pp. 115–153. Kluwer Academic/Plenum Press, New York.

Drennan, Robert D.
1987   Regional Demography in Chiefdoms. In *Chiefdoms in the Americas*, edited by Robert Drennan and Carlos A. Uribe, pp. 307–324. University Press of America, Lanham.

Earle, Timothy
1978   *Economic and Social Organization of a Complex Chiefdom, the Halelea District, Kaua'i, Hawaii*. Anthropological Papers No. 63, Museum of Anthropology, University of Michigan, Ann Arbor.
1991   *Chiefdoms: Power, Economy and Ideology*. Cambridge University Press, Cambridge.
1997   *How Chiefs Come to Power*. Stanford, Palo Alto.
2001   Exchange and Social Stratification in the Andes: The Xauxa Case. In *Empire and Domestic Economy*, edited by Terence D'Altroy and Christine Hastorf, pp. 297–314. Kluwer Academic/Plenum Press, New York.

Earle, Timothy, Terence D'Altroy, Catherine LeBlanc, Christine Hastorf, and Terry Y. LeVine

1980   Changing Settlement Patterns in the Upper Mantaro Valley, Peru. *Journal of New World Archaeology* 4:1–49.

Earle, Timothy, Terence D'Altroy, Christine Hastorf, Catherine Scott, Cathy Costin, Glenn S. Russell, and Elsie Sandefur

1987   *Archaeological Field Research in the Upper Mantaro, Peru, 1982–1983: Investigations of Inka Expansion and Exchange.* Monograph 28, Institute of Archaeology, University of California, Los Angeles.

Espinoza Soriano, Waldemar

1971   Los Huancas, aliados de la conquista. *Anales científicos de la Universidad del Centro del Perú* 1:9–407.

Flores Espinoza, I.

1959   El sitio arqueológico Wari Willca, Huancayo. *Actas u trabajos del II Congreso National de Historica del Perú* V. 1:177–186.

Gillespie, Susan

2000   Rethinking Ancient Maya Social Organization: Replacing 'Lineage' with 'House.' *American Anthropologist* 102:467–484.

Hagstrum, Melissa

1989   Technological Continuity and Change: Ceramic Ethnoarchaeology in the Peruvian Andes. Ph.D. dissertation, Department of Anthropology, University of California, Los Angeles.

Hastorf, Christine

1983   Prehistoric Agricultural Intensification and Political Development in the Jauja Region of Central Peru. Ph.D. dissertation, Department of Anthropology, University of California, Los Angeles.

1993   *Agriculture and the Onset of Political Inequality before the Inka.* Cambridge University Press, Cambridge.

2001a   Agricultural Production and Consumption. In *Empire and Domestic Economy*, edited by Terence D'Altroy and Christine Hastorf, pp. 155–178. Kluwer Academic/Plenum Press, New York.

2001b   The Xauxa Andean Live. In *Empire and Domestic Economy*, edited by Terence D'Altroy and Christine Hastorf, pp. 315–324. Kluwer Academic/Plenum Press, New York.

Hastorf, Christine, and Timothy Earle

1985   Intensive Agriculture and the Geography of Political Change in the Upper Mantaro Region of Central Peru. In *Prehistoric Intensive Agriculture in the Tropics*, edited by Ian Farrington, pp. 569–595. British Archaeological Reports, International Series 323, Oxford.

Hastorf, Christine, Timothy Earle, H. Wright, Lisa LeCount, Glenn Russell, and Elsie Sandefur

1989   Settlement archaeology in the Jauja region of Peru. *Andean Past* 2: 81–130.

Hillier, Bill, and J. Hanson
1984   *The Social Logic of Space*. Cambridge University Press, Cambridge.
Hyslop, John
1977   Hilltop Cities in Peru. *Archaeology* 30: 281–225.
Johnson, Allen, and Timothy Earle
2000   *The Evolution of Human Societies*, 2nd ed. Stanford University Press, Stanford.
Krzanowski, Andresz
1977   Yuraccama: the Settlement Complex in the Alto Chicama Region (Northern Peru). In *Polish Contributions in New World Archaeology*, edited by Janusz Kozlowski, pp. 29–58. Zakla Narodowy im Ossolinskich Krakow.
Lavallée, Danielle
1967   Types céramiques des Andes Centrales du Pérou. *Journal de Société des Americanistes* 65:411–447.
LeBlanc, Catherine J.
1981   Late Prehispanic Huanca Settlement Patterns in Yanamarca Valley, Peru. Ph.D. dissertation, Department of Anthropology, University of California, Los Angeles.
LeVine, Terry
1979   Prehistoric Political and Economic Change in Highland Peru: An Ethno-historical Study of the Mantaro Valley. Master's thesis, Archaeology Program, University of California, Los Angeles.
Lumbreras, Luis G.
1957   La cultura Wanka. *Ondas Isabelinas, Organo de la Gran Unidad Escolar Santa Isabel de Huancayo* 1:15–18. Huancayo, Peru.
Matos Mendiete, Ramiro
1959   Los Wankas, datos históricos u arqueológicos. In *Actas y trabajos del II Congreso National de Historica del Perú*, Vol. 1, pp. 187–210. Lima, Peru.
1966   La economia durante el periodo de reinos y confederaciónes en Mantaro. *Actas y memorias del XXXVI Congreso Internacional de Americanistas*. Vol. 2, pp. 95–99. Seville.
1975   Prehistoria y ecología humana en las punas de Junín. *Revista del Museo Nacional* 41:37–80.
McIntosh, Susan (editor)
1999   *Beyond Chiefdoms: Pathways to Complexity in Africa*. Cambridge University Press, Cambridge.
Owen, Bruce
1986   The Role of Common Metal Objects in the Inka State. Master's thesis, Department of Anthropology, University of California, Los Angeles.
2001   The Economy of Metal and Shell Wealth Goods. In *Empire and Domestic Economy*, edited by Terence D'Altroy and Christine Hastorf, pp. 265–293. Kluwer Academic/Plenum Publishers, New York.

Owen, Bruce, and M.A. Norconk.

1987   Appendix 1: Analysis of the Human Burials, 1977–1983 Field Seasons: Demographic Profiles and Burial Practices. In *Archaeological Field Research in the Upper Mantaro, Peru, 1982–1983: Investigations of Inka Expansion and Exchange*, edited by Timothy Earle, Terence D'Altroy, Christine Hastorf, Catherine J. Scott, Cathy L. Costin, Glenn S. Russell, and Elsie C. Sandefur, pp. 107–123. Monograph 28, Institute of Archaeology, University of California, Los Angeles.

Parsons, Jeffrey

1971   *Prehistoric Settlement Patterns in the Texcoco Region, Mexico.* Memoirs No. 3, Museum of Anthropology, University of Michigan, Ann Arbor.

1978   El complejo hidaulico de Tunanmarca: Canales, acueductos y reservorios. In *El hombre u la cultura Andina: Actas y trabajos del III Congreso II*, edited by Ramiro Matos, pp. 556–566. Universidad Nacional Mayor de San Marcos, Lima.

Parsons, Jeffrey, and Charles Hastings

1987   The Late Intermediate Period. In *Peruvian Prehistory*, edited by Richard Keating, pp. 190–229. Cambridge University Press, Cambridge.

Parsons, Jeffrey, Charles Hastings, and Ramiro Matos

2000   *Prehistoric Settlement Patterns in the Upper Mantaro and Tarma Drainages, Junín, Peru.* Memoirs No. 34, Museum of Anthropology, University of Michigan, Ann Arbor.

Parsons, Jeffrey, and Ramiro Matos

2001   Forward. In *Empire and Domestic Economy*, edited by Terence D'Altroy and Christine Hastorf, pp. *vii–xi*. Kluwer Academic/Plenum Publishers, New York.

Russell, Glenn

1988   The Effect of Inka Administrative Policy on the Domestic Economy of the Wanka, Peru: the Production and Use of Stone Tools. Ph.D. dissertation, Department of Anthropology, University of California, Los Angeles.

Sahlins, Marshall

1972   *Stone Age Economics.* Aldine, Chicago.

Sandefur, Elsie C.

1988   Andean Zooarchaeology: Animal Use and the Inka Conquest of the Upper Mantaro Valley. Ph.D. dissertation, Archaeology Program, University of California, Los Angeles.

2001   Animal Husbandry and Meat Consumption. In *Empire and Domestic Economy*, edited by Terence D'Altroy and Christine Hastorf, pp. 179–202. Kluwer Academic/Plenum Publishers, New York.

Sikkink, Lynne

2001   Ethnoarchaeology and Contemporary Domestic Economy in the Mantaro Valley. In *Empire and Domestic Economy*, edited by Terence D'Altroy and Christine Hastorf, pp. 97–111. Kluwer Academic/Plenum Publishers, New York.

Steponaitis, Vincus
　1978　Locational Theory and Complex Chiefdoms: a Mississippian Example. *Mississippian Settlement Pattern*, edited by B. Smith, pp. 417–453. Academic Press, New York.

Toledo, Francisco de
　1940 [1570]　Información hecha por Orden de Don Francisco de Toledo en su Visita de las Provincias del Perú, el la que Declaran Indios Ancianos sobre el Derecho de los Caciques y sobre el Gobierno que Tenían Aquellos Pueblos antes que los Incas los Conquitasen. Concepción de Xauxa, 20 Noviembre 1570. In *Don Francisco de Toledo, supremo organizador del Peru: Su vida, su obra (1515–1582)*, Vol. 2, edited by Roberto Levillier, pp. 14–37. Espasa-Calpe, Buenos Aires.

Vega, Andrés de
　1965 [1582]　La Descripción que se hizo en la Provincia de Xauxa por la instrucción de su Majestad que a la Dicha Provincia se Invio de Molde. In *Relaciones geográficas de Indias*. Biblioteca de Autores Españoles, Vol. 183:166–175. Ediciones Atlas, Madrid.

EARLY CHIEFDOM COMMUNITIES COMPARED:

THE SETTLEMENT PATTERN RECORD FOR CHIFENG, THE ALTO MAGDALENA, AND THE VALLEY OF OAXACA

ROBERT D. DRENNAN AND CHRISTIAN E. PETERSON
University of Pittsburgh

No early chiefdom society was exactly like that of another region, but all represented the initial development of permanent hierarchical social relations in their respective regions. In these societies, those who would be chiefs were successful enough at forging unequal social relationships with other members of their own communities that the fundamental organizing principles of those communities were transformed. The communities involved in this transformation existed at varying social and spatial scales; we commonly think of small local communities composed of those in face-to-face interaction on a daily basis nested within higher-order communities, which were sometimes nested within yet larger communities. From this perspective, the emergence of chiefdoms is marked by the emergence of larger, more tightly integrated communities than had existed previously. Settlement pattern research on a regional scale provides an opportunity to delineate and compare these communities, based on the assumption that they are reflected in the way human settlement is distributed across the landscape at a given time.

Even as a settlement pattern perspective in archeology was still taking shape, Parsons (1972) observed both that human communities were recognizable in the archeological record and that identifying and delineating them were tasks that required explicit analytical attention—as opposed to simply assuming implicitly that whatever was identified as an archaeological site automatically represented a human community. He also stressed the importance of focusing separately, but in complementary fashion, at a range of different scales. All these observations are fundamental to the analytical approach central to the comparisons undertaken in this chapter (Peterson and Drennan 2005).

THE CHIFENG REGION IN EASTERN INNER MONGOLIA

Complex patterns of social organization in northeastern China emerged during Hongshan times (ca. 4500–3000 BC) (Barnes 1993:108–110; Chang 1986:181–188; Guo 1995; Nelson 1990, 1994, 1997; Shelach 1997, 1999). Spectacular objects, such as jade sculpture and finely painted pottery, give evidence of craft specialization, and the inclusion of such objects in a few elaborate burials is taken to reflect considerable social inequality, although the exact nature of this system of social ranking remains to be clearly determined (Childs-Johnson 1991; Chiou-Peng 1994; Guo 1995, 1997; Liaoning 1997; Nelson 1994:9–10, 1997:60, 2001). Possible ceremonial structures suggest large coordinated groups of workers for their construction and substantial centralized communities for their use (Barnes and Guo 1996; Guo 1995; Guo and Zhang 1984; Fang and Liu 1984; Liaoning 1986, 1997). While the term "state" has been applied to the entire Hongshan phenomenon as if it were a single polity (Guo 1995; Nelson 1994:4, 1996), the archaeological "culture" clearly represents a large number of more local polities or societies generally consistent in demographic scale and degree of social hierarchy with what are sometimes called "chiefdoms." Detailed settlement pattern information is available for an area of 765 km^2 west of Chifeng city (Figure 6-1), a small part of the area through which the Hongshan culture is spread (Chifeng 2003a, 2003b; Chinese-American 2002; Linduff, Drennan, and Shelach 2004). The map of locations where Hongshan ceramics have been recovered in the Chifeng survey region (Figure 6-2) reveals a pattern of small farming settlements, usually near what are, today, the most productive agricultural zones of the valley. The length of the survey area is roughly a day's walk, so its 4,000 to 8,000

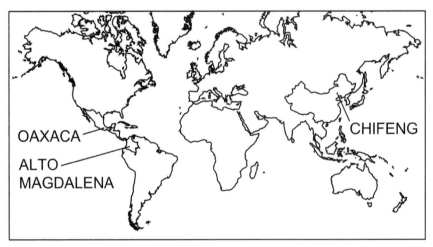

Figure 6-1. Locations of the three archaeological regions compared in this chapter.

inhabitants (Drennan et al. 2003) were surely in contact with each other. This population could easily have been supported within a small part of the survey area, and social interaction would have been greatly facilitated by concentration in one or a few places. Occupation was widely spread through the entire region, however, so social interaction of only moderate intensity involving the entire regional population is suggested.

Figure 6-2 shows spatially separate areas of occupation tending to cluster close to each other with greater separation from other clusters. Systematic

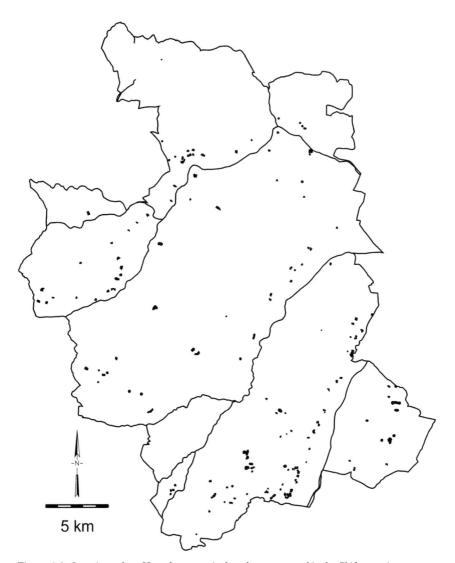

5 km

Figure 6-2. Locations where Hongshan ceramics have been recovered in the Chifeng region.

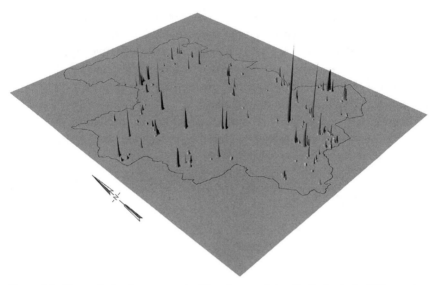

Figure 6-3. Unsmoothed surface representing Hongshan population distribution in the Chifeng region.

delineation of these clusters offers an opportunity to look more deeply into patterns of social interaction and community formation. Peterson and Drennan (2005) suggest using surfaces representing population distribution (reconstructed for Chifeng primarily from area and density of surface remains [Drennan et al. 2003]) as a basis for delineating human interaction communities, assuming that, broadly speaking, human interactions are more intense at shorter distances than at longer ones. Such a surface for the Hongshan occupation of Chifeng (Figure 6-3) is undoubtedly a better representation of population distribution than Figure 6-2, since Figure 6-2 reflects only areas where Hongshan remains were found, while Figure 6-3 also reflects their density. In some cases, a single peak in Figure 6-3 represents several nearby, but spatially separate occupation areas, and this occurs especially where larger, denser occupations are involved. This provides a natural way of clustering very closely spaced occupations. If the surface is represented as a contour map, a single very low contour level can be selected that outlines the bases of the peaks representing Hongshan occupation where they rise up from the flat (unoccupied) terrain around them. This contour line clearly demarcates some 125 clusters of Hongshan occupation areas (Figure 6-4). The smallest are likely the isolated farmsteads of single families, but the larger ones may range up to as many as several hundred inhabitants. The clarity of these clusters suggests that human interaction at this scale is strongly structured around small communities. Since these clusters are all less than 900 m long, their inhabitants were probably in face-to-face contact with each other on a

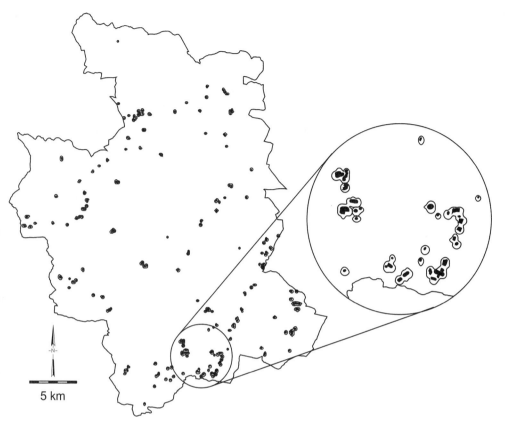

Figure 6-4. Cutoff contour delineating the bases of the occupational peaks in Figure 6-3 and clustering Hongshan occupation areas into small local communities.

virtually daily basis. Hongshan occupation distribution, then, suggests a fundamental social building block in the form of a local community, of variable size but averaging some 10 to 12 households, who may well have been related to each other through kinship, and who shared daily routines and activities. These social interactions were important enough to Hongshan households that they chose to facilitate them by locating their residences in close proximity rather than, for example, directly adjacent to the specific plots of land that they cultivated.

Some, although not all, of the small Hongshan communities show clustering at a larger scale as well, occurring as groups of several closely spaced communities. To identify interaction structure at this larger-than-local scale, Peterson and Drennan (2005) smoothed the surfaces representing population distribution mathematically. As the Hongshan surface is smoothed, the occupation peaks become progressively larger, and some of them merge together

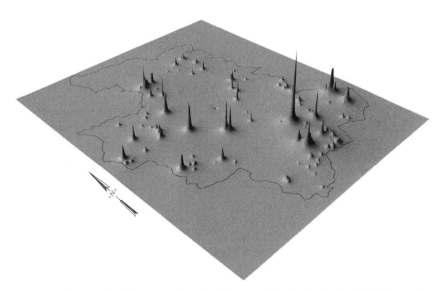

Figure 6-5. Smoothed surface representing Hongshan population distribution in the Chifeng region.

(Figure 6-5). A very low contour level again delineates clusters of occupation, although now the pattern is more complicated (Figure 6-6). Toward the north and west, roughly circular shapes delineate clusters of the small communities identified in the less smoothed surface, although some of the small communities remain separate and individual. Toward the southeast one very large cluster is delineated, but another look at the surface (Figure 6-5) reveals this to be an oversimplification. In fact, several smaller occupational peaks occur in the southeast as well, but they are close together so the smoothing of the surface has caused a general uplift of the "flat" surface from which the peaks rise sharply up. Thus we should choose a higher contour level (also shown in Figure 6-6) to define the bases of the six major occupational peaks in this sector. The surface between these two contour levels in the southeast (Figure 6-6), shows "valleys" that separate occupational peaks and ridges. Some of the smaller scattered settlements that are especially numerous here clearly cluster with one or another of the peaks, forming what might be called "districts"—units of social interaction like the larger communities in the northwest, but with an added territorial dimension.

Altogether there are 65 clusters of small local communities, of which the largest 14 (with estimated populations over 150) are clearly set off from the smaller ones in the frequency distribution of cluster populations. It is these 14 that suggest further community structure above the level of the small local community involved in face-to-face interaction on a daily basis. It appears that not all the Hongshan inhabitants of the region were involved in such higher-

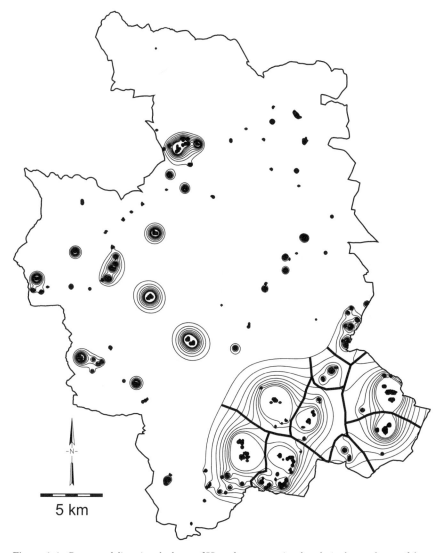

Figure 6-6. Contours delineating the bases of Hongshan occupational peaks in the northwest of the smoothed surface (Figure 6-5) and more complicated occupational landscape to the southeast, where heavy lines indicate division into districts.

order communities. About one-fourth of the estimated regional population lived in the 51 small local communities not included in larger clusters. In most of the higher-order communities, where the other three-fourths of the regional population lived, the small local communities occupy the role of building blocks, as the higher-order communities consist of clusters of up to 10 small local communities, although in two instances the higher-order communities are single settlements. The clusters are as much as 3 km across, a spatial scale

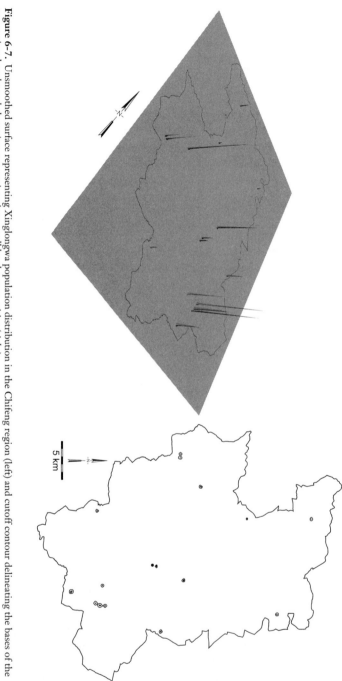

Figure 6-7. Unsmoothed surface representing Xinglongwa population distribution in the Chifeng region (left) and cutoff contour delineating the bases of the occupational peaks and clustering occupations into small local communities (right).

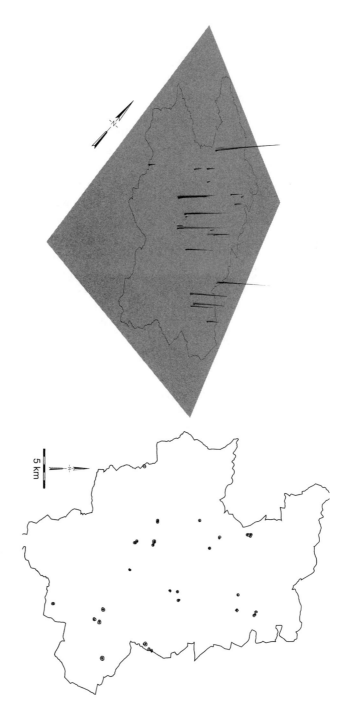

Figure 6-8. Unsmoothed surface representing Zhaobaogou population distribution in the Chifeng region (left) and cutoff contour delineating the bases of the occupational peaks and clustering occupations into small local communities (right).

too large to involve face-to-face interaction on a daily basis. We attribute the formation of these clusters to more intensive interaction among the small local communities within each cluster than with communities outside it.

Such richness of higher-order structure is not present in the settlement distributions of earlier periods in Chifeng. At about 6000 BC, in Xinglongwa times, the earliest sedentary agricultural population of perhaps 300 inhabitants (Figure 6-7), formed small local communities with only a little clustering of the individual occupation areas. These small local communities may group together by twos or threes in a few places in the survey area, but their number is so small that there is simply no prospect of the complex multi-scalar clustering delineated for Hongshan. In the Zhaobaogou period, from about 5250 BC, regional population increased to between 800 and 1,600, and occupation areas were, again, broadly distributed across the survey area, with only slightly greater clustering into small local communities (Figure 6-8). Higher-order clustering is still very weak. The 14 clearly defined higher-order Hongshan communities and districts, then, represent a newly emerged structure. Their populations varied from about 150 for the smallest to as high as 1,000 for the largest. In many of them, a single local community can be identified that is by far the largest constituent community in the cluster. Rank-size graphs for the individual communities and districts (Figure 6-9) nearly all show the log-normal or primate patterns generally assumed to reflect centralized social units. The rank-size graph for the entire survey area, however, is strongly convex (Figure 6-10), and probably indicates the presence in the survey area of multiple independent units not centralized under any single organization at a yet higher level.

We thus see directly in the settlement patterns the kinds of communities previously postulated from less direct evidence. These communities could have been produced by increased economic interdependence emerging with specialized production. Such communities might engage in the activities for which public structures were desired, and they could provide the labor forces to build them. Such communities could well be organized according to the hierarchical principle of social ranking. Whether the specific higher-order communities and districts delineated in this analysis of the Chifeng area had such structures or social ranking remains to be confirmed by excavation, since direct evidence of these characteristics would not necessarily remain on the surface. Stone mounds, however, do still exist on the surfaces of Hongshan sites immediately to the west of the area included in this analysis (Shelach 1999:79–83).

THE ALTO MAGDALENA IN THE ANDES OF COLOMBIA

Archaeological indicators of complex social organization in the Alto Magdalena (Figure 6-1) occur during the Regional Classic period (AD 1–900) in the

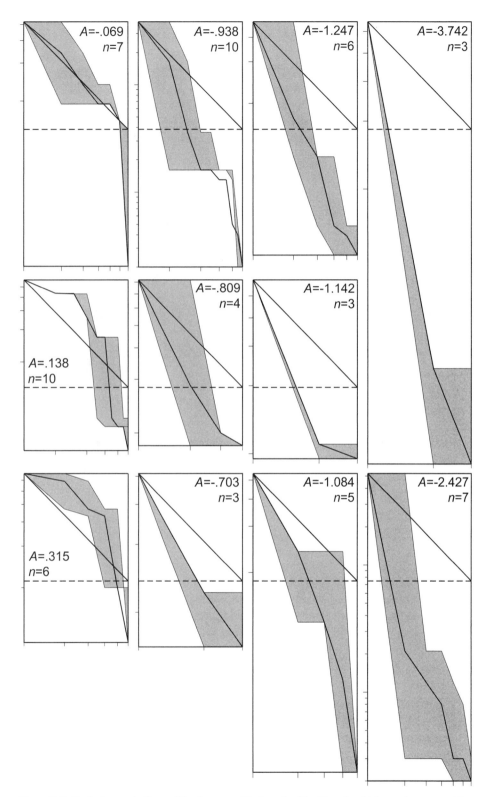

Figure 6-9. Rank-size graphs for small local communities in each of the Hongshan higher-order communities or districts. Higher-order communities made up of fewer than three distinct local communities are omitted. *A* values and 67% confidence zones for the rank-size lines are included (Drennan and Peterson 2004).

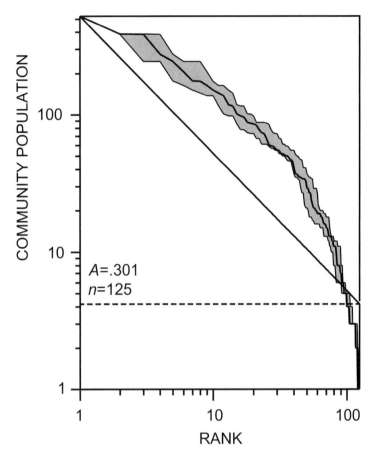

Figure 6-10. Rank-size graph for all Hongshan local communities in the Chifeng survey region. The *A* value and a 67% confidence zone for the rank-size line are included (Drennan and Peterson 2004).

form of elaborate tombs, often surrounded by monumental stone statues depicting human, animal, and supernatural figures (Duque 1964; Duque and Cubillos 1979, 1983, 1988; Cubillos 1980; Reichel-Dolmatoff 1972; Llanos 1995). Clearly only individuals of special importance received such treatment in death, although (as with Hongshan societies) we do not know the exact nature of their special positions. Unlike the prehistoric tombs of many parts of northern South America, the elaborate, monumental Classic period tombs of the Alto Magdalena do not contain many items of personal wealth, perhaps suggesting a social hierarchy based more on symbolic or ritual prestige than on accumulation of wealth (Drennan 1995). Here we will focus on settlement information from one of four separate areas of regional survey (Drennan 2000;

Drennan ed. 1985; Drennan and Quattrin 1995; Drennan, Taft, and Uribe eds. 1993; Drennan et al. 1991; Herrera, Drennan, and Uribe eds. 1989). The total Classic period population of this area of 317 km^2 was probably between 7,000 and 14,000, compared to the 4,000 to 8,000 estimated for Hongshan in a much larger area. This population density (20 to 40 people per km^2), while substantially higher than that for Hongshan (5 to 10 per km^2), was apparently still easily supported by the resources of the Alto Magdalena.

Instead of a small number of compact settlements surrounded by large amounts of unoccupied space, as for Hongshan, the Alto Magdalena Classic period occupation spreads across broad areas of the landscape (Figure 6-11). In this survey area, Classic period remains occur on 7.3% of the total surface area. By comparison, Hongshan artifacts are found on only 0.3% of the Chifeng landscape. When we view the Classic period distribution as a surface (Figure 6-11), delineating small local communities does not work as it did for Hongshan. While the bases of some peaks are small and separate, other peaks merge together and their combined bases sprawl irregularly across areas of over 2 km^2 without any noticeable gap. Individual households here simply did not uniformly choose to locate their residences in spatial clusters as Hongshan households did. Classic period interaction between households was probably not especially intensive within clearly defined small local communities as opposed to between them, since it is not even possible to identify such communities in the spatial distribution of occupational remains. The large areas of continuous Classic period occupation extend nearly 3 km from one side to the other—too great a distance to facilitate daily face-to-face interaction. More detailed studies of Classic period residential areas (e.g. González 1998) suggest households living directly on the land they cultivated, a pattern resembling present-day settlement in the Alto Magdalena. The Hongshan settlement pattern, in turn, might well have resembled the modern settlement pattern of the Chifeng region, with compact villages separated by tracts of open farmland, although Hongshan villages were smaller and spaced much farther apart than modern ones (Peterson and Drennan 2005).

While the local community is easy to identify in the archaeological record for Hongshan, and likely served as an important social interaction building block in the formation of higher-order communities (which take the form of clusters of small local communities), such small local communities are evidenced in the Alto Magdalena Classic only in the most sparsely settled peripheries; large agglomerations of dispersed occupation sprawl amorphously over sizeable areas without any indication of small-scale spatial structure. The Alto Magdalena settlement distribution can also be viewed as a more smoothed surface (Figure 6-12), in just the way we looked for larger-scale structure in the Hongshan settlement pattern. In this surface, the multitude of tiny

132

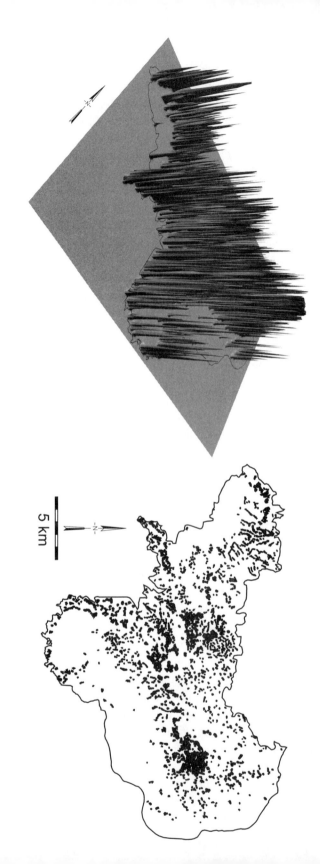

Figure 6-11. Unsmoothed surface representing Regional Classic population distribution in one survey region of the Alto Magdalena (left), based on locations where Regional Classic period materials have been located (right).

5 km

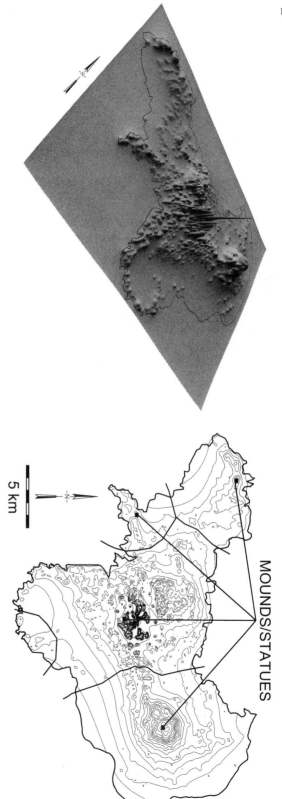

Figure 6-12. Smoothed surface representing Regional Classic period population distribution in one survey area of the Alto Magdalena (left) and contour map of the same surface (right) showing division into districts.

MOUNDS/STATUES

5 km

peaks visible in the unsmoothed surface have merged together into two principal and three somewhat lower "hills" of denser occupation. Alto Magdalena occupation is so widespread that, unlike the Hongshan smoothed surface, there is no unoccupied flat surface from which separate occupational peaks rise up in any part of the survey area. Rather, the entire area has the characteristics that led us to use occupational valleys to define districts in the southeastern sector of the Hongshan settlement distribution studied. The valleys of less dense occupation in the Classic period Alto Magdalena surface delineate two large and apparently relatively complete districts (Figure 6-12), along with perhaps three others that are only partially included in the survey area.

For the Alto Magdalena Classic, additional evidence supports an interpretation of this larger-scale spatial patterning as territorial communities or districts. Both of the two relatively complete districts, and two of the three only partially contained within the survey area, have a single site with monumental tombs and statues—each a possible ceremonial center for its district. The sociopolitical identities of the Alto Magdalena districts could have been created and maintained in the funerals of individuals of high social rank and in the ceremonies for which the plazas and statues around their monumental tombs appear to have been designed. In a similar way, ceremonial centers (with some of the characteristics of Hongshan ritual sites excavated outside the Chifeng survey area) may have exerted centripetal social forces in the Chifeng Hongshan districts. As of now, however, the presence of such centers in the Chifeng Hongshan districts remains to be demonstrated. The Alto Magdalena Classic districts are larger than the Hongshan districts—10 to 12 km from one side to the other, as opposed to 4 to 6 km for Hongshan. District populations in the Alto Magdalena are also substantially larger; the two districts that are complete in the survey area each had a population of several thousand inhabitants (perhaps as many as 7,000) compared to 1,000 or less for Hongshan districts.

The earliest sedentary occupation in the Alto Magdalena at about 1000 BC (Formative 1) was much smaller than that of the Classic, although within about 400 years after the establishment of agriculture the population had already grown to at least 1,500. Although population was much sparser than later on, its distribution does not make it easy to define small local communities, even when viewed as an unsmoothed surface (Figure 6-13). Instead, while there are some isolated population peaks, many of them run together, especially in four main areas. Just as in the Classic, spatial structure is most visible in a smoothed surface, whose undulations suggest three or possibly four districts (Figure 6-14). The territorial extents of the two included more or less completely in the survey area are quite similar to those defined for the Classic period, although their populations are much smaller. The basic characteristics of this larger-scale spatial structure, then, are present in Alto Magdalena settlement patterns from

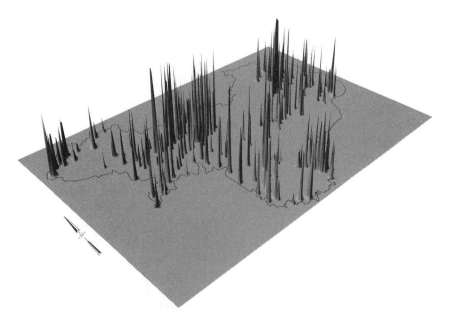

Figure 6-13. Unsmoothed surface representing Formative 1 period population distribution in one survey region of the Alto Magdalena.

the beginning of sedentary living. Population did grow through subsequent centuries, and the centripetal social forces of the districts drew population more tightly together toward their centers, probably as the ceremonial centers of tombs and statues developed in the Regional Classic or slightly before. Unlike Hongshan higher-order communities and districts, however, the Alto Magdalena ones do not emerge at some point in the sequence as a larger-scale socio-spatial phenomenon built up of smaller building blocks that already existed in earlier periods.

THE VALLEY OF OAXACA IN THE SOUTHERN MEXICAN HIGHLANDS

Archaeological evidence of early chiefdoms is less conspicuous on the landscape in the Valley of Oaxaca (Figure 6-1) than in the Alto Magdalena, and its appearance is not clearly associated with a single period as it is for Hongshan. Sedentary agricultural life was established about 1500 BC (Blanton et al. 1982; Flannery 1983; Kowalewski et al. 1989; Winter 1976). There are clear indications of social hierarchy by 300 years later, when some individuals were buried entirely without offerings while others received ceramic vessels, figurines, and ornamental objects of bone, shell, magnetite, jade, and other materials. The highest-ranking families came to live in large stone houses raised on platforms.

136

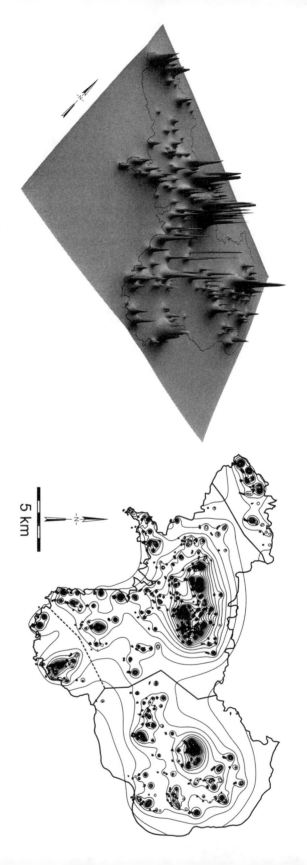

Figure 6-14. Smoothed surface representing Formative 1 period population distribution in one survey area of the Alto Magdalena (left) and contour map of the same surface (right) showing division into districts.

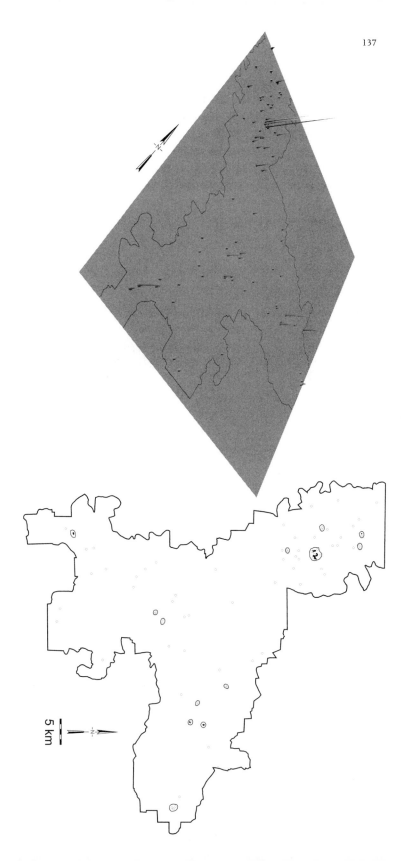

137

Figure 6-15. Unsmoothed surface representing Rosario phase population distribution in the Valley of Oaxaca (left) and cutoff contour delineating the bases of the occupational peaks and clustering occupations into local communities (right).

5 km

Households of part-time craft specialists were often adjacent to high-ranking households (Drennan and Flannery 1983; Flannery and Marcus 1983a; Flannery and Winter 1976). These indications of complex social organization intensified gradually during 700 years divided into three archaeological periods (San José, Guadalupe, and Rosario). By the end of this time, sculptural evidence shows that high-ranking people wielded considerable coercive power over subordinates (Flannery and Marcus 1983a).

The population of the entire Valley of Oaxaca survey area (2,125 km^2) during the Rosario phase (700–500 BC) was only 1,000 to 2,500 inhabitants (Kowalewski et al. 1989), for a population density (0.5–1.2 persons per km^2) far below that of either Classic Alto Magdalena or Hongshan Chifeng. Oaxaca's agricultural resources vastly exceeded the needs of this tiny Rosario phase population. The unsmoothed surface for Rosario phase population distribution (Figure 6-15) resembles that for Hongshan Chifeng; 65 small local communities can be distinctly identified. Most are single contiguous occupation areas, but occasionally two or three nearby occupations are combined. One community at San José Mogote is strikingly different from the others; here eight settlements cluster, with a total population of 400 to 800 (Kowalewski et al. 1989). This is about the population of the largest Hongshan local community, and far larger than any other local community in Rosario Oaxaca. In Chifeng and Oaxaca, then, small local communities of people in face-to-face interaction on a daily basis are very easily recognized, whereas in the Alto Magdalena there is no evidence of such local communities having served as small-scale sociospatial building blocks. The clearly defined small local communities of Rosario were present from the earliest sedentary occupation, and the emergence of a single much larger local community occurred within about 300 years after the beginning of sedentary life (well before the Rosario phase).

A smoothed surface delineates clustering of local communities at a larger scale, but the Oaxaca pattern is strikingly different from either Chifeng or the Alto Magdalena (Figure 6-16). The dominant feature is a single occupational peak rising up from an otherwise flat landscape. The lower slopes of the large peak engulf numerous smaller outlying settlements, defining a district of 30 small local communities around San José Mogote containing more than half the region's population, but little clustering of local communities occurs elsewhere in the survey area. Nothing about the surface encourages subdivision of this district, as there are no occupational valleys separating peaks. This district is about 20 km across, so it covers a considerably larger area than either the Hongshan or Alto Magdalena districts, but its population (between 600 and 1,400 people) is similar to the largest of the Hongshan districts and much smaller than either of the Alto Magdalena districts. The rank-size graph for the local communities within this district is much the same as for the survey area as a whole (Figure

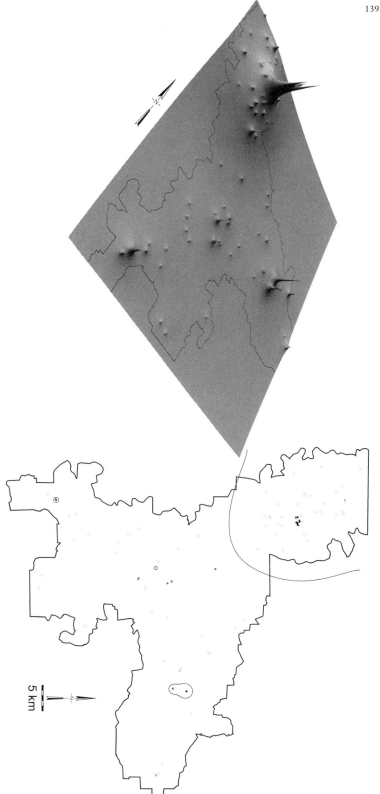

Figure 6-16. Smoothed surface representing Rosario phase population distribution in the Valley of Oaxaca (left) and a cutoff contour for the bases of occupational peaks in the same surface (right).

5 km

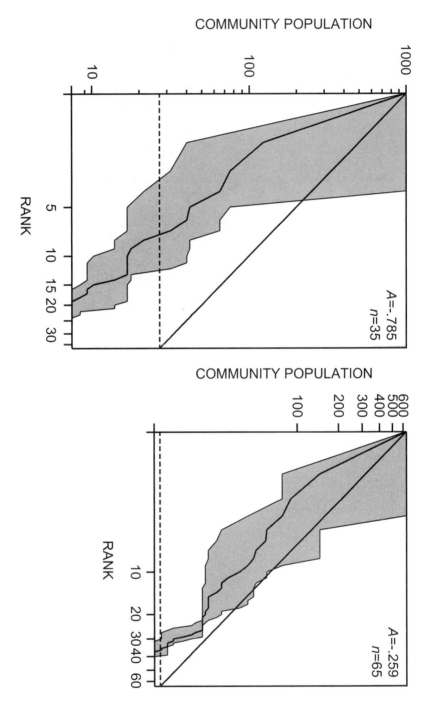

Figure 6-17. Rank-size graphs for local communities in the Rosario phase San José Mogote district (left) and for all local communities in the Valley of Oaxaca survey area (right). *A* values and 67% confidence zones for the rank-size lines are included (Drennan and Peterson 2004).

6-17). Both show the strong and significant primate pattern of a highly centralized district, whose largest community has no demographic rival in the valley.
By contrast, in Chifeng and the Alto Magdalena, multiple higher-order communities or districts of comparable size shared their respective regions.

EARLY CHIEFDOM COMMUNITIES IN THREE REGIONS

In all three regions, broadly similar social changes occurred within one or
two thousand years after the establishment of sedentary agricultural life.
Initial agricultural settlements grew into larger, more inclusive communities
with hierarchical organizing principles. Comparison of settlement patterns,
however, reveals differences in the nature of these communities and in the trajectories of their development. In all three areas there were at least some small
isolated farmsteads of only one or two households, and excavations at larger
settlements consistently reveal that they are composed of small households.
In Chifeng and Oaxaca, small local communities—mostly between about 5
and 15 households—are easy to identify and are usually clearly separate from
each other. In Oaxaca, one of these local communities, and in Chifeng several
of them, are larger, reaching 100 households or more. In the Alto Magdalena,
population densities are higher, and other households are seldom very far away,
but separate small local communities are not identifiable. This may reflect more
diffuse and less structured patterns of social interaction than those focused in
the well-defined small local communities of Chifeng and Oaxaca.

If the small local communities of Chifeng and Oaxaca reflect more intensive interaction, we can ask what the nature of this interaction was and how
it differed from interaction in the Alto Magdalena. One possibility is more
economic interaction within the local communities of Chifeng and Oaxaca.
Oaxaca has yielded concentrations of tools and production waste indicating different households that produced pottery, bone implements, lithic tools, cloth,
and ornaments of shell, jade, and other materials (Flannery and Winter 1976).
We do not know by what mechanisms these goods were interchanged, but this
interchange clearly occasioned considerable interaction of importance between
households, especially within small local communities (as opposed to between
them, since the ethnographically well-known pattern of specialization by village
is of modern origin in Oaxaca [Kowalewski 2003:17]). Hongshan finely painted
pottery and jade sculpture must have been produced by specialists, but we do
not know where, how production was organized, or whether utilitarian goods
were involved as well. In the Alto Magdalena, fairly good evidence about the
nature and range of productive activities by household suggests little economic
specialization at all (Drennan 2000; González 1998). The economic component
of face-to-face interaction on a daily basis, then, may have been much less

developed in the Alto Magdalena than in Chifeng or Oaxaca, and this may help account for the more diffuse character of such interaction there.

The organization of land tenure and/or agricultural production may also be related to the formation of tightly integrated, clearly defined local communities. Two very different patterns characterize occupation in different parts of the Alto Magdalena today. In the survey area we have discussed here, most inhabitants live on the land that they own and farm as a family, and residences are widely scattered through cultivated land without clear local communities. At lower elevations, however, most inhabitants live in compact villages surrounded by large expanses of cultivated lands largely devoid of houses. These lands are divided into large holdings, owned by a very few families; they are cultivated by groups of hired laborers who live with their families in the compact villages. Land-tenure and cultivation are also organized by supra-household groups today in Chifeng and Oaxaca, and the modern settlement patterns of both regions show compact local communities in landscapes of cultivated land devoid of houses. The exact political and economic arrangements were surely different, but the local community may have been an extremely important unit from the beginnings of agricultural life in Oaxaca and Chifeng. Kowalewski (2003) has argued that the autonomy of modern villages in Oaxaca does not have prehispanic antecedents, but such villages, autonomous or not, undeniably existed as interaction communities in the Rosario phase. While larger political structures are indeed necessary to guarantee the stability of land-tenure systems, the actual land-holding units are smaller, and in the case of prehispanic Oaxaca, may well have been local communities rather than individual households. The absence of well-defined local communities in the Alto Magdalena, by the same token, probably indicates a much greater role for individual households in the organization of land tenure and cultivation.

It has long been noted that population size and density correlate broadly with sociopolitical complexity: more complex societies generally have larger and denser populations than less complex societies (e.g. Carneiro 1972). All three regions do show substantial demographic growth following the shift to agriculture, but there are differences as well (Figure 6-18). At earliest agricultural settlement, the Alto Magdalena's population density was more than 10 times greater than that of either Chifeng or Oaxaca, and this already high population density grew very rapidly, compared to the other two regions. Population density started much lower and rose more slowly in Chifeng, although by Hongshan times it reached much higher levels than Oaxaca in Rosario times. In Oaxaca, population density rose for some 300 or 400 years following the beginning of agriculture, and by this time evidence of a single larger community with substantial social hierarchy is quite clear. This community grew, and social organization became considerably more

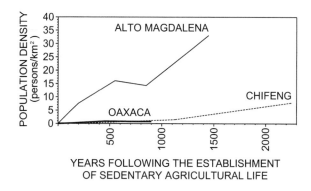

Figure 6-18. Change in regional population density for the three regions discussed from the establishment of sedentary agricultural life up through the chiefdoms dealt with in the text (Hongshan for Chifeng, Rosario for Oaxaca, and Regional Classic for the Alto Magdalena).

complex and hierarchical through the next 500 years, while population density did not rise at all. The Rosario societies of Oaxaca, then, developed very quickly, even though population density was low and, after a point, no longer growing. Hongshan societies, of course, are the oldest of the three, but their development took by far the longest time after the beginnings of sedentary living. In the Alto Magdalena, although small local communities cannot be identified, higher-order communities or districts are in evidence soon after sedentary living begins, and social organization continues to become more complex on into the Classic period. This fairly rapid development in the Alto Magdalena is associated with high population densities and rapid demographic growth. The demographic scale of the higher-order communities is similar for Hongshan and Rosario Oaxaca, and much larger for Classic Alto Magdalena, but, in this latter region, the larger demographic scale of higher-order communities in the Alto Magdalena was not accompanied by more complex social organization. Indeed, however highly respected and prestigious the high-ranking individuals buried in the Alto Magdalena's tombs may have been, economic specialization and interdependence seem to have been less developed in the Alto Magdalena than in Oaxaca and probably Chifeng. Archaeological population estimates, of course, are very approximate, but the differences observed between these three regions are much larger than can be attributed to the sources of estimation error.

SUBSEQUENT DEVELOPMENTS

In Chifeng, the end of the Hongshan period is not completely understood, but by about 2200 BC, the 14 higher-order Hongshan communities and districts in the Chifeng survey area had been replaced by 21 such units in the Lower Xiajiadian period (Figure 6-19). The Lower Xiajiadian districts were about the same area as the Hongshan ones, but each contained a population several times greater. Internal organization of these districts had become more state-like (Shelach 1997, 1999), but each was a cluster of small local communities, like the Hongshan higher-order communities before them. In the Alto Magdalena, the Classic period districts persisted into the following Recent period (Figure 6-20), although district populations grew. Important individuals were no longer buried in monumental tombs surrounded by statues, but the deep shaft burials that were made may contain more offerings, possibly suggesting that the supernatural and symbolic basis of Classic period social hierarchy had given way to greater accumulation of personal wealth (Drennan 1995). Just how else economic organization may have changed after the Classic period is still unknown, but settlement distribution continues to be extremely dispersed with no evidence that individual households were grouped into small local communities. Following the Rosario phase the Valley of Oaxaca continued to be dominated by a single large center (Figure 6-21), but it was the newly founded city of Monte Albán whose population quickly grew to 20,000 or more, and whose armies' conquests were recorded in stone carvings (Blanton 1978; Flannery and Marcus 1983b; Marcus 1983).

The trajectories of social change in Chifeng and Oaxaca go on to substantially greater scale and complexity of organization. In both there is evidence of the bureaucratic and political activity that is a criterion of state-level organization. In the Alto Magdalena, sociopolitical change after the Classic period is quite modest by comparison. The two regions with more dramatic organizational change this time are the two with the greatest population increases, while the Alto Magdalena's modest organizational change is matched by its modest population growth (Figure 6-22). The Alto Magdalena's population density, though, continued to be substantially higher than that of the Valley of Oaxaca, where the largest and probably most complex political entity emerged of any of the three sequences examined here. The pace of change in Chifeng continued to be very slow, compared to the other two regions; altogether, the sequence discussed covers more than 4000 years, compared to about 2200 for the Alto Magdalena and about 1500 for Oaxaca. The Valley of Oaxaca continued to be dominated after Rosario by a single sociopolitical unit, as had been the case since early in the sequence, while both the Alto Magdalena and Chifeng were divided into multiple sociopolitical units with no one spatially or demographically much

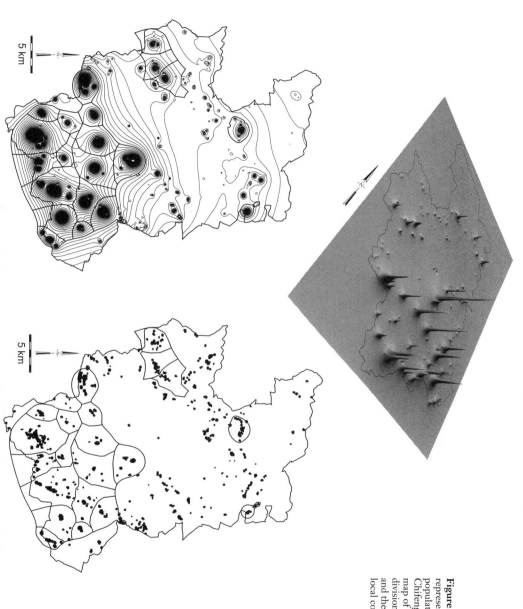

Figure 6-19. Smoothed surface representing Lower Xiajiadian population distribution in the Chifeng region (top), contour map of the same surface with division into districts (lower left), and the way the districts group local communities (lower right).

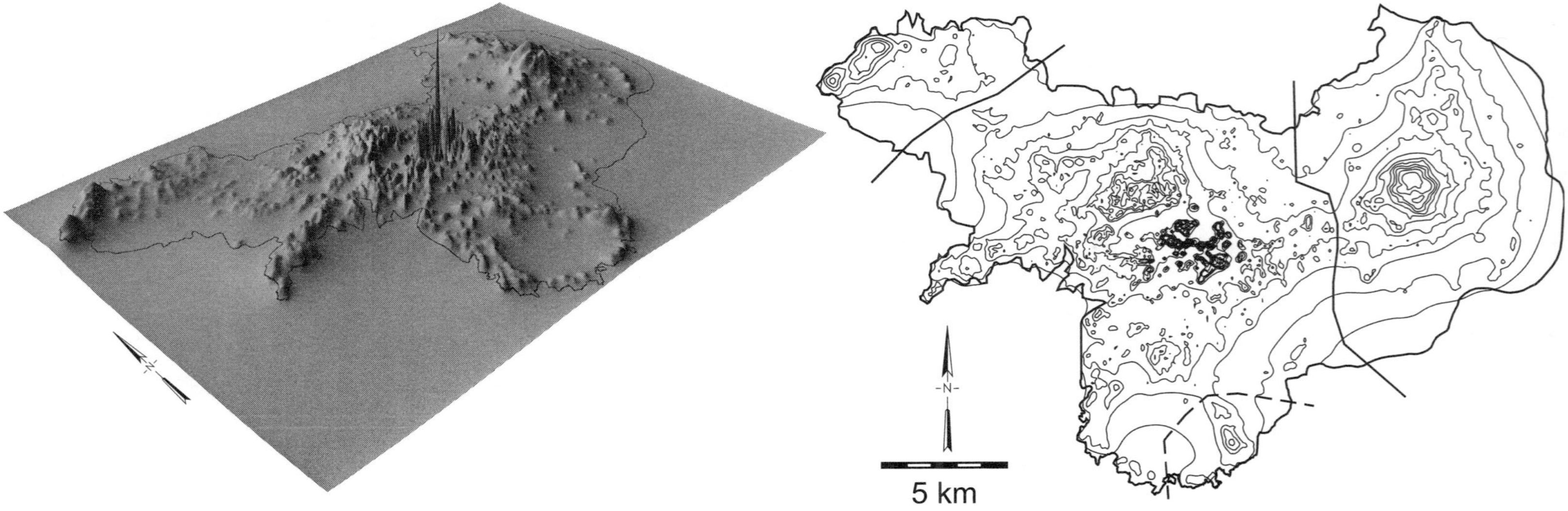

Figure 6-20. Smoothed surface representing Recent period population distribution in one survey area of the Alto Magdalena (left) and contour map of the same surface (right) showing division into districts.

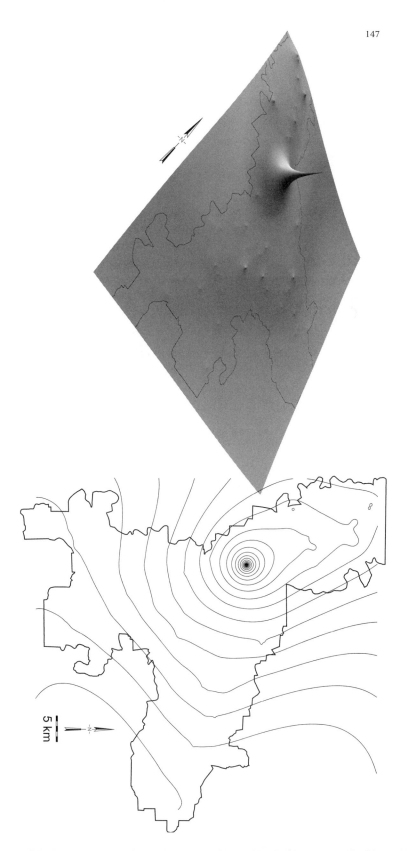

Figure 6-21. Smoothed surface representing Monte Albán II population distribution in the Valley of Oaxaca (left) and contour map of the same surface (right).

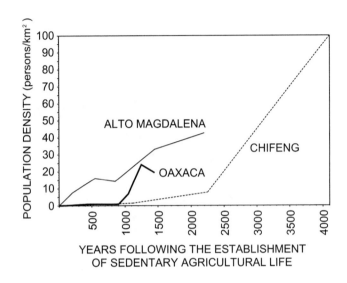

Figure 6-22. Change in regional population density for the three regions discussed, from the establishment of sedentary agricultural life through developments subsequent to initial chiefdoms (Lower Xiajiadian for Chifeng, Monte Albán II for Oaxaca, and Recent for the Alto Magdalena).

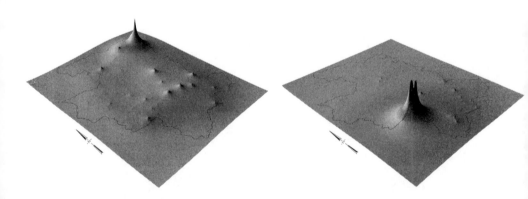

Figure 6-23. Smoothed surfaces representing Zhanguo-Han (left) and Liao (right) population distribution in the Chifeng region.

larger than its neighbors. It was not until substantially later (after 600 BC), that overall integration into a single sociopolitical unit was effected in Chifeng, with the intrusion of external power (Figure 6-23). This came only with the Spanish Conquest (after AD 1530) in the Alto Magdalena.

CONCLUSION

The emergence of politically integrated hierarchical societies from simpler egalitarian patterns happened repeatedly and independently in many parts of the world, exemplified here by three regions far enough apart that they could not have had much contact or any real influence on each other. Although these processes were broadly parallel, the roughly similar changes took place in different ways in the three sequences and produced hierarchical societies of somewhat different character in each. The presence of clearly identifiable small local communities in Chifeng and Oaxaca, and their absence in the Alto Magdalena, is one observation that seems especially worth pursuing. It challenges the implicit assumption that such local communities always form a basic social building block of complex social organization. Investigation of the kinds of interaction that formed clear community patterns in Chifeng and Oaxaca and of whether these kinds of interaction were absent or just organized differently in the Alto Magdalena might help us understand the basis for the particular dynamic of chiefdoms in each region as well as how larger political formations came to emerge in Chifeng and Oaxaca but not in the Alto Magdalena.

Acknowledgments
We thank Stephen Kowalewski for providing data from the Valley of Oaxaca survey in electronic form, and Gideon Shelach for reading and commenting on an earlier version of this paper.

REFERENCES CITED

Barnes, Gina L.
  1993   *China, Korea, and Japan: The Rise of Civilization in East Asia*. Thames and Hudson, London.
Barnes, Gina L., and Guo Dashun
  1996   The Ritual Landscape of 'Boar Mountain' Basin: The Niuheliang Site Complex of Northeastern China. *World Archaeology* 28(2):209–219.
Blanton, Richard E.
  1978   *Monte Albán: Settlement Patterns at the Ancient Zapotec Capital*. Academic Press, New York.

Blanton, Richard E., Stephen Kowalewski, Gary Feinman, and Jill Appel
  1982   *Monte Albán's Hinterland, Part I: The Prehispanic Settlement Patterns of the Central and Southern Parts of the Valley of Oaxaca, Mexico.* Memoirs No. 15, Museum of Anthropology, University of Michigan, Ann Arbor.

Carneiro, Robert L.
  1972   From Autonomous Villages to the State, a Numerical Estimation. In *Population Growth: Anthropological Implications,* edited by Brian Spooner, pp. 64–77. MIT Press, Cambridge, Massachusetts.

Chang, Kwang-Chih
  1986   *The Archaeology of Ancient China.* Yale University Press, New Haven.

Chifeng Collaborative Archaeological Survey Team
  2003a   Neimenggu Chifeng diqu 1999 nian quyu xing kaogu diaocha baogao [Regional Archaeological Surveys in the Chifeng Region, Inner Mongolia in 1999]. *Kaogu* 2003(5):24–34.

Chifeng International Collaborative Archeological Research Project
  2003b   *Regional Archeology in Eastern Inner Mongolia: A Methodological Exploration.* Science Press, Beijing.

Childs-Johnson, Elizabeth
  1991   Jades of the Hongshan Culture: The Dragon and Fertility Cult Worship. *Arts Asiatiques* 46.82–95.

Chinese-American Chifeng Collaborative Archeological Team
  2002   Neimenggu Chifeng diqu quyu xing kaogu diaocha jieduan xing baogao (1999–2001) [A Phased Report of Full-Coverage Regional Archeological Survey in Chifeng, Inner Mongolia (1999–2000)]. *Bianjiang Kaogu Yangjiu [Research on China's Frontier Archaeology]* 1:357–368.

Chiou-Peng, Tze-Huey
  1994   Jade Carving in Neolithic China: A Review of Recent Discoveries. In *Archaic Chinese Bronzes, Jades, and Works of Art.* J. J. Lally, New York.

Cubillos, Julio César
  1979   *Arqueología de San Agustín: El Estrecho, El Parador, y Mesita C.* Fundación de Investigaciones Arqueológicas. Nacionales del Banco de la República, Bogotá.

Drennan, Robert D.
  1995   Mortuary Practices in the Alto Magdalena: The Social Context of the "San Agustín Culture". In *Tombs for the Living: Andean Mortuary Practices,* edited by Tom D. Dillehay, pp. 79–110. Dumbarton Oaks, Washington, D.C.

  2000   *Las Sociedades Prehispánicas del Alto Magdalena.* Instituto Colombiano de Antropología e Historia, Bogotá.

Drennan, Robert D. (editor)
  1985   *Regional Archaeology in the Valle de la Plata, Colombia: A Preliminary Report on the 1984 Season of the Proyecto Arqueológico Valle de la Plata.* Technical Reports No. 16, Museum of Anthropology, University of Michigan, Ann Arbor.

Drennan, Robert D., and Kent V. Flannery
1983   The Growth of Site Hierarchies in the Valley of Oaxaca: Part II. In *The Cloud People: Divergent Evolution of the Zapotec and Mixtec Civilizations*, edited by Kent V. Flannery and Joyce Marcus, pp. 65–71. Academic Press, New York.

Drennan, Robert D., Luis Gonzalo Jaramillo, Elizabeth Ramos, Carlos Augusto Sánchez, María Angela Ramírez, and Carlos A. Uribe
1991   Regional Dynamics of Chiefdoms in the Valle de la Plata, Colombia. *Journal of Field Archaeology* 18:297–317.

Drennan, Robert D., and Christian E. Peterson
2004   Comparing Archaeological Settlement Systems with Rank-Size Graphs: A Measure of Shape and Statistical Confidence. *Journal of Archaeological Science* 31:533–549.

Drennan, Robert D., Christian E. Peterson, Gregory G. Indrisano, Teng Mingyu, Gideon Shelach, Zhu Yanping, Katheryn M. Linduff, and Guo Zhizhong
2004   Chapter 4: Approaches to Regional Demographic Reconstruction. In *Regional Archeology in Eastern Inner Mongolia: A Methodological Exploration*, pp. 152–165. Science Press, Beijing.

Drennan, Robert D., and Dale W. Quattrin
1996   Social Inequality and Agricultural Resources in the Valle de la Plata, Colombia. In *The Foundations of Social Inequality*, edited by Gary M. Feinman and T. Douglas Price, pp. 207–231. Plenum, New York.

Drennan, Robert D., Mary M. Taft, and Carlos A. Uribe (editors)
1992   *Prehispanic Chiefdoms in the Valle de la Plata, Vol. 2: Ceramics—Chronology and Craft Production*. Memoirs in Latin American Archaeology No. 5, Department of Anthropology, University of Pittsburgh, Pennsylvania.

Duque Gómez, Luis
1964   *Exploraciones arqueológicas en San Agustín. Revista Colombiana de Antropología*, Suplemento No. 1. Imprenta Nacional, Bogotá.

Duque Gómez, Luis, and Julio César Cubillos
1980   *Arqueología de San Agustín: Alto de los Idolos, montículos y tumbas*. Fundación de Investigaciones Arqueológicas Nacionales del Banco de la República, Bogotá.

1983   *Arqueología de San Agustín: Exploraciones y trabajos de reconstrucción en las Mesitas A y B*. Fundación de Investigaciones Arqueológicas Nacionales del Banco de la República, Bogotá.

1987   *Arqueología de San Agustín: Alto de Lavapatas*. Fundación de Investigaciones Arqueológicas Nacionales del Banco de la República, Bogotá.

Fang Dianchun, and Liu Baohua
1984   Liaoning Fuxin xian Hutougou Hongshan wenhua yuqi mu de faxian [Discovery of the Hongshan Jade Tombs at Hutougou, Fuxin County in Liaoning]. *Wenwu* 1984(6):1–5.

Flannery, Kent V.

1983   The Tierras Largas Phase and the Analytical Units of the Early Oaxacan Village. In *The Cloud People: Divergent Evolution of the Zapotec and Mixtec Civilizations*, edited by Kent V. Flannery and Joyce Marcus, pp. 43–50. Academic Press, New York.

Flannery, Kent V., and Joyce Marcus

1983a   The Growth of Site Hierarchies in the Valley of Oaxaca, Part I. In *The Cloud People: Divergent Evolution of the Zapotec and Mixtec Civilizations*, edited by Kent V. Flannery and Joyce Marcus, pp. 53–65. Academic Press, New York.

1983b   The Earliest Public Buildings, Tombs, and Monuments at Monte Albán, with Notes on the Internal Chronology of Period I. In *The Cloud People: Divergent Evolution of the Zapotec and Mixtec Civilizations*, edited by Kent V. Flannery and Joyce Marcus, pp. 87–91. Academic Press, New York.

Flannery, Kent V., and Marcus C. Winter

1976   Analyzing Household Activities. In *The Early Mesoamerican Village*, edited by Kent V. Flannery, pp. 34–47. Academic Press, New York.

González Fernández, Víctor

1997   Prehispanic Change in the Mesitas Community: Documenting the Development of a Chiefdom's Central Place in San Agustín, Colombia. Unpublished Ph.D. Dissertation, Department of Anthropology, University of Pittsburgh, Pennsylvania.

Guo Dashun

1995   Hongshan and Related Cultures. In *The Archaeology of Northeast China: Beyond the Great Wall*, edited by Sarah M. Nelson, pp. 21–64. Routledge, London.

1996   Understanding the Burial Rituals of the Hongshan Culture through Jade. In *Chinese Jades*, edited by Rosemary E. Scott, pp. 27–36. Colloquies on Art & Archaeology in Asia, No. 18. Percival David Foundation of Chinese Art, London.

Guo Dashun, and Zhang Keju

1984   Liaoning sheng Kezuo xian Dongshanzui Hongshan wenhua jianzhu qunzhi fajue jianbao [Excavation Report of the Hongshan Site at Dongshanzui in Kezuo County, Liaoning]. *Wenwu* 1984(11):1–11.

Herrera, Luisa Fernanda, Robert D. Drennan, and Carlos A. Uribe (editors)

1988   *Prehispanic Chiefdoms in the Valle de la Plata, Vol. 1: The Environmental Context of Human Habitation.* Memoirs in Latin American Archaeology, No. 2, Department of Anthropology, University of Pittsburgh, Pennsylvania.

Kowalewski, Stephen A.

2003   What is the Community? The Long View from Oaxaca, Mexico. *Social Evolution and History* 2:4–24.

Kowalewski, Stephen A., Gary M. Feinman, Laura Finsten, Richard E. Blanton, and Linda M. Nicholas

1989   *Monte Albán's Hinterland, Part II: Prehispanic Settlement Patterns in Tlacolula, Etla, and Ocotlán, the Valley of Oaxaca, Mexico.* Memoirs No. 23, Museum of Anthropology, University of Michigan Ann Arbor.

Liaoning Sheng Wenwu Kaogu Yanjiusuo

1985   Liaoning Niuheliang Hongshan wenhua "nushenmiao" yu jishi zhong qun fajue jianbao [Excavation Report of the Hongshan "Goddess Temple" and Cairn Group at Niuheliang]. *Wenwu* 1986(8):1–17.

1997   *Niuheliang Hongshan wenhua yizhi yu yuqi jingcui [The Niuheliang Hongshan Culture Site and Its Wonderful Jades].* Wenwu Chubanshe, Beijing.

Linduff, Katheryn M., Robert D. Drennan, and Gideon Shelach

2004   Early Complex Societies in NE China: The Chifeng International Collaborative Archaeological Research Project. *Journal of Field Archaeology* 29:45–73.

Llanos Vargas, Héctor

1995   *Los chamanes jaguares de San Agustín: Génesis de un pensamiento mitopoético.* H. Llanos Vargas, Santafé de Bogotá.

Marcus, Joyce

1983   The Conquest Slabs of Building J, Monte Albán. In *The Cloud People: Divergent Evolution of the Zapotec and Mixtec Civilizations,* edited by Kent V. Flannery and Joyce Marcus, pp. 106–109. Academic Press, New York.

Nelson, Sarah M.

1990   The Neolithic of Northeastern China and Korea. *Antiquity* 64:234–248.

1994   The Development of Complexity in Prehistoric North China. *Sino-Platonic Papers* 63:1–17.

1995   Ideology and the Formation of an Early State in Northeast China. In *Ideology and the Formation of Early States,* edited by Henri J. M. Claessen and Jarich G. Oosten, pp. 153–169. Brill, Leiden.

1996   Hongshan: An Early Complex Society in Northeast China. In *Indo-Pacific Prehistory: The Changmai Papers,* Vol. 3, edited by Peter Bellwood and Dianne Tilloson, pp. 57–62. Indo-Pacific Prehistory Association, Australian National University, Canberra.

2001   Hongshan. In *Encyclopedia of Prehistory, Vol. 3: East Asia and Oceania,* edited by Peter N. Peregrine and Melvin Ember, pp. 77–81. Kluwer Academic/Plenum, New York.

Parsons, Jeffrey R.

1972   Archaeological Settlement Patterns. *Annual Review of Anthropology* 1:127–150.

Peterson, Christian E., and Robert D. Drennan

2005   Communities, Settlements, Sites, and Surveys: Regional-Scale Analysis of Prehistoric Human Interaction. *American Antiquity* 70:5–30.

Reichel-Dolmatoff, Gerardo

1972   *San Agustín: A Culture of Colombia*. Praeger, New York.

Shelach, Gideon

1997   A Settlement Pattern Study in Northeast China: Results and Potential Contributions of Western Theory and Methods to Chinese Archaeology. *Antiquity* 71:114–127.

1998   *Leadership Strategies, Economic Activity, and Interregional Interaction: Social Complexity in Northeast China*. Kluwer Academic/Plenum, New York.

Winter, Marcus C.

1976   The Archaeological Household Cluster in the Valley of Oaxaca. In *The Early Mesoamerican Village*, edited by Kent V. Flannery, pp. 25–31. Academic Press, New York.

PAST LIVES IN DIFFERENT PLACES:

THE ORIGINS AND RELATIONSHIPS OF TEOTIHUACAN'S FOREIGN RESIDENTS

MICHAEL W. SPENCE
CHRISTINE D. WHITE
University of Western Ontario

EVELYN C. RATTRAY
Universidad Nacional Autónoma de México

FRED J. LONGSTAFFE
University of Western Ontario

INTRODUCTION

Teotihuacan, situated some 45 km northeast of modern Mexico City, grew rapidly through the terminal formative period to become the largest urban center in the New World during the classic period. Jeffrey Parsons (1974), in his summary of the settlement pattern studies executed in the Basin of Mexico in the 1960s and early 1970s, has demonstrated that immigration to the city from the rest of the Basin fueled much of this growth. He has also suggested that nearby parts of Tlaxcala and Puebla may have contributed substantially to its population (Parsons 1968:876–877).

However, the terminal formative people of those regions probably had much in common culturally with their contemporaries in the Valley of Teotihuacan (Cowgill 1997:139; Plunket and Uruñuela 2002). Of concern here is a rather different sort of immigration, one that may have contributed less in demographic terms to the city's growth but that would have had the potential to introduce more distinctive and exotic elements into its cultural mix. These migrants came from further away, from societies in different environments and with quite different cultures and languages. Their integration into the city may have presented a greater challenge.

Most of these foreign immigrants probably arrived somewhat after the large-scale early movements from nearby areas that initially propelled urban growth. They would have been attracted by an already viable and expanding city (Spence et al. 2004). Many of them, arriving in relatively small groups and perhaps maintaining only limited contact with their homelands, would have been absorbed within a few generations. Even those who maintained a distinctive identity may have become archaeologically invisible, relying on the specialized workshops and market system of Teotihuacan for their material goods and living in the standardized apartment compounds that, probably with some state intervention, became the universal residential format in the city (Spence 1996:334–336). One example is the site 33:S3W1, Tlajinga 33 (Widmer 1987; Storey 1992). A single shaft tomb and very few figurines are the only material traces of a West Mexico heritage, but stable oxygen isotope analysis shows that a number of the occupants had moved to the compound from at least two distant regions, one of which has an isotopic signature consistent with West Mexico (White et al. 2004a). Another apartment compound, 19:N1W5, initially had several ceramic and mortuary indicators of Michoacán ancestry, but these were not retained in the later stage of the compound's existence (Gómez 1998, 2002).

Two areas of Teotihuacan with less ephemeral expressions of a foreign presence are the Tlailotlacan enclave (also known as the "Oaxaca Barrio") near the west edge of the city and the Merchants' Barrio by the east edge. René Millon initially identified both during the course of the Teotihuacan Mapping Project surveys (Millon 1967:45; 1970, 1973, 1981). From the outset, it was recognized that the two areas differed not only in their derivation from quite different parts of Mesoamerica, but also in their structure and functions (Millon 1981; Rattray 1987; Spence 1996). The general impression in the literature is that, on one hand, migrants from the Valley of Oaxaca occupied Tlailotlacan, some becoming involved in the extraction and importation of lime and perhaps the movement of other goods (Crespo and Mastache 1981; Rattray 1987). The Merchants' Barrio, on the other hand, was seen as a multiethnic base for long-distance merchants who traded with (and likely were from) societies in the Gulf Coast, Yucatan, Campeche, Belize, and perhaps Guatemala (Rattray 1987).

These interpretations have been based largely on archaeological evidence such as ceramics, lithics, architecture, and mortuary practices. When osteological analyses have been conducted, they have been oriented primarily toward supplying data for the reconstruction of mortuary practices, like information on age, sex, and postmortem treatment (Spence 1976, 1994; Spence and Gamboa 1999; Rattray and Civera 1999). In some cases, internal social reconstruction (Spence 1976, 1994), pathology, and cultural modification (Rattray and Civera 1999) were also considered. However, no attempt to biologically relate these enclave series to their presumed ancestral or homeland populations has been made, although the lamentable condition of most of the skeletal material would certainly make this difficult.

Recently, though, physical anthropologists have added a new analytical methodology to their repertoire: stable isotope analysis (White et al. 1998; Price et al. 2000). The ratios of particular stable isotopes in human skeletal phosphate and collagen reflect the ratios of those isotopes in the region's water (oxygen isotopes) and bedrock (strontium isotopes). As these vary significantly by region, they are in effect geographic markers for individuals at various points in their lifespan. The isotopic ratio will be locked in a particular tooth at the time of that tooth's mineralization and will resist change thereafter, since dental tissues do not remodel after formation. In comparison, the isotopic ratio in a bone will change constantly as the bone remodels throughout life. Thus, a person's origin and interregional movements in early life can be identified through the varying isotopic ratios in their sequentially developing teeth, while such data for their bones will provide their location in the years immediately preceding death.

This methodology offers a powerful new way to consider the questions of enclave origin and structure. Indeed, some work has already been performed along these lines. Price et al. (2000) have tested a small sample of individuals from Tlailotlacan and the Merchants' Barrio for strontium-isotope ratios and determined that most originally came from foreign regions. Spence and colleagues (2004), using stable oxygen isotope ratios in skeletal and dental phosphate, have examined a larger Merchants' Barrio series. They had also previously published some limited data on Tlailotlacan (White et al. 1998), but have now completed a much larger series from that enclave (White et al. 2004b). After a brief outline of the two enclaves, the insights derived from these studies are discussed below.

THE MERCHANTS' BARRIO

Settlement Patterns and Architecture

The Merchants' Barrio extends along both sides of the San Juan River, on the northeast periphery of the city (Millon 1973:27, 34, 40; Millon, Drewitt, and Cowgill 1973: maps of N3E4, N4E4). Rattray's extensive excavations there form the basis for the following summary (Rattray 1987, 1988, 1989, 1990, 1992:51–52, 65, 76, 204–221, Table 1, Figures 15–21, plus *xvi–xix*; 2001:379, 381, 389, 393, 395, 399, 403; Rattray and Civera 1999; see also Iceland 1989; Limon 1990; Spence 1996).

The area covered by the Merchants' Barrio is approximately four hectares. The excavated parts show a number of circular structures interspersed with rectangular structures, plazas, and altars. Both the circular and rectangular structures are generally small and relatively simple in construction, with foundations and walls of adobe blocks. Burials are frequently associated with the circular structures and altars, more occasionally with the rectangular structures. There are no examples of the distinctive Teotihuacan talud-tablero architectural facade, and features do not always follow the standard Teotihuacan orientation. In a later period of the barrio, a multiroom, stone-wall rectangular structure overlies some of the circular structures and appears somewhat more similar to the standard Teotihuacan apartment compound (Rattray 1987, 1988:169, Figure 4).

The circular structures range from 5 to 9.5 m in diameter, indicating floor areas of 20 to 70 m², adequate for residence only by a nuclear or, in a few cases, small extended family. The rectangular structures are no larger, most having one or two rooms with maximum dimensions of about 6 m per room (e.g. Rattray 1988: Figure 6). If we assume that all circular and rectangular structures were nuclear family residences (with five people per family) and extrapolate from the excavated portions of the area, the total population of the Merchants' Barrio might have been approximately 1,700 people.

However, it seems unlikely that all the structures were residences. Circular structure 8, for example, has only about 19 m² of floor space and no burials or offerings, so it was probably not a residence. Pollen analyses of floor samples indicate that circular structures 5 and 7 were more probably storage facilities than residences (Limon 1990). Three rectangular features, by comparison, have pollen profiles expected of residential use (Limon 1990:322–324). Given this variability in function, it is unlikely that the barrio had a population of 1,700; half that number seems more plausible.

The rectangular structures are different from the usual Teotihuacan apartment compound, which was a large and complex mix of rooms, temples, patios, courtyards, and passageways, housing some 60 to 100 people (Millon 1976). The circular structures are quite unique. The only comparable features are two structures in the Cuadrangulo Norte, an area associated with the Ciudadela in the center of the city. These, however, are low semicircular platforms considered to be primarily mortuary features (Rodríguez 1982:59, Plan 1).

Circular structures with burials are known from the Huasteca (Stresser-Peán 1977; Rattray 1990). However, the Huasteca touches only on the northernmost part of the Gulf Coast, and little evidence exists of Teotihuacan influence there or of a Huastec presence in Teotihuacan (Yarborough 1992:228–237). The Maya region is another possible source for these enigmatic structures (Rattray 1990:125). The foreign ceramics associated with their appearance in the Merchants' Barrio include Maya pottery from the coastal lowlands. It is also possible, however, that the circular structures have no external referent, but rather were an indigenous development.

The organization of the barrio as a whole may not have been highly centralized. The relatively even distribution of structures and plazas suggests some planning (Rattray 1990:120). The tendency for a few circular and small rectangular structures to cluster around a plaza, often with an altar in it, suggests the existence of a social unit comprised of a few nuclear families that apparently practiced communal rituals and shared storage facilities. The barrio as a whole contains no obvious public structures. The best candidate for one is circular structure 4, at the south edge of the excavated area. It stands out from the others because of its larger size, superior construction, and the presence of a shaft tomb (Rattray 1990:119–120, Figure 2f). Others, however, are only slightly smaller. Rather than being devoted to public functions, structure 4 may simply have been the residence of some elite members of the community.

Material Culture

Most of the material culture recovered in the Merchants' Barrio excavations is typical of Teotihuacan. The most striking exception is the relatively high proportion of foreign ceramics, 9 to 12% for Gulf Coast and Maya wares and another 15% for Thin Orange ware from the southern Puebla workshops some 150 km to the southeast of Teotihuacan. Less common, but nonetheless notable, are jade, amber, and Belizean chert (Iceland 1989:108–110).

There is some temporal variation in the presence of foreign ceramics. The Maya wares were most common in the earliest occupation of the area, in the Late Tlamimilolpa phase (see Table 7-1), and, for the most part, their seeming origins were in Yucatan, Campeche, and Belize (Ball 1983:131, 137–138). In the following Xolalpan period, ceramics from the Gulf Coast increased in quantity, becoming more common than the Maya wares were even at their peak. All of these foreign wares were apparently imported, rather than produced locally in the Merchants' Barrio as copies of "homeland" pottery.

Table 7-1.
Chronology of Teotihuacan*

Phase	Dates
Tzacualli	0–150 AD
Miccaotli	150–200 AD
Early Tlamimilolpa	200–250 AD
Late Tlamimilolpa	250–350 AD
Early Xolalpan	350–450 AD
Late Xolalpan	450–550 AD
Metepec	550–650 AD

*after Rattray 2001: Figure 1b

The Teotihuacan assemblage of the barrio shows only a few unusual features. One is the paucity of *comales*, common elsewhere in the city. Apparently, the barrio occupants did not accept Teotihuacan culinary practices, or at least not those based on the consumption of maize tortillas. *Comales* were not present in the Maya or Gulf Coast regions in the classic period (Rattray 1990:126–127). Also, there were an unusual number of *amphoras*, vessels for transporting liquids, associated with the larger multiroom structure (Rattray 1988:169). Some of these were of a common local ware, San Martín Orange, while others were of a variant of Thin Orange ware.

Rituals

As noted above, no structure in the barrio is obviously devoted to communal rituals. Circular structure 4, the only plausible candidate, is better explained as an elite residence. Rituals, then, may not have played a prominent role in the integration of the barrio, at least at the public level. Lesser social units may have shared some ritual practices, but these seem largely drawn on Teotihuacan materials and ideas. Most of the exterior altars have a T-shape plan, a common form among the altars of the Teotihuacan apartment compounds (e.g. Rattray 1992: Figure 19; Séjourné 1966:Figures 87–88). Also, the only specialized ritual paraphernalia found in the barrio are items of Teotihuacan style and manufacture. Burial 13a-b, for example, includes a Tlaloc vase, a puppet figurine, numerous miniature Fine Matte vessels, and four miniature censer *adornos* (Rattray 1992:215–216). Other burials contain *candeleros* and parts of Teotihuacan censers. Most of the nonburial offerings in the barrio included Teotihuacan theater censers, complete with the elaborate Teotihuacan iconography typically displayed in their masks and *adornos*. The prevalence of these Teotihuacan forms suggests the acceptance by barrio residents of Teotihuacan ritual practices and, considering the censer iconography, Teotihuacan beliefs.

Mortuary practices form a significant exception to this (Rattray and Civera 1999). The proportion of secondary burials in the barrio is much higher than usual for Teotihuacan. Also, there are more double and multiple burials than expected. Outstanding in these respects is burial 5-8, in a pit under the ramp of circular structure 2. Burial 5-8 included 34 individuals, of whom all but one adult female were secondary. Most of the barrio burials were in simple pits, like those found elsewhere in Teotihuacan, but the two individuals of burial 13a and 13b, a perinatal and an adult female, respectively, were in a small shaft tomb (Rattray and Civera 1999:Figure 8).

External Relations and Economy

Long distance trade was probably a principal economic activity in the Merchants' Barrio (Rattray 1990). A number of goods available in the Gulf Coast and Maya littoral lowlands would have been welcome in Teotihuacan: cacao, rubber, cotton, decorated ceramic vessels, marine shell, etc. Materials from more distant regions, like jade and amber, may have been transshipped to Teotihuacan through sites participating in the network. An increased frequency of amphoras in the later years of the barrio may reflect the importation or export of liquids like honey, *agua miel*, or *pulque* (Rattray 1992:65).

The nature of the wider network associated with the Merchants' Barrio is not clear. Matacapan, in the Tuxtlas region of Veracruz, may have been involved in economic exchanges between Teotihuacan and the Gulf Coast (Santley et al. 1987; Santley 1989, 1994). However, its relationship with Teotihuacan, let alone with the Merchants' Barrio, is not entirely clear (Yarborough 1992; Cowgill 1997:135; Daneels 2002). Some of the ceramic types of Matacapan appear in the Merchants' Barrio, but others do not (Yarborough 1992:395–396; Santley 1994:261; Rattray 2001:403). It has even been suggested that the presence of some Gulf Coast and Maya ceramics in the Merchants' Barrio may have resulted from their distribution to the barrio through the Great Compound or some other Teotihuacan institution responsible for their initial importation into the city (Yarborough 1992:257). Certainly, the flow of Gulf Coast goods to Teotihuacan (and vice versa) was not conducted exclusively through either Matacapan or the Merchants' Barrio (Stark et al. 1998; Daneels 2002). Furthermore, if Matacapan and the Merchants' Barrio were linked in an ongoing exchange network, it was not one based on a shared or mutually constructed ethnic identity (Spence 1996:344–345). The distinctive features of the Merchants' Barrio (circular structures, an emphasis on multiple secondary burial, high proportions of imported ceramics) contrast with Matacapan's (rectangular structures, talud-tablero temple facades, individual primary burial, imitations of a variety of Teotihuacan ceramic forms but few imports).

The occupants of the Merchants' Barrio possibly had economic specialties other than trade. In particular, the frequent occurrence of tools for textile manufacture, like weaving picks and bone needles, suggests that some of the residents may have been involved in the conversion of incoming raw cotton into fabrics (Rattray 1989:124; 1990:129). While long-distance exchange may have been primarily a male affair, textile production probably fell more in the domain of women (but see Padró and Manzanilla 2004 for evidence of male textile working in Teotihuacan).

Gender and Status

In the broader Teotihuacan society, men often had higher status than women, though not markedly so (Sempowski 1994:260–261). Gender roles and status distinctions are difficult to identify in the Merchants' Barrio. The principal form of evidence lies in the burials, but because these were so often multiple and secondary, and so poorly preserved, it was not always possible to link the grave goods or mortuary treatment with a particular individual or gender.

Women, however, were frequently associated with mortuary contexts that suggest high status. In three cases, they were buried in or beside altars. In two others, they were associated with unique burial features. The shaft tomb in circular structure 4 held burial 13a-b, a perinatal and a young adult female. The grave offering included many items indicating the importance of the burial: two Maya polychrome bowls, a stuccoed polychrome vase, three Gulf Coast vessels, six cylindrical vases, a Tlaloc vase, a marine shell artifact, and a large puppet figurine. It is interesting to note that, despite the high proportion of foreign vessels in the offering, the high status of the woman was apparently not based on a foreign origin; her dental and bone oxygen isotope values are all local (Spence et al. 2004).

The other unusual burial is the large burial 5-8. Its 34 individuals included both males and females. All were secondary burials except for one young adult female with a jade pectoral. It is possible that her death triggered the reburial event. The offering included foreign vessels, jade, marine shell, amber and weaving tools, but it is impossible to say whether or not the goods (other than the jade pectoral) were associated with any particular individual.

Five of the barrio interments included only adult males, and another five only females or females with perinatals (see Table 7-2). The distribution of grave goods among these ten burials indicates that men and women were about equally likely to receive marine shell, items of pyrite, slate, Thin Orange pottery, and Maya vessels (Rattray 1992:204–220). A total of two miniature vessels were present with two male burials, but forty miniatures were divided among four female burials. Found only in the burials of women were *candeleros* (three burials), theater censer parts (four burials), and the enigmatic clay "finger rolls" (a total of 31 in four burials). Although the sample is small, it seems that men

Table 7-2.
Merchants' Barrio: Gender and Grave Offerings

	Male burials	Female burials
number	5	5
with candeleros	0	3
with censer elements	0	4
with "finger rolls"	0	4
with miniature ceramics	2	4
with marine shell	3	3
with pyrites	2	1
with slate	3	2
with greenstone*	0	1*
with Tlaloc vases	0	1
with bone needles	1	1
with Teotihuacan vases	1	3
with Teotihuacan bowls	4	5
with Thin Orange ceramics	4	2
with Gulf Coast vessels	0	1
with Maya vessels	1	1

*does not include jade pectoral with primary woman of burial 5-8.

and women had roughly equivalent access to exotic goods, but women were much more likely to buried with ritual equipment and goods prepared specifically for mortuary ceremonies.

These data suggest that women in the Merchants' Barrio had high status, perhaps equivalent to that of the barrio men. This may have been due, in part, to their role in textile production, if indeed they did play a major part in that industry. It is also possible, given the frequent inclusion of *candeleros* and censers in their burials, that they played specialized ritual roles in the community, giving them independent or even preferential access to some supernatural forces. As will be discussed below, the isotopic data raise still other possibilities.

TLAILOTLACAN

Settlement Patterns and Architecture

Tlailotlacan is near the west edge of the city, extending through Teotihuacan Mapping Project square N1W6 into N2W6 (Spence 2002:Figure 6.1). A smaller, culturally related area is located in square N2W5, separated from the main area by about 850 m (Rattray 1987:253). Several of the structures in the larger area have been partially excavated over the years. The following summary draws on the various accounts of these projects (Millon 1967, 1973:35–36, 41–42, Figures 58–60; Spence 1976, 1989, 1990, 1994:354–366; 1998, 2002; Quintanilla 1982, 1993; Rattray 1987, 1992:27, 39, 70, 75, 201–203, Figures 11–14, pls. *xiii-xv*; 1993; Gamboa 1995; Ortega and Palomares 2003).

Immigrants first settled in Tlailotlacan about AD 200. Oaxacan archeologists have noted that the ceramic assemblage they brought has its closest counterpart in the Monte Albán Late Period II culture of the Valley of Oaxaca, generally identified as Zapotec (Paddock 1983; Winter 1998; Winter et al. 1998, 2002). We will follow that usage here. However, the ethnic identity of the Tlailotlacanos was not, strictly speaking, Zapotec. Although clearly derived from a Valley of Oaxaca Zapotec antecedent, it was, in fact, a construct developed in good part in response to the new cultural environment of the immigrants (Spence 1992:76–79).

To judge by the surface distribution of Zapotec-style ceramics and the Zapotec features exposed in excavations, the enclave covered about 6 to 7 hectares, excluding the small N2W5 outlier. Its population was approximately 700 people (Rattray 1993:Figure 2; Spence 2002:Figure 6.1). At one point in its history, it may have extended further to the east. Structure 19:N1W5, just beyond the east edge of the enclave, had a Zapotec tomb and displayed the Zapotec *escapulario* version of the *talud-tablero* facade on its platforms, although it also seems to have been home to some immigrants from Michoacán (Gómez 1998, 2002).

Although the earliest structures in the enclave may not have been typical Teotihuacan structures (Spence 1998; Ortega and Palomares 2003), by at least the Late Tlamimilolpa phase, everybody in the area lived in standard Teotihuacan multifamily apartment compounds (see Millon 1976, 1981; Cowgill 1997:137). This residential format was not the one favored in the Valley of Oaxaca, where most people lived in nuclear or small extended family compounds (Winter 1986), but the residents of Tlailotlacan may not have had much choice in the matter. The thoroughness with which apartment compounds replaced earlier residences everywhere in the city raises the possibility of some degree of coercion by the state. In at least one of the structures, site 7:N1W6, the main platform bore the typical Teotihuacan *talud-tablero* facade (Millon 1973:41–42). However, in other sites, the Oaxacan *escapulario* version, distinguished by the absence of a lower projecting border on the *tablero* component, was used (Gómez 2002:574).

Over time, the Tlailotlacanos would have adapted socially to this new residential format. Patterns of interaction and interrelationship within the structure, shaped by the architectural environment, would have created a new and larger social unit, or promoted a weak existing one to a new level of relevance in the lives of the people. This new group was probably still articulated through kin ties. The Valley of Oaxaca practice of tomb burial was brought to Tlailotlacan, where the senior couples of the enclave apartment compound were buried in Zapotec-style tombs. Furthermore, these tombs were constructed to allow continued access, as newly deceased individuals were interred in them and additional rituals were performed over the corpses of their predecessors (Spence 1976, 1994:354–366). This continued relevance of previous leaders, now ancestors, testifies to the formal structure and kin basis of the new social unit. In fact, this elevated level of cohesion would have served the interests of the Tlailotlacanos well, giving them a social vehicle to better address their concerns about cultural survival (Spence 2002:53–54).

At a still higher level, the dozen or so apartment compounds of the enclave were probably integrated in a larger sociopolitical unit that would have managed the external relationships of the community with the broader Teotihuacan society and with related groups beyond Teotihuacan. Unfortunately, we have little direct evidence of this level. What was once thought to be a circular temple in the enclave, site 69:N2W6, turned out to be another apartment compound upon excavation (Quintanilla 1982, 1993). Structure 34:N1W6, located at the south edge of the enclave where it could have monitored access from West Avenue, has been interpreted as a small platform, although this awaits verification from excavation. However, site 5:N1W6 includes a Zapotec temple that likely had community-wide functions (Michelle López-Croissier, personal communication, 2004).

Material Culture

The Tlailotlacanos adopted much of the material culture of Teotihuacan. The bulk of their pottery and all of their chipped and ground stone tools came from Teotihuacan workshops. There were, however, some significant ceramic exceptions. A minor proportion of the pottery used in the enclave was manufactured there, but in Valley of Oaxaca styles (Rattray 1987, 1993; Spence 1992, 2002). These local products included both ritual and domestic utilitarian forms. The latter included a variety of storage, food preparation and serving vessels (among them, a number of *comales*) and were most common, but figurines and three censer forms were also manufactured.

Statistical analysis indicates that this local industry continued at least well into the Xolalpan period, with no discernible change in form or technique throughout this lengthy span (Gibbs 2001). Part of the broad Zapotec inventory carried by the immigrants to Teotihuacan, these forms survived the challenges presented by the city to become fixed (orthodox, *sensu* Bourdieu 1977:169–171) elements in the enclave assemblage. Why these particular forms were retained while others were discarded is not clear, but their variety and their impingement on both the domestic and public spheres suggest that there is more than one answer. The domestic wares may reflect the continued preparation and consumption of favored Zapotec foods, and would have been important components in the presentation of a Zapotec domestic environment to facilitate the proper enculturation of the young.

The ritual forms raise different questions (Spence 2002). The Zapotec items retained in Tlailotlacan included handled censers, braziers, urns, and figurines (some of which may have been toys). At the same time, Teotihuacan *candeleros*, theater censers, and figurines were also employed in enclave rituals. Some of these bore a heavy symbolic load, but this was apparently recognized and accepted by the Tlailotlacanos (Spence 2002:64). This syncretism should not be surprising. Religions throughout central Mexico had enough features in common that many of the beliefs, symbols, and practices of one group would have been intelligible to others.

Rituals

Several ritual deposits in the 6:N1W6 apartment compound probably represent the ceremonial disposal of the afterbirth of infants who survived birth. Each deposit consisted of a ceramic vessel placed in a small pit, with another vessel or simply fragments placed over it as a cover. Similar features described in Zapotec ethnographies were intended to hold and protect the afterbirth of newborns (Parsons 1936:76; Berg 1976:5, 132; Spence 2002:58–59). The fact that most of these features were located in the public sectors of the structure reflects the importance attached to birth, or more precisely, recruitment, by the wider community. This broad concern is visible also in the treatment of subadults who died (Spence and Gamboa 1999). They were buried in public areas, often near or inside altars, and often with grave offerings.

A number of adults were also interred in public areas. Others were placed in residential space. However, the number of recovered burials in structure 6: N1W6 is, like elsewhere in Teotihuacan, well below the number of individuals who would once have lived and died there. The location of the missing burials, which must number in the hundreds, is unknown. Many were probably accidentally exhumed and scattered in the renovation and restructuring episodes that the building frequently experienced, but it is suspected that others were disposed of in ways still unidentified. Hopefully, the recovered burials offer an accurate representation of the total, though we have no real assurance of this.

The mortuary practices seem more Zapotec than Teotihuacan. Certainly, the tombs are Zapotec features. Also alien to Teotihuacan, but common in the Valley of Oaxaca, are the burial of single individuals in stonewalled cists and burial in the extended position. Nevertheless, the Tlailotlacan mortuary program was not completely Zapotec. As might be expected, it was also responsive to the pressures and concerns the new environment created. Teotihuacan ritual items were placed with some burials, and more individuals were buried in the public areas of the apartment compound than was the case either in the Valley of Oaxaca or elsewhere in Teotihuacan.

External Relations and Economy

Unlike the Merchants' Barrio, Tlailotlacan did not stand alone in central Mexico. It was apparently part of a broader network, one based on a shared ethnic identity (Hirth and Swezey 1976; Díaz 1980, 1981; Crespo and Mastache 1981; Rattray 1987; Mastache et al. 2002:52–59; Spence 2005). In the Tula region, some 60 km northwest of Teotihuacan, three sites show a mixture of Teotihuacan and Zapotec ceramics, and at least one of them has a Zapotec tomb (Hernández 1994). Crespo and Mastache (1981) have suggested that these sites were linked with Tlailotlacan in the procurement and processing of lime for use in Teotihuacan plaster (see also Barba and Córdova 1999).

The three sites are by no means homogeneous. The proportion of Zapotec-style ceramics in surface collections ranges from 63% at the El Tesoro site, where the tomb was found, to about 7% at the much larger Chingú site (Díaz 1980; Crespo and Mastache 1981). Further, considerable variation exists in the Zapotec types present on each site, though some of this may result from the vagaries of surface collection. Díaz (1980) has suggested that Chingú, where the ratio of Zapotec to Teotihuacan ceramics is very similar to that of Tlailotlacan, was a regional administrative center for Teotihuacan. The two smaller sites may have had closer and more direct ties to Tlailotlacan.

Elsewhere in central Mexico, still other sites with possible Zapotec ties have been identified (Hirth and Swezey 1976). Los Teteles, in Puebla, is a particularly convincing candidate for inclusion in a Zapotec diaspora network. Three Zapotec tombs, producing a mixture of Zapotec-style, Teotihuacan, and Thin Orange ceramics, have been reported there (Hirth and Swezey 1976; Noyola 1993:23; Plunket and Uruñuela 1998:106; Figure 3). Sites in Tehuacan and Morelos may also have been involved, but are less understood.

This network would have certainly had important economic functions, acting as a trade diaspora in some respects (Cohen 1969, 1971; Curtin 1984). Goods circulating through it may have included lime, green obsidian, Thin Orange ware, and perhaps other materials (Spence 1992:80; Rattray 1993:70). However, we should not allow these economic functions to eclipse the major social roles that the network would also have played (Spence 2005; White et al. 2004b). The communities participating in the network were relatively small and were often embedded in much larger, culturally distinct populations. Their survival would have depended on the continued health of the network, from which each would have drawn spouses with the "proper" cultural background and a wider support system for their distinctive cultural practices. The network must have been continually affirmed and recreated through collective social and ritual practices, though these may not be as visible in the archaeological record as its economic correlates.

Gender and Status

In a study of burials throughout the enclave, Spence and Gamboa (1999) noted the highly favorable treatment accorded to the burials of women. They appear to have been considered, at least in those archaeologically visible respects, equal in status to men (see Table 7-3). They were more likely to be buried in public space and to have been given grave offerings. These offerings were as likely as those of men to include items of wealth (marine shell, Thin Orange vessels, and greenstone), items indicating access to the supernatural world (censers, urns), and Zapotec-style artifacts that presented the salient cultural identity of the community. Also, women were included in the tombs, in some cases, clearly as mortuary events distinct from the burials of male leaders (Spence and Gamboa 1999:193).

It is very rare in Mesoamerican societies to find that women were assigned such high status, in all observable respects equal to that of men. This exceptional situation may have been due to the unusual circumstances of the enclave. As a relatively small community in the midst of a far larger and more powerful

Table 7-3.
Burial Practices and Gender in Tlailotlacan

	Male burials	Female burials
number	14	9
in public space	4	5
in domestic space	10	4
with offerings	9	9
without offerings	5	0
with Zapotec urn elements	2	0
with Zapotec handled censers	1	1
with other Zapotec vessels	0	1
with Teotihuacan censers	1	2
with Teotihuacan miniatures	5	3
with Thin Orange ceramics	2	2
with marine shell	2	3
with greenstone	1	4

society, its cultural survival was always an open question. It was necessary not only to maintain the numbers of the enclave residents, but also to ensure that they consisted of people with the appropriate cultural background. The pivotal roles of women in these respects, as the primary agents of both the physical production of new members and their initial enculturation in the enclave's ways, made them essential to the community's survival. This fact was apparently recognized and respected in the enclave. Beyond that, however, the oxygen isotope data indicate that women were also instrumental in the articulation of identity and practice in the wider diaspora network (White et al. 2004b).

THE OXYGEN ISOTOPE EVIDENCE

Archaeological and osteological data allow the reconstructions outlined above of the two principal areas of foreign occupation in Teotihuacan. However, these data are mute with respect to some fundamental questions. In particular, we do not know the patterns of interaction with related communities elsewhere: the degree to which relationships were maintained through time with them and with the homeland, the practices that perpetuated these relationships, the geographic (and cultural) sources of spouses or other new members recruited into the community, the gender structure of intercommunity movement, etc. For answers to these sorts of questions, we turn to the evidence provided by stable oxygen isotopes.

In the following discussion, we shall differentiate between the Merchants' Barrio and Tlailotlacan by referring to them as, respectively, the barrio and the enclave. This is not simply for convenience; these terms seem to capture some real differences between the two areas. Tlailotlacan was an ethnic enclave, occupied by a group that shared a common identity. The Merchants' Barrio, by comparison, may have been home to a variety of people from different cultural backgrounds. The barrio was clearly distinct, a neighborhood or district apart from the rest of Teotihuacan, but that distinction may not have been founded on a uniform ethnic identity.

Oxygen Isotope Analysis

The use of oxygen isotope ratios to identify geographic relocations from skeletal material is based on the premise that "we are what we drink" i.e., our tissues reflect the isotopic composition of the water we imbibe (mainly from liquid), which is, in turn, determined by the physical and climatic environment in which we live. Further details of the theoretical basis and methodology for oxygen isotope analysis may be found in previous publications (White et al. 2000a, 2002). Oxygen isotope values ($\delta^{18}O$) are determined relative to the Vienna Standard Mean Ocean Water (VSMOW) standard (Coplen 1994) and expressed as parts per thousand (‰) using the formula:

$$\delta^{18}O = \frac{(^{18}O/^{16}O\text{sample} - {}^{18}O/^{16}O\text{standard})}{(^{18}O/^{16}O\text{standard})} \times 1000$$

The $\delta^{18}O$ values of imbibed water are incorporated into body water and then into bones and teeth during the process of mineralization (Longinelli 1984; Luz et al. 1984). Because tooth enamel does not remodel after it is formed (unlike bone), it provides a permanent record of the environmental water imbibed during its formation. Bone continuously remodels, and therefore, its isotopic composition slowly changes to reflect that of any new environment. By comparing teeth formed at different times during growth and development or teeth with bone in the same individual, it is possible to determine not only if a person has relocated, but also the approximate age(s) when they moved. The length of time it takes for bone to completely change its isotopic composition varies by age, i.e., it will happen more quickly in children than in adults. Although the precise time required for complete turnover is still not well defined, it is estimated to be in the order of 10 to 25 years for cortical bone (Libby et al. 1964; Stenhouse and Baxter 1979; Parfitt 1983) and much less for trabecular bone (Fazzalari et al. 1997; Parfitt 1983; Manolagas 2000). We have chosen to analyze the phosphate portion of the skeletal material ($\delta^{18}O_P$) because it is generally very well preserved (Bryant et al. 1994, 1996; Koch et al. 1989; McArthur and Herczig 1990; Quade et al. 1992; Reinhard et al. 1996).

The main source of water for breastfeeding children is mother's milk, which is enriched in ^{18}O relative to the water consumed by the mother (White et al. 2000a; 2004c; Williams et al. 2003; Wright and Schwarcz 1998). Although controlled studies have not yet been conducted to determine the precise degree of enrichment, previous analyses at other Mesoamerican sites and at Tlailotlacan indicate that the $\delta^{18}O$ values of bones and teeth from breastfeeding children are elevated by about .7‰ relative to their mothers (White et al. 2002; Wright and Schwarcz 1998). Because children in most Mesoamerican populations are typically breastfed until about 3 to 4 years old (Dolphin 2000; Song 1997; Storey 1992; White 1994; Williams 2000; Williams et al. 2003; Wright and Schwarcz 1998), dental values reflecting this age span were adjusted downward, by .7‰ for deciduous molars and permanent first molars, and by .35‰ for permanent canines and premolars.

Previous studies of archaeological skeletons have established a baseline range of $\delta^{18}O$ values, i.e., 14.0 to 16.0‰, for the Teotihuacan environment, which identifies individuals as coming from this area (White et al. 1998; 2000a; 2002; 2004a). The 2‰ variability in this range is also typical of archaeological sites elsewhere in Mesoamerica where it was possible to control for local residency (White et al. 2000b), and the Teotihuacan range has been used to identify those who had lived in Teotihuacan versus elsewhere in a number of Mesoamerican sites (White et al. 2000a, 2001, 2002, 2004a; Spence et al. 2004). A number of factors could contribute to the breadth of this range, including climatic seasonality, the inclusion of individuals who had moved from nearby and similar microenvironments, the presence of foreigners from more distant regions who had not yet fully equilibrated to local values, or the consumption of large quantities of imported foods with high water contents. Most sites analyzed so far have $\delta^{18}O$ values distinct from Teotihuacan (see Figure 7-1), but there is some overlap between sites.

Tests for alteration previously conducted on the Merchants' Barrio and Tlailotlacan samples have demonstrated postmortem processes do not affect their $\delta^{18}O$ values (Spence et al. 2004; White et al. 1998).

Temporal Variation in External Relations and Economy

The sample from the Merchants' Barrio spans the Late Tlamimilolpa (AD 250 to 350) to Late Xolalpan periods (ending AD 550) (Table 7-4), whereas the Tlailotlacan sample covers a broader time period, i.e., from the Miccoatli-Early Tlamimilolpa transition (c. AD 200) to the Metepec period (ending AD 650) (Table 7-5). The modal $\delta^{18}O$ values for all time periods at both the barrio and the

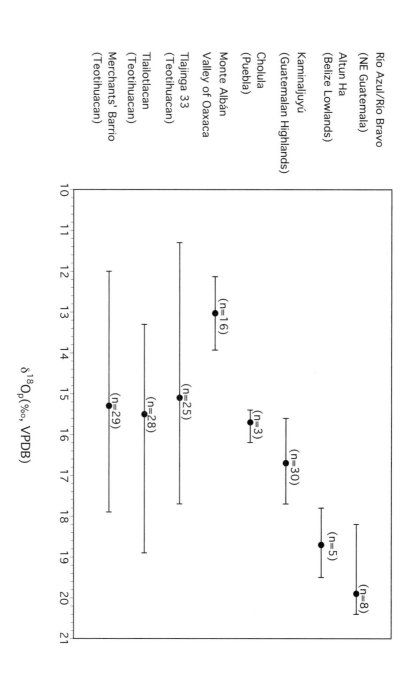

Río Azul/Río Bravo
(NE Guatemala)

Altun Ha
(Belize Lowlands)

Kaminaljuyú
(Guatemalan Highlands)

Cholula
(Puebla)

Monte Albán
Valley of Oaxaca

Tlajinga 33
(Teotihuacan)

Tlailotlacan
(Teotihuacan)

Merchants' Barrio
(Teotihuacan)

δ¹⁸O_p(‰, VPDB)

Figure 7-1. Comparison of ranges of δ¹⁸O values from the Merchants' Barrio and Tlailotlacan with those used for controls at a variety of Mesoamerican sites.

Table 7-4.
$\delta^{18}O$ Values for the Merchants' Barrio Burials

Phase	Burial	Sex	Age[1]	Sample[2]	$\delta^{18}O(\text{‰})$
L. Tlam.	9		s	bone	15.3
	22a		a	bone	15.4
	22b		s	bone	16.6
E. Xol.	5-8		a	bone	13.9
	5-8		a	bone	14.2
	5-8	F	a	bone	14.2
	5-8	F	a	bone	14.7
	5-8	F	a	bone	14.4
	5-8	F	a	bone	14.2
	5-8		a	bone	14.5
	5-8		s	bone	15.9
	5-8	F	a	bone	14.0
	14b	F	a	bone	15.2
	14c/e		a	PM	17.9
	24-25		a	C	16.5
	24-25d	F	a	bone	13.9
L. Xol.	10a	M	a	bone	15.7
	10a	M	a	PM1	17.9
	10c		s	bone	16.6
	11a	M	a	bone	15.2
	11b		s	bone	15.6
	13b	F	a	bone	15.1
	13b	F	a	bone	15.6
	13b	F	a	M2	15.9
	17	F	a	bone	17.8
	17	F	a	C	16.8
	33a	M	a	bone	14.2
	33a	M	a	C	12.1
	33b	M	a	bone	16.3

[1] s = subadult; a = adult
[2] for teeth, I=incisor, C=canine, PM=premolar, M=molar

Table 7-5.
$\delta^{18}O$ Values for the Tlailotlacan Burials

Phase	Burial	Sex	Age	Sample[1]	$\delta^{18}O(‰)$
Micc./E. Tlam.	408INF		s	bone	15.2
	408/1		s	dI1	15.6
	408/1		s	dM2	17.1
	408/1		s	M1	15.5
	408/2		s	dI1	15.0
	408/2		s	dM2	17.1
	409		s	bone	15.0
	409		s	dI1	14.7
	409		s	dM2	16.9
E. Tlam.	284A	F	a	bone	15.3
	284A	F	a	M2	15.2
	284B	M	a	bone	15.4
	261	F	a	C	16.3
	261	F	a	M3	15.4
	322	F	a	bone	15.1
	322	F	a	PM2	15.5
	322	F	a	C	16.2
	322	F	a	M3	18.5
	345S		s	bone	15.6
	345S		s	dI1	15.5
	345S		s	dM2	16.4
L. Tlam.	223		s	bone	15.5
	223		s	dI1	16.0
	223		s	dM2	13.3
	223		s	M1	15.5
	223		s	M2	16.1
	345N		s	bone	16.4
	345N		s	dI1	16.0
	345N		s	dM2	15.2
	345N		s	M1	15.3
E.–L. Tlam.	#841		a	bone	13.4
L. Tlam.-E. Xol.	130		s	bone	15.3
	130		s	dI1	17.1
	130		s	dM2	15.4
	381	F	a	bone	15.6
	381	F	a	C	15.4
	381	F	a	M3	15.1
	S. Tomb				
	20		a	bone	15.1
	1954	M	a	C	16.2
	140		a	C	15.8
E. Xol.	133		s	bone	16.5
	133		s	dI1	15.6
	133		s	dM2	15.5
	133		s	M1	16.4
	113	F	a	bone	14.1
	113	F	a	M3	17.0
E.-L. Xol.	E. Tomb				
	ent.	M	a	bone	15.2
	ent.	M	a	M1	14.9
	#774a		a	M2	15.5
Xol.-Met.	372	M	a	bone	14.2
	372	M	a	M3	18.9
Met.	N. Tomb				
	#68		a	bone	15.6
	#8		a	C	15.4
	#31	M	a	PM1	14.4
	#31	M	a	C	16.2
	#33	M	a	C	16.6

[1] deciduous teeth distinguished by prefix d; I = incisor, C = canine, PM = premolar, M = molar

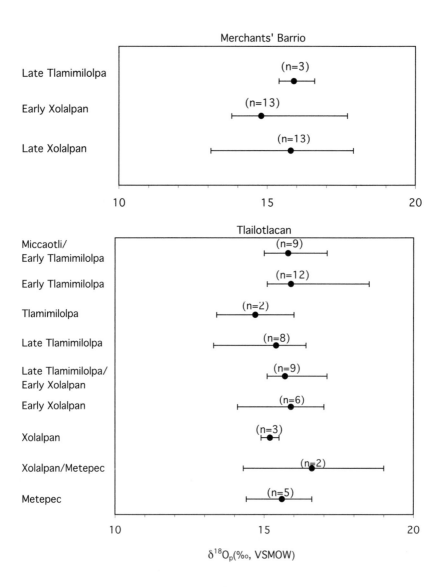

Figure 7-2. Comparison of δ¹⁸0 values by time period.

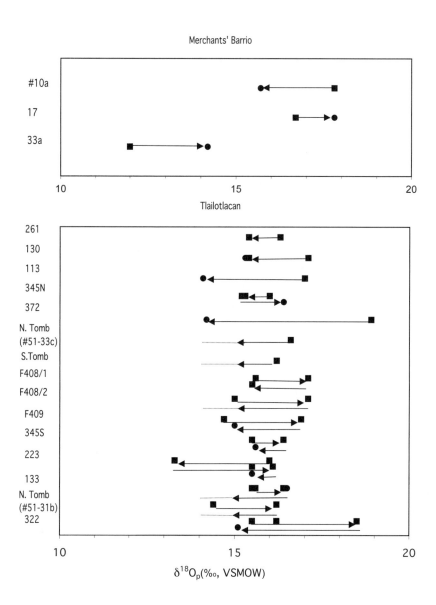

Figure 7-3. Illustration of individuals who relocated, showing the direction of movement from earliest to latest sampled δ¹⁸0 values in the course of their lifetimes. ■ dental ● bone

enclave fall within the range established for Teotihuacan, but there are also foreign values found throughout the entire sequence of both samples including the earliest and latest periods (Figure 7-2).

The majority of the Teotihuacan $\delta^{18}O$ values were obtained from bone. Of the 24 individuals with bone samples from the Merchants' Barrio, 17% had foreign values. Of the 16 individuals with bone from Tlailotlacan, 13% had foreign values. The dominance of local $\delta^{18}O$ values in bone means that most of the inhabitants of both locations had dwelt in Teotihuacan for a long time before their death. Their teeth, however, tell stories of past lives in different places.

Both the barrio and the enclave appear comprised of similar proportions of immigrants. Of the teeth (n = 6, each belonging to a different individual) from the Merchants' Barrio, four (67%) had foreign values. Of the 22 individuals represented by teeth (n = 39) from Tlailotlacan, 14 (64%) had foreign values. Therefore, the majority of inhabitants of both locations had either migrated to Teotihuacan or spent substantial periods of their childhood, i.e., during tooth formation, in a different environment. These percentages are probably under-estimated. If teeth and bone were available for all individuals, the percentage of migrants would likely rise. For example, among individuals represented by both tissues at the Merchants' Barrio, 75% had foreign signatures, and at Tlailotlacan 83% had dwelt elsewhere. Of the three Merchants' Barrio individuals with both bone and teeth who show relocation, two moved to Teotihuacan from elsewhere, and one moved from one foreign location to another (Figure 7-3). Of the 15 Tlailotlacan individuals who show movement, nine individuals moved more than once. There were eight relocations from Teotihuacan to a foreign location, 15 relocations from a foreign area to Teotihuacan, and one from one foreign area to another (Figure 7-3). The contrast between the foreign values found in enamel and the dominance of Teotihuacan values in bone provides a means of extrapolating economic behavior and the fate of ethnic identities in the big city.

In terms of the Merchants' Barrio, it appears that foreign traders arrived in the city with the purpose of permanently establishing themselves personally or corporately. This process continued throughout the entire temporal sequence of the site, so there was continuous renewal of foreign representation in the economy of the barrio. By extension, this may mean that the trade relationships established by immigrants in Teotihuacan were not taken over by local inhabitants or the state upon their death. More likely, someone else from their homeland replaced them. In essence, they were more like foreign trade ambassadors or factors (though perhaps not regulated by their homelands), rather than traveling Teotihuacan merchants using a common base of operations run by the state. It, therefore, appears that the trade model of the Aztecs, which was characterized by the *pochteca*, merchants who made circuits between their homes in the Basin of Mexico and other regions, was a significant deviation from the antecedent model that existed at Teotihuacan. The difference between the two systems may lie in the political identities of the merchants. The *pochteca*, however ambiguous their relationship with the Aztec nobility may have been, were nevertheless Aztecs. Their political allegiance to the Triple Alliance was never in question, and indeed, they often acted as agents of the state (Berdan 1982). In contrast, we believe that the traders of the Merchants' Barrio came there from a number of other regions; if they recognized any political allegiance at all, it was to their various homeland states rather than to Teotihuacan.

The Zapotec migrants to Tlailotlacan were probably not attracted to Teotihuacan for purposes of trade in quite the same way, although their presence would have facilitated economic exchange with the homeland and with related communities. Although perhaps attracted to Teotihuacan by its power and opportunities, we cannot say why they originally left their homeland in the Valley of Oaxaca. They may have been only one segment of a broader diaspora, impelled by a search for new opportunities or by political upheaval in the homeland. Once this particular group had settled in Tlailotlacan, they maintained their identity through a continuous influx of immigrants and, as we shall see below, by enculturating their youth in their traditional ethnic identity.

Both the barrio and the enclave provide an interesting contrast with the apartment compound of Tlajinga 33, where a much smaller percentage of the sample (29%) had foreign values (White et al. 2004a). Tlajinga 33 was thought to have been comprised of local people, and many were artisans (Widmer 1991). Some of the individuals identified as foreign had $\delta^{18}0$ values consistent with West Mexico, which is also represented in the construction of a shaft tomb (Widmer 1987). Nonetheless, to judge by the relative lack of non-Teotihuacan artifacts or structures, the inhabitants of this pocket of Teotihuacan appear to have experienced greater assimilation than either the Merchants' Barrio or Tlailotlacan. They may also have been more subject to state control of their production (Storey 1991) and may not have had the continual contact with their homeland(s) experienced by those living in the barrio and the enclave. Although the percent of foreigners in Tlajinga 33 is higher than might have been expected, it is consistent with Storey's (1992) demographic analysis; because of an extremely high infant mortality rate, the community would have needed immigrants to maintain its population.

The Tlailotlacan dental sample is more extensive than that from the Merchants' Barrio, both in terms of individuals represented and the number of teeth from each individual. It has, therefore, allowed a much more detailed analysis of patterns and timing of relocations (White et al. 2004b). For example, several individuals had been born in Tlailotlacan but moved to other regions where they sojourned during periods of their childhood. In these sojourns, they must have been accompanied by adults, certainly by their mothers since most of them would still have been nursing at the time. We believe that this pattern of behavior was a major mechanism in the maintenance of Zapotec ethnicity at Tlailotlacan. Unfortunately, the Merchants' Barrio sample does not allow us to examine any age-related patterning of relocation.

The locations of these other relevant regions cannot be specifically identified at this point, but we can speculate on how many there were. There were probably three represented at the Merchants' Barrio, one with a single very low $\delta^{18}O$ value (12.1‰), one with $\delta^{18}O$ values between 16.3 and 16.8‰ (n=5), and one with values of 17.8-17.9‰ (n=3). The homeland indicated by the 12.1‰ value may not be represented by anyone from Tlailotlacan.

At Tlailotlacan, there are at least three regions represented by the $\delta^{18}O$ values obtained. One of these (see burial 223) is consistent with Monte Albán in the Valley of Oaxaca (around 13‰), the homeland of the Tlailotlacanos. Another set of values falls between 16 and 18‰, and still another location (found in burial 322) has a very high $\delta^{18}O$ value (18.5‰). The latter value is outside the range found in the Merchants' Barrio. We suggest that these foreign locations may represent Zapotec diaspora communities with which the diaspora segment in Teotihuacan was connected. There is clearly an overlap in $\delta^{18}O$ values between the Merchants' Barrio and Tlailotlacan that may represent the same areas of origin. However, we must remember that quite different regions may have similar isotopic values. Given the different functions of the two Teotihuacan neighborhoods, it would not be surprising to find that their foreign connections were not shared.

The samples are not large enough to determine any strong association between homelands and time period (Figure 7-2), so it is not possible to say, for example, that immigration from the Valley of Oaxaca or the Gulf Coast was restricted to a particular time period. Both ceramic and isotopic data indicate that one of the earliest (Late Tlamimilolpa) burials at the Merchants' Barrio is foreign (burial 22). By contrast, there are no foreign materials in the latest Merchants' Barrio burial (burial 10-12), but this burial does contain individuals with foreign isotopic signatures, one of whom (burial 10a) has a very high $\delta^{18}O$ value that might indicate a Gulf Coast location.

The earliest known Tlailotlacan in situ burials, from the Miccaotli-Early Tlamimilolpa transition (AD 200), were children whose values indicate local birth, which supports the idea that the founders of the enclave had migrated earlier. The latest burials are from the North Tomb and contain two individuals who were probably foreigners. Only two Tlailotlacan values fall in the range for Monte Albán, one (burial 223) of the Late Tlamimilolpa phase and the other (#841) an undated but probably early secondary burial in mixed fill.

Gender, Status, and Age

One of the most striking aspects of the data from the Merchants' Barrio is that for all the skeletons that could be sexed, all but one of those with foreign $\delta^{18}O$ values were males (Figure 7-4). The one woman (burial 17) with foreign values grew up (6 months to 5 or 6 years) in one foreign location and moved to another, where she had lived for quite a long time before her death. She was probably either visiting or had recently moved to the city when she died, and was perhaps the homeland wife or other relative of a trader. Regardless, she was located next to a shrine in a primary burial, which suggests that she was accorded high status in death. Women in general appear to have had high status at the Merchants' Barrio. Although further testing using both bone and enamel from more individuals would be useful, the patterns of mobility seem to suggest that the majority of women and children were local and that the majority of immigrants were adult males. The combination of apparent high status for women and the greater proportion of male immigrants suggests an uxorilocal marriage pattern where the women maintained the stability of the population and perhaps its economic functioning within the city. Also, the frequent presence of ritual paraphernalia in the burials of women (Table 7-2) suggests that they may have been primarily responsible for ritual practices in the barrio.

These roles alone could have been responsible for the high status of women, but an additional factor might have existed. The Merchants' Barrio was similar in several respects to the *k'rum*, or merchants' ward, in the Anatolian city of Kanesh (Veenhof 1995; Stein 2005). The *k'rum* merchants came from several regions, including the Assyrian city of Asshur, and maintained their homeland political identities while residing in Kanesh. A number of them took Anatolian wives, selected from local elite families to enhance their security and opportunities. By analogy, some of the Merchants' Barrio women with local isotopic signatures may have been Teotihuacan wives, their status reflecting in part the prominence of their Teotihuacan families.

These same gender, age, and status distinctions were not present at Tlailotlacan. The dental $\delta^{18}O$ values tell us that children were being often relocated, presumably with one or both their parents. For those individuals who have tissues representing infancy and childhood, 80% had moved during their early years and had sojourned elsewhere for substantial periods of time, i.e., long enough to register in a forming tooth. Because of this high frequency and because adult skeletons of both sexes have foreign values in their teeth, we assume that both male and female children were taken elsewhere for sojourns. Furthermore, because many of the teeth representing preweaning ages had foreign $\delta^{18}O$ values, we can reasonably assume that nursing mothers were moving across the landscape with the subadults. In general, the $\delta^{18}O$ values of enamel are

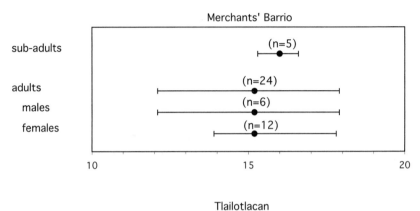

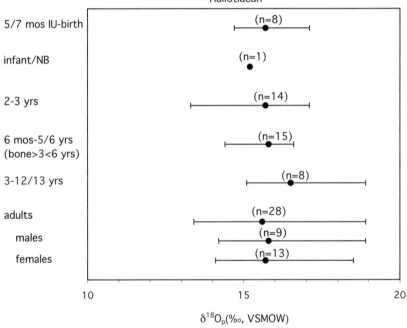

$\delta^{18}O_p$(‰, VSMOW)

Figure 7-4. Comparison of $\delta^{18}O$ values by sex and age. Subadult ages in Tlailotlacan are ages of dental crown development. Adult data include dental and bone values.

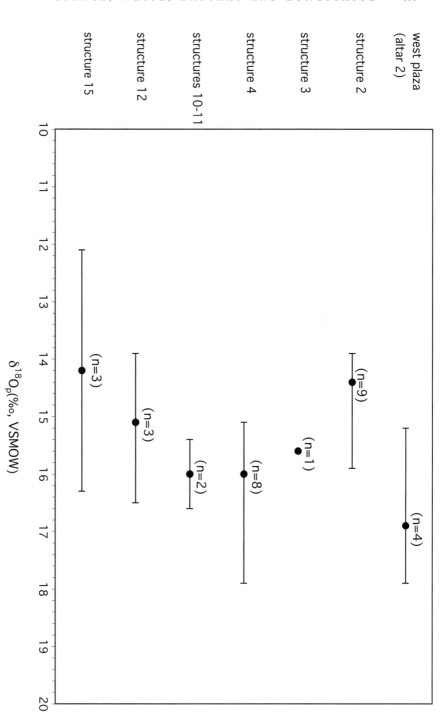

Figure 7-5. Comparison of δ¹⁸O values by area and structure at the Merchants' Barrio.

much more variable than the bone $\delta^{18}O$ values. The contrast can be explained by a tendency to dwell primarily in Tlailotlacan after reaching adulthood.

Because bone turnover is a continuous and slow process, it is difficult to determine relocations in adult life with any fine definition. Sojourns in foreign locations might be too short to register in bone, or longer ones could be obliterated through isotopic exchange upon return to the city. Bone $\delta^{18}O$ values that fall outside the Teotihuacan range do indicate time spent in foreign locations, but could also reflect varying degrees of equilibration to the Teotihuacan environment.

There is no support for a gender-based marital residence pattern at Tlailotlacan. Both sexes were migrating to Teotihuacan from the same locations either in early childhood or after, and both sexes were also found to be local to Teotihuacan. We have speculated that the absence of a specific marital residence pattern and the active role played by women in taking their children for sojourns in their natal communities not only empowered women in diaspora networks, but also helped to maintain the Zapotec identity of the enclave. Although both the Merchants' Barrio and Tlailotlacan provide evidence that women wielded respected forms of power, the sources of female power appear different.

Settlement Pattern and Architecture

Because the relationship between foreigners and residence type and location within the Merchants' Barrio appears to have been quite complex, the interpretations here are preliminary. The barrio will need further sampling to affirm or clarify the patterning that may exist.

The three locales sampled in the Merchants' Barrio may represent distinct ethnic groups. Xocotitla and Mezquititla on the west side of San Juan River contain more individuals with high $\delta^{18}O$ values compared with Nopalera (circular structure 15) on the east side of the river, which has the only individual with a low $\delta^{18}O$ value (Figure 7-5). Only an expanded sample will provide the means of further testing this hypothesis.

Some evidence suggesting group identity is found in structures within these locales (Figure 7-5). For example, circular structure 2 (near the north limit of Xocotitla) has a significantly lower mean ($\delta^{18}O$ = 14.4 ± 0.60‰, n = 9) than circular structure 4 (near the south limit of Xocotitla) ($\delta^{18}O$ = 15.9 ± 0.91‰, n = 8), which is different again from altar 2 of West Group Plaza ($\delta^{18}O$=16.8‰, n = 4). Notably, altar 2 is located only a few meters west of circular structure 2. Although these data suggest that ethnic groupings may have been localized within structures rather than general areas, the distribution of foreign isotopic values seems to contradict this in some cases. For example, the two individuals of burial 33, in Nopalera circular structure 15, include the very low value of 12.1‰, but also the higher value of 16.3‰. Similarly, burial 10 to 12 of

Xocotitla circular structure 4 produced five values, of which three are local, one is 16.6‰ and one is 17.9‰. Also, the idea that structures grouped around a plaza and altar may have housed an extended family is not corroborated, though the sample is too small to be definitive.

Some evidence supports our earlier suggestion that, on the death of a merchant, the trade connections that had been established remained within the family or "house". Burials 14 and 17 are both associated with altar 2, but burial 14 was earlier than burial 17. The premolar of a burial 14 adult produced a $\delta^{18}O$ value of 17.9‰. Burial 17, a woman of high status who we have suggested was the homeland wife of a trader, had a bone value of 17.8‰ and a dental value of 16.8‰, indicating her birth in one foreign region but her movement, as an older child or adult, to a different foreign region, the same one where the burial 14 individual had lived.

Unfortunately, at present, we cannot examine the relationship between $\delta^{18}O$ values and settlement pattern at Tlailotlacan as the material analyzed has come from a single structure. Plans are underway, however, to analyze skeletons from other structures in the enclave.

Material Culture and Mortuary Ritual

Foreign artifacts, generally uncommon in Teotihuacan burials, were found in burials at both the barrio and the enclave (Sempowski 1994; Spence 1994). Of the nine burials from both locations that contain foreign ceramics, seven also have foreign $\delta^{18}O$ values (Table 7-6). Unfortunately, at present, it is not possible to determine if these values are consistent with the place of artifact manufacture because we do not yet have enough isotopic compositions for possible source areas. However, one of the $\delta^{18}O$ values of burial 223 at Tlailotlacan is consistent

Table 7-6.
Imported Ceramics and Associated $\delta^{18}O$ Values

Burial	Origins of Ceramics	Local	Foreign
MB5-8[1]	Gulf, unidentified	14.0–15.9	13.9
MB9	Puebla[2], Gulf, unidentified	15.3	none
MB13b	Maya, Gulf	15.1–15.9	none
MB14[1]	Puebla[2]	15.2	17.9
MB17[1]	Puebla[2]	none	16.8, 17.8
MB22[1]	Puebla[2], Maya, Gulf	15.4	16.6
MB33[1]	Puebla[2]	14.2	12.1, 16.3
TL223	Oaxaca	15.5, 16.0	13.3, 16.1
TL NTomb[1]	Puebla[2]	14.4–15.6	16.2, 16.6

[1] multiple individuals; not clear with which person ceramics are associated.
[2] All Puebla ceramics are Thin Orange ware.

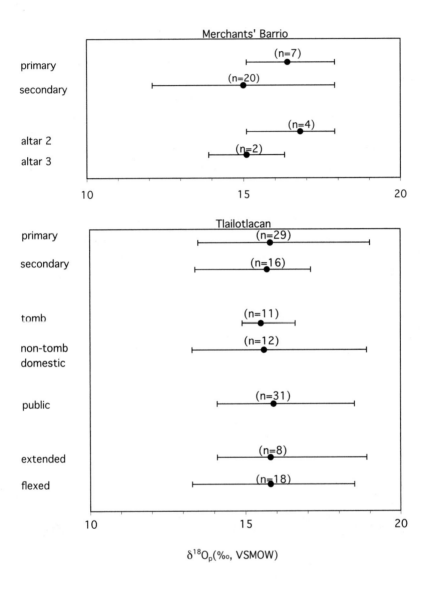

Figure 7-6. Comparison of δ¹⁸O values by mortuary treatment.

with Monte Albán in the Valley of Oaxaca (White et al. 1998; 2004b) and this individual had a micaceous vase of Oaxacan manufacture. Analyses of samples from other areas of Mesoamerica should help clarify these relationships in the future. At present, it is probably more informative to examine patterning in mortuary variables (Figure 7-6).

The Merchants' Barrio contains a large number of secondary burials, a mortuary behavior uncharacteristic of indigenous Teotihuacan society. Secondary burials with foreign $\delta^{18}0$ values may be the remains of relatives brought from their homelands by immigrants to rest close by or the remains of travelers who died while on the road (White et al. 1998; 2004b). The subadults 10c and 22b are likely examples of transported deceased children. However, most of the secondary burials appear to reflect the Teotihuacan environment (mean $\delta^{18}0$ = 15.0‰ ± 1.3, n = 20), and primary burials are statistically more likely to have foreign values (Student's t = 3.3, p < 0.005, df = 25) (Figure 7-6). Almost half the primary burials from the Merchants' Barrio had $\delta^{18}0$ values higher (mean $\delta^{18}0$ = 16.4‰ ± 1.0, n = 8) than those from Teotihuacan. The large number of secondary burials and the patterning of foreign values within primary/secondary types lend further support for the proposed movement of foreign traders to the barrio, where they stayed to establish communities and, no doubt, provided a base within the city for economic activity with their various homelands.

Six burials from two shrines are also included in the Merchants' Barrio sample. Five of these exhibit foreign $\delta^{18}0$ values (Figure 7-6). Because shrines are normally thought to represent high status burial locations, we conclude that individuals of foreign origin may often have been accorded high status in death. The inhabitants may have revered these people as successful merchants or community leaders.

The mortuary data and $\delta^{18}0$ values at Tlailotlacan provide a number of strong points of contrast (Figure 7-6). Unlike the Merchants' Barrio, the number of foreign signatures does not differ between primary and secondary burials. Some of the secondary burials were probably deceased relatives brought with migrating families who, like those who moved to the Merchants' Barrio, must have done so with the express purpose of committing to life in Teotihuacan. High-status locations in Tlailotlacan would have been tombs and public areas, such as near altars and in courtyards accessible to all inhabitants. However, burials in these locations show no correlation with foreign $\delta^{18}0$ values. Similarly, burial position is not associated with either foreign or local $\delta^{18}0$ values. Both flexed or seated burials, which are characteristic of Teotihuacan, and extended burials characteristic of Oaxaca (Romero 1983) are found at Tlailotlacan. Thus, the distribution of foreign $\delta^{18}0$ values appears to be fairly homogeneous within the apartment compound. From this, we conclude that, unlike the Merchants' Barrio, no evidence indicates that foreign-born individuals at Tlailotlacan were accorded greater status than locally born individuals.

CONCLUSIONS

The oxygen isotope evidence provides important new data on the foreign residents of Teotihuacan. Both the Merchants' Barrio and Tlailotlacan clearly maintained active relationships, including the movement and residential relocation of people, with a number of other regions throughout their existence. In the case of the Merchants' Barrio, this interaction seems largely to have involved the movement of adult men, who came from foreign regions to settle in the barrio. Most of the women, in contrast, were lifelong residents. This gendered pattern of movement is what would be expected of a barrio of merchants who came from a variety of homelands, and whose purpose in Teotihuacan was the establishment of trading houses. The Middle Eastern *k'rum* seems to be an appropriate analogy (Veenhof 1995).

In the case of Tlailotlacan, however, both men and women were on the move. Furthermore, a clear pattern of subadult relocation exists, in which infants and very young children born in Tlailotlacan sojourned for a year or more in another region, then returned to Tlailotlacan. Because they were not yet of weaning age, they must have been accompanied on these sojourns by their mothers. This practice may have conferred on the infant formal recognition of his or her "citizenship" in the diaspora network. Equally important, however, adult women were moving around in the network and spending considerable time in other communities. They probably played a significant role in the integration and maintenance of the network, smoothing over the discontinuities in practice and social memory that would inevitably have developed among the communities as a result of their distinct migration experiences and life in rather different host societies.

Women in both the Merchants' Barrio and Tlailotlacan seem to have enjoyed unusually high status. However, the foundations for their status were different, reflecting differences in the fundamental priorities of the two areas. The Tlailotlacanos were concerned with the survival of their ethnic community, and by extension with the continued health of the larger network that helped to sustain it. Women played a major part in this effort. They were crucial to both the physical and cultural reproduction of the enclave, and their involvement in infant sojourning made them instrumental in the harmonization of practice throughout the network.

By comparison, the Merchants' Barrio may never have developed a strong overarching structure or communal identity. External relationships were probably not community affairs but rather the concern of smaller groups. If the *k'rum* analogy holds true, the most important ties would have been between traders and related groups in their homelands. Men would have traveled frequently, leaving the women to manage things in their absence. This responsibility might explain the high status of the women, who seem, for the most part, to have been lifelong residents of the barrio (or in some cases, may have married into it from the wider Teotihuacan society). Their management of local affairs apparently included the conduct of ritual, to judge by the restriction of ritual paraphernalia to the graves of women. Elements of Teotihuacan theater censers occurred only with women, linking them also to the numerous nonburial offerings in the barrio, most of which contained theater censers.

The ideas expressed here are still somewhat tentative. The database on which they are constructed suffers from two deficiencies. One is the lack of good samples from other regions of Mesoamerica, limiting our ability to specifically identify some of the foreign communities that interacted with Tlailotlacan and the Merchants' Barrio. Given the overlap in oxygen isotope values between some regions, it would also be prudent to include other approaches, like strontium isotope analysis (Price et al. 2000), to further refine our geographic focus.

The other drawback is the inadequate coverage of the samples from the two areas. In the case of the Merchants' Barrio, it would be desirable to sample more teeth to obtain better data on relocation at earlier points in barrio residents' lives. In Tlailotlacan, that sort of evidence has proved surprisingly informative, revealing the striking pattern of subadult sojourning. However, to date, we have only sampled one of the dozen or so apartment compounds in Tlailotlacan. It is important to determine if the other structures in the enclave show the same web of connections, or if they differ in the direction or intensity of their external contacts. In this respect, it is interesting to note that only two of the Tlailotlacan values point to the Valley of Oaxaca, the homeland of the Tlailotlacanos. It may be that one of the other apartment compounds played a larger role in mediating that relationship. Alternatively, it may simply be that, after the initial founding of Tlailotlacan, the homeland relationship played no larger part in enclave life than did ties with the other diaspora communities.

Acknowledgments

We wish to thank the Consejo de Arqueología of the Instituto Nacional de Antropología e Historia of Mexico and its presidents Joaquín García-Bárcena and Lorena Mirambell for permission to export the samples used in this study, and numerous colleagues in Mexico, Guatemala, and the United States for providing samples from their sites. We are also grateful for the support of the Social Sciences and Humanities Research Council of Canada and the Natural Sciences and Engineering Research Council of Canada. Jay Maxwell created Figures 7-1 through 7-6.

REFERENCES

Ball, Joseph
  1983   Teotihuacan, the Maya, and Ceramic Interchange: A Contextual Perspective.
          In *Highland-Lowland Interaction in Mesoamerica: Interdisciplinary Approaches*,
          edited by Arthur Miller, pp. 125–145. Dumbarton Oaks Research Library,
          Washington, D.C.

Barba, Luis, and José Luis Córdova
  1999   Estudios energéticos de la producción de cal en tiempos Teotihuacanos y sus
          implicaciones. *Latin American Antiquity* 10:168–179.

Berdan, Frances
  1982   *The Aztecs of Central Mexico: an Imperial Society.* Harcourt Brace Jovanovich
          College Publishers, Toronto.

Berg, Richard
  1976   *Shwan, a Highland Zapotec Woman.* Vantage Press, New York.

Bourdieu, Pierre.
  1977   *Outline of a Theory of Practice.* Cambridge University Press, Cambridge.

Bryant, J. Daniel, Boaz Luz, and Philip N. Froelich
  1994   Oxygen Isotope Composition of Fossil Horse Phosphate as a Record of
          Continental Palaeoclimate. *Palaeogeography, Palaeoclimatology, Palaeoecology*
          107:303–316.

Bryant, J. Daniel, Paul Koch, Philip N. Froelich, William J. Showers, and Bernard J.
          Genna
  1996   Biologic and Climatic Signals in the Oxygen Isotope Composition of Eocene-
          Oligocene Equid Enamel Phosphate. *Palaeogeography, Palaeoclimatology,
          Palaeoecology* 126:75–89.

Cohen, Abner
  1969   *Custom and Politics in Urban Africa: a Study of Hausa Migrants in Yoruba Towns.*
          University of California Press, Berkeley.
  1971   Cultural Strategies in the Organization of Trading Diasporas. In *The Devel-
          opment of Indigenous Trade and Markets in West Africa*, edited by Claude
          Meillassoux, pp. 266–281. Oxford University Press, Oxford.

Coplen, Tyler B.
  1994   Reporting of Stable Hydrogen, Carbon and Oxygen Isotopic Abundances.
          Pure and Applied Chemistry 66:271–276.

Cowgill, George L.
  1997   State and Society at Teotihuacan, Mexico. *Annual Review of Anthropology*
          26:129–161.

Crespo, Ana, and Alba Guadalupe Mastache
  1981   La presencia en el área de Tula, Hidalgo, de grupos relacionados con el barrio
          de Oaxaca en Teotihuacan. In *Interacción cultural en México central*, edited by

Evelyn Rattray, Jaime Litvak King, and Clara Díaz, pp. 99–106. Universidad Nacional Autónoma de México, Mexico, D.F.

Curtin, Philip

1984   *Cross-Cultural Trade in World History.* Cambridge University Press, Cambridge.

Daneels, Annick

2002   Presencia de Teotihuacan en el centro y Sur de Veracruz. In *Ideología y política a través de materiales, imágenes y símbolos: Memoria de la Primera Mesa Redonda de Teotihuacan,* edited by María Elena Ruiz Gallut, pp. 655–683. Instituto Nacional de Antropología e Historia, Mexico, D.F.

Díaz, Clara

1980   *Chingú, un sitio Clásico del área de Tula, Hgo.* Instituto Nacional de Antropología e Historia, Mexico, D.F.

1981   Chingú. In *Interacción cultural en México central,* edited by Evelyn Rattray, Jaime Litvak King, and Clara Díaz, pp. 112–120. Universidad Nacional Autónoma de México, Mexico, D.F.

Dolphin, Alexis

2000   A Comparison of Two Postclassic Communities Using Enamel Hypoplastic Indicators of Juvenile Health: Marco Gonzalez and San Pedro. Master's thesis, University of Western Ontario, London.

Fazzalari, N.L., A.J. Moore, S. Byers, and R.W. Byard

1997   Quantitative Analysis of Trabecular Morphogenesis in the Human Costochondral Junction During the Postnatal Period in Normal Subjects. *Anatomical Records* 248:1–12.

Gamboa, Luis

1995   Proyecto San Juan Teotihuacan: Drenaje sanitario. Report to the Instituto Nacional de Antropología e Historia, Mexico, D.F.

Gibbs, Kevin

2001   Time and Ethnicity in the Oaxaca Barrio, Teotihuacan: The TL6 Ceramics. Master's thesis, University of Western Ontario, London.

Gómez, Sergio

1998   Nuevos datos sobre la relación de Teotihuacan y el occidente de México. In *Antropología e historia del occidente de México III:1461–1493.* XXIV Mesa Redonda of the Sociedad Mexicana de Antropología, Mexico, D.F.

2002   Presencia del Occidente de México en Teotihuacan. Aproximaciones a la política exterior del estado Teotihuacano. In *Ideología y política a través de materiales, imágenes y símbolos. Memoria de la Primera Mesa Redonda de Teotihuacan,* edited by María Elena Ruiz Gallut, pp. 563–625. Instituto Nacional de Antropología e Historia, Mexico, D.F.

Hernández, Carlos

1994   Rescate de una tumba Zapoteca en Tepeji del Rio. In *Simposium sobre arqueología en el estado de Hidalgo. Trabajos recientes, 1989*, edited by Enrique Fernández, pp. 125–142. Instituto Nacional de Antropología e Historia, Mexico, D.F.

Hirth, Kenneth, and William Swezey

1976   The Changing Nature of the Teotihuacan Classic: A Regional Perspective from Manzanilla, Puebla. In *Las fronteras de Mesoamérica*, XIV Mesa Redonda, pp. 12–23. Sociedad Mexicana de Antropología, Mexico, D.F.

Iceland, Harry

1989   Lithic Artifacts at the Teotihuacan Merchants' Barrio. Ph.D. dissertation, University of Texas at San Antonio, San Antonio.

Koch, P.L., D.C. Fisher, and D. Dettman

1989   Oxygen Isotope Variation in the Tusks of Extinct Proboscideans: A Measure of Season of Death and Seasonality. *Geology* 17:515–519.

Libby, W.F., R. Berger, J.F. Mead, G.V. Alexander, and J.F. Ross

1964   Replacement Rates for Human Tissue from Atmospheric Radiocarbon. *Science* 146:1170–1172.

Limon, Amie

1990   Interpretación funcional de estruturas arquitectónicas en Xocotitla, Teotihuacan, por medio de análisis de polen. In *Etnoarqueología, Primer coloquio Bosch-Gimpera*, edited by Yoko Sugiura and Mari Carmen Serra, pp. 305–328. Universidad Nacional Autónoma de México. Mexico, D.F.

Longinelli, Antonio

1984   Oxygen Isotopes in Mammal Bone Phosphate: A New Tool for Paleohydrological and Paleoclimatological Research? *Geochimica et Cosmochimica Acta* 48:385–390.

Luz, Boaz, Yehoshua Kolodny, and Michal Horowitz

1984   Fractionation of Oxygen Isotopes Between Mammalian Bone-Phosphate and Environmental Drinking Water. *Geochimica et Cosmochimica Acta* 48:1689–1693.

Manolagas, S.

2000   Birth and Death of Bone Cells: Basic Regulatory Mechanisms and Implications for the Pathogenesis and Treatment of Osteoporosis. *Endocrine Reviews* 21:115–137.

Mastache, Alba Guadalupe, Robert Cobean, and Dan Healan

2002   *Ancient Tollan: Tula and the Toltec Heartland*. University Press of Colorado, Boulder.

McArthur, J.M., and A. Herczeg

1990   Diagenetic Stability of the Isotopic Composition of Phosphate-Oxygen: Paleoenvironmental Implications. Phosphorite Research and Development, *Geological Society Special Publication* No. 52:119–124.

Millon, René
  1967   Urna de Monte Albán IIIA encontrada en Teotihuacan. *Instituto Nacional de Antropología e Historia Boletín* 29:42–44.
  1970   Teotihuacan: Completion of Map of Giant Ancient City in the Valley of Mexico. *Science* 170:1077–1082.
  1973   *Urbanization at Teotihuacan, Mexico, Vol. One: The Teotihuacan Map, Part 1: Text.* University of Texas Press, Austin.
  1976   Social Relations in Ancient Teotihuacan. In *The Valley of Mexico: Studies in Pre-Hispanic Ecology and Society,* edited by Eric Wolf, pp. 205–248. University of New Mexico Press, Albuquerque.
  1981   Teotihuacan: City, State, and Civilization. In *Supplement to the Handbook of Middle American Indians, Volume 1: Archaeology,* edited by J. Sabloff, pp.198–243. University of Texas Press, Austin.

Millon, René, Bruce Drewitt, and George L. Cowgill
  1973   *Urbanization at Teotihuacan, Mexico, Vol. 1: The Teotihuacan Map, Part 2: Maps.* University of Texas Press, Austin.

Noyola, Andrés
  1993   Unidades habitacionales prehispánicas excavadas en el estado de Puebla. *Notas Mesoamericanas* 14:19–36.

Ortega, Verónica, and Teresa Palomares
  2003   Nuevas evidencias sobre el barrio Oaxaqueño de Teotihuacan. *Arqueología Mexicana* 61:6.

Paddock, John
  1983   The Oaxaca Barrio at Teotihuacán. In *The Cloud People: Divergent Evolution of the Zapotec and Mixtec Civilizations,* edited by Kent Flannery and Joyce Marcus, pp. 170–175. Academic Press, New York.

Padró, Johanna, and Linda Manzanilla
  2004   Attire Manufacture at Teotihuacan: a Possible Tailor's Shop at Teopancazco. Paper presented at the 69th Annual Meeting, Society for American Archaeology, Montreal.

Parfitt, A.M.
  1983   The Physiologic and Clinical Significance of Bone Histomorphometric Data. In *Bone Histomorphometry: Techniques and Interpretation,* edited by R.R. Recker, pp. 143–223. CRC Press, Boca Raton.

Parsons, Elsie
  1936   *Mitla, Town of the Souls, and other Zapoteco Speaking Pueblos of Oaxaca, Mexico.* University of Chicago Press, Chicago.

Parsons, Jeffrey R.
  1968   Teotihuacan, Mexico, and its Impact on Regional Demography. *Science* 162:872–877.
  1974   The Development of a Prehistoric Complex Society: a Regional Perspective

from the Valley of Mexico. *Journal of Field Archaeology* 1:81–108.

Plunket, Patricia, and Gabriela Uruñuela

1998   Cholula y Teotihuacan: Una consideración del occidente de Puebla durante el Clásico. In *Rutas de intercambio en Mesoamérica: III Coloquio Pedro Bosch Gimpera*, edited by Evelyn Rattray, pp. 101–114. Universidad Nacional Autónoma de México, Mexico, D.F.

2002   Antecedentes culturales de los conjuntos de Tres Templos. In *Ideololgía y política a través de materiales, imágenes y símbolos: Memoria de la Primera Mesa Redonda de Teotihuacan*, edited by María Elena Ruiz Gallut, pp. 529–546. Instituto Nacional de Antropología e Historia, Mexico, D.F.

Price, T. Douglas, Linda Manzanilla, and William D. Middleton

2000   Immigration and the Ancient City of Teotihuacan in Mexico: A Study Using Strontium Isotope Ratios in Human Bone and Teeth. *Journal of Archaeological Science* 27:903–913.

Quade, Jay, Thure E. Cerling, John C. Barry, Michele E. Morgan, David R. Pilbeam, Allan R. Chivas, Julia A. Lee-Thorp, and Nikolaas J. van der Merwe

1992   A 16-Ma Record of Paleodiet Using Carbon and Oxygen Isotopes in Fossil Teeth from Pakistan. *Chemical Geology* 94:183–192.

Quintanilla, Patricia

1982   Estructura 69. In *Memoria del proyecto arqueológico Teotihuacan 80 82*, edited by Rubén Cabrera, Ignacio Rodríguez, and Noel Morelos, pp. 355–360 Colección Científica 132. Instituto Nacional de Antropología e Historia, Mexico, D.F.

1993   Superposición de estructuras habitacionales en San Juan Teotihuacan. Thesis, Escuela Nacional de Antropología e Historia, Mexico, D.F.

Rattray, Evelyn

1987   Los Barrios Foráneos de Teotihuacan. In *Teotihuacan: Nuevos Datos, Nuevas Síntesis, Nuevos Problemas*, edited by Emily McClung de Tapia and Evelyn Rattray, pp. 243–273. Universidad Nacional Autónoma de México, Mexico, D.F.

1988   Nuevas interpretaciones en torno al barrio de los comerciantes. *Anales de Antropología* XXV:165–180.

1989   El Barrio de los comerciantes y el conjunto Tlamimilolpa: Un estudio comparativo. *Arqueología* 5:105–129

1990   The Identification of Ethnic Affiliation at the Merchant's Barrio, Teotihuacan. In *Etnoarqueología: Coloquio Bosch-Gimpera*, edited by Y. Sugiura and Mari Carmen Serra Puche, pp. 113–138. Universidad Nacional Autónoma de México, Mexico, D.F.

1992   *The Teotihuacan Burials and Offerings: A Commentary and Inventory*. Publications in Anthropology 42. Vanderbilt University, Nashville.

1993   *The Oaxaca Barrio at Teotihuacan*. Monografías Mesoamericanas 1. Universidad de las Américas-Puebla, Cholula.

2001   *Teotihuacan: Cerámica, cronología y tendencias culturales.* Instituto Nacional de Antropología e Historia, Mexico, D.F.

Rattray, Evelyn C., and Magalí Civera

1999   Los entierros del Barrio de los Comerciantes. In *Prácticas funerarias en la Ciudad de los Dioses: Los enterramientos humanos de la antigua Teotihuacan*, edited by Linda Manzanilla and Carlos Serrano, pp. 149–172. Universidad Nacional Autónoma de México, Mexico, D.F.

Reinhard, E., T. de Torres, and J.R. O'Neil

1996 $^{18}O/^{16}O$ Ratios of Cave Bear Tooth Enamel: A Record of Climate Variability during the Pleistocene. *Palaeogeography, Palaeoclimatology, Palaeoecology* 126:45–59.

Rodríguez, Ignacio

1982   Frente 2. In *Memoria del Proyecto Arqueológico Teotihuacan 80-82*, edited by Rubén Cabrera, Ignacio Rodríguez, and Noel Morelos, pp. 55–73. Insituto Nacional de Antropología e Historia, Mexico, D.F.

Romero, Javier

1983   Tumbas y los entierros prehispánicos de Oaxaca. *Anales de antropología* 20:91–113.

Santley, Robert

1989   Obsidian Working, Long-Distance Exchange, and the Teotihuacan Presence on the South Gulf Coast. In *Mesoamerica after the Decline of Teotihuacan, AD 700–900*, edited by Richard Diehl and Janet Berlo, pp. 131–151. Dumbarton Oaks Research Library and Collection, Washington, D.C.

1994   The Economy of Ancient Matacapan. *Ancient Mesoamerica* 5:243–266.

Santley, Robert, Clare Yarborough, and Barbara Hall

1987   Enclaves, Ethnicity, and the Archaeological Record at Matacapan. In *Ethnicity and Culture*, edited by R. Auger, M. Glass, S. MacEachern and P. McCartney, pp. 85–100. University of Calgary Archaeological Association, Calgary.

Séjourné, Laurette

1966   *Arquitectura y pintura en Teotihuacan.* Siglo XXI Editores, Mexico, D.F.

Sempowski, Martha

1994   Mortuary Practices at Teotihuacan. In *Mortuary Practices and Skeletal Remains at Teotihuacan*, edited by Martha Sempowski and Michael W. Spence, pp. 1–311. Urbanization at Teotihuacan, Mexico, Volume 3, edited by René Millon. University of Utah Press, Salt Lake City.

Song, Rhan Ju

1997   Developmental Defects of Enamel in the Maya of Altun Ha, Belize: Implications for Ancient Maya Childhood Health. Unpublished Master's thesis, Department of Anthropology, Trent University, Peterborough, Ontario.

Spence, Michael W.

1976   Human Skeletal Material from the Oaxaca Barrio in Teotihuacan, Mexico.

In *Archaeological Frontiers: Papers on New World High Cultures in Honor of J. Charles Kelley*, edited by Robert Pickering, pp. 129–148 University Museum Research Records 4. Southern Illinois University, Carbondale.

1989   Excavaciones recientes en Tlailotlacan, el barrio Oaxaqueño de Teotihuacan. *Arqueología* 5:81–104.

1990   Excavaciones en Tlailotlacan, Teotihuacan. Segunda temporada. *Consejo de arqueología boletín* 1989:128–130.

1992   Tlailotlacan, a Zapotec Enclave in Teotihuacan. In *Art, Ideology, and the City of Teotihuacan*, edited by Janet Berlo, pp. 59–88. Dumbarton Oaks Research Library and Collection, Washington, D.C.

1994   Human Skeletal Material from Teotihuacan. In *Mortuary Practices and Skeletal Remains at Teotihuacan*, edited by Martha Sempowski and Michael W. Spence, pp. 312–427. Urbanization at Teotihuacan, Mexico, Vol. 3, edited by René Millon. University of Utah Press, Salt Lake City.

1996   A Comparative Analysis of Ethnic Enclaves. In *Arqueología Mesoamericana: Homenaje a William T. Sanders*, edited by Alba Guadalupe Mastache, Jeffrey Parsons, Robert Santley, and Mari Carmen Serra Puche, pp. 333–353. Universidad Nacional Autónoma de México, Mexico, D.F.

1998   La cronología de radiocarbono de Tlailotlacan. In *Los ritmos de cambio en Teotihuacán: Reflexiones y discusiones de su cronología*, edited by Rubén Cabrera and Rosa Brambila, pp. 283–297. Colección Científica 366. Instituto Nacional de Antropología e Historia, Mexico, D.F.

2002   Domestic Ritual in Tlailotlacan, Teotihuacan. In *Domestic Ritual in Ancient Mesoamerica*, edited by Patricia Plunket, pp. 53–66. Monograph 46, Cotsen Institute of Archaeology University of California, Los Angeles.

2005   A Zapotec Diaspora Network in Classic-Period Central Mexico. In *The Archaeology of Colonial Encounters*, edited by Gil Stein, pp. 173–205. School of American Research, Santa Fe, New Mexico.

Spence, Michael W., and Luis Gamboa

1998   Mortuary Practices and Social Adaptation in the Tlailotlacan Enclave. In *Prácticas funerarias en la Ciudad de los Dioses: Los enterramientos humanos de la antigua Teotihuacan*, edited by Linda Manzanilla and Carlos Serrano, pp. 173–201. Universidad Nacional Autónoma de México, Mexico, D.F.

Spence, Michael W., Christine D. White, Fred J. Longstaffe, Evelyn C. Rattray, and Kim R. Law

2004   Un análisis de las proporciones de los isótopos del oxígeno en los Entierros del barrio de los comerciantes. In *La costa del golfo en tiempos Teotihuacanos: Propuestas y perspectivas*, edited by María Elena Ruiz Gallut and Arturo Pascual Soto, pp. 469–492. Instituto Nacional de Antropología e Historia, Mexico, D.F.

Stark, Barbara, Lynette Heller, and Michael Ohnersorgen
  1999   People with Cloth: Mesoamerican Economic Change from the Perspective
          of Cotton in South-Central Veracruz. *Latin American Antiquity* 9:7–36.
Stein, Gil
  2005   The Political Economy of Mesopotamian Colonial Encounters. In *The
          Archaeology of Colonial Encounters*, edited by Gil Stein, pp. 143–171. School of
          American Research, Santa Fe, New Mexico.
Stenhouse, M.J., and M.S. Baxter
  1978   The Uptake of Bomb ^{14}C in Humans. In *Radiocarbon Dating*, edited by R.
          Berger and H. Suess, pp. 324–341. University of California Press, Berkeley.
Storey, Rebecca
  1991   Residential Compound Organization and the Evolution of the Teotihuacan
          State. *Ancient Mesoamerica* 2:107–118.
  1992   *Life and Death in the Ancient City of Teotihuacan*. University of Alabama Press,
          Tuscaloosa.
Stresser-Peán, Guy
  1997   *San Antonio Nogalar*. Mission Archéologique et Ethnologique Française au
          Mexique, Mexico.
Veenhof, Klaas
  1995   Kanesh: an Assyrian Colony in Anatolia. In *Civilizations of the Ancient Near
          East*, edited by Jack Sasson, pp. 859–871. Simon and Schuster MacMillan,
          New York.
White, Christine D.
  1994   Dietary Dental Pathology and Cultural Change in the Maya. In *Strength in
          Diversity: A Reader in Physical Anthropology*, edited by Ann Herring and Leslie
          Chan, pp. 279–302. Canadian Scholars' Press, Toronto.
White, Christine D., Fred J. Longstaffe, and Kimberley R. Law
  2001   Revisiting the Teotihuacan Connection at Altun Ha: Oxygen Isotope Analysis
          of Tomb F-8/1. *Ancient Mesoamerica* 12:65–72.
White, Christine D., Fred J. Longstaffe, and Kimberley R. Law
  2004c   Exploring the Effects of Environment, Physiology and Diet on Oxygen
          Isotope Ratios in Ancient Nubian Bones and Teeth. *Journal of Archaeological
          Science* 31:223–250
White, Christine D., Fred J. Longstaffe, Michael W. Spence, and Kimberley R. Law
  2000a   Teotihuacan State Representation at Kaminaljuyú: Evidence from Oxygen
          Isotopes. *Journal of Anthropological Research* 56:535–558.
White, Christine D., Michael W. Spence, and Fred J. Longstaffe
  2000b   The Identification of Foreigners in Mortuary Contexts using Oxygen-Isotope
          Ratios: Some Mesoamerican Examples. Paper presented at the 69th Annual
          Meeting, American Association of Physical Anthropologists, San Antonio.

White, Christine D., Michael W. Spence, Fred J. Longstaffe, and Kimberley Law
  2004b Demography and Ethnic Continuity in the Tlailotlacan Enclave of Teotihuacan: The Evidence from Stable Oxygen Isotopes. *Journal of Anthropological Archaeology* 23:385–403.

White, Christine D., Michael W. Spence, Fred J. Longstaffe, Hilary Le-Q. Stuart-Williams, and Kimberley R. Law
  2002 Geographic Identities of the Sacrificial Victims from the Feathered Serpent Pyramid, Teotihuacan: Implications for the Nature of State Power. *Latin American Antiquity* 13:217–236.

White, Christine D., Michael W. Spence, Hilary Le Q. Stuart-Williams, and Henry P. Schwarcz
  1998 Oxygen Isotopes and the Identification of Geographical Origins: The Valley of Oaxaca versus the Valley of Mexico. *Journal of Archaeological Science* 25:643–655

White, Christine D., Rebecca Storey, Michael W. Spence, and Fred J. Longstaffe
  2004a Immigration, Assimilation and Status in the Ancient City of Teotihuacan: Isotopic Evidence from Tlajinga 33. *Latin American Antiquity* 15:176–198.

Widmer, Randolph
  1987 The Evolution of Form and Function in a Teotihuacan Apartment Compound. In *Teotihuacan: Nuevos datos, nuevas síntesis, nuevos problemas*, edited by Emily McClung de Tapia and Evelyn Rattray, pp. 317–368. Universidad Nacional Autónoma de México, Mexico, D.F.
  1991 Lapidary Craft Specialization at Teotihuacan: Implications for Community Structure at 33:S3W1 and Economic Organization in the City. *Ancient Mesoamerica* 2:131–147.

Williams, Jocelyn
  2000 The People Who Ate the Sea: a Stable Isotopic Analysis of Diet at Marco Gonzalez and San Pedro, Belize. Master's thesis, Department of Anthropology, The University of Western Ontario, London.

Williams, Jocelyn, Christine White, and Fred Longstaffe
  2003 Trophic Level and Macronutrient Shift Effects Associated with the Weaning Process in the Maya Postclassic. Unpublished manuscript in the hands of the authors.

Winter, Marcus
  1986 Unidades Habitacionales Prehispánicas en Oaxaca. In *Unidades habitacionales Mesoamericanas y sus areas de actividad*, edited by Linda Manzanilla, pp. 325–374. Universidad Nacional Autónoma de México, Mexico, D.F.
  1998 Monte Alban and Teotihuacan. In *Rutas de intercambio en Mesoamérica: III Coloquio Pedro Bosch Gimpera*, edited by Evelyn Rattray, pp. 153–184. Universidad Nacional Autónoma de México, Mexico, D.F.

Winter, Marcus, Cira Martínez López, and Alicia Herrera Muzgo
2002   Monte Albán y Teotihuacan: Política y ideología. In *Ideololgía y política a través de materiales, imágenes y símbolos: Memoria de la Primera Mesa Redonda de Teotihuacan*, edited by María Elena Ruiz Gallut, pp. 627–644. Instituto Nacional de Antropología e Historia, Mexico, D.F.

Winter, Marcus, Círa Martínez López, and Damon Peeler
1998   Monte Albán y Teotihuacán: Cronología y interpretaciones. In *Los ritmos de cambio en Teotihuacán: Reflexiones y discusiones de su cronología*, edited by Rubén Cabrera and Rosa Brambila, pp. 461–475. Colección Científica 366. Instituto Nacional de Antropología e Historia, Mexico, D.F.

Wright, Lori E., and Henry P. Schwarcz
1998   Stable Carbon and Oxygen Isotopes in Human Tooth Enamel: Identifying Breastfeeding and Weaning in Prehistory. *American Journal of Physical Anthropology* 106:1–18.

Yarborough, Clare
1992   Teotihuacan and the Gulf Coast: Ceramic Evidence for Contact and International Relationships. Ph.D. dissertation, University of Arizona, Tucson.

MEN, WOMEN, AND MAGUEY:

THE HOUSEHOLD DIVISION OF LABOR AMONG AZTEC FARMERS

SUSAN TOBY EVANS

The Pennsylvania State University

In the Basin of Mexico during the Late Postclassic period (AD 1430–1520), settlement on the sloping piedmont zone was substantial, and many of these communities specialized in maguey farming. Maguey farmers terraced the slopes and planted maguey as an embankment crop, while other staples such as maize were grown on the level terraces, and there the farmers built their houses, as well. Despite somewhat harsh conditions—many of these areas lacked sources of potable water—these families lived well. Maguey provided a significant proportion of their caloric needs, earning its modern nickname of *la vaca verde* (Jeffrey Parsons, personal communication) by furnishing refreshing drink of high nutritional value. And, like that of the cow, the maguey's body also provided raw materials for artisanal purposes—its leaves gave fibers for baskets and woven fabrics.

Another contribution this versatile plant made to the lives of maguey farmers is less obvious: Maguey's cultivation and exploitation requirements set up a schedule of tasks that could best be accomplished by the cooperative efforts of the whole farming family. Many of the tasks could be done by any able-bodied adult, while others were more specifically the domain of men or women, or could use the more limited strength and skills of a family's children. The household cooperation required by maguey farming offers insights into the family farm in Aztec culture and into the nature of gender relations between the adults of the family. In this paper, these larger patterns are described and then compared to archaeological evidence from maguey-farming household remains from Cihuatecpan, a Late Postclassic village in the Teotihuacan Valley.

FARMERS AND ROBUST WOMEN: NAHUA GENDER AND ROLES

Gender relations during the Late Postclassic period in the Central Highlands of Mexico have been variously characterized as complementary or hierarchical.[1] This issue is difficult to resolve, because available evidence is limited and can be selectively mustered to argue either perspective. Clearly, Nahua political structures were seldom ruled by women, but women—even commoner women—held positions of authority, owned property, enjoyed legal rights, and conducted significant entrepreneurial activity. Women were by no means sequestered or forbidden from partaking in public activities, including speaking on their own behalf in legal cases (see the Codex Mendoza 69R for an illustration) and in the arbitration of domestic problems (Nuttall 1926:72–73).

In the larger realm of cross-cultural comparison, such activities on the part of commoner women are not present in those cultures wherein a man's rights always supercede those of a woman. While an adequate reconstruction of gender relations in Nahua society would necessarily include features that are present in both hierarchical *and* complementary relationships, commoner women seemed not to have led significantly more constrained lives than did their husbands and brothers, and this high level of relative independence would indicate complementary relations.

Ethnohistorical sources of Aztec society provide evidence of complementarity, and ethnographic studies of gender relations within small-hold farming families in other cultures provide a model of how complementarity operates in that setting.[2] Thus, we can examine the household division of labor within and among Aztec-period maguey-farming families in order to understand the extent to which women and men were partners in the complex, full-time work of maguey farming.

In these farming households, the skills of each gender were critical to the household's economic success. Maguey (*Agave* spp.) provided its farmers not just nourishment, but shelter, clothing, and medicine. Its sap was a potable liquid where clean water was scarce; its roots held the soil so that other plants could grow. Its products were essential to daily life, and entered the larger economic world as tribute and trade items. The tasks involved in exploiting this plant took place all year and were most effectively carried out within the framework of a gender-based division of labor in a joint-family, monogamous household.

Ethnohistorical descriptions of sixteenth-century Nahua mores, social organization, and job specialization reveal single standards of behavior for commoner men and women, but there were different kinds of productive activities appropriate to each gender. Maguey-farming tasks have traditionally included some that were largely gender-specific and many that were shared, and observations of maguey farmers today provide insight into how social and economic roles interacted in the past. The houses and tools of Aztec period maguey-farming households in the Teotihuacan Valley substantiate the gender-based division of labor and its association with maguey farming.

How maguey-farming households functioned and allotted tasks along gender lines calls forth the larger perspective on appropriate male and female behavior, because in any culture, these mores influence acquisition of skills, as do an individual's potential strength and dexterity. Sixteenth-century Mexican sources are consistent in portraying ideal commoner citizens of both sexes as industrious, hard working, modest, and sober. Book 10 (The People) of the Florentine Codex describes ideal individuals (and their "bad" counterparts) of many statuses and occupations. Sahagún's informants described both "the farmer" (Sahagún 1961:41) and the "robust woman" (Sahagún 1961:51) in identical terms: "strong, rugged, energetic, wiry"[3] and both are also industrious and long suffering. Descriptions of stalwart members of society (and their sin-mired antitheses) reveal the importance of conformity and thrift, and the social ills that ensue when immoderation, slovenliness, and sloth rule the personality.[4] The moral lessons of the Florentine Codex and the Codex Mendoza show a broad single standard of appropriate attitudes and bearing for both men and women of the Aztec commoner class.

In the work lives of adults, however, there is a more marked distinction along gender lines.[5] The textile arts are clearly the domain of women of all classes, even noblewomen (Anawalt 1981:11). Rulers admonished their daughters to prepare themselves for useful lives: "What wilt thou seize upon as thy womanly labors? ... the spindle whorl, the weaving stick" (Sahagún 1969:95), because other work, like trading in the marketplace, lacked the requisite dignity for noblewomen. Midwives greeted all newborn baby girls with "the equipment of women, the little reed basket, the spinning whorl, the batten." (1969:205, Illustration 30). The same spinning implements (Figure 8-1) are shown in Folio 57R of the Codex Mendoza (1992:3:121), which depicts the naming ceremony of infants. The associated gloss notes that "if the infant was a girl, the symbol they gave her ... was a distaff with its spindle and its basket ... which were the things she would use when she grew up." (Berdan and Anawalt 1992:4:118). Subsequent pages (Folios 58R and 59R) of the Codex Mendoza depict girls of ages four, five, and six becoming familiar with the handling of spindle and distaff and, at age 14, being able to weave (Figure 8-2).

The Florentine Codex and the Codex Mendoza, compiled from accounts by urban informants, reflect Tenochtitlan's cosmopolitan milieu. Sahagún's Primeros Memoriales was compiled in Tepeapulco, a country town on the northeastern edge of the Basin of Mexico in a region famous for maguey cultivation. It described the common woman's work equipment as "stone used for

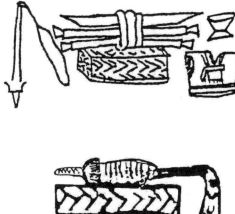

Figure 8-1. Spinning equipment was included in the naming ceremony for infant girls.
Top: In the Florentine Codex: A bundle of weaving battens lies atop a work basket. To the left is the distaff loaded with its spindle whorl (incompletely drawn by the Codex artist) and above that, spun thread; unspun fibers spill off to the right.
Bottom: Codex Mendoza: the distaff, filled with spun thread, lies atop the workbasket, and unspun fibers spill off to the right. The spindle whorl shown here has a hemispherical shape.

age 4

age 5

age 6

age 14

Figure 8-2. Aztec girls being taught spinning and weaving. At age 14, the daughter has mastered the whole range of basic textile-production techniques. She will probably wed before her sixteenth birthday, and good spinning and weaving skills will greatly enhance her marriageability. (Illustrations after Codex Mendoza, Folio 58R and 60R.)

scraping the maguey plant. Her palmleaf basket. Batten for maguey threads. A stout cane is her [instrument to work the maguey threads]. Her skeins, her heddles are thick. Board on which maguey leaves are prepared for combing and cleaning fibers. ... Her jar of ground corn preparation for dressing textiles."[6]

Thus virtually all women were spinners and weavers who learned their skills at home and continued to work in that context, and these circumstances define textile skills as "general" rather "restricted" in the analytical terms of economic specialization,[7] which are based on setting and intensity of production, the overall requirements for products, the availability of raw materials, and range of circulation. Textile production typically comes to be regarded as an institutionalized economic specialization when it takes place in workshops (for example, at Huánaco Pampa in Peru [Morris 1974:55]), as may have occurred in the palaces of Aztec cities (Monzón 1983, citing Motolinía's Historia).

Yet, in analyzing the role of specialization in society, we should not ignore a basic distinction between skills that are "general" because any able-bodied adult can readily master them, and skills that have been acquired in the "general" setting of home and family, but through long and rigorous "specialized" training (as the Codex Mendoza illustrates for spinning and weaving). It would be impossible for another adult untrained in spinning and weaving (by definition, in Aztec society, a man) to produce thread and fabric acceptable for tribute or exchange. However, as Brumfiel (1991:226) noted, "the ethnohistoric record conspires with Western culture to encourage us to treat women's production as a nondynamic element in Aztec history."

Men were also trained from childhood toward mastery of certain skills (Calnek 1992). All young men trained for, and then served in, the army, a duty owed to the state, but few men were full-time professional soldiers. Men raised in rural farming families would have learned, from childhood, the routine of farming tasks by helping their parents (Figure 8-3). The Florentine Codex and Codex Mendoza show commoner men engaged in woodworking and building construction, and Codex Mendoza also shows artisan fathers demonstrating techniques to their sons. In maguey-farming families, many tasks no doubt were shared by men and women, and others would have fallen into the regular daily routines of one group or the other.

MAGUEY-FARMING HOUSEHOLDS: SOCIAL ORGANIZATION

The gender-based division of labor within the household was conditioned by patterns of land holding, kin reckoning, and mate choice, as well as by training in gender-related skills and tasks. Many maguey-farming households had particular use-rights to their house plots and farm lots, as part of village-wide corporate holdings, the *calpullis* (Carrasco 1971). Other

Figure 8-3. From The Florentine Codex, Earthly Things, comes this summary of maguey tending: "I plant ... transplant ... set out the maguey ... sow the maguey ... press the maguey in. The maguey takes hold, takes root, buds, sets a node, grows, sends out fresh leaves, enlarges, matures, forms a stalk. I break up ... the maguey. I pierce the center. I pierce the stalk. I clean the surface. I scrape it. I remove the maguey syrup ... I heat the maguey syrup. I make wine. I scrape the maguey leaf. I dress the maguey leaf to extract the fiber." (1963:217)

farming communities included tenant farmers working land held by nobles or attached to civic or religious offices.

All commoners followed the same general flexible rules of social structure, reckoning descent bilaterally and avoiding only nuclear family members when choosing marriage partners. These practices, plus the inertia of propinquity, probably resulted in community endogamy. Postmarital residence was either neolocal or bilocal (see Carrasco 1971 for summary treatment of Aztec social structure).

Household Organization

Our best information on household organization comes from the several decades right after the Spanish Conquest, when Nahua cultural patterns were still in force, but before the devastating demographic effects of disease and overwork had greatly reduced the population. Family size and household size differ, but both were fairly small: The nuclear family in the Texcoco region of the Basin Mexico averaged 4 to 4.3 people (Harvey 1985; Offner 1983, 1984; Williams 1984; Williams and Harvey 1988). Household size varied more, according to regional and community averages from various parts of Mesoamerica (Table 8-1), which range from 4.8 persons/household in the Mixteca Alta to 8.2 in Molotla (the last two entries on the table, from Mexico City, are ranges for which no average was given). Basin of Mexico rural examples are 5.3 and 6.0 persons per household.

If known census data can be accurately generalized, then households were comprised of one or two nuclear families. Over half the households in the Texcoco region censuses were joint, extended family households, which tended to link the nuclear families of related men (such as father and sons, or brothers). Another one-third of households were nuclear families, and the remaining few households were polygynous.[8] For the average household, the

Table 8-1.
Commoner Household Size in Early Colonial Mesoamerica

Household Size	Community	Region	Source
4.8	average of 7 communities	Mixteca Alta	Spores 1984:104
5.2	Tlacatecpan, Tepoztlan (calpulli)	Valley of Morelos	Carrasco 1964
5.3	Cuauhtepoztla, Tepetlaoztoc (calpulli)	Texcoco region, Basin of Mexico	Harvey 1985
5.4	various	Patzcuaro	Cook and Borah 1971:128
6.0	San Geronimo, Tepetlaoztoc (tenant–farmer)	Texcoco region, Basin of Mexico	Offner 1984:138
6.2	Tlacatecpan, Tepoztlan (tenant–farmer)	Valley of Morelos	Carrasco 1971:368–369
8.2	Molotla, Yautepec (tenant–farmer)	Valley of Morelos	Carrasco 1972, 1976
10–15*	Mexico City, chinampa zone (tenant–farmer)	Basin of Mexico	Calnek 1972:111
2–8*	Mexico City	Basin of Mexico	Kellogg 1988:489

*No average given.

gender ratio would be roughly equal and each couple would have relatives living within the community.

.Flexible in size and form, the maguey-farming household inevitably varied over time, but it had to maintain a general equality in the sex ratio of adults, given the many steps of maguey processing and their strong gender associations. If the sex ratio were to become unbalanced, several fallback strategies could be used. For short-term needs, neighbors (who might also be family members) could be recruited to help, but they could not neglect their own duties for long. If basic extractive tasks could continue, then the extracted materials could be traded in a relatively unprocessed state: maguey leaves rather than fibers, fibers rather than thread, cord, etc., thread rather than woven fabric, raw sap rather than processed syrup or sugar.

Eventually, however, a labor imbalance or shortage would necessitate reorganization of the household, either by recruiting new permanent members, or joining other established households and turning the house and its adjacent land back to the corporate village administration for redistribution to another family. These changes were established features of the cycle of household life for Nahua families. The village's landholding organization maintained the social and economic functions of the household, promoting a moral economy at the local level, as would be expected, given the subsistence agricultural base (see Cheal 1989:18).

Tribute, Commodities, and the Farming Village

Maguey products were required as tributes throughout the central highlands of Mexico. Each maguey-farming household owed tributes to civil and religious offices within the village, the city-state, and the major capitals. Extant community and regional tribute summaries[9] provide a general idea of these obligations, which include maguey items (woven textiles and maguey leaves for firewood [Paso y Troncoso 1979:213, 221, 233–234]), and also cotton textiles, of interest in this study because they were an essential part of the household economy and were manufactured by women, using nonlocal raw materials. Raw cotton was available in the marketplace, or possibly rulers procured the cotton for their subjects to weave (Brumfiel 1991:229). In the Teotihuacan Valley, the amount of tribute in textiles owed by each household may have been quite low—perhaps less than one length of woven fabric each year.[10] Motecuzoma I's dictum that "common people will not be allowed to wear cotton clothing, under pain of death" (Durán 1964:131) apparently did not forbid commoners the ownership of cotton textiles, which, as an accepted medium of exchange, would have been a valued commodity and would have provided a means of increasing the household's wealth by making (that is, weaving) money.

MAGUEY-FARMING DIVISION OF LABOR

Maguey farming was widely practiced in the Aztec period, but only recently has its importance been appreciated. An extensive study by Jeffrey and Mary Parsons (1990) combined original ethnographic research into sap and fiber processing in the central highlands of Mexico with an exhaustive literature review summarizing findings on agricultural productivity, nutritional value, ethnohistorical reports, and archaeological evidence. The brief outline of maguey processing summarized below is drawn from their study and will provide an understanding of the tasks shared within the Aztec-period household.

The tasks of maguey farming include particular skills and general knowledge, with certain tasks being habitually performed by some people and most being accomplished, at times, by virtually any able-bodied household member. The biological imperative of childbearing and nursing, usually combined with the rearing of other children, would seem to predispose women to perform tasks close to home, but in fact, countless ethnographically known cases document women farmers working in the fields and carrying very heavy loads. Common women in Nahua culture were valued for energy and willingness to work, and were not confined by any traditions of *purdah*. Yet illustrations in sources such as the Florentine Codex, and descriptions that include gender attribution, cite men as commonly working in the fields, women working at home, and tasks being taught to children by their same-sex parents. With all due respect to common situations of shared labor, we must grant, as Conkey argued regarding the Magdalenian of Europe, "some particular divisions of labor to account for the archaeological materials" (1991:78).

Maguey's growth pattern clarifies the division of labor. Unlike most other plant crops, maguey is cultivated and harvested regularly throughout the year, and requires the coordinated efforts of several adults to tend the plants and process their products. There are four general domains of tasks: cultivation, sap production, fiber production, and distribution of products.

1) Cultivation: As the young plant grows to maturity, some leaves will be pruned and used. Men probably tended the maturing plants in the course of other farming duties such as cultivating grain crops interplanted among maguey. After 8 to 12 years of growth, a plant's stem bud begins to emerge and is removed to provoke sap production.

2) Sap processing: The plant's interior cavity is scraped and drained of sap twice daily, each time producing over a liter of sap, which is carried back to the house. A household with 150 to 200 plants would have 8 to 10 (about 5%) in production at any time, so the total weight of the sap plus the traditional ceramic carrying jar might be 12 to 15 kg. Farmers might collect sap as they

performed other tasks in the fields, or make special collection rounds, but every day, there would be sap to gather and transport.

Production of sap products took place at the house, with tasks shared among household members. Fresh sap (*aguamiel*) required no processing and was drunk within a day; this may have been the use of most of the sap collected (Evans 1992:110–111). Further processing was required for production of sugar or syrup for long-term storage or sale, or of fermented *pulque* for use or sale. *Pulque* is extremely short lived and requires careful tending as it ferments, rapid delivery to users if it is to be distributed, and meticulous care of fermentation equipment, lest future batches be spoiled by impurities.

3) Fiber processing: As leaves were harvested, their fibers were extracted and processed. Men tending the plants probably harvested leaves situationally, depending on a plant's maturity, the need to keep the naturally ungainly plants from hindering work in the fields, and the needs of the fiber-processing artisans of the household. Most leaves were harvested after sap extraction was completed. To extract fiber, leaves were steamed in a pit and then scraped, which may have taken place in the fields, in a special workshop, or in an activity area adjacent to the house. Hauling leaves and extracted fiber from place to place could be done by any able-bodied household member recruited for the task, but may often have been done by men as they returned from their other field tasks. Carding fibers may well have been shared work, along with twisting fibers into cords and ropes. Spinning and weaving were done by women, usually in the home, but spinning was also portable handwork, the reflexive activity of the model housewife wherever her other duties took her.

4) Distribution: Maguey products were used by the household (and probably also situationally shared or exchanged with neighbors), they were given as tributes, and they were exchanged in the marketplace. Tribute contributions would have been delivered to the headman's house (the *tecpan*) by the household head. Ethnohistorical censuses from the Texcoco region indicate that women were sometimes heads of household for census and tribute purposes (Harvey 1985:287–288), even when their husbands were still alive, but that the great majority of household heads were men. Taking maguey products to the marketplace and exchanging them would have been done by men and women; Illustrations 116-132 in Book 10 of the Florentine Codex indicate that women sellers were common, and there are no intimations that marketplace exchange was not a respectable occupation for a commoner woman.

In summary, adults in maguey-farming households would have been familiar with a range of jobs and could have provided general help when necessary. Likewise, adolescents would have been general helpers, being given greater responsibility when they showed skill and initiative. At the heart of the maguey-farming household was a balance of jobs and adult skills that suited the other responsibilities of members of each sex. The commitment of all adult members to maguey farming suggests that decision-making was shared, and this may have contributed to the long-term stability of these maguey-farming villages (as Wilk suggests for the Kekchi, 1989:43–44).

CIHUATECPAN, AN AZTEC PERIOD MAGUEY-FARMING VILLAGE

The village of Cihuatecpan was one of scores of Aztec-period maguey-farming settlements in the Teotihuacan Valley and other regions of the Central Highlands. Such communities blanketed the piedmont zones with tiers of farming terraces, dotted by houses of the farmers dispersed over their fields (Sanders, Parsons, and Santley 1979:166–168). At the time of European contact, half the population of the Teotihuacan Valley lived in settlements of this type (Evans 1980:155), but with postcontact demographic collapse and Colonial government policies of *congregación* of survivors into fewer communities, dispersed villages were largely abandoned. Their remains—fossil terraces, house mounds, artifacts—were relatively undisturbed until the 1970s and 1980s, when development using bulldozers effectively destroyed much of this part of the archaeological record (Parsons 1989:222–223). Fortunately, extensive survey and mapping operations in the 1960s by the Teotihuacan Valley Project (Sanders 1965) documented these dispersed sites, their layouts, and samples of artifacts. More detailed studies have been made of several surviving sites in the Otumba area (Charlton 1972), including the city-state capital of Otumba itself (Charlton and Nichols 1990; Nichols 1990), and of the nearby village of Cihuatecpan, about 5 km to its east (Evans 1988b).

Cihuatecpan had been relatively unscathed by recent agricultural intensification, and in 1984, eight of its 200 mounds were excavated,[11] revealing remains of six commoner houses, an elite residence, and a storehouse or workshop. Maguey-processing tools were prominent among the artifacts. Archaeological remains of commoner households support the assumption that they operated as cooperative productive units and generally performed the same range of tasks, while different patterns in the material culture record of the nonresidential building and the elite residence indicate other behavioral patterns.

Maguey farming at Cihuatecpan has already been the focus of an investigation of sap extraction and productivity (Evans 1990 and 1992), revealing that the villagers could have derived a significant proportion of their caloric needs from maguey sap. Moreover, they could have used fresh sap as their potable beverage during much of the year, when no pure water was available to them (1990:127). For Cihuatecpan and other dispersed villages in the semiarid central highlands, maguey was not just the versatile source of a host of products, but also the basic means of their survival.

Size and Layout of the Village

Cihuatecpan extended over an area of about 3 km²; the excavated structures were all on the more densely settled southwest slope (Figure 8-4). Variation in size and layout among the eight excavated structures is demonstrated in Figure 8-5 and Table 8-2. The plans of the buildings show considerable variety, but there are striking similarities. All commoner houses have some sort of entry

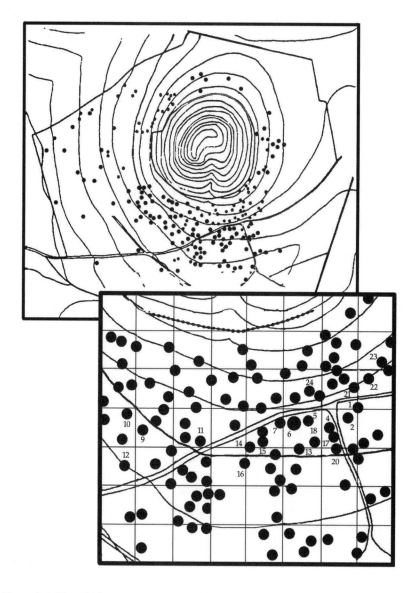

Figure 8-4. Plan of Cihuatecpan, with detail of densely settled south slope. (each square = one hectare). Excavated structures are numbers 1, 2, 4, 5, 6, 7, 9, and 10. Operation 3, to the right of structure 1, was the *jagüey* (pond).

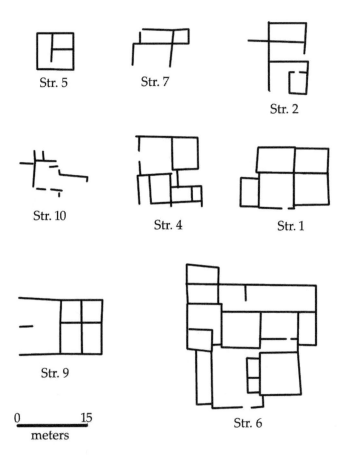

Figure 8-5. Plans of Cihuatecpan excavated structures. Top row: 5, 7, and 2. Middle row: 10, 4, and 1. Bottom row: 9 and 6.

courtyard, oriented toward the south or southwest and flanked by habitation and other rooms. The courtyard would have been unroofed, a workspace for various household activities. All houses have habitation rooms, where families slept, warmed their food, ate, and stored their belongings. The more elaborate houses had kitchens, passageways, storerooms, extra courtyards, and niches that may have served as shrines.

What were the households like? Commoner households probably consisted of single nuclear families or joint families (Evans 1989:435; 1992:183). The estimated number of residents (see Table 8-2) includes a fairly wide plus-or-minus range, reflecting the flexible nature of household arrangements

Table 8-2.
Cihuatecpan Structures and Households

Op. #	5	7	2	10	4	1	9	6
Function	workshop storage	house	house	house	house	house	house	house, administration
Exterior m x m	6.8 x 7.0	6.8 x 10.2	11.5 x 12.8	9.0 x 13.0	11.2 x 12.0	10.7 x 16.4	14.6 x 9.8	24.0 x 25.0
Size: sum of rooms	26.2 m3	41.8 m3	65.3 m3	<100m3	92.8 m3	108.7 m3	119.7 m3	363.1 m3
rank	*8*	*7*	*6*	*5*	*4*	*3*	*2*	*1*
#rooms / #room types	3 / ?	3 / 2	5+ / 3	3 / ?	8 / 4	5 / 3	6 / 2–3	21 / 6
# habitation rooms	2	3	2?	3	3	4		10
# inhabitants	6 + 4	9 + 6	6 + 4	9 + 6	9 + 6	12 + 8		28 + 12
house hold composition		nuclear	nuclear or joint	nuclear or joint	joint	joint	joint	polygyny

Table based on Evans 1989:435 and 1993:183.

as each underwent the changes typical of its normal life cycle. Structure 6, at some point, may have served as the headman's house, the *tecpan*, with its range of community-house functions (Evans 1991), its residents, the polygynous family of the headman, plus house servants. Cihuatecpan was probably a *calpulli* village with a noble headman, based on archaeological evidence interpreted with the help of the ethnohistorical studies cited above (Evans 1989, 1991, 1993).

Attribution of function to these buildings is largely based on their artifact assemblages and on architectural features such as building layout and the number, size, and functions of the rooms, but the locations of the buildings relative to each other can also indicate function. As Figure 8-4 shows, Structures 7 and 5 flank Structure 6. Structure 5's size and layout indicate that it may have been a workshop and/or storehouse associated with Structure 6. Structure 7 was probably a residence—small and poorly built. Perhaps its household was attached to the possible *tecpan*; and its residents, "*tecpanpouhque . . . (tecpan* people), who paid no tribute but served in the repair of the . . . *tecpan*" (Gibson 1964:259). The other residences (Structures 1, 2, 4, 9, and 10) are assumed to have housed farmer–artisan tribute-paying families.

As maguey farmers, members of these households worked together to harvest and process the crop. What architectural features or facilities, and what artifacts are identifiable as integral to sap or fiber processing? Parsons and

Parsons (1990:269–359) show that ethnographic and ethnohistorical sources provide clues to expected patterns in the material culture remains, but many facilities and tools served more than one purpose and thus are difficult to distinguish as particularly related to maguey processing. Courtyards, for example, are common to all houses, and would have offered space for maguey sap and fiber processing, and for many other tasks as well.

Sap Extraction and Processing

Tools germane to these operations (Parsons and Parsons 1990:289–297) include discoidal (plano-convex) scrapers made of black obsidian, probably used to scrape the cavity, and three-handled jars used to transport sap: Both "almost certainly had multiple functions and uses" (1990:293) and were common at Cihuatecpan. The percentage of recognizable jar sherds (relative to those from the other major utility ware categories, griddles, and basins) was 31% overall (range = 28% to 41%); Figure 8-6 compares the percentages of these utility vessel sherds: Note that jar sherds account for a relatively constant proportion from house to house.

The percentages of sherds from basins vary more, perhaps indicating a *pulque*-making specialization at Structure 1 (Evans 1994). In studying the *pulque*-making process, Parsons and Parsons (1990:294) found that "[l]arge,

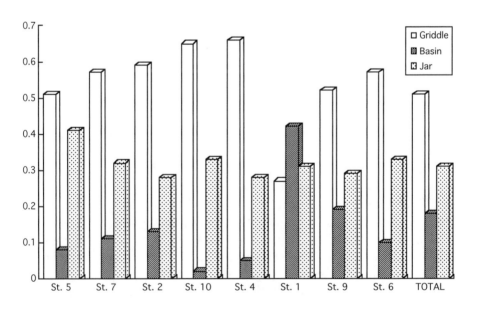

Figure 8-6. Cihuatecpan utility vessel sherd percentages, by structure.

wide-mouthed basins are probably the best candidates for prehispanic fermentation vats." Overall, basins accounted for 18% of utility sherds recognizable as griddles, basins, or jars (Figure 8-6). The variation in proportion of basin sherds among the houses is remarkable: Only Structure 9 has roughly the same proportion as the overall average, and all the rest except Structure 1 show a much lower than average proportion. Structure 1 was probably a joint-family house (Table 8-2), and it was located next to a pond that existed on the site in Aztec times (Figure 8-4; see also Evans 1994; Evans and Abrams 1988:84–86). The location of the house next to the pond is important evidence of possible *pulque*-making specialization, as is the presence of so many basins, because "[i]n terms of fermentation . . . perhaps the most salient factor . . . is the need for numerous containers and plenty of water" (Parsons and Parsons 1990:294). Impurities wreak havoc on the fermentation process, and all equipment must be cleaned after each use.

Pulque production was probably not a common household activity, and this is an important point to consider in any assessment of the extent of pre-Columbian *pulque* production and consumption among the general population. The many constraints on *pulque* use go far beyond the famous death penalty illustrated at the end of the Codex Mendoza.[12] The fermentation process is labor intensive and uses up quantities of water, an extremely valuable resource that was only occasionally renewable, and difficult to stockpile in the semiarid conditions favoring maguey growth; furthermore, *pulque* is so unstable that it must be quickly transported to the imbibers. *Pulque* was an integral part of curing, rituals, and the festivities that accompanied them, and structure 1's household may have specialized in *pulque* production for the village. Analysis of the basin sherds for residual remains of *pulque* would clarify this.

Fiber Processing and Products

There are two basic sets of operations: extracting the fibers from the leaves and crafting the fibers into thread, cord, and textiles. Parsons and Parsons make a strong case for pit-steaming as the probable prehispanic method of preparing maguey for scraping, and note that archaeological features associated with this method would be a cooking hearth and rotting pit (their ethnographic examples are roughly 2 m and 1 m wide, respectively [Parsons and Parsons 1990:164]), a large pounding stone, and midden with spiny waste. They note that "permanent workshops, at or near the place of residence, are . . . likely in the prehispanic archaeological record. Maguey-fiber processing is quite labor intensive. . . . labor is most efficient in the workshop when more than one individual is available most of the time" and peak efficiency is achieved with three workers (1990:299).

At Cihuatecpan, leaves may have been processed in residential courtyards. We did not note the configuration of features described above in the course of our excavations, but a review of the layout of the site's known features may reveal some of these patterns. The workshop operates best with several workers in attendance, so it is a strong argument for location in, or adjacent to, the house, where the workforce of the joint family could be used.

The tool used to extract the fibers from the cooked leaves was probably the well-known ground stone "hoe" (named for its shape, not its function), a flat trapezoidal piece of basalt or felsite. Following suggestions by Brumfiel (1976) and Serra (1985) that this tool was used for fiber scraping, Parsons and Parsons conducted ethnoarchaeological experiments that substantiated its effectiveness (1990:160, 175, 299–300).

At Cihuatecpan, scrapers were found associated with all structures. The histogram of fiber-related tools shows their "relative proportion" (Figure 8-7, first column for each structure). This value (also calculated for the spindle whorls) shows the relationship between actual and expected frequencies, the latter based on the percent of sherds from all structures accounted for by any one structure. Structure 1's share of total sherds was 10.7%; its seven scrapers account for 23.3% of all scrapers found associated with structures, 2.18 times the expected proportion of scrapers, based on proportion of sherds.

Note that Structure 6, the possible *tecpan*, has the lowest relative proportion of scrapers, and this is understandable, given its hypothesized status as a polygynous household. A *tecpan* would not have had farming plots like other houses,

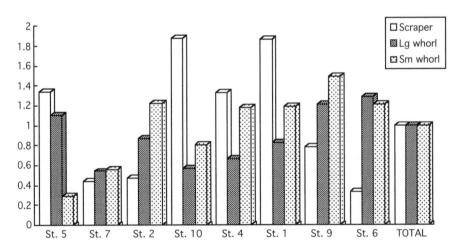

Figure 8-7. Cihuatecpan fiber processing tools, all structures. Scraper and spindle whorl relative proportions, by structure.

but instead would have been supported by crops from special fields (Gibson 1964:259). The tasks of fiber extraction, up to spinning, demand a ready supply of maguey leaves and involve the work of men (or men and women working together); the disproportionately large number of high-status adult women living here, and the many other functions served by the building would argue against its use in fiber extraction. Structure 5, a possible workshop/storehouse associated with Structure 6, has a high relative proportion of scrapers, consistent with the functional interpretation.

The six commoner residences account for 22 of the scrapers, and the relative proportions of scrapers among them (lower rows, Table 8-3 and Figure 8-7) reveal a skewed distribution of scrapers, and Structure 6's relatively low proportion of them. Structures 7 and 2, and to a lesser extent, 9, have below-average frequencies of scrapers, while Structures 1 and 10 have more scrapers than the average. While inferences based on so few data are obviously fragile, Structure 1's household (*pulque* makers) may have specialized to a greater extent than normal in maguey processing. Structure 7, with its possible "*tecpanpouhque*" household of nontribute-paying servants, may have had little reason—or time—to process maguey fiber for their own uses, and if they did so for Structure 6, they may have used the possible workshop, Structure 5.

The second set of fiber-processing activities is the manufacturing of thread, cord, rope, and textiles out of maguey fiber. Rope-making could have taken place in courtyards or adjacent to the houses; there would be few distinctive archaeological traces in terms of facilities or tools. Spinning, on the other hand, involved use of spindle whorls to weight the distaff, and these ceramic artifacts are virtually indestructible and fairly abundant in the archaeological record of the Aztec period. Parsons and Parsons note that unlike fiber processing, "spinning and weaving are particularly well adapted to small-scale, individualized production" (1990:313); the activities are also clearly women's work. Spindle whorls from surface collections throughout the Teotihuacan Valley were studied by Mary Parsons (1972, 1975), who noted that the bimodal distribution of

Table 8-3.
Frequency Values for Fiber-Processing Artifacts from Structures at Cihuatecpan, and X^2 Calculation

Tool Type: Structure Type	Maguey Scrapers	Spindle Whorls	Totals
Commoner house	22	52	**74**
Workshop	3	5	**8**
Elite house	5	61	**66**
	30	**118**	**148**

calculated $X^2 = 12.141701$, with 2 df
X^2 at 0.005 level, with 2 df = 10.5966

whorl size and weight probably reflected use for cotton and maguey fiber. Use of the larger whorls for spinning maguey thread was substantiated by Parsons and Parsons's ethnoarchaeological work (1990:180–181, 314–332).

Both kinds of whorls were recovered from excavations at Cihuatecpan in roughly equal proportions (58 large whorls, 60 small ones from the excavations under study here). They were found in all structures at Cihuatecpan (Figure 8-7). In addition to whorls, sherds from miniature bowls (used to support the cotton spinning distaff,[13] see Figure 8-2) were found in various contexts at the site; half the miniature bowl sherds were found at Structure 6.

Structure 6 had a greater-than-average-relative proportion of both kinds of whorls, and it accounted for roughly half the spindle whorls found in structural contexts at Cihuatecpan. This is commensurate with the assumption that this was a polygynous household, and thus would have had a greater-than-average proportion of adult women for whom spinning would have been a habitual activity. If this house was, in fact, the *tecpan* of a noble headman, then the high frequency of maguey whorls may indicate that even though nobles were permitted to wear cotton clothes, maguey textiles had many household uses and were part of the materials produced in palaces, as well as in modest homes.

The adjacent structure, 5, shows anomalies in a higher-than-expected frequency of maguey whorls and much lower-than-expected frequency of cotton whorls. One could imagine a workshop scene of men and women processing fiber, the women spinning maguey thread in free moments, but not bringing the finer and more expensive cotton into the workshop.

Looking now at the set of six commoner residences, compared only to each other (Figure 8-8), we see that Structure 9 was a hot spot of spinning of both kinds. Structure 7 has the lowest relative values, with the fewest scrapers and whorls among these houses; this might reflect the nontributary status of this household. Structure 10's spindle whorl collection is somewhat smaller than would be expected, and the other three houses show modest variation around average.

Changes over time in relative proportions of spindle whorls have been hypothesized to reflect broad changes in Aztec-period economic organization (Brumfiel 1991), but this issue remains unresolved as long as surface-sampled collections of spindle whorls are the basis for inference. Surface samples are inadequate to address this problem because only by chance do they accurately reflect the proportions of excavated materials at the same site or locus, possibly because the cotton whorls are small (Hershey Kiss size) and dust-colored, difficult for surface collectors to see. For example, Parsons's 1972 study of Aztec-period spindle whorls from the Teotihuacan Valley showed that 72% of whorls in surface collections were large, but large whorls accounted for only 56% of those from excavations (Parsons 1972:44). Cihuatecpan (T.A. 81) was unusual among surface-collected sites because large whorls accounted for 57%

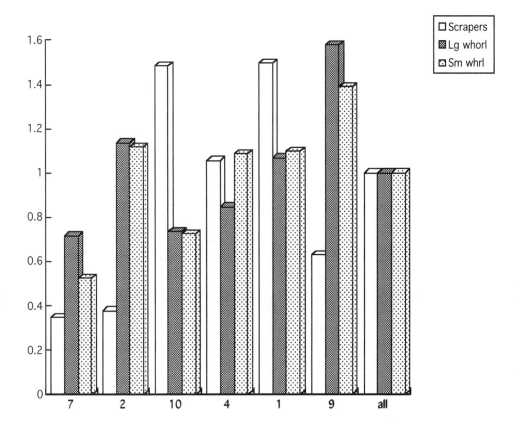

Figure 8-8. Cihuatecpan fiber processing tools, commoner residences only. Scraper and spindle whorl relative proportions, by structure.

of those recovered from the 1964 surface collections (20 large, 15 small).[14] The occasional coincidence of similar relative proportions of surface-collected whorls and those from excavations is just that: a coincidence.

The larger issue Brumfiel raises is whether Late Aztec Basin of Mexico women wove less than their great-grandmothers, and instead bought imported textiles in the marketplace to give as tribute payments (1991:230–234). Such a temporally based comparison must have much stronger evidence than surface-sampled materials, and I assert that even our excavated materials at this point are inadequate to address this issue. The shallowness of deposits at the site in general, and the high proportion of plowzone and other disturbed contexts render the identification of such trends impossible. Most buildings featured a plowzone layer of ca. 30 cm overlying a compacted sterile layer, sometimes with a remnant of floor and shallow stratum of subfloor fill. Structure 6 had slightly more complex stratigraphy, and I examined its contexts and associated ceramics and obsidian hydration dates, and isolated an Aztec III component bearing Black-on-Orange IIID and IIIE ceramics, and 13 large whorls and 13 small ones, the same rough parity of proportion as for the site as a whole. Before we claim revolutionary changes in the work lives of half the Aztec population, we need additional solid evidence.

Statistical Significance

Returning to the gender-based division of labor at Cihuatecpan, do the pertinent variations in artifact frequencies among the different buildings signify actual patterns of task allocation? We can use the two general categories of fiber-processing tools, spindle whorls, and scrapers to represent, respectively, female labor and male (or shared male and female) labor. The distribution of these two tool categories over the three different kinds of structures—commoner residence (Structures 1, 2, 4, 7, 9, and 10), workshop/storehouse (5), and elite residence (6)—would show no significant difference among them if no patterning existed. But, in fact, the differences are highly significant, with a calculated X^2 statistic at the 0.005 level, a 200-to-1 probability that this distribution occurred due to random chance.

In calculating the x^2 statistic, each cell (Table 8-3) contributes to the whole. Most of the value, in this case, came from frequencies of scrapers: Many were found in commoner residences, and few were found at the elite residence. This accords with the assumption that Structure 6 was an administrative residence with one high-status adult male, several high-status women, and few (or no) teams of commoner fiber processors working within the building.

Relatively little of the value of the calculated statistic was derived from the spindle-whorl frequencies. This accords with the notion of spinning as a universal household activity, pursued by all women regardless of the composition of the household and other workshop activities taking place in the house, and it also indicates that, in all households, women were spinning both cotton and maguey. For Structure 6, it cannot be determined whether all women, regardless of rank, were spinning both fibers, or higher-ranking women spun cotton while their servants spun maguey.

OVERVIEW

As we try to understand actual behavior from these material traces, we must bear in mind that a few dozen artifacts, none found in a context of activity, can only *suggest* such patterns. The most solid inferences we can draw from these data and their interpretation through the ethnohistorical and ethnographic records are that:

• all the tribute-paying commoner households (those living in Structures 1, 2, 4, 9, and 10) processed maguey and produced a variety of goods from it;

• maguey-fiber processing was widespread, but concentrations of scrapers may indicate workshops of particularly intense activity at some houses, and in the workshop/storehouse (Structure 5);

• Structure 1 may have been a locus of *pulque* production, and this was not a regular activity in other houses;

• variations in artifact frequencies support the identification of special purpose buildings and substantiate social status differences among households: At Structure 6, less-than-normal maguey-fiber production (though not production of spun thread) would befit an administrative building; Structure 7's low frequencies of fiber production and processing artifacts accord with a household of workers assigned to special duties and freed of textile tribute obligations; Structure 5's high proportions of maguey scrapers and whorls, but low proportion of cotton whorls, indicate maguey-fiber processing or storage of equipment;

• women spun maguey and cotton in all houses. They also probably wove these fibers into cloth, but Cihuatecpan has yielded no material evidence of weaving;

• there is no evidence of a diminution of textile production over time; and

• while the work of women is rendered visible by spindle whorls, the role of men in the work of the household requires reconstruction from various lines of evidence. When these are taken together, the cooperative work force of the maguey-farming household is revealed.

THE FARMERS AND THE FARMED

Case studies in ecological symbiosis sometimes describe *mutualism*, in which interaction between two species is mutually beneficial, and also obligatory for the success of both species (Boughey 1973:99). The concept of mutualism is also germane to understanding the interaction between humans and those plant and animal species on which they depend for food: Particular food crops support human life, and their growth habits shape the social organizational patterns of their exploiters, which in turn, encourage certain food species.[15] Maguey farming is a good example of a mutualistic symbiosis, since the plants provide a wide range of necessary products for human life, and their cultivation as a staple crop structures the composition of the farming family and the yearly round of activities of the farmers. The set of tasks involved in tending and processing maguey favored an equal sex ratio among adults in the household, and also may have favored an extended family joint household form.

It is not overstating maguey's importance to say that without it, pre-Columbian farmers could not have cultivated and lived on the piedmont zones of the Basin of Mexico. Parsons and Darling (1993) noted that maguey is not just "supplementary and secondary" in comparison with seed crops, but "complementary and primary," playing a role analogous to that of herd animals in the Old World and South America.

At the same time, the plant constrained the family and household composition options open to maguey farmers by the range of tasks associated with its exploitation. As in so many other cases (Netting 1989:222), household organization and agricultural practice had a close and mutually well-adapted relationship.

Maguey's raw materials provided occupations for men and women, and the economic partnership forged in maguey-farming families deserves our understanding. Here is a societal form that lent much to the stability of Aztec period city-states, but it is often obscured behind the glorious shadow of the male-dominated violent world of the Aztec elite. In Aztec Mexico, women seemed to have had little voice in most high-level policymaking in politics or religion (Rodríguez Valdés 1988:195–198), but the policymakers in Aztec society, like the elites in traditional societies elsewhere in the world, formed only a small percent of the society as a whole. Farmer–artisans were the broad base and massive midsections of the social organization pyramid, and they produced basic commodities (Sanders and Killion 1992:20). Contrasting the relative value of the products of the farmer–artisans with the better-known elite materials and products (precious metals, feather work, fine sculpture, etc.), it is obvious that the survival of Aztec society as a whole depended most on the mundane necessities produced by countless farming households. The pattern of Aztec male dominance may have been another "luxury good" common to elites but little in evidence in the daily lives of the mass of producers in the Basin of Mexico.

Acknowledgments
This paper evolved from a presentation in the symposium "Household Organization: Empirical Approaches to Continuity and Change," organized by Patricia Lyons Johnson and Elliot Fratkin for the American Anthropological Association meetings, New Orleans, 1990. I appreciate the comments on earlier versions from Frances Berdan, Richard Blanton, Elliot Fratkin, Nancy Howell, Patricia Lyons Johnson, Robert Netting, David Webster, and James W. Wood, and encouragement by Jeffrey Parsons to develop this version. Excavations at Cihuatecpan and materials storage and research were approved by the Instituto Nacional de Antropología e Historia of Mexico, and by the

Municipio de Otumba, Estado de México, and were supported by National Science Foundation Grants BNS–8317830 and BNS–8519834. Further analysis of materials was supported by National Endowment for the Humanities Grant FE–22957–89.

NOTES

1. Ohnersorgen 1994 distinguished between these two perspectives in Aztec gender studies, citing McCafferty and McCafferty (1991) as an example of the complementary view, while Nash (1978) and Rodríguez Valdés (1988) focus on hierarchy.

2. Tribute-paying Aztec farmers had long-term rights to lands that were communally held by their villages. Thus they were "smallholders" in Netting's (1989:221-222) sense: intensively cultivating free-held land, as households. Such smallholders today account for 80% of the world's farmers (1989:221) and display remarkable cross-cultural regularities, among them strong social sanctions against carelessness and irresponsibility (1989:224) and the development of a high degree of loyalty, trust, and mutual respect among members of the smallholding household (1989:228-229).

3. Nahuatl: "*chicoac, vapaoac, popuxtli, ichtic*" (1961:41) "*chicoac, oapaoac, popuxtli, ichtic*" (1961:51)

4. The contrast is graphically depicted in the Codex Mendoza, Part 3. Calnek's (1992) study of this "daily life" section outlined two parallel stories, relating the respective consequences of rectitude and self-indulgence, leading either to a happy old age (surrounded by doting offspring and eased by quantities of fermented maguey sap, *pulque*), or to an early death by execution for crimes of excess.

5. The lives of pre-Columbian women artisans are difficult to reconstruct without ethnohistoric sources. Introducing her edited collection of studies of women in ancient New World art, Miller noted that "[o]ne female role that is not explored ... here is that of ... craft specialist. The accomplishments of such women will probably never be fully recognized." (1988:xi)

6. Translation by Thelma Sullivan of Primeros Memoriales, Chapter 3, Paragraph 8, published in Berdan and Anawalt 1992:2:155.

7. Otis Charlton et al. (1993) distinguish between "general or restricted" skill in discussing textile production at Otumba in order to identify workshops. This distinction is useful in this regard, but perhaps obfuscates the related issue of the amount of training required to master textile-production skills.

8. The practice of polygyny was a major difference between nobles and commoners. Polygyny was legally the right of any man sufficiently affluent to support more than one wife (Anonymous Conqueror 1917:77), but in fact it was a prerogative of nobles. It would not have been suited to the economic needs of maguey farmers, since it disrupted the gender balance of available labor to perform various tasks.

9. (Codex Mendoza, the Matrícula de Tributos, the Información of 1554 [these are

described in Berdan 1992:I], Motolinía's Memoriales, and the Relaciones Geográficas [Paso y Troncoso 1979])

10. This estimate is based on the amount of cloth tribute from the province of Acolhuacan, of which the Teotihuacan Valley was a part, to the Triple Alliance, according to the Codex Mendoza, 8,000 textile items (80% of them *mantas*) each year (Berdan 1992; Berdan and Anawalt 1992a:37-40; other discussion in Rodríguez Vallejo 1982:39; Drennan 1984). Given an Acolhua domain population of ca. 250,000 (Offner 1983:17) with perhaps 20,000 elites and other non-tributaries, and household size averaging 6, this amounts to about 1 *manta* each year, from every five families. Several more would be required for other tribute obligations. See also Hicks 1994 for a discussion of this issue.

11. The surveyed and excavated remains of Cihuatecpan, designated T.A. 81 by the Teotihuacan Valley Project, have been described in Abrams 1988, Evans 1988a, 1988b, 1989, Evans and Abrams 1988, McCoy and Evans 1988.

12. Clendinnen makes the important point that strictures against pulque drinking weren't simply based on the offense given to the well-developed Aztec sense of propriety, but that Aztecs saw themselves as part of a universe of spiritual forces, not all benign. "The Mexica knew pulque's capacity to demoralize the individual and to disrupt social relations ... But its deeper import and its deeper danger was its capacity to lay humans open to the sacred" (1991:50), thus endangering them and the community.

13. For a general discussion of miniature bowls, their distribution and function, see Smith and Hirth 1988.

14. Parsons reported 2 large and 11 small whorls for this site (the only site collection to show such an imbalance toward small whorls) but a recent review of Teotihuacan Valley surface collections (Evans, Parsons, and Charlton 1995) yielded 16 more large whorls and 4 small ones.

15. Flannery's (1968) concepts of seasonality and scheduling in the evolution of food production in the Tehuacan Valley broadly trace the dynamics of mutualism among human groups and their food plants.

REFERENCES CITED

Abrams, Elliot M.
    1988   Investigation of an Obsidian Midden At Cihuatecpan, Mexico. In *Excavations at Cihuatecpan, An Aztec Village in the Teotihuacan Valley*, edited by Susan T. Evans, pp. 235–239. Vanderbilt University Publications in Anthropology No. 36, Vanderbilt University, Nashville.
Anawalt, Patricia Rieff
    1981   *Indian Clothing Before Cortes*. University of Oklahoma Press, Norman.
Anonymous Conqueror
    1917   *Narrative of Some Things of New Spain and of the Great City of Temestitan Mexico*. Translated by M.H. Saville. The Cortes Society, New York.

Berdan, Frances F.

1992 The Imperial Tribute Roll of the Codex Mendoza. In *The Codex Mendoza, Vol. 1: Interpretation*, edited by Frances F. Berdan and Patricia R. Anawalt, pp. 55–79. University of California Press, Berkeley.

Berdan, Frances F., and Patricia R. Anawalt (editors)

1992a *The Codex Mendoza, Vol. 2, Description of Codex Mendoza*. University of California Press, Berkeley.

1992b *The Codex Mendoza, Vol. 4, Pictorial Parallel Image Replicas of Codex Mendoza, with Transcriptions and Translations*. University of California Press, Berkeley.

Boughey, Arthur S.

1973 *Ecology of Populations*. The Macmillan Co., New York.

Brumfiel, Elizabeth

1976 *Specialization and Exchange at the Late Postclassic (Aztec) Community of Huexotla, Mexico*. Ph.D. dissertation, University of Michigan. University Microfilms, Ann Arbor.

1991 Weaving and Cooking: Women's Production in Aztec Mexico. In *Engendering Archaeology*, edited by Joan M. Gero and Margaret W. Conkey, pp. 224–251. Basil Blackwell, Oxford.

Calnek, Edward E.

1972 Settlement Pattern and Chinampa Agriculture at Tenochtitlan. *American Antiquity* 37:104–115.

1992 The Ethnographic Context of the Third Part of the *Codex Mendoza*. In *The Codex Mendoza, Vol.1, Interpretation*, edited by Frances F. Berdan and Patricia R. Anawalt, pp. 81–91. University of California Press, Berkeley.

Carrasco, Pedro

1964 Family Structure of Sixteenth Century Tepoztlan. In *Process and Pattern in Culture: Essays in Honor of Julian H. Steward*, edited by R.A. Manners, pp. 185–210. Aldine, Chicago.

1971 Social Organization of Ancient Mexico. In *Handbook of Middle American Indians*, Vol. 10, edited by Gordon Ekholm and Ignacio Bernal, pp. 349–375. University of Texas Press, Austin.

1972 La Casa y la hacienda de un señor Tlahuica. *Estudios de Cultura Náhuatl* 10:225–244.

1976 The Joint Family in Ancient Mexico: The Case of Molotla. In *Essays on Mexican Kinship*, edited by H.C. Nutini, P. Carrasco, and J. Taggart, pp. 45–64. University of Pittsburgh Press, Pittsburgh.

Charlton, Thomas H.

1972 *Post-Conquest Developments in the Teotihuacan Valley, Mexico*. Report 5. Office of the State Archaeologist, Iowa City.

Charlton, Thomas H., and Deborah L. Nichols

1990 *Preliminary Report on Recent Research in the Otumba City-State*. Mesoamerican

Research Colloquium, Research Report No. 3, Department of Anthropology, University of Iowa, Iowa City.

Cheal, David
1989   Strategies of Resource Management in Household Economies: Moral Economy or Political Economy? In *The Household Economy: Reconsidering the Domestic Mode of Production*, edited by Richard Wilk, pp. 11–22. Westview Press, Boulder.

Clendinnen, Inga
1991   *Aztecs: An Interpretation*. Cambridge University Press, Cambridge.

Codex Mendoza
1992 [1541–1542]   *Codex Mendoza*. Vol. 3, *A Facsimile Reproduction of* Codex Mendoza, edited by Frances F. Berdan and Patricia R. Anawalt. University of California Press, Berkeley.

Conkey, Margaret W.
1991   Contexts of Action, Contexts for Power: Material Culture and Gender in the Magdalenian. In *Engendering Archaeology*, edited by Joan M. Gero and Margaret W. Conkey, pp. 57–92. Basil Blackwell, Oxford.

Cook, Sherburne F., and Woodrow Borah
1971   *Essays in Population History: Mexico and the Caribbean*, Vol. 1. University of California Press, Berkeley.

Drennan, Robert D.
1984   Long Distance Transport Costs in Pre–Hispanic America. *American Anthropologist* 86:105–112.

Durán, Fray Diego
1964   *The Aztecs: The History of the Indies of New Spain*. Translated, with notes, by Doris Heyden and Fernando Horcasitas. Orion, New York.

Evans, Susan T.
1980   *A Settlement System Analysis of the Teotihuacan Region, Mexico, A.D. 1350–1520*. Ph.D. dissertation, Department of Anthropology, The Pennsylvania State University. University Microfilms, Ann Arbor.

1988a   Cihuatecpan: The Village in Its Ecological and Historical Context. In *Excavations at Cihuatecpan, An Aztec Village in the Teotihuacan Valley*, edited by Susan T. Evans, pp. 1–49. Vanderbilt University Publications in Anthropology No. 36, Vanderbilt University, Nashville.

1989   House and Household in the Aztec World: The Village of Cihuatecpan. In *Households and Communities*, edited by S. MacEachern, D.J.W. Archer, and R.D. Garvin, pp. 430–440. The Archaeological Association of the University of Calgary, Calgary.

1990   The Productivity of Maguey Terrace Agriculture in Central Mexico During the Aztec Period. *Latin American Antiquity* 1:117–132.

1991   Architecture and Authority in an Aztec Village: Form and Function of the

Tecpan. In *Land and Politics in the Valley of Mexico*, edited by Herbert Harvey, pp. 63–92. University of New Mexico Press, Albuquerque.

1993   Aztec Household Organization and Village Administration. In *Prehispanic Domestic Units in Western Mesoamerica*, edited by Robert Santley and Kenneth Hirth, pp. 173–189. CRC Press, Boca Raton.

1994   The Drinking Problem of the Aztecs. Paper presented at the 1994 Annual Meeting of the American Society for Ethnohistory, Tempe.

Evans, Susan T., and Elliot M. Abrams

1988   Archaeology at the Aztec Period Village of Cihuatecpan, Mexico: Methods and Results of the 1984 Field Season. In *Excavations at Cihuatecpan, An Aztec Village in the Teotihuacan Valley*, edited by Susan T. Evans, pp. 50–234. Vanderbilt University Publications in Anthropology No. 36, Vanderbilt University, Nashville.

Evans, Susan T., Jeffrey R. Parsons, and Thomas H. Charlton

1995   Aztec Period Ceramics of the Rural Teotihuacan Valley. A paper presented at the 60th Annual Meeting of the Society for American Archaeology, Minneapolis.

Flannery, Kent

1968   Archeological Systems Theory and Early Mesoamerica. In *Anthropological Archaeology in the Americas*, edited by Betty J. Meggers, pp. 67–87. Anthropological Society of Washington, Washington D.C.

Gibson, Charles

1964   *The Aztecs Under Spanish Rule*. Stanford University Press, Stanford.

Harvey, Herbert R.

1985   Household and Family Structure in Early Colonial Tepetlaoztoc: An Analysis of the Códice Santa María Asunción. *Estudios de Cultura Náhuatl* 18: 275–294.

Hicks, Frederic

1994   Cloth in the Political Economy of the Aztec State. In *Economies and Polities in the Aztec Realm*, edited by Mary G. Hodge and Michael Smith, pp. 89–111. University of Texas Press for SUNY Institute of Mesoamerican Studies, Austin.

Kellogg, Susan

1988   Households in Late Prehispanic and Early Colonial Mexico City. *The Americas* 44:483–494.

McCafferty, Sharisse D., and Geoffrey G. McCafferty

1991   Spinning and Weaving as Female Gender Identity in Postclassic Mexico. In *Textile Traditions of Mesoamerica and the Andes: An Anthology*, edited by M.B. Schevill, J.C. Berlo, and E.B. Dwyer, pp. 19–44. Garland Publishing, New York.

McCoy, Bruce Gregory, and Susan T. Evans

1988   Preliminary Description of Flotation Sample Materials from Cihuatecpan, Mexico. In *Excavations at Cihuatecpan, An Aztec Village in the Teotihuacan Valley*, edited by Susan T. Evans, pp. 239–245. Vanderbilt University Publications in Anthropology No. 36, Vanderbilt University, Nashville.

Miller, Virginia E.

1988   Introduction. In *The Role of Gender in PreColumbian Art and Architecture*, edited by V.E. Miller, pp. *vii–xviii*. University Press of America, Lanham.

Monzón, Arturo

1983   *El calpulli en la organización social de los Tenocha*. Clásicos de la Antropología Colección No. 15. Instituto Nacional Indigenista, Mexico, D.F.

Morris, Craig

1974   Reconstructing Patterns of Non-Agricultural Production in the Inca Economy: Archaeology and Documents in Institutional Analysis. In *Reconstructing Complex Societies*, edited by C.B. Moore, pp. 49–68. Supplement to the Bulletin of the American Schools of Oriental Research, No. 20, Case Western Reserve University, Cleveland.

Motolinía, Fray Toribio de

1971   *Memoriales*. Edited by Edmundo O'Gorman. UNAM Instituto de Investigaciones Históricas, Mexico, D.F.

Nash, June

1978   The Aztecs and the Ideology of Male Dominance. *Signs* 4:349–362.

Netting, Robert McC.

1989   Smallholders, Householders, Freeholders: Why the Family Farm Works Well Worldwide. *The Household Economy: Reconsidering the Domestic Mode of Production*, edited by Richard Wilk, pp. 221–244. Westview Press, Boulder.

Nichols, Deborah L.

1990   Maguey Fiber Production in the Aztec City–State of Otumba, Mexico. Paper presented at the 55th Annual Meeting of the Society for American Archaeology, Las Vegas.

Nuttall, Zelia

1926   Official Reports on the Towns of Tequizistlan, Tepechpan, Acolman, and San Juan Teotihuacan Sent by Francisco de Castaneda to His Majesty, Phillip II, and the Council of the Indies, in 1580. *Papers of the Peabody Museum, Harvard University* 11:45–86. Cambridge, Massachusetts.

Offner, Jerome

1983   *Law and Politics in Aztec Texcoco*. Cambridge University Press, Cambridge.

1984   Household Organization in the Texcocan Heartland: The Evidence in the Codex Vergara. In *Explorations in Ethnohistory*, edited by H. Harvey and H. Prem, pp. 127–146. University of New Mexico Press, Albuquerque.

Ohnersorgen, Michael A.

1994   Multiple Roles, Multiple Statuses: Reexamining Gender Relations in Prehispanic Aztec Society. Paper presented at the 1994 Annual Meeting of the American Society for Ethnohistory, Tempe.

Otis Charlton, Cynthia, Thomas H. Charlton, and Deborah Nichols

1993   Aztec Household–Based Craft Production: Archaeological Evidence from the City–State of Otumba, Mexico. In *Prehispanic Domestic Units in Western Mesoamerica*, edited by Robert Santley and Kenneth Hirth, pp. 147–171. CRC Press, Boca Raton.

Parsons, Jeffrey R.

1989   Arqueología regional en la cuenca de México: Una estrategía para la investigación futura. *Anales de Antropología* 26:157–257.

Parsons, Jeffrey R., and J. Andrew Darling

1993   A Reconsideration of Maguey in Mesoamerican Civilization. Paper presented at the 13th International Congress of Anthropological and Ethnological Sciences, Mexico City.

Parsons, Jeffrey R., and Mary H. Parsons

1990   *Maguey Utilization in Highland Central Mexico.* Anthropological Papers No. 82, Museum of Anthropology, University of Michigan, Ann Arbor.

Parsons, Mary H.

1972   Spindle Whorls from the Teotihuacan Valley, Mexico. In *Miscellaneous Studies in Mexican Prehistory*, edited by M. Spence, J.R. Parsons, and M.H. Parsons, pp. 45–80. Anthropological Papers No. 45, Museum of Anthropology, University of Michigan, Ann Arbor.

1975   The Distribution of Late Postclassic Spindle Whorls in the Valley of Mexico. *American Antiquity* 40:207–215.

Paso y Troncoso, Francisco del (compiler)

1979   *Papeles de nueva España: Relaciones geográficas de la diócesis de México, 1579–1582.* Editorial Cosmos, Mexico, D.F.

Rodríguez Valdés, María J.

1988   *La mujer azteca.* Universidad Autónoma del Estado de México, Toluca.

Rodríguez Vallejo, José

1982   *Ixcatl, el algodon mexicano.* Fondo de Cultura Económica, Mexico, D.F.

Sahagún, Fray Bernardino de

1961   *The Florentine Codex, Book 10: The People.* Translated, with notes, by C.E. Dibble and A.J.O. Anderson. The School of American Research and University of Utah, Santa Fe, New Mexico.

1963   *The Florentine Codex, Book 11: Earthly Things.* Translated, with notes, by C.E. Dibble and A.J.O. Anderson. The School of American Research and University of Utah, Santa Fe, New Mexico.

1969   *The Florentine Codex, Book 6: Rhetoric and Moral Philosophy.* Translated, with notes, by C.E. Dibble and A.J.O. Anderson. The School of American Research and University of Utah, Santa Fe, New Mexico.

Sanders, William T.

1965   *The Cultural Ecology of the Teotihuacan Valley.* Department of Sociology and

Anthropology, Pennsylvania State University, University Park.

Sanders, William T., and Thomas W. Killion

1992   Factors Affecting Settlement Agriculture in the Ethnographic and Historic Record of Mesoamerica. In *Gardens of Prehistory*, edited by T.W. Killion, pp. 14–31. University of Alabama Press, Tuscaloosa.

Sanders, William T., Jeffrey R. Parsons, and Robert Santley

1979   *The Basin of Mexico: The Cultural Ecology of a Civilization*. Academic Press, New York.

Serra Puche, Mari Carmen

1985   *Terremote Tlaltenco: Los recursos lacustres de la cuenca de México durante el Formativo*. Thesis, UNAM Facultad de Filosofía y Letras, Mexico, D.F.

Smith, Michael E., and Kenneth G. Hirth

1988   The Development of Prehispanic Cotton-Spinning Technology in Western Morelos, Mexico. *Journal of Field Archaeology* 15:349–358.

Spores, Ronald

1984   *The Mixtecs in Ancient and Colonial Times*. University of Oklahoma Press, Norman.

Wilk, Richard R.

1989   Decision Making and Resource Flows within the Household: Beyond the Black Box. In *The Household Economy: Reconsidering the Domestic Mode of Production*, edited by Richard Wilk, pp. 23–52. Westview Press, Boulder.

Williams, Barbara J.

1984   Mexican Pictorial Cadastral Registers. In *Explorations in Ethnohistory*, edited by H.R. Harvey and H. Prem, pp. 103–105. University of New Mexico Press, Albuquerque.

Williams, Barbara J., and Herbert R. Harvey

1988   Content, Provenience, and Significance of the Codex Vergara and the Códice de Santa María Asunción. *American Antiquity* 53:337–351.

MORE THAN ALLUVIAL LAND AND WATER:

THE LATE PRE-HISPANIC EMERGENCE OF EASTERN TLACOLULA, OAXACA, MEXICO

GARY M. FEINMAN AND LINDA M. NICHOLAS

The Field Museum

INTRODUCTION

We recognize the fundamental efforts and inspirations of Jeffrey R. Parsons as key to the early implementation, vast coverage, and subsequent theoretical contributions that pedestrian, full-coverage, archaeological surveys have achieved in highland Mesoamerica (e.g., J. Parsons 1971, 1972, 2002; Parsons et al. 1982). The impact of Parsons' studies, as well as those of other highland Mexican settlement pattern pioneers (e.g., Blanton 1978; Sanders 1999; Spores 1972), has prompted massive reconsiderations of the manner in which archaeologists envision the demographic and spatial scales of the early polities and civilizations that arose in such core regions as the Basin of Mexico, the Valley of Oaxaca, and intermontane areas in between and adjacent to them. Building on these studies, we have gained a far better empirical foundation to evaluate which factors and processes were associated with urbanism and state formation and the waves of socioeconomic changes that followed in pre-Hispanic Mexico (e.g., Blanton et al. 1993). At the same time, systematic settlement pattern surveys have yielded the most complete picture of long-term demographic change (over several millennia) that archaeologists are apt to achieve for highland Mesoamerica (e.g., Kowalewski 2003), one of the global regions where ancient states indigenously developed.

The thematic focus of this paper has its genesis in the settlement pattern and demographic findings from one of the largest highland Mexican survey blocks, the Valley of Oaxaca (Blanton et al. 1982; Feinman and Nicholas 1990; Kowalewski et al. 1989) (Figure 9-1). The systematic, full-coverage archaeological survey of this Y-shaped valley has generated a vantage on population

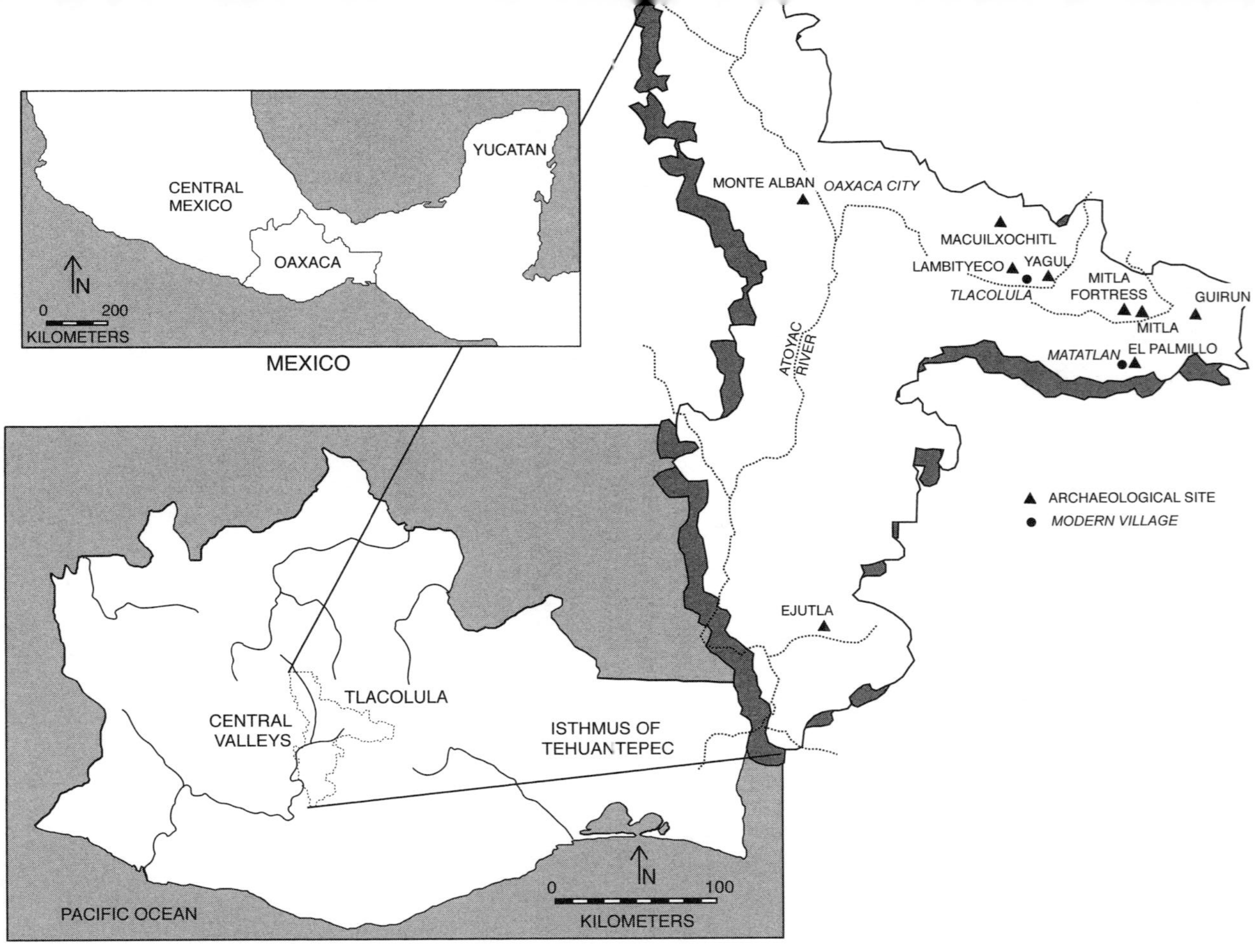

Figure 9-1. Map of Oaxaca, showing places mentioned in the text.

and settlement pattern shifts over the last three millennia of the pre-Hispanic era (c. 1500 BC–AD 1500). With our colleagues (Feinman et al. 1985; Feinman and Nicholas 1990; Kowalewski 1990), we have recorded and analyzed shifts in the densities and distributions of past settlement at a series of analytical and temporal scales. We also have compared long-term patterns of settlement and demographic change with the dispersal of land and water resources in the region (Nicholas 1989), since the latter are key to the production of the Mesoamerican food staple—maize—in this semiarid valley (Kirkby 1973). Based on these studies, we found that the distribution of population shifted significantly over space and time during the pre-Hispanic era. Valleywide settlement did not map onto (or spatially correlate with) the distribution of fertile land and available water in any neat or simple manner (cf. Sanders and Nichols 1988). The nature of the spatial relationship between these two variables shifted in important ways over space and time.

Specifically, this discussion is focused on the driest sector of the Valley of Oaxaca—the eastern end of the Tlacolula arm—and an apparent demographic conundrum. Compared with the rest of the Valley of Oaxaca, it is in eastern Tlacolula that we generally see the greatest discrepancies between estimates for pre-Hispanic population and the distribution of flat arable land and reliable water resources. In other words, despite being the subvalley with the lowest yields and least reliable productivity of maize (Druijven and Kruithof 1992; Kirkby 1973; Nicholas 1989), population densities in Tlacolula during the Classic period (AD 200-800) were as high or higher than they were in any other valley subregion (Nicholas 1989:497). By the Postclassic period (c. AD 800–1520), Tlacolula was the most densely occupied subvalley (Kowalewski et al. 1989:312). Archaeological estimates based on settlement pattern findings are consistent with evidence from sixteenth-century documents, indicating that two of the valley's most important Postclassic communities, Macuilxochitl and Mitla, as well as the highest demographic densities were situated in eastern Tlacolula (Asensio 1905 [1580]; Canseco 1905 [1580]; Kowalewski 2003:319; Kowalewski et al. 1989:317).

Yet significantly, looking at the *longue durée*, pre-Hispanic populations were not always denser in Tlacolula as compared with other sectors of the valley. When early villages were first established in the Valley of Oaxaca during the Formative period (c. 1600 BC–AD 200), eastern Tlacolula was sparsely settled (Blanton et al. 1993:55–59; Kowalewski et al. 1989:63–64). Populations continued to be relatively dispersed there when the early hilltop city of Monte Albán was founded around 500 BC in the center of the valley and during the centuries following when rapid demographic expansion occurred immediately surrounding the nascent hilltop city (Blanton et al. 1993:73–74). A dramatic growth spurt did not occur in Tlacolula until after AD 200 (the beginning of the Classic period), a time when the Valley of Oaxaca was becoming more integrated politically and economically (Feinman et al. 1985:351–353) under an expanding and architecturally monumental Monte Albán (Blanton 1978). Nevertheless, the dense populations in Tlacolula lasted for longer than a millennium, persisting through major political transitions, including the fall of Monte Albán at the end of the Classic period.

The high Classic–Postclassic population densities in eastern Tlacolula are hard to account for based on the distribution of agrarian resources (flat alluvial land and available water). Following broadly held assumptions regarding the importance of maize in pre-Hispanic Mexico (e.g., Kirkby 1973; Kowalewski 1980; Sanders and Price 1968:9, 87; Wolf 1959), detailed land use studies in Oaxaca (Nicholas 1989) illustrated that a significant proportion of the populace in eastern Tlacolula during the Classic and Postclassic periods (well more than in any other valley subregion) would have required imports of food produced outside their immediate vicinity. That is, on a local scale, many communities in Tlacolula could not have grown sufficient maize from their immediate catchment area, year after year, to sustain their local populations. Rainfall in much of eastern Tlacolula today is barely sufficient for maize cropping during a relatively wet year, and crops in this part of the valley fail frequently in drier years (Kirkby 1973). Even in years when the total rainfall is adequate, the specific periodicity of precipitation is not always suitable for bountiful corn yields.

Given the deployment of agricultural land and water, how can the magnitude and timing of the demographic growth in this driest part of the valley be explained? At present, there is no evidence for major climatic changes that would have affected the relative availability of land and water resources in eastern Tlacolula as compared with the remainder of the valley (Schoenwetter 1974). So why was the population denser in Tlacolula than in other parts of the valley for most of a millennium (during the Classic and Postclassic periods) or even longer? Why did this growth occur when it did? And how did these populations, particularly in eastern Tlacolula, support themselves?

One likely activity that possibly helped sustain the Tlacolula populations is craft production (Blanton et al. 1993; Feinman et al. 2002a; Finsten 1983, 1995; Kowalewski et al. 1989). During the regional surveys, more surface indications of craft activities were recorded in Tlacolula, especially at Classic and Postclassic hilltop terrace sites in that subvalley, than in the other valley arms. Because these hilltop towns often were situated far from productive well-watered land on the valley floor, craft activities may have been a critical aspect of their local economies.

Yet at the same time, recent findings from central Mexico (Evans 1990; Parsons and Parsons 1990) have spurred doubts regarding the overwhelming and universal importance generally given to maize agriculture in pre-Hispanic highland Mexico. As some are beginning to suspect regarding the central highlands (Parsons and Parsons 1990:6), perhaps the role of maize as an agricultural staple throughout the Valley of Oaxaca has been overemphasized. Did the populations in the dry Tlacolula arm of the valley engage in other kinds of agricultural production and intensification so that their subsistence dependence on maize was less than once thought? If so, how did those strategies relate to the growth of population in Tlacolula, especially eastern Tlacolula, during the Classic and Postclassic periods?

In the following sections, we draw on recent archaeological and botanical studies in Oaxaca (and beyond) to build the case that local xerophytic plants likely were heavily exploited in eastern Tlacolula. Many of these plants are known to have economic uses both as food and raw materials for crafts. Because of the abundance of these economically useful drought-resistant plants in drier parts of the valley, the lack of fit between resources and population may not be as great as we previously thought. With integrative mechanisms in place to ensure exchange between communities and valley subregions, these plants, along with other craft industries, may have provided a strong economic base for the large communities and dense pre-Hispanic populations that were situated in eastern Tlacolula.

RECENT ARCHAEOLOGICAL RESEARCH IN EASTERN TLACOLULA

Over the past decade, we have carried out intensive terrace-by-terrace surveys at three large hilltop terrace sites in eastern Tlacolula: Guirún, El Palmillo, and the Mitla Fortress (Feinman and Nicholas 2004a; Holmes 1897; Saville 1900, 1909). Based on findings from earlier regional surveys, all three sites were thought to have been loci of craft production (especially stone working) (Kowalewski et al. 1989), and all three had extensive Classic and Postclassic (AD 200-1500) occupations (Feinman and Nicholas 1996).

The three sites are situated on defensible hilltops at the edge of the valley, located on or near chert sources of variable quality (Whalen 1986; Williams and Heizer 1965). Significantly, the intensive surveys provided a preliminary picture of the different economic specializations (especially stone working and plant processing) practiced at each settlement (Feinman and Nicholas 2004a). Stone tool processing and utilization were more evident at these three sites than at communities in most other parts of the valley (Kowalewski et al. 1989; Robles 1994; Whalen 1986; Williams and Heizer 1965).

Distinctive scraping tools—scraper planes, or *raspadores* (Hester and Heizer 1972; Robles G. 1994)—were noted on the surfaces of all three sites (Figure 9-2). These tools likely were used to process plants for fiber (e.g., Evans 1990; Fish et al. 1992:84; Parsons and Parsons 1990). Such stone tools are far more

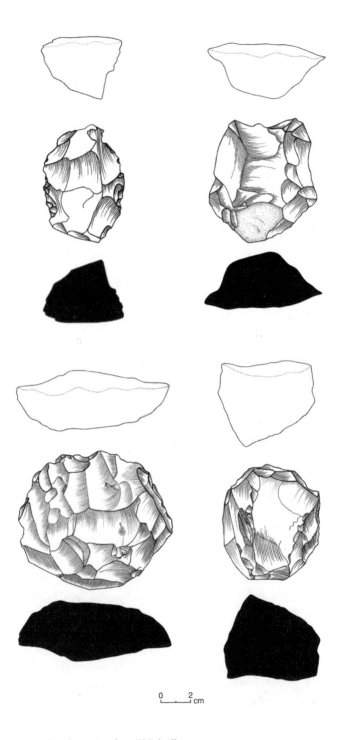

Figure 9-2. Examples of *raspadores* from El Palmillo.

abundant at sites in eastern Tlacolula than elsewhere in the Valley of Oaxaca (Hester and Heizer 1972; Messer 1978:77–80). We suspect that the inhabitants of the ancient sites utilized the economically useful xerophytic plants found commonly in eastern Tlacolula today, including maguey (*Agave sp.*) and *nopal* (*Opuntia pilifera*) . El Palmillo and the Mitla Fortress both lacked flat land on-site and had little well-watered terrain nearby where maize could have been farmed reliably and produced in quantity.

In 1999, following these intensive surveys, we implemented excavations focused on a series of residential terraces at El Palmillo (Feinman et al. 2002a). With more than 1,400 residential terraces, El Palmillo is the largest Classic-period terrace site in the Tlacolula subvalley and likely one of the biggest in the Valley of Oaxaca at that time (Feinman and Nicholas 2004a). Over six field seasons (1999–2004), we uncovered large sections of seven terraces (uncovering six distinct residential compounds) (Feinman and Nicholas 2001; Feinman et al. 2002a, 2002b, 2003). We have investigated four contiguous terraces near the base of the site (terraces 1147, 1148, 1162, 1163); two separate terraces in intermediate positions on the hill (terraces 925 and 507), and one large residential complex located adjacent to the public precinct at the apex of the site (terrace 335). This research has served to examine (and begin to define) the nature of spatial variation in domestic life/status and household economic activities at the site.

The terraces were excavated to expose as much as possible of the top residential surface on each terrace, including domestic architecture and outdoor workspaces and refuse areas. Each residential complex was composed of a patio group that included two or more rectangular rooms bordering a lime-plastered patio. The uppermost terrace had the most elaborate domestic architecture, a residential complex composed of 11 rooms that enclosed two sunken patios in the uppermost surfaces, similar in form to elaborate residences at Lambityeco (Lind and Urcid 1983; Paddock et al. 1968). On earlier occupation surfaces on this terrace, the residential complexes consisted of a series of rooms around a single patio, similar to palace-like compounds at Monte Albán (Caso 1938; Flannery 1983a; Marcus and Flannery 1996:208–212). On all the other terraces, the basic architectural plan was retained throughout several minor remodeling and more major rebuilding episodes. With the exception of two small adjacent terraces in the lower terrace group that we suspect sustained one domestic unit (terraces 1147 and 1148), each excavated terrace housed a separate domestic unit. Human burials were placed under house and patio floors, in terrace retaining walls, and in subfloor tombs.

Craft Production at El Palmillo

Of the excavated domestic units at El Palmillo, the residents of all but the uppermost investigated terrace were involved in production activities. Chert working and the utilization of xerophytic plant materials are repeatedly evidenced, although some ceramic manufacture, lapidary work, and ground stone tool production also have been noted in association with specific residences. As observed during the prior surveys (intensive and regional), the manufacture of chipped stone implements and tools from local chert materials was a key economic activity at the site. The stone assemblage at El Palmillo is dominated by chert and metaquartzites, with production waste constituting roughly three-quarters of the assemblage. The percent of formal chert tools at El Palmillo (2.5% of the entire chert assemblage) is low, in line with reduction/production contexts. Chipped stone nodules and chunks were being reduced into cores, usable flakes, and tools. On the lower terraces, the quantities of chert production waste were especially high, and the occupants of these houses likely engaged in a high intensity or volume of stone working, producing usable chipped stone for exchange to other households on site or other settlements in the region.

Another important economic activity at El Palmillo was xerophytic plant processing. Today, centuries after the abandonment of pre-Hispanic El Palmillo, the site has a wealth and diversity of xerophytic plants that are of contemporary economic importance (or were important in the past). The remnant plant community at the site appears to be a relict of the pre-Hispanic habitation of the hill (Middleton et al. 2001). Maguey likely was the most important of those plants. Eight different varieties of maguey were recorded on site, each having its own economic and subsistence uses. Today, just one of these varieties (*Agave angustifolia*) is the economic backbone of the contemporary village (Santiago Matatlán) where the site is situated, as it is used to manufacture the alcoholic beverage, mescal. Many of the scraping tools at El Palmillo, especially the *raspadores*, likely were used to process maguey.

Fiber-working tools, including spindle whorls, also were relatively abundant in the domestic excavations at El Palmillo. Although variable in size, most of the El Palmillo whorls are large, in the size range typically used for maguey fiber (rather than cotton) (Parsons and Parsons 1990; M. Parsons 1972). Many of the bone tools recovered in the El Palmillo excavations, including battens, needles, perforators, and spindle whorls, also are related to the manufacture of textiles (Feinman et al. 2003; Middleton et al. 2002).

Residents of El Palmillo (as well as neighboring hilltop sites in eastern Tlacolula) were involved in craft manufacture for circulation or, in other words, for consumption outside their own household (Feinman and Nicholas 2004b). During the Classic period, even settlements on the valley floor in eastern

Tlacolula appear to have been involved in production activities, such as salt production at Lambityeco (Peterson 1976), that went beyond maize agriculture. Although much of this nonagrarian production may have been less than full time, it still clearly was part of the region's economic foundation, helping sustain the dense local populations and apparent discrepancies between potential maize productivity and archaeologically derived population estimates.

XEROPHYTIC PLANTS: SUBSISTENCE AND CRAFTS

According to colonial-era accounts (Paso y Troncoso 1905 [1579–1581]:149–150), maize was seldom consumed in the eastern Tlacolula subvalley near Mitla and Matatlán. Even in the early twentieth century, maize was more costly in the Tlacolula arm than in other parts of the Valley of Oaxaca (Malinowski and de la Fuente 1982:100). Given the absence of reliable water sources and adjacent flat farmland near the base of El Palmillo, it seems doubtful that maize could have been grown in sufficient quantities to support the thousands of occupants that likely inhabited the site during the Classic period. Because of the scarcity of published artifact assemblages from Classic-period houses in Oaxaca, it is difficult to compare El Palmillo with other sites. Yet there is some artifactual evidence that maize consumption may have been less important there.

One site that we can compare with El Palmillo is Ejutla (see Feinman and Nicholas 2000, 2004b), a large Classic-period community situated in an alluvial setting in the wetter, southern edge of the Valley of Oaxaca. There, we excavated one house that is roughly contemporaneous with the residential complexes at El Palmillo. At the Ejutla site, the number of stone grinding tools (including *manos* and *metates* that likely were used to prepare maize) in the domestic assemblage (114) is more than twice as high as for any one residential complex at El Palmillo (13–55). A similar pattern was noted for *comales* (used in tortilla preparation). We recovered between 591 and 1,426 *comal* rims in the six El Palmillo houses compared to 4,759 rims during the excavations of a single residence at Ejutla. These basic patterns (a relatively greater number of grinding implements in Ejutla as compared with El Palmillo residences) do not change if the data are standardized by the volumes excavated. No archaeological complexes are strictly comparable, and the number of *comales* at the Ejutla site may well be overweighted by the production of this ceramic form in the excavated residence (Balkansky et al. 1997; Feinman 1999). Yet each of the El Palmillo domestic compounds was rebuilt and occupied for a longer duration than was the Ejutla house, and this occupational difference would tend to strengthen the observation that maize preparation implements were indeed less abundant at El Palmillo.

To supplement maize, El Palmillo's Classic-period residents most likely depended on a range of xerophytic plants. Although most of the flattened space on the residential terraces at El Palmillo was occupied by domestic architecture, plants adapted to rocky terrain could have been fostered and cultivated along terrace walls. Currently, these walls support dense xerophytic vegetation, particularly during the wet season. Cacti and maguey could easily have been planted on the sloping retaining walls of the residential terraces in the past, providing not only some privacy (Parsons 1936:9) but also reinforcing the walls and preventing erosion (Ortiz de Montellano 1990:97; Patrick 1985; Wilken 1987:105). These plants also do well on the unterraced rocky slopes of the site.

The use of xerophytic plants as food, medicine, and sources of fiber has a long history in the Valley of Oaxaca (Flannery 1983b, 1986; Flannery and Spores 1983; King 1986; Smith 1978, 1986). Archaic-period (c. 9000–2000 BC) occupants of the Valley of Oaxaca relied on a variety of xerophytic plants in their diet, including seeds from *nanche* (*Malpighia* sp.) and *nopal*/prickly pear (*Opuntia* sp.), *biznaga* (*Ferocactus recurvus*), maguey (*Agave* spp.), and *susí* nuts (*Jatropha* sp.) (Flannery and Spores 1983:22). Evidence of *nopal* also is found at later Formative period (c. 1500–200 BC) villages (Whalen 1981:192).

Botanical studies at Yagul (Martínez y Ojeda 1996) and El Palmillo (Middleton et al. 2001) have confirmed the presence of many of these same plants at later sites in eastern Tlacolula. The vegetation at El Palmillo includes a variety of economically useful plants that are present throughout the immediate area and form the backbone of the local natural floral community (Middleton et al. 2001; see also Martínez y Ojeda 1996). Yet during the botanical survey, we documented that several plant species are more common at El Palmillo than in the surrounding hills (Middleton et al. 2001). The most significant of these plants are several varieties of *Agave* ssp. (maguey) (Figure 9.3), *Yucca periculosa* (yucca, locally known as *palmillo*) (Figure 9.4), and *Opuntia pilifera* (Figure 9.5).

The distribution and diversity of maguey (*Agave* spp.) at El Palmillo are especially intriguing. Specific varieties of maguey often prefer narrow, specific locales and microenvironmental conditions (Gentry 1982). Of the eight species of *Agave* that Sánchez López (1989:34) lists for the Tlacolula subvalley, all of which were used for food and/or fiber in the past (and most still are today), no community in his study had more than three to five species of *Agave*. Yet we have recorded the same eight species of maguey on a single promontory site, El Palmillo. While two species (*Agave karwinskii* and *A. potatorum)* also are present on hills near El Palmillo, the other six (*Agave angustifolia*, *A. americana*, *A. kerchovei*, *A. macroacantha*, *A. marmorata*, and *A. rhodacantha*) are not (Middleton et al. 2001). Given the large number of *Agave* species that still grow at El

Figure 9-3. Wild maguey plant (*Agave marmorata*) at El Palmillo.

Palmillo today and not on nearby hills, we suspect that some of the magueys at El Palmillo were taken to the site from other locales in pre-Hispanic times and were fostered or husbanded on site for their economic and food value. Similar techniques to expand the range and foster agave varieties have been documented for the pre-Hispanic North American Southwest (Hodgson 2001; Hodgson and Slauson 1995; see also Folan et al. 1979).

The marked abundance of *Agave* spp., *Opuntia* sp., and other economically useful plants at El Palmillo, especially in comparison with nearby hills that lack the surface vestiges of pre-Hispanic occupation, lead us to believe that El Palmillo's plant community is a relict of the pre-Hispanic habitation of the hill. No other hills in the area, including hills closer to the modern village or the colonial-period hacienda, have this suite or range of economically useful plants. Given the economic and dietary usefulness of the identified xerophytic plant community, we believe these plants were an integral part of the economy and subsistence base of El Palmillo. Here we focus on three economically important xerophytic plants—maguey, yucca, and *nopal*—that are particularly abundant at El Palmillo.

Maguey, Yucca, and Nopal

Maguey (*Agave* spp.) has long been recognized as a highly versatile and economically important plant in highland Mexico, where its use is well

Figure 9-4. Palmillo (*Yucca periculosa*) at El Palmillo.

Figure 9-5. Nopal (*Opuntia pilifera*) at El Palmillo.

documented ethnohistorically (Beals 1975; Malinowski and de la Fuente 1982; Parsons 1936; Parsons and Parsons 1990) and pre-Hispanically (Anawalt 1981; Callen 1965, 1967; Ebeling 1986; Evans 1990; Gonçalves de Lima 1956; King 1986; MacNeish 1967; Ortiz de Montellano 1990; Smith 1967, 1986; Smith and Kerr 1968). According to a sixteenth-century account, "[maguey], by itself, could easily furnish all that is needed for a simple, frugal life . . . There is nothing which gives a higher return" (Hernández 1959 [1577], vol. 1, p. 349).

Different parts of the maguey plant can be harvested or exploited to fulfill a diversity of needs. The sap can be processed into diverse liquids and alcoholic beverages (Brumen 2000), the flesh can be roasted and eaten, the pulpy leaves can be stripped to produce fibers or mashed into medicinal poultices, and what remains can be burned for fuel or even used as a construction material. Maguey sap, or *aguamiel*, is one of the most versatile dietary components of agave (Evans 1990; Hough 1908; Parsons and Darling 2000; Parsons and Parsons 1990). When freshly extracted from the plant, *aguamiel* is a thin, watery liquid with a pleasant sweet, tart flavor that can be consumed raw and, in arid areas, may serve as a substitute for water (Evans 1990:125). *Aguamiel* is not only refreshing but also nutritious; the sap contains protein, carbohydrates, and a variety of vitamins and minerals including calcium, iron, and vitamin C.

Aguamiel can be fermented into a nondistilled, mildly alcoholic beverage called *pulque*. One liter of this nutritious drink contains roughly 600 calories and supplies important minerals, amino acids, and vitamins (Parsons and Darling 2000:83). Studies conducted in the 1940s among Otomí villagers revealed that *pulque* contributed as much as 12% of their total calories (second only to tortillas) and 48% of their total vitamin C (Anderson et al. 1946:888, table 2). Taken in moderation, *pulque's* nutritional value makes it a reasonable substitute for meat (Gentry 1982:11). *Aguamiel* also can be boiled down into a sugar that can be formed into cakes for easy portability; these cakes are highly caloric and can be stored for long periods of time (Evans 1990:126–127; Parsons and Darling 2000:83). The highly nutritious flesh contains roughly 350 calories and 4.5 grams of protein per 100 grams (about a 3.5 ounce serving) (Fish et al. 1985:112).

A fermented beverage (almost certainly *pulque*) was consumed in Oaxaca in the sixteenth century (Paso y Troncoso 1905 [1580]:145), and the Postclassic consumption of *pulque* is documented in the Codex Vindobonensis (a Mixtec document from Oaxaca) (Furst 1978:201–203). Similar images also are present in the Codex Nuttall (Nutall 1975:plate 82). Later in the nineteenth century, maguey was grown in almost all eastern Tlacolula towns, with Matatlán the largest producer of these plants in the eastern part of this arm (Taylor 1972:103).

In our findings from El Palmillo, several classes of evidence indicate maguey's significance as a food source. Two large ovens similar to present-day maguey ovens in Matatlán (Feinman et al. 2001) were excavated on the lower terraces. Soil sampled from the El Palmillo ovens is compositionally similar to soil collected from modern ovens in Matatlán (Middleton et al. 2001; Serra Puche et al. 2000). In addition, coarse, maguey-like fibers were found adhering to sooted stones and ceramics from the El Palmillo ovens. We suspect these ovens were used for roasting maguey hearts. In addition, the artifact assemblages from the excavated terraces at El Palmillo contain a range of stone scrapers that resemble tools used today for processing maguey into food and fiber.

The extraction of the maguey fibers is a labor-intensive process that requires the leaves to be sheared from the plant and then either roasted or placed in a rotting pit to allow the flesh to soften; the fibers are then extracted by washing and scraping the leaves (Parsons and Parsons 1990). We recovered many obsidian blades on the excavated terraces, which were possibly used to cut the leaves free from the plant (Evans 1990; Nichols et al. 2000). The aforementioned scraper planes (*raspadores*) likely could have been used to remove fibers from maguey leaves.

Ceramic spindle whorls used to spin fibers into thread were recovered from all the excavated terraces at El Palmillo (Feinman et al. 2002a, 2003). Different types, or grades, of thread can be produced based on the size and weight of the spindle whorl and the dimension of the central hole (Evans 1990; Nichols et al.

2000; Parsons and Parsons 1990; Parsons 1972, 1975). According to Parsons and Parsons (1990:328–330), midweight whorls (between 11 to 23 g) can be used to spin the finer maguey fibers into a fine thread; heavier and larger whorls (above 23 g) are unsuited for the finer fibers and instead were most likely used to spin coarser thread. Spindle whorls recovered at El Palmillo include sizes suitable for spinning both fine and coarse threads. In addition, several stone bark beaters recovered during the excavations may have been employed to make maguey-fiber paper (Gonçalves de Lima 1956:195).

The El Palmillo site derives its contemporary name from the large stands of *Yucca periculosa* (locally referred to as *palmillo*) that dot the hill where the site is situated. In addition to El Palmillo, this plant is present at other archaeological sites today, such as the Mitla Fortress and Yagul (Martínez y Ojeda 1996), although it is not commonly noted elsewhere in the eastern Tlacolula subvalley. Like maguey, yucca was used pre-Hispanically as both a food (the fruit) and for fiber (the leaves) (Sheldon 1980). As a food, the fruits and seeds could have been dried and stored (Ebeling 1986:472–474). Among the later Aztecs, yucca fibers were woven into mantles, skirts, cord, and cloaks or jackets (Anawalt 1981:27, 33, 45; Berdan 1987:245). The abundance of yucca at El Palmillo—where a great grove of the plant still stands at the apex of the hill, and its presence at other sites (while rare elsewhere)—provides support that this plant was utilized and, perhaps, fostered pre-Hispanically.

Like yucca, *nopal* (or prickly pear) is far more abundant at El Palmillo than in the surrounding hills. This cactus also has a variety of economic uses; virtually all parts of the plant (fruit, juice, flesh, and sap) can be consumed in some manner. Sap from *nopal* (*zumo*) can serve as a beverage when water is scarce, or it can be mixed with other substances as a salve for burns (Donkin 1977:12). Still today in Matatlán, *nopal* pads are a key dry-season staple, especially for village inhabitants of lesser means, and stands of *nopal* are cultivated in agricultural fields.

Nopal also is the host plant for an economically important insect that produces the vibrant red dye, cochineal. Cochineal was highly prized by both the Spanish (Donkin 1977; Evans 1990; Gibson 1964:354; Lee 1947–1948) and the Aztecs (Durán 1994[1581]; Evans 1990). The dye is produced from the dried bodies of the female scale insect, *Dactylopius coccus* Costa (Baranyovits 1978:88; Lee 1947–1948:450). The desiccated remains closely resemble small seeds or grains (Baranyovits 1978; Lee 1947–1948), which led to the colloquial term *grana* (grain) being used to describe the raw dye.

Pre-Hispanically, cochineal had many uses, the most important of which was dying textiles. But at the same time, cochineal was employed for painting codices (Donkin 1977:20), decorating tomb walls (Franco Brizuela 1997), and coloring wood, stone, and ceramics (Lee 1947–1948:453). By 1572 (following

Spanish conquest), cochineal production in Oaxaca was important enough to the Spanish export economy to warrant the establishment of a separate weighing and registration office in the valley (Lee 1947–1948:note 116). Cochineal was Mexico's second most valuable export commodity (after silver) for much of the colonial period (Baskes 2000:9). For Oaxaca, however, it was the region's most important economic product by the mid-eighteenth century (Taylor 1972:14), when as many as one-third of the province's households were involved in some aspects of its production (Baskes 2000:12). As much as 40% of the cochineal was produced in the central valleys, including the district that encompassed Matatlán (Baskes 2000:17). Colonial-period documents mention peasant cochineal producers from Matatlán (Baskes 2000:84; Taylor 1972:65). Even into the mid-1900s, cochineal was still easy to obtain in the Tlacolula and Oaxaca markets (Parsons 1936:45).

At present, Classic-period cochineal production at El Palmillo can only be inferred from the dense concentrations of its host plant, *Opuntia pilifera* (*nopal*), on site. There is no question that cochineal was important in Oaxaca in the Postclassic period; this red dye was a major tribute item exacted from Oaxaca by the Aztecs (Berdan and Anawalt 1997:108; Schmieder 1930:19). Its role in Classic-period Oaxaca is less clear. Although we have noted bright red pigment on figurines, urns, and a tomb wall at El Palmillo, we have not yet established whether cochineal was the source of this red dye (but see Franco Brizuela 1997). Yet arguments for a Classic-period cochineal industry at El Palmillo are strengthened by the archaeologically documented presence of the spinning and weaving of maguey and other fibers (Feinman et al. 2001, 2002a), materials on which the dye could have been applied. Given its later importance in Postclassic and colonial-period Oaxaca, cochineal was likely to have been economically important at El Palmillo during the Classic period.

Maguey, yucca, and *nopal* are just three of the dozens of economically important plants still found at El Palmillo today (Feinman et al. 2002a; Middleton et al. 2001). Many of these plants are good potential sources of calories, vitamins, and even some protein that have been exploited in highland Oaxaca for millennia. Based on the presence of the maguey roasting ovens at El Palmillo, the identification of little crystal rods in agave, called raphides, in sediment samples from these excavated ovens, the abundance of agave and other plants on site, the associated tool kits, and other information, we suspect that these xerophytic plants composed a significant portion of the diet at El Palmillo and, by extension, other later pre-Hispanic Eastern Tlacolula settlements. If the people of eastern Tlacolula did indeed eat little maize at the cusp of the colonial period (Paso y Troncoso 1905 [1579–1581]:149–150), then it is difficult to see how they could have grown and relied on maize as a staple during the Classic and Postclassic periods. The xerophytic plants also yielded the raw materials for fiber, weaving, and other craft industries in this dry sector of the valley (Feinman and Nicholas 2004b). Together with other crafts such as stone working, household weaving and fiber industries provided an economic foundation for the residents of El Palmillo and other eastern Tlacolula terrace sites (Feinman and Nicholas 2004a) that likely enabled them to procure through exchange some maize and other plant foods that would have been difficult to grow in great quantities, year after year, in this dry sector of the valley. Yet if xerophytic plants and other available resources were able to support the high demographic densities that resided in eastern Tlacolula during the Classic and Postclassic periods, then why was the population of this area so sparse earlier (Feinman et al. 1985; Feinman and Nicholas 1990; Kowalewski 2003), and why was the demographic collapse in this part of the valley even steeper than elsewhere in the Valley of Oaxaca during the sixteenth through eighteenth centuries (Kowalewski 2003:319)?

ECONOMIC LINKAGES IN THE VALLEY AND BEYOND

Although domestic producers in eastern Tlacolula during the Classic period relied on fiber and stone-related crafts (Feinman and Nicholas 2004a, 2004b), the findings from the El Palmillo excavations indicate that each household was associated with a somewhat different artifactual assemblage, and so likely had different economic foci or emphases. For example, the occupants of the lowest excavated terraces at the site seem to have been involved in basic lithic reduction activities, as well as some ground stone tool manufacture less evident elsewhere at the site, while the residents of terrace 507 appear to have executed lapidary production not found elsewhere (Haines et al. 2004). In general, residents of the lower terraces spun greater quanties of coarse maguey fiber, while finer yarns tended to be spun farther up the hill (Feinman and Nicholas 2004b). These differences in production activities between sites (Feinman and Nicholas 2004a, 2004b; Kowalewski et al. 1989; Middleton et al. 2002) and even within sites (Feinman and Nicholas 2002a; Haines et al. 2004), where householders were producing distinct craft goods for circulation, require that there were active means by which goods moved across different spatial scales. Given the scale of the regional population (estimated at considerably over 70,000 throughout the Classic period) and the active circulation of utilitarian as well as rarer more valued goods, we suspect that the means of circulation and economic connectivity had to involve more than just face-to-face reciprocity between known exchange partners and/or kin.

There is no question that the economic circulation of goods was part and parcel of life in the Valley of Oaxaca for centuries before the Classic period (e.g., Flannery 1976; Kowalewski et al. 1983). Yet there seems little doubt that exchanges and economic interdependence in the region intensified early in the Classic period, a time when the valley population increased markedly and a ring of hilltop sites was situated along the physiographic edges of the valley (Kowalewski et al. 1989). At this time, the region was at least partly under the political hegemony of Monte Albán, the centrally located center whose public architectural grandeur and size were unmatched in the region (e.g., Blanton 1978). Although there is no indication that the rulers at Monte Albán directly controlled exchange or production, various kinds of evidence can be used to imply that the volume of economic circulation and interconnection increased in the Valley of Oaxaca at the outset of the Classic period. In eastern Tlacolula, as well as elsewhere, periodic (albeit local) imbalances and reliance on food exchanges likely became more common than at any time previously (Nicholas 1989). Based on the regional surveys, we argued in 1989 (Kowalewski et al. 1989:213) that there was "more evidence for specialized craft production—in the form of technological attributes, the distribution of goods, and work areas—for IIIA [the Early Classic] than any prior phase." Subsequent excavations at El Palmillo and the Ejutla site (Feinman and Nicholas 2000) have only strengthened these findings.

At the same time, as outlined earlier (Kowalewski et al. 1989:213), we suspect that the changes in the Classic-period economy were not simply quantitative (related to the larger valley population) but qualitative. With a greater degree of valleywide political unification, the modes and means of production and exchange appear to have intensified and shifted in ways we do not yet fully comprehend. For example, during the Classic period, if we look at a durable and datable good—ceramics—mold-made figurines largely replaced modeled figurines, while urns incorporated cookie-cutter molded appliques that were used in lieu of more handcrafted forms. Basic ceramic vessels, particularly bowls, also became progressively less elaborate, more formalized, and easier to transport (Feinman 1982; Kowalewski et al. 1989:213–221, 226). We suspect that the domestic economic options selected in eastern Tlacolula during the Early Classic period could have succeeded and endured for generations only in the context of a burgeoning network of circulation and exchange. With the development of high-volume modes of exchange, eastern Tlacolula households could have reliably depended for at least part of their living on the production for exchange of woven garments, fiber footwear, rope, cloth, dye, chert cores, alcohol, and a range of other goods, some of which were still made in this part of the valley into the twentieth century. Of course, this perspective is not in conflict with the notion that the "demands" for some of these goods and products, such as alcohol, red dye, and various vestments, may have been fostered or encouraged through overarching changes in customs and cultural conventions. Such changes in tradition, whether prompted by design or serendipity, may have expanded or shifted the kinds of goods that were socially valued. As a consequence, the consumption patterns for such products and, ultimately, the degree of intraregional economic connectivity also were affected.

Although the political consolidation of the valley under Monte Albán early in the Classic period served to spur demographic expansion in eastern Tlacolula, the fall of Monte Albán (c. AD 800) did not prompt population decline in this region. In fact, during the late pre-Hispanic period, more people lived in Tlacolula than any other arm of the valley (Feinman et al. 1985). The continued demographic expansion during the Postclassic period in Tlacolula, along with an increasing emphasis on craft manufacture, temporally coincided with overall demographic growth in the valley and the increasing movement of goods and people across both polity boundaries and the surrounding mountains that define this region (Drennan 1989; Feinman 1997; Kowalewski et al. 1983, 1989). With the rise of major Postclassic-era Tlacolula Valley centers at Mitla and Macuilxochitl, craft production in that region (as well as the valley as a whole) appears to have intensified with intra- and interregional flows of goods increasing in volume (e.g., Feinman et al. 1989).

It was only following Spanish conquest that the population in eastern Tlacolula declined dramatically, seemingly at a proportional rate even greater than the rest of the valley (Kowalewski 2003:319). Significantly, the more dramatic drop-off in Tlacolula population co-occurred with the great overall decline in valley population and a breakdown in regional exchange networks. With less active intra- and interregional linkages, making a living in eastern Tlacolula became somewhat tenuous, and the population in this sector of the valley declined more precipitously than elsewhere. During the seventeenth and eighteenth centuries, native communities had large tracts of land and comparatively little interaction with Spanish estates (as compared with other parts of the valley) (Taylor 1972:102–107). Despite the colonial-era Spanish demand for cochineal, householders in Tlacolula could not reliably get the basic goods and staples they needed, leading to food shortages and population loss (Hamnett 1971:14). In fact, Baskes (2000:186–187) argues that during the colonial period, the Spanish—in their desire to control the lucrative cochineal trade—established numerous restrictions on production activities and built protectionist walls limiting the rights of certain classes to participate in exchange. The colonial-period cochineal trade brought wealth to the state of Oaxaca, but it apparently benefited a limited few.

Only in the nineteenth century, when economic interaction within the region and with other parts of Mexico increased in volume and the overall population of the Valley of Oaxaca as a whole began to reach pre-Hispanic levels again (Cohen 1999:27–35; Murphy and Stepick 1991:26–43), did the population of eastern Tlacolula experience a marked and proportional increase compared with the other valley sectors (although it is still not the demographic center of gravity that it was in AD1500) (Kowalewski 2003:319). Significantly, manufacturing basic goods, such as woven items, fiber products, and alcohol, remains key to the household productive economy and regional exchange in this part of the valley (e.g., Beals 1979; Parsons 1936; Rothstein and Rothstein 2002). At the same time, the late twentieth-century Sunday market in Tlacolula is second in size and activity only to the Saturday market in Oaxaca City (Beals 1979:129–131). No other market in the central valley even compares. A view across the last two millennia provides strong support for the view that the population of eastern Tlacolula and that area's artisan producers appear to have thrived when active exchange networks linked them with their neighbors, as well as with people living farther away. Consequently, we would venture that the consolidation and increased economic integration of the valley that occurred by the outset of the Early Classic period was seemingly a necessary, albeit not a sufficient, condition for eastern Tlacolula's demographic take-off.

CONCLUDING THOUGHTS

This paper serves to honor the extremely impressive and highly influential contributions of Jeff and Mary Parsons. Their dedication to systematic regional settlement pattern survey, as well as their more recent detailed studies of contemporary crafts, pre-Hispanic cloth production, and the utility of xerophytic plants in Mesoamerica, have provided fundamental insights and consistent inspirations for our own investigations as well as the more specific arguments presented here.

More broadly, we also see this presentation as a testament to the critical importance of full-coverage archaeological survey. Questions spurred a quarter century ago regarding the surprisingly high late pre-Hispanic population of arid eastern Tlacolula served as the intellectual genesis of this effort, stimulating the implementation of finer-grain intensive site surveys and residential excavations in this part of the valley. Through this multiscalar approach, we now better understand that the presumed nutritional centrality of maize was probably overstated in many past interpretations. At the same time, we see how domestic-scale craft production and a link into active spheres of economic circulation underpinned the demographic expansion of eastern Tlacolula during the Early Classic period, thereby serving as a foundation for the region's additional growth and socioeconomic development in the later Postclassic. Finally, we hope that these findings will help the people of eastern Tlacolula gain a fuller understanding of their long and rich history: why craft, cloth, and the juice of the agave are so central to the millennial record that they share with their ancestors.

Acknowledgments

It is our distinct privilege to contribute to this volume in honor of Jeff and Mary Parsons. They have been thoughtful teachers and generous colleagues to us both through their writings and during insightful conversations at Midwest Mesoamericanist meetings and other conferences and get-togethers through the decades. We also wish to thank Richard Blanton for inviting us to participate in this well-deserved festschrift. We gratefully acknowledge the National Science Foundation support given to the first author for the excavations at El Palmillo (SBR–9805288) and Ejutla (BNS 89–19164, BNS 91–05780, SBR–9304258). We also appreciate the valuable support received from the National Geographic Society, the H. John Heinz III Fund of the Heinz Family Foundation, The Field Museum, the Graduate School of the University of Wisconsin–Madison, and Arvin B. Weinstein. This study would not have been possible without the dedicated assistance of our Oaxacan and North American field and laboratory crews. We profoundly thank the Instituto Nacional de Antropología e Historia of Mexico, the Centro Regional de Oaxaca, and the local authorities of Santiago Matatlán and Ejutla de Crespo for the necessary permissions to implement these field studies, as well as for their essential support.

REFERENCES CITED

Anawalt, Patricia Rieff
   1981   *Indian Clothing Before Cortes: Mesoamerican Costumes from the Codices.* University of Oklahoma Press, Norman.
Anderson, Richmond K., Jose Calvo, Gloria Serrano, and George C. Payne
   1946   A Study of the Nutritional Status and Food Habits of Otomí Indians in the Mezquital Valley of Mexico. *American Journal of Public Health and the Nation's Health* 36:883–903.
Asensio, Gaspar
   1905 [1580]   Relación de Macuilsúchil y su Partido. In *Papeles de Nueva España: Segunda serie, geografía y estadística, Vol. 4*, edited by Francisco del Paso y Troncoso, pp. 100–104. Est. Tipográfico "Sucesores de Rivadeneyra," Madrid.
Balkansky, Andrew, Gary M. Feinman, and Linda M. Nicholas
   1997   Pottery Kilns of Ancient Ejutla, Oaxaca, Mexico. *Journal of Field Archaeology* 24:139–160.
Baranyovits, F.L.C.
   1978   Cochineal Carmine: An Ancient Dye with a Modern Role. *Endeavour n.s.* 2:85–92.

Baskes, Jeremy
  2000 *Indian, Merchants, and Markets: A Reinterpretation of the Repartimiento and Spanish–Indian Economic Relations in Colonial, Oaxaca 1750–1821.* Stanford University Press, Stanford.

Beals, Ralph L.
  1975 *The Peasant Marketing System of Oaxaca, Mexico.* University of California Press, Berkeley.
  1979 Economic Adaptations in Mitla, Oaxaca. In *Mesoamerica: Homenaje al Doctor Paul Kirchhoff,* edited by Barbro Dahlgren, pp. 165–193. Instituto Nacional de Antropología e Historia, Mexico, D.F.

Berdan, Frances F.
  1987 Cotton in Aztec Mexico: Production, Distribution, and Uses. *Mexican Studies/ Estudios Mexicanos* 3:235–262.

Berdan, Frances F., and Patricia Rieff Anawalt
  1997 *The Essential Codex Mendoza.* University of California Press, Berkeley.

Blanton, Richard E.
  1978 *Monte Albán: Settlement Patterns at the Ancient Zapotec Capital.* Academic Press, New York.

Blanton, Richard E., Stephen A. Kowalewski, Gary M. Feinman, and Laura M. Finsten
  1993 *Ancient Mesoamerica: A Comparison of Change in Three Regions.* 2nd ed. Cambridge University Press, Cambridge.

Blanton, Richard E., Stephen A. Kowalewski, Gary M. Feinman, and Jill Appel
  1982 *Monte Albán's Hinterland, Part 1: Prehispanic Settlement Patterns of the Central and Southern Parts of the Valley of Oaxaca, Mexico.* Memoirs No. 15, Museum of Anthropology, University of Michigan, Ann Arbor.

Brumen, Henry J.
  2000 *Alcohol in Ancient Mexico.* University of Utah Press, Salt Lake City.

Callen, Edward O.
  1965 Food Habits of Some Pre-Columbian Mexican Indians. *Economic Botany* 9:334–343.
  1967 Analysis of Tehuacan Coprolites. In *Prehistory of the Tehuacan Valley, Volume One: Environment and Subsistence,* edited by Douglas S. Byers, pp. 261–289. University of Texas Press, Austin.

Canseco, Alonso de
  1905 [1580] Relación de Tlacolula y Mitla hecha en los días 12 y 23 de agosto respectivamente. In *Papeles de Nueva España: segunda serie, geografía y estadística, Vol. 4,* edited by Francisco del Paso y Troncoso. Est. Tipográfico "Sucesores de Rivadeneyra," Madrid.

Caso, Alfonso
  1938 *Exploraciones en Oaxaca, quinta y sexta temporadas 1936–1937.* Publicación 34, Instituto Panamericano de Geografía e Historia, Mexico, D.F.

Cohen, Jeffrey H.
1999   *Cooperation and Community: Economy and Society in Oaxaca.* University of Texas Press, Austin.

Donkin, Robin A.
1977   *Spanish Red: An Ethnographical Study of Cochineal and the Opuntia Cactus.* Transactions of the American Philosophical Society, Vol. 67, Part 5, The American Philosophical Society, Philadelphia.

Drennan, Robert D.
1989   The Mountains North of the Valley. In *Monte Albán's Hinterland, Part II: Prehispanic Settlement Patterns in Tlacolula, Etla, and Ocotlán, the Valley of Oaxaca, Mexico*, by Stephen A. Kowalewski, Gary M. Feinman, Laura Finsten, Richard E. Blanton, and Linda M. Nicholas, pp. 367–384. Memoirs No. 23, Museum of Anthropology, University of Michigan, Ann Arbor.

Druijven, Peter, and Annette Kruithof
1992   Tlacolula Valley, Oaxaca, Mexico. In *Coping with Semiaridity: How the Rural Poor Survive in Dry-Season Environments*, edited by Henk Reitsma, Ton Dietz, and Leo de Haan, pp. 132–152. Netherlands Geographic Studies 146, Amsterdam.

Durán, Fray Diego
1994 [1581]   *The History of the Indies of New Spain.* Translated, annotated, and with an introduction by Doris Heyden. University of Oklahoma Press, Norman.

Ebeling, Walter
1986   *Handbook of Indian Foods and Fibers of Arid America.* University of California Press, Berkeley.

Evans, Susan T.
1990   The Productivity of Maguey Terrace Agriculture in Central Mexico during the Aztec Period. *Latin American Antiquity* 1:117–132.

Feinman, Gary M.
1982   Patterns in Ceramic Production and Distribution: Periods Early I through V. In *Monte Albán's Hinterland, Part 1: Prehispanic Settlement Patterns of the Central and Southern Parts of the Valley of Oaxaca, Mexico*, by Richard E. Blanton, Stephen A. Kowalewski, Gary M. Feinman, and Jill Appel, pp. 181–210. Memoirs No. 15, Museum of Anthropology, University of Michigan, Ann Arbor.

1997   Macro–Scale Perspectives on Settlement and Production in Ancient Oaxaca. In *Economic Analysis beyond the Local System*, edited by Richard E. Blanton, Peter N. Peregrine, Deborah Winslow, and Thomas D. Hall, pp. 13–42. Monographs in Economic Anthropology 13, University Press of America, Lanham.

1999   Rethinking Our Assumptions: Economic Specialization at the Household Scale in Ancient Ejutla, Oaxaca, Mexico. In *Pottery and People: Dynamic*

Interactions, edited by James M. Skibo and Gary M. Feinman, pp. 81–98. University of Utah Press, Salt Lake City.

Feinman, Gary M., Sherman Banker, Reid F. Cooper, Glen B. Cook, and Linda M. Nicholas

1989   A Technological Perspective on Changes in the Ancient Oaxaca Grayware Ceramic Tradition: Preliminary Results. *Journal of Field Archaeology* 16:331–344.

Feinman, Gary M., Stephen A. Kowalewski, Laura Finsten, Richard E. Blanton, and Linda M. Nicholas

1985   Long–Term Demographic Change: A Perspective from the Valley of Oaxaca, Mexico. *Journal of Field Archaeology* 12:333–362.

Feinman, Gary M., and Linda M. Nicholas

1990   At the Margins of the Monte Albán State: Settlement Patterns in the Ejutla Valley, Oaxaca, Mexico. *Latin American Antiquity* 1:216–246.

1996   Defining the Eastern Limits of the Monte Albán State: Systematic Settlement Pattern Survey in the Guirún Area, Oaxaca, Mexico. *Mexicon* 18:91–97.

2000   High–Intensity Household-Scale Production in Ancient Mesoamerica: A Perspective from Ejutla, Oaxaca. In *Cultural Evolution: Contemporary Viewpoints*, edited by Gary M. Feinman and Linda Manzanilla, pp. 119–142. Kluwer Academic/Plenum Publishers, New York.

2001   Excavations at El Palmillo: A Hilltop Terrace Site in Oaxaca, Mexico. *In The Field* 72(2):2–5.

2004a   *Hilltop Terrace Sites of Oaxaca, Mexico: Intensive Surface Survey at Guirún, El Palmillo, and the Mitla Fortress*. Fieldiana: Anthropology, new series No. 37. Field Museum of Natural History, Chicago.

2004b   Unraveling the Prehispanic Highland Mesoamerican Economy: Production, Exchange, and Consumption in the Classic Period Valley of Oaxaca. In *Archaeological Perspectives on Political Economies*, edited by Gary M. Feinman and Linda M. Nicholas, pp. 167–188. University of Utah Press, Salt Lake City.

Feinman, Gary M., Linda M. Nicholas, and Helen R. Haines

2002a   Houses on a Hill: Classic Period Domestic Life at El Palmillo, Oaxaca, Mexico. *Latin American Antiquity* 13:251–277.

Feinman, Gary M., Linda M. Nicholas, Helen R. Haines, and Jennifer A. Clark

2002b   El Palmillo: una perspectiva doméstica del período clásico en el valle de Oaxaca. Final report of the 2002 field season prepared for the Instituto Nacional de Antropología e Historia, Mexico, D.F.

Feinman, Gary M., Linda M. Nicholas, Helen R. Haines, and Jennifer A. Clark

2003   El Palmillo: una perspectiva doméstica del período clásico en el valle de Oaxaca. Final report of the 2003 field season prepared for the Instituto Nacional de Antropología e Historia, Mexico, D.F.

Feinman, Gary M., Linda M. Nicholas, and William D. Middleton
2001   Domestic Life at Classic Period Hilltop Terrace Sites: Perspectives from El
        Palmillo, Oaxaca. *Mexicon* 23:42–48.
Finsten, Laura
1983   The Classic-Postclassic Transition in the Valley of Oaxaca, Mexico. Unpub-
        lished Ph.D. dissertation, Department of Sociology and Anthropology, Purdue
        University, West Lafayette.
1995   *Jalieza, Oaxaca: Activity Specialization at a Hilltop Center.* Publications in
        Anthropology No. 48, Vanderbilt University, Nashville.
Fish, Suzanne K., Paul R. Fish, and John H. Madsen
1992   Evidence for Large-scale Agave Cultivation in the Marana Community. In
        The Marana Community in the Hohokam World, edited by Suzanne K. Fish,
        Paul R. Fish, and John H. Madsen, pp. 73–87. Anthropological Papers No.
        56, University of Arizona, Tucson.
Fish, Suzanne K., Paul R. Fish, Charles Miksicek, and John Madsen
1985   Prehistoric Agave Cultivation in Southern Arizona. *Desert Plants* 7:107–112.
Flannery, Kent V.
1983a   The Legacy of the Early Urban Period: An Ethnohistoric Approach to Monte
        Albán's Temples, Residences, and Royal Tombs. In *The Cloud People: Divergent
        Evolution of the Zapotec and Mixtec Civilizations*, edited by Kent V. Flannery and
        Joyce Marcus, pp. 132–136. Academic Press, New York.
1983b   Settlement, Subsistence, and Social Organization of the Proto-Otomangueans.
        In *The Cloud People: Divergent Evolution of the Zapotec and Mixtec Civilizations*,
        edited by Kent V. Flannery and Joyce Marcus, pp. 32–36. Academic Press,
        New York.
1986   Wild Food Resources of the Mitla Caves: Productivity, Seasonality, and Annual
        Variation. In *Guilá Naquitz: Archaic Foraging and Early Agriculture in Oaxaca,
        Mexico*, edited by Kent V. Flannery, pp. 255–264. Academic Press, New York.
Flannery, Kent (editor)
1976   *The Early Mesoamerican Village.* Academic Press, New York.
Flannery, Kent V., and Ronald Spores
1983   Excavated Sites of the Oaxaca Preceramic. In *The Cloud People: Divergent
        Evolution of the Zapotec and Mixtec Civilizations*, edited by Kent V. Flannery
        and Joyce Marcus, pp. 20–26. Academic Press, New York.
Folan, William J., Laraine A. Fletcher, and Ellen R. Kintz
1979   Fruit, Fiber, Bark, and Resin: Social Organization of a Maya Urban Center.
        Science 204:697–701.
Franco Brizuela, María Luisa
1997   La tumba de Huijazoo: privilegio zapoteco. In *Historia del arte de Oaxaca: arte
        prehispánico, Volumen 1*, edited by Margarita Dalton, pp. 151–173. Govierno
        del Estado de Oaxaca, Oaxaca, Mexico.

Furst, Jill Leslie
   1978   *Codex Vindobonensis Mexicanus I: A Commentary.* Publication No. 4, Institute
           for Mesoamerican Studies, State University of New York at Albany, Albany.
Gentry, Howard S.
   1982   *Agaves of Continental North America.* University of Arizona Press, Tucson.
Gibson, Charles
   1964   *The Aztecs Under Spanish Rule: A History of the Indians of the Valley of Mexico,
           1519–1810.* Stanford University Press, Stanford.
Gonçalves de Lima, Oswaldo
   1956   *El maguey y el pulque en los códices mexicanos.* Fondo de Cultura Económica,
           Mexico City.
Haines, Helen R., Gary M. Feinman, and Linda M. Nicholas
   2004   A Perspective on Household Economic Specialization and Social Dif-
           ferentiation: The Stone–Tool Assemblage at El Palmillo, Oaxaca. *Ancient
           Mesoamerica* 15:251–266.
Hamnett, Brian R.
   1971   *Politics and Trade in Southern Mexico 1750–1821.* Cambridge University Press,
           Cambridge.
Hernández, Francisco
   1959 [1577]   *Historia natural de la Nueva España.* 2 vols. Universidad Nacional
           Autónoma de México, Mexico, D.F.
Hester, Thomas R., and Robert F. Heizer
   1972   Problems in the Functional Interpretation of Artifacts: Scraper Planes from
           Mitla and Yagul, Oaxaca. *University of California Archaeological Research Facility*
           14:107–123.
Hodgson, Wendy C.
   2001   Taxonomic Novelties in American Agave (Agavaceae). *Novon* 11:410–
           416.
Hodgson, Wendy C., and Liz Slauson
   1995   *Agave delamateri* (Agavaceae) and Its Role in the Subsistence Patterns of
           Pre-Columbian Cultures in Arizona. *Haseltonia* (Yearbook of the Cactus and
           Succulent Society of America) 3:130–140.
Holmes, William H.
   1897   *Archaeological Studies among the Ancient Cities of Mexico: Part II, Monuments of
           Chiapas, Oaxaca, and the Valley of Mexico.* Anthropological Series Vol. 1, No.
           1, Field Columbian Museum, Chicago.
Hough, Walter
   1908   The Pulque of Mexico. *Proceedings of the United States National Museum
           (Smithsonian)* 33(1579):577–592.
King, Mary Elizabeth
   1986   Preceramic Cordage and Basketry from Guilá Naquitz. In *Guilá Naquitz:*

Archaic Foraging and Early Agriculture in Oaxaca, Mexico, edited by Kent V. Flannery, pp. 157–161. Academic Press, Orlando.

Kirkby, Anne V.T.

1973   *The Use of Land and Water Resources in the Past and Present Valley of Oaxaca, Mexico*. Memoirs No. 5, Museum of Anthropology, University of Michigan, Ann Arbor.

Kowalewski, Stephen A.

1980   Population Resource Balances of Period I of Oaxaca Mexico. *American Antiquity* 45:151–165.

1990   The Evolution of Complexity in the Valley of Oaxaca. *Annual Review of Anthropology* 19:39–58.

2003   Scale and the Explanation of Demographic Change: 3,500 Years in the Valley of Oaxaca. *American Anthropologist* 105:313–325.

Kowalewski, Stephen A., Richard E. Blanton, Gary M. Feinman, and Laura Finsten

1983   Boundaries, Scale, and Internal Organization. *Journal of Anthropological Archaeology* 2:32–56.

Kowalewski, Stephen A., Gary M. Feinman, Laura Finsten, Richard E. Blanton, and Linda M. Nicholas

1989   *Monte Albán's Hinterland, Part II: Prehispanic Settlement Patterns in Tlacolula, Etla, and Ocotlán, the Valley of Oaxaca, Mexico*. Memoirs No. 23, Museum of Anthropology, University of Michigan, Ann Arbor.

Lee, Raymond L.

1947–1948   Cochineal Production and Trade in New Spain to 1600. *The Americas* 4:449–473.

Lind, Michael, and Javier Urcid

1983   The Lords of Lambityeco and Their Nearest Neighbors. *Notas Mesoamericanas* 9:78–111.

MacNeish, Richard S.

1967   Summary of Subsistence. In *Prehistory of the Tehuacan Valley, Volume One: Environment and Subsistence*, edited by Douglas S. Byers, pp. 290–309. University of Texas Press, Austin.

Malinowski, Bronislaw, and Julio de la Fuente

1982   *Malinowski in Mexico: The Economics of a Mexican Market System*. Routledge and Kegan Paul, London.

Marcus, Joyce, and Kent V. Flannery

1996   *Zapotec Civilization: How Urban Society Evolved in Mexico's Oaxaca Valley*. Thames and Hudson, London.

Martínez y Ojeda, Enrique

1996   *Guía ilustrada de las plantas de Yagul. Proyecto Yagul 96: conservación de los recursos ecológicos*. Centro INAH, Oaxaca, Mexico.

Messer, Ellen
  1978   *Zapotec Plant Knowledge: Classification, Uses, and Communication about Plants in Mitla, Oaxaca, Mexico.* Memoirs No. 10, Part 2, Museum of Anthropology, University of Michigan, Ann Arbor.

Middleton, William D., Gary M. Feinman, and Linda M. Nicholas
  2001   An Investigation of the Use of Xerophytic Plant Resources in the Economy and Subsistence of El Palmillo, Oaxaca, Mexico. Project report submitted to the Heinz Family Foundation, Pittsburgh.

  2002   Domestic Faunal Assemblages from the Classic Period Valley of Oaxaca, Mexico: A Perspective on the Subsistence and Craft Economies. *Journal of Archaeological Science* 29:233–249.

Murphy, Arthur D., and Alex Stepick
  1991   *Social Inequality in Oaxaca: A History of Resistance and Change.* Temple University Press, Philadelphia.

Nicholas, Linda M.
  1989   Land Use in Prehispanic Oaxaca. In *Monte Albán's Hinterland, Part II: Prehispanic Settlement Patterns in Tlacolula, Etla, and Ocotlán, the Valley of Oaxaca, Mexico,* by Stephen A. Kowalewski, Gary M. Feinman, Laura Finsten, Richard E. Blanton, and Linda M. Nicholas, pp. 449–505. Memoirs No. 23, Museum of Anthropology, University of Michigan, Ann Arbor.

Nichols, Deborah L., Mary Jane McLaughlin, and Maura Benton
  2000   Product Intensification and Regional Specialization: Maguey Fibers and Textiles in the Aztec City–State of Otumba. *Ancient Mesoamerica* 11:267–291.

Nuttall, Zelia
  1975   *The Codex Nuttall: A Picture Manuscript from Ancient Mexico.* Dover Publications, New York.

Ortiz de Montellano, Bernard R.
  1990   *Aztec Medicine, Health, and Nutrition.* Rutgers University Press, New Brunswick.

Paddock, John, Joseph R. Mogor, and Michael D. Lind
  1968   Lambityeco Tomb 2: A Preliminary Report. *Boletín de Estudios Oaxaqueños* 25. Museo de Frissell de Arte Zapoteca, Mitla, Oaxaca, Mexico.

Parsons, Elsie C.
  1936   *Mitla: Town of the Souls.* University of Chicago Press, Chicago.

Parsons, Jeffrey R.
  1971   *Prehistoric Settlement Patterns in the Texcoco Region, Mexico.* Memoirs No. 3, Museum of Anthropology, University of Michigan, Ann Arbor.

  1972   Archaeological Settlement Patterns. *Annual Review of Anthropology* 1:127–150.

  2002   Geological Mapping with Rob Scholten in the Beaverhead Range, SW Montana and Adjacent Idaho, Summer 1960. *Department of Geosciences Newsletter* 1:4, 6, 9, 10, 11.

Parsons, Jeffrey R., Elizabeth Brumfiel, Mary H. Parsons, and David J. Wilson

1982   *Prehispanic Settlement Patterns in the Southern Valley of Mexico: The Chalco-Xochimilco Region.* Memoirs No. 14, Museum of Anthropology, University of Michigan, Ann Arbor.

Parsons, Jeffrey R., and J. Andrew Darling

2000   Maguey (*Agave* spp.) Utilization in Mesoamerican Civilization: A Case for Precolumbian 'Pastoralism.' *Boletín de la Sociedad Botánica de México* 66:81–91.

Parsons, Jeffrey R., and Mary H. Parsons

1990   *Maguey Utilization in Highland Central Mexico: An Archaeological Ethnography.* Anthropological Papers No. 82, Museum of Anthropology, University of Michigan, Ann Arbor.

Parsons, Mary H.

1972   Spindle Whorls from the Teotihuacan Valley, Mexico. In *Miscellaneous Studies in Mexican Prehistory*, by Michael W. Spence, Jeffrey R. Parsons, and Mary H. Parsons, pp. 45–79. Anthropological Papers No. 45, Museum of Anthropology, University of Michigan, Ann Arbor.

1975   The Distribution of Late Postclassic Spindle Whorls in the Valley of Mexico. *American Antiquity* 40:207–215.

Paso y Troncoso, Francisco del

1905 [1579–1581]   *Papeles de Nueva España: Segunda serie, geografía y estadística, Vol. 4.* Est. Tipográfico "Sucesores de Rivadeneyra," Madrid.

Patrick, Larry L.

1985   Agave and Zea in Highland Central Mexico: The Ecology and History of the Metepantli. In *Prehistoric Intensive Agriculture in the Tropics*, edited by I.S. Farrington, pp. 539–546. BAR International Series 232, Part 2, British Archaeological Reports, Oxford.

Peterson, David A.

1976   Ancient Commerce. Unpublished Ph.D. dissertation, Department of Anthropology, State University of New York, Binghamton.

Robles G., Nelly M.

1994   *Las canteras de Mitla, Oaxaca: tecnología para la arquitectura monumental.* Publications in Anthropology No. 47, Vanderbilt University, Nashville.

Rothstein, Arden Aibel, and Anya Leah Rothstein

2002   *Mexican Folk Art: From Oaxacan Artist Families.* Schiffer Publishing, Atglen, Pennsylvania.

Sánchez López, Alberto

1989   *Oaxaca tierra de maguey y mezcal.* Instituto Tecnológico de Oaxaca, Oaxaca, Mexico.

Sanders, William T.

1999   Three Valleys: Twenty–Five Years of Settlement Archaeology in Mesoamerica. In *Settlement Pattern Studies in the Americas: Fifty Years Since Virú*, edited by Brian

R. Billman and Gary M. Feinman, pp. 12–21. Smithsonian Institution Press, Washington, D.C.

Sanders, William T., and Deborah L. Nichols
 1988   Ecological Theory and Cultural Evolution in the Valley of Oaxaca. *Current Anthropology* 29:33–52.

Sanders, William T., and Barbara J. Price
 1968   *Mesoamerica: The Evolution of a Civilization.* Random House, New York.

Saville, Marshall H.
 1900   Cruciform Structures near Mitla. *American Museum of Natural History, Bulletin* 13:201–218, New York.
 1909   The Cruciform Structures of Mitla and Vicinity. In *Anthropological Essays Presented to Frederic Ward Putnam in Honor of his Seventieth Birthday*, pp. 151–190. New York.

Schmieder, Oscar
 1930   *The Settlements of the Tzapotec and Mije Indians State of Oaxaca, Mexico.* University of California Press, Berkeley.

Schoenwetter, James
 1974   Pollen Records of Guilá Naquitz Cave. *American Antiquity* 39:292–303.

Serra Puche, Mari Carmen, J. Carlos Lazcano Arce, and Samuel Hernández Hernández
 2000   ¿Hornos para la producción de mezcal en un sitio del Formativo de Tlaxcala? *Arqueología* 24:149–157.

Sheldon, Sam
 1980   Ethnobotany of *Agave lecheguilla* and *Yucca carnerosana* in Mexico's Zona Ixtlera. *Economic Botany* 34:376–390.

Smith, C. Earle, Jr.
 1967   Plant Remains. In *Prehistory of the Tehuacan Valley, Volume One: Environment and Subsistence*, edited by Douglas S. Byers, pp. 220–255. University of Texas Press, Austin.
 1978   *The Vegetational History of the Oaxaca Valley.* Memoirs No. 10, Part 1, Museum of Anthropology, University of Michigan, Ann Arbor.
 1986   Preceramic Plant Remains form Guilá Naquitz. In *Guilá Naquitz: Archaic Foraging and Early Agriculture in Oaxaca, Mexico*, edited by Kent V. Flannery, pp. 265–274. Academic Press, Orlando.

Smith, C. Earle, Jr., and Thomas Kerr
 1968   Pre-conquest Plant Fibers from the Tehuacán Valley, Mexico. *Economic Botany* 22:354–358.

Spores, Ronald
 1972   *An Archaeological Settlement Survey of the Nochixtlán Valley, Oaxaca.* Publications in Anthropology No. 1, Vanderbilt University, Nashville.

Taylor, William B.
 1972   *Landlord and Peasant in Colonial Oaxaca.* Stanford University Press, Stanford.

Whalen, Michael E.

1981   *Excavations at Santo Domingo Tomaltepec: Evolution of a Formative Community in the Valley of Oaxaca*. Memoirs No. 12, Museum of Anthropology, University of Michigan, Ann Arbor.

1986   Sources of the Guilá Naquitz Chipped Stone. In *Guilá Naquitz: Archaic Foraging and Early Agriculture in Oaxaca, Mexico*, edited by Kent V. Flannery, pp. 141–156. Academic Press, Orlando.

Wilken, Gene C.

1987   *Good Farmers: Traditional Agricultural Resource Management in Mexico and Central America*. University of California Press, Berkeley.

Williams, Howel, and Robert F. Heizer

1965   Geological Notes on the Ruins of Mitla and Other Oaxacan Sites, Mexico. *Contributions of the University of California Archaeological Research Facility* 1:40–54.

Wolf, Eric R.

1959   *Sons of the Shaking Earth*. University of Chicago Press, Chicago.

THE MESOAMERICAN WORLD OF GOODS AND ITS TRANSFORMATIONS

RICHARD E. BLANTON
LANE F. FARGHER
VERENICE Y. HEREDIA ESPINOZA
Purdue University

INTRODUCTION

"World-system" denotes a territorially expansive economy characterized by a division of labor between polities and cultural groups. Stemming from Wallerstein's (1974) original formulation, a modified world-system approach to macroregional interaction (e.g., Stein 2002) has proven a useful complement to the region-centered cultural ecology that dominated archaeological thought during the mid-twentieth century (e.g., Schortman and Urban 1992). A developing world-system is saturated with the potential for sociocultural, environmental, and technological change in diverse social settings. This occurs as work-time is reallocated away from subsistence production and toward export production, as imported goods are substituted for local goods, as modes of labor mobilization are altered, as new sociocultural modes of goods exchange are developed, and as wealth disparities become more pronounced (cf. Chase-Dunn and Hall 1997; Chase-Dunn and Hall 1991; Frank and Gills 1993). Researchers interested in economic change in early civilizations, for example, in greater Mesopotamia (Algaze 1993) and the Mediterranean (Woolf 1990), have found world-system ideas a useful starting point. Mesoamericanists also have been a critical but receptive audience for these ideas (e.g., Blanton and Feinman 1984; Feinman and Nicholas 1992; Finsten 1996; Kepecs 1999; McAnany et al. 2002; Santley and Alexander 1992; Stark 1990; Stark, et al. 1998; Whitecotton 1992; cf. Peregrine and Feinman 1996).

The robustness and creativity of world-system theory is evident in a recent volume edited by Michael Smith and Frances Berdan (2003), *The Postclassic Mesoamerican World*. Smith, Berdan, and coauthors provide a detailed description of the structure and function of a complex world-system as it operated over several centuries prior to the Spanish Conquest. Their volume testifies to the advanced state of theory development and the growth of substantive knowledge about pre-Hispanic Mesoamerican economy, society, and culture. This chapter will not attempt to match the richness and complexity of *The Postclassic Mesoamerican World*, rather, we will try to build on it by proposing several hypotheses that serve to contextualize the Postclassic world-system within the history and sociocultural evolution of Mesoamerican civilization.

A GOODS-BASED APPROACH TO WORLD-SYSTEMS

In his original formulation of world-system theory, Wallerstein posits a structural opposition of luxury and staple goods (Wallerstein 1974:41-42). Luxury goods are "symbols of conspicuous consumption" consumed by an elite, but their exchange is not "systemic" (i.e. system-shaping). The exchange of staples, however, is systemic because they "account for more of men's economic thrusts than luxuries" (ibid.) In this chapter, we use a more empirical mode of inquiry by comparison with Wallerstein's stark dichotomy, built on descriptive summaries of a selection of Mesoamerican goods. From these summaries we derive several broad and overlapping goods categories, one of which we found strongly linked with world-system growth. Our categories are then ordered in an evolutionary scheme that allows us to place world-system development within its temporal and sociocultural contexts.

In developing our goods-based approach, we drew from the insights of world-system theory, but augmented it with studies of goods found in sources such as Appadurai (1986), Blanton (1994), Douglas and Isherwood (1979), Gregory (1982), McCracken (1988), Mintz (1985), Parsons and Parsons (1990), Parsons (2001), Sahlins (1994), and Schneider (1987). These authors illustrate the value of goods analysis as a stepping stone to understanding the complex interactions of environment, technology, society, and culture within an overarching framework of human agency. The perspectives developed in sources such as these suggest the need for a more nuanced and complex approach than Wallerstein's structural opposition of luxuries and staples. Schneider (1977:21), for example, points to the false dichotomy of luxuries and staples "which obscures the systemic properties of the luxury trade" (cf. Schneider 1978). In the scheme of Mesoamerican goods developed here, the systemicity of a good pertains to the degree to which its increased production results in significant social, demographic, technological, and agroecological change. As we point out below, all the goods considered, whether luxuries or staples, were "systematic," but the consequences of their production and use were quite distinct.

Rather than study a single good, as Mintz (1985) did in his enlightening discussion of sugar in early modern Europe, our goal here is more broadly evolutionary, deriving its conclusions from a comparison of several Mesoamerican goods used over a time span of 2,700 years from the latter Early Formative Period through the Late Postclassic Period (Table 10-1). For each good, we first identify major innovative episodes in its production, distribution and use that represent, in Adams's (2000:96) terminology, phases of "great irregularities in rates of change." Next, we investigate these innovative episodes, identifying those social, technological, and cultural processes that reveal its systemic properties. Our discussion of process elucidates relationships among technology, labor allocation, agroecology, exchange, demography, and consumption as they may play out under conditions of production intensification. We summarize process by asking the following questions about each good:

(1) Is it likely, within households, that inherent labor and time allocation bottlenecks would result in increased production specialization?

(2) Did increased production entail phases of population growth, migration, or altered modes of labor mobilization?

(3) Did the good place pressure on distribution systems, for example, a need for markets or other institutions linking production specializations? and

(4) Did production or use intensification of the good eventuate in the development of secondary products or markets?

Table 10-1. Archaeological periods mentioned in text

Period	Dates
	1520
Late Postclassic	
	1200
Early Postclassic	
	900
Epiclassic	
	700
Classic	
	AD 200
Terminal Formative	
	200 BC
Late Formative	
	500
Middle Formative	
	900
Early Formative	
	1400

A SAMPLE OF PRE-HISPANIC MESOAMERICAN GOODS

Given the complexity of the Mesoamerican economy, its great diversity of goods, and the vast literature on its goods, our approach can become unwieldy, so we restricted our investigation by briefly summarizing the literatures of a small sample of the many hundreds of pre-Hispanic Mesoamerican goods. We benefited from previous summaries such as Smith (2003a), who provides a functional categorization of 54 Postclassic goods. Goods of the Early and Middle Formative Periods are not well represented in our selection, given our analytical emphasis on the world-system evolution of subsequent periods. Even for later periods, we include only a small sample of the total number of goods in use. We limit our discussion to five goods—obsidian, salt, cacao, cotton cloth, and pottery—a selection we think illustrates the main features of broad evolutionary changes in the Mesoamerican world of goods and the evolution of its world-system.

I. Pottery
Transformation Period(s):

(a) Early and Middle Formative: New technologies making possible highly decorated vessels and large hollow figurines, including differentially fired black and white wares, specular hematite, and fine white pastes, were developed in the context of a phase of rapid social change after 1200 BC (e.g., Flannery and Marcus 1994), although technological changes in valuable pottery types are also evident later in the pre-Hispanic sequence (e.g. Plumbate, in Neff [1989]).

(b) Later Formative and Classic Periods: Production specialization and standardization of utilitarian vessel types are both evident in several regions (e.g., in Oaxaca [Blanton et al. 1999:chapter 4; Feinman 1982, 1999; Feinman, Kowalewski, and Blanton 1984], and at Teotihuacan [Rattray 1988]). These changes brought technological improvements in some regions, including more formalized pit kilns and up-draft kilns (Arnold III et al. 1993; Balkansky et al. 1997; Santley et al. 1993; Santley and Kneebone 1993; Winter and Payne 1976)

Labor/time bottlenecks? None are evident in an industry that featured a high degree of specialization in some regions, but at the same time, continued as an intensive but small-scale household industry with some exceptions that involved larger-scale production units (Feinman 1999; cf. Fargher 2004; Santley et al. 1989).

Demographic pressure (e.g., migration/labor mobilization)? Not likely.

Pressure on distribution, including markets? Specialist-produced ceramics were probably distributed primarily through market channels by the Postclassic (e.g., Díaz del Castillo 1956:216) and perhaps by as early as the Late

Formative in some areas (Feinman et al. 1984). Producer households probably would have been dependent on markets for subsistence goods, at least in part, especially in situations where large-scale production units were involved (e.g., Fargher 2004). But in other areas (e.g., in the Mixteca Alta [Heredia Espinoza 2005]), household production for home use remained common throughout the pre-Hispanic sequence. Even where specialization is likely, production technologies remained simple (including small kilns or surface firing), and generally household-based.

Secondary industries? Not well studied.

II. Salt
Transformation Period(s):

(a) Terminal Formative and Classic: During the Terminal Formative in the Basin of Mexico, large-scale salt production became increasingly important, probably related to the rise of regional centers at Teotihuacan and Cuicuilco (Parsons 2001:265). The primary center of salt production in the eastern Basin of Mexico at this time may have been El Tepalcate (Parsons 2001:303). This site covers 19 ha and is littered with probable salt production facilities, including large rectangular enclosures that may have been evaporation pans, and concentrations of pottery associated with stone piles that possibly functioned as leaching vessels placed on stone supports (Parsons 2001:261, 265). Production at El Tepalcate did not continue into the Classic Period and few locations of salt production have been identified for that period (Parsons 2001). There is also some evidence of Terminal Formative brine boiling from central and coastal Guatemala (Parsons 2001:270–271). Minor production changes, focused on boiling methods to extract salt from brine collected from springs or leached from soils, are evident by the Classic Period. Evidence for intensified production of salt through boiling at this time comes from Oaxaca, coastal Belize, Tehuacan, north-central Guatemala, and Chiapas (Andrews and Mock 2002; Castellón 1998; Dillon et al. 1988:44–7; Fargher 2004; Mackinnon and Kepecs 1989; Parsons 2001:270–272; Peterson 1976). A few localities saw an expansion in the scale and complexity of solar evaporation for salt production. They include northern Yucatan, Lake Sayula, Jalisco, Hierve el Agua, Oaxaca, and Tehuacan (Hewitt, et al. 1987; Kepecs 1999:383; Parsons 2001:272,274). According to Kepecs (1999:386) the large-scale solar evaporation pans were used to produced salt at the regional scale in the northern and southern Maya lowlands, but salt from northern Yucatan did not enter trade networks connecting highland and lowland Mesoamerica (Kepecs 1999:386).

(b) Postclassic Period: By the Late Postclassic Period, salt-making sites lined the edges of the saline lakes in the Basin of Mexico in a density far higher than any prior period, and a specialized ceramic type, fabric-marked (Blanton and Parsons 1971:312–313), is found in high densities on them (Parsons 2001:259, 266). The salt produced on these sites was probably not highly valued as a food additive, but had other purposes, including fish preservation and dye mordant (Parsons 2001:157–158). The nature of salt production at these sites has not been clearly determined, and the relative importance of solar evaporation versus brine boiling remains an open question (Parsons 2001:266). In the Valley of Oaxaca, solar evaporation and high-temperature boiling in ovens were used (Peterson 1976:101–103). Large-scale evaporation facilities were constructed in northern Yucatan during the Postclassic that supplied the Mesoamerican world with a high quality, pure, white sea salt, distributed through long-distance trade networks, which was probably available in Aztec markets (Kepecs 2003:129). During the Epiclassic And Early Postclassic, 25 hectares of salt pans were constructed at the famous salt making site of Emal (Kepecs 1999:410). These salt pans consisted of a series of large and small solar evaporation pans fed by a complex network of canals (Kepecs 1999:315). A second complex of similar salt pans was constructed at the northern Yucatan site of Otro Sacboh during the Late Postclassic Period (Kepecs 1999:516).

Labor/time bottlenecks? Not known.

Demographic pressure (e.g., migration/labor mobilization)? Kepecs (1999:422) suggests the possibility of seasonal labor migration in the large-scale Postclassic production systems of northern Yucatan.

Pressure on distribution, including markets? Distribution systems for the Formative and Classic Periods are not known, but by the Late Postclassic salt was sold in several grades in the Basin of Mexico marketplaces (Sahagún 1961, Book 10:84).

Secondary industries? Not clear. A specialized fabric-marked pottery was used in salt-making sites during the Basin of Mexico Late Postclassic (Parsons 2001:249-259), but it is not known if this was produced by specialists or available in markets.

III. Obsidian

Transformation Period(s):

(a) Classic Period Central Mexico: While obsidian prismatic blade technology was primarily a limited elite good in the Formative Period, by the Classic Period, blades were more widely available, including in areas distant from sources (Clark 1985). The central Mexican industry grew substantially and was socially transformed through the centralization of production and distribution. Mining focused on three primary source areas, among others, in Central Mexico—Pachuca (Cruz de Milagro), Otumba, and Paredon (Charlton

1978:1230; Spence and Parsons 1972:8,18)—and involved mining from shallow pits (e.g., Charlton 1978:1229). Tool production was concentrated at Teotihuacan and Tepeapulco, indicating a major reorganization of production, contrasting with the more dispersed pattern found during the Formative Period (Charlton 1978). Workshops indicating specialized production are abundant at Teotihuacan (Santley 1983, 1989; Spence 1967, 1981).

(b) Postclassic Period: By the Late Postclassic, the scale of obsidian mining in Central Mexico had increased significantly. At Pachuca (e.g., Cruz de Milagro) and Pico de Orizaba (e.g., Valle de Ixtetal), extensive shaft and tunnel mines have been discovered that required substantially more skill and organization than the excavation of surface pits (Charlton and Spence 1982:24; Cobean 2002). Changes in blade production technology between the Classic and Postclassic Periods are evident. During the Postclassic, specialists increasingly prepared blade cores by grinding the striking platforms (Clark 1985; MacNeish, et al. 1967:18; Spence and Parsons 1972:18; Tolstoy 1971:274). This is a technological improvement over earlier periods when platforms either lacked preparation or were chipped (MacNeish, et al. 1967:18), because ground platforms are much more uniform, allowing the worker to remove blades from the core using hard slick bits with more consistency and fewer errors (Clark 1985:9). Also, once the platform has been prepared, the knapper can remove blades from the core until the core has been exhausted unless an error damages the core's striking platform (Clark 1985:9,11; Crabtree 1968:463). During the Postclassic, most of the grey obsidian tools produced in the Otumba-San Marcos area and around Texcoco were distributed to consumers at the regional level through the market system (Berdan and Anawalt 1997:39; Blanton 1996; Spence and Parsons 1972:27). In contrast, green obsidian blades not only were distributed through the regional market system, but also were distributed through long-distance trade networks supplying market systems in other regions. They may have also, for a time, been collected as tribute by the Aztec Triple Alliance (Barlow 1949; Spence and Parsons 1972:26–27; but cf. Berdan and Anawalt 1997:39). Obsidian from these and other sources (e.g., from the Valle de Ixtetal source [Cobean 2002]) were distributed across Mesoamerica (e.g., Fargher 2004; Kepecs 1999; Kowalewski et al. 1989). Green obsidian blades were available outside the Basin of Mexico in such a large quantity and were so easily accessible in various regional markets that they were consumed in utilitarian activities by people from across social sectors and hence functioned as what we term a bulk luxury, a goods category we discuss below.

Labor/time bottlenecks? Not known.

Demographic pressure (e.g., migration/labor mobilization)? Little information is available on the demographic or settlement pattern changes in the key production zones.

Pressure on distribution, including markets?

(a) Classic period: The quarried obsidian was initially worked at mine sites to produce polyhedral cores (Charlton 1978:1230; Spence and Parsons 1972:6). The polyhedral cores were then transported from the obsidian source areas to two sites primarily, Teotihuacan and Tepeapulco. There, they were worked to produce finished tools including scrapers, points, and knives or prismatic cores and blades (Charlton 1978:1230; Spence and Parsons 1972:28). Production appears to have been centralized at these two sites and intensified to supply growing regional and macroregional demand (Charlton 1978:1234; Santley 1984; Spence 1984). Household specialization at Teotihuacan probably developed (Spence 1981). Green obsidian produced by this system was exported as far away as Guatemala, including Tikal (Moholy-Nagy 2003; Spence and Parsons 1972:28).

(b) Postclassic: Production was more widely dispersed than had been the case for the Classic Period (Spence 1985). The primary mechanism for the movement of obsidian tools during the Late Postclassic appears to have been through the Basin of Mexico market system and long-distance trade that linked markets across Mesoamerica (Berdan and Anawalt 1997:39; Blanton 1996; Spence and Parsons 1972:27). Green and clear obsidian blades have been recovered from Late Postclassic sites throughout Mesoamerica, including Oaxaca, northern Yucatán, and various other locations outside the Basin of Mexico (Fargher 2004; Kepecs 1999:408-9,425; Kowalewski, et al. 1989:357).

Secondary industries? None evident.

IV. Cacao
Transformation Period(s):

(a) Classic period: The archaeobotanical history of cacao domestication is not well known (Coe and Coe 1996:26; Young 1994), but Mesoamerican people likely used cacao since at least the Classic Period. Cacao had special importance to the Classic Maya elite, who incorporated it into their pantheon of deities and developed special preparation and serving vessels for elite chocolate drinking (Coe and Coe 1996:43-50; McAnany et al. 2002). Cacao was known at Teotihuacan, but figures only to a minor degree in symbolic representation on some fancier ceramic vessels (e.g., Coe and Coe 1996:54), and the quantity and nature of its consumption there is not known. Coe and Coe (1996:53-54) propose a cacao for obsidian exchange system linking Teotihuacan with coastal Guatemala, but this cannot be confirmed.

(b) Postclassic Period: It is likely that during the Postclassic cacao's uses had transcended the domain of the political elite, and it had emerged as a good more likely to be consumed by elite and nonelite alike. Growth in consumer demand brought an increase in cacao production by populations of suitable wet tropical areas (Gasco 2003:295). Based on early Colonial Period sources that describe a situation probably little changed from late pre-Hispanic times, Bergmann (1969:94) estimates the total production in Guatemala at six million pounds per year. Vast quantities flowed to the Aztec centers through tribute channels (ibid), but it was also available for sale in markets (e.g., Feldman 1978:221), in varying grades of cost and quality including as a lower-cost beverage (*pinole*) (Coe and Coe 1996:87-89). It also played a role in rituals of household social reproduction such as birth ceremonies and weddings (Bergmann 1969:93; Coe and Coe 1996:61-63; Millon 1955:174), and it served as one of the most important categories of commodity money (Bergmann 1969:86-87; Millon 1955:159–162).

Labor/time bottlenecks? Coe and Coe (1996:60) describe a pattern of small scale production, probably for home use, in parts of Yucatán, but the main aboriginal production areas described in early European sources were large, densely planted, and, evidently, monocrop patches described variously as groves, plantations, or estates (Bergmann 1969; Millon 1955:130–133), which could be privately owned (Millon 1955:133). Large, comparatively special-ized plantation-based production would imply the possibility of production bottlenecks in relation to subsistence production and other tasks for plantation workers, especially since cacao production requires nearly year-round effort. Harvesting was intermittent over the whole year (although with two major periods of heavier yields [Millon 1955:24]), and maturing seeds had to be guarded to prevent losses from monkeys and other animals (ibid.) Once har-vested, preparation tasks require several weeks and must be completed quickly to prevent spoilage and to enhance quality (Coe and Coe 1996:23–25). Labor and time allocation issues have not been sufficiently addressed (e.g., Gasco 2003:293), so it is not known how labor was organized or mobilized. Given the impressive scale of this industry, the transformation of vast areas of wet tropical forest to monocrop plantations would have entailed one of the most significant agroecological alterations of lowland Mesoamerican landscapes during the pre-Hispanic period.

Demographic pressure (e.g., migration/labor mobilization)? We suggest there would have been substantial demographic consequences of Postclassic cacao production, but little information is available. Bergmann (1969:91) men-tions migratory wage labor, and some sources point to the possibility of slave labor in production (Berdan 1975:182; Millon 1955:130). The Early Colonial Period sources suggest the possibility of other modes of labor mobilization for pre-Hispanic cacao production, for example, exchange relationships between laborers and the "Lords of Atitlan" in southwestern Guatemala (Millon 1955:131). Working on cacao plantations may have been a corvée obligation to elite plantation owners (e.g., Millon 1955:134).

Pressure on distribution, including markets? If plantation work was highly specialized and subsistence production was displaced by it, local markets or other distribution systems would have developed in response to provide household goods and food to part- or full-time plantation workers, but the nature of regional economies in cacao-producing areas is unknown (but see McAnany et al. 2002). At the world-system scale, cacao was an important local and imperial tribute good (Bergmann 1969), but it also moved in substantial quantities through commercial networks including the international trade centers (Gasco and Berdan 2003) and local markets (Bergmann 1969:86).

Secondary industries? Millon (1955:110) mentions cacao tree nurseries for transplanting as a possible secondary industry. Various specialized beaters and spoons were used to foam the cacao beverage.

V. Cotton Cloth

Transformation Period(s):

(a) Classic Period: In most Mesoamerican regions, figural images were typically clothed by the Classic Period, illustrating a growing use of cloth compared to earlier Formative Periods when human figures were more typically portrayed nude (e.g., Stark et al 1998). While the cloth content of clothing is not easy to discern from these images, cotton cloth was likely in use as it was a highly esteemed Mesoamerican good (Berdan 1987). Cotton cloth has been found archaeologically prior to the Classic Period (King 1979:267), even in the central highlands well above the usual 1,000 masl limit for its cultivation. Increased cotton-related production is archaeologically indicated by evidence for spinning and weaving dating to Terminal Formative and Classic Periods in central and southern Veracruz and other Gulf lowland locations that may reflect a growth in exports to Central Mexico (Hall 1997; Stark et al 1998:17). A technological improvement, the mold-formed spinning whorl, is evident by the Classic Period in south-central Veracruz (Stark et al 1998:19). Hirth (1980) and Hirth and Angulo (1981) propose that an irrigated cotton industry in eastern Morelos grew in response to demand by Classic Period Teotihuacan. Another technological innovation would have been annual cotton, which produces a higher quality product, is more consistent with control of insect infestations, and can be grown in cooler climates than perrenial cotton, but its archaeobotanical history is not well known (Stark et al. 1998:10).

(b) Postclassic: During the Late Postclassic, cotton was one of the most important tribute and market commodities in Mesoamerica (Berdan 1987; Hicks 1994). Weaving methods grew in complexity from the Classic to the Postclassic. King (1979:267) was able to identify only a few weaving patterns for the Classic Period, but in the Postclassic materials, she sees an "explosion of weaving techniques" (p. 268). The growth of the cotton industry is detectable archaeologically, even in areas far from cotton cultivation zones, for example, as an increased frequency of mold-made whorls in the Basin of Mexico and other central highlands areas (Parsons and Parsons 1990:356; Smith and Hirth 1988:354), and spinning bowls that allow for greater control of thread size (e.g., in Morelos; [Smith and Hirth 1988:355]). The diverse uses of cotton cloth in Late Postclassic culture and society are well documented in many sources (Berdan 1987; Hicks 1994; Stark et al. 1998), including clothing, household utilitarian, medicinal, decorative hanging, religious offering, mummy bundling, gifting (including those given to commemorate rites of passage), and as armor; in addition, cotton was an important commodity form of money (e.g., Hicks 1994:100–102).

Labor/time bottlenecks? Labor and time conflicts between cotton and subsistence production are not well studied (Berdan 1987:237). Cotton requires a frost-free growing period of 200 days (Stark et al. 1998:11), but these same authors imply the possibility, in central and southern Veracruz, of dry-season cotton intercropped with a rainy-season *milpa* (food production crops), owing to excess summer rains that damage cotton. This would imply a very tight work schedule if an entire maize crop cycle had to be carried out in roughly 150 days, given the time costs of field preparation and final harvest. At least four to six months (120 to 180 days) are required for a maize crop (e.g., Kirkby 1973:chapter 5), and at least six months for a cotton crop when accounting for field preparation and final harvesting (Saindon 1977:9). In regions more arid than Veracruz, an annual intercrop strategy would be even more problematic, since both maize and cotton benefit from a rainy-season developmental period extending into a dry season phase for final maturation and harvesting (Kirkby 1973:54-55; Saindon 1977:9). A multicrop of maize and cotton would present problems, also, since cotton requires three or four harvests to avoid deterioration of ripe bolls (Stark et al. 1998:11), implying work periods that might conflict with *milpa* operations.

The technology of cotton cloth weaving remained simple throughout the pre-Hispanic sequence, with the back-strap loom as the basic production tool. This limited the width of pieces to less than 1m, but also kept production costs low. As a result, spinning and weaving remained largely household industries, but we suggest that an increase in household spinning and weaving production would have required time and labor reallocations to meet production goals. Hicks (1994:98-99) suggests 34 weeks of surplus household labor (mostly adult female labor) would be required to meet domestic and tribute requirements for cotton cloth, with an additional 18 weeks to produce cloth for market sale. He seems to imply that in the "domestic mode of production," this could have been easily achieved by deploying household labor, apparently with no significant economic consequences. But we find it unlikely that this level of production could have been achieved without substantial changes in task priorities and time allocation unless we are willing to accept that in prior periods, household members, especially females who did most of the cloth production, had large blocks of leisure or nonwork time. This is unlikely since, for example, tortilla preparation alone is estimated to require five to six hours per day (Smith 2003b:131; cf. Brumfiel 1991).

Demographic pressure (e.g., migration/labor mobilization)? Little is known about labor mobilization for crop production, although slave labor is not mentioned in the sources we reviewed. Stark and her coauthors (1998:11, 14) emphasize the high year-around labor requirements of a maize-cotton intercrop in Veracruz. Growing demand for labor for cotton export might have had demographic consequences resulting in increasing household size or labor immigration. Increased cotton spinning and weaving in the Mixtequilla region of Veracruz was accompanied by substantial population growth (Stark et al. 1998:20). Similarly, population grew in eastern Morelos corresponding to an increase in interaction with Teotihuacan (Hirth 1980:94).

Pressure on distribution, including markets? By the Late Postclassic, cotton was one of the most important Mesoamerican goods counted in terms of both tribute and market exchange (Berdan 1987). Wholesale cotton markets were established at Hueypuchtla and Tepeaca (Saindon 1977:61). We conclude that a substantial commitment to cotton production would require some degree of local-level specialization and increased market participation as farmers substituted cotton for subsistence production and when households committed more time and labor to spinning and weaving.

Secondary industries? According to Anawalt (1990:104), by the Late Postclassic, although some very fancy cotton garments may have been restricted to elite consumption, almost everyone had decorated cotton clothing (cf. Anawalt 2001). Woven-in or other decoration stimulated secondary industries, particularly in dyes and dyeing of several types (Sahagún 1961, Volume 10:77), as well as in the production of the "alum" or mordant used to fix the dyes. Parsons (2001:248) suggests that the proliferation of salt-making sites around the fringes of the saline lakes in the Basin of Mexico Late Postclassic may reflect, in part, the booming demand for the low-grade salt used as a dye-fixing mordant, and that the dyeing itself may have occurred at these sites.

Red dyes based on cochineal were probably the most significant secondary dye industry (Wallert 1997). This was a large-scale and complex biotechnological and agroecological system primarily built around a domesticated insect, *Dactylopius coccus*, which uses nopal leaves (*penca*) as a host. According to Donkin (1977:15) "...the domestic *Dactylopius* is a delicate and vulnerable insect, closely dependent on humans. Improvement has come about through the selection and care of breeding populations, management of the host nopals, and partial protection from a large number of enemies, besides inclement weather." Cultivating both the host nopals and the insects was a labor-intensive process requiring two to three harvests per year (done nearly continuously on large Colonial-Period plantations). Nopal joints populated with insects required protection from heavy rain, with a two- to three-week period when the insects are stored inside shelters. Following the wet season, the insects are laboriously returned to live nopals (Donkin 1977:16-17), a production step probably coinciding with the *milpa* harvest and thus requiring scheduling adjustments or specialization. The Triple Alliance collected cochineal tribute from 25 towns, of which the primary provinces were Tlaxiaco, Coixlahuaca, and Cuilapan, amounting to 9,750 lbs of dye (ibid:21), but cochineal was also available in market places (Díaz del Castillo 1956:216). We estimate the tribute quantity alone would have required roughly 150,000 young soft nopal *pencas* with insect colonies, representing a total of nearly 300 million insects that had to be hand-harvested to meet the tribute demand (modified from productivity values given in Nobel [1994:58–60]).

THREE "GREAT TRANSFORMATIONS" OF THE MESOAMERICAN WORLD AND ITS GOODS

Each of the previously discussed goods can be implicated in the evolution of pre-Hispanic Mesoamerican civilization in some way, but they differed in how and when they penetrated society and culture. We identify three "Great Transformations" (with apologies to Karl Polanyi) over the nearly 3,000 years of Mesoamerican history considered here, each associated with a distinct pattern of change in the technological, social, and cultural properties of what we call "prestige goods," "regional goods," and "bulk luxury goods." Rather than representing categories derived through a logic of structural opposition, such as Wallerstein's luxury/staple dichotomy, our categories are empirically derived, loosely defined, and have sometimes overlapping characteristics. Our categories are also flexible in membership, with some goods inhabiting multiple categories depending on the social context of their use. And some goods shifted between our categories over time, as we discuss next.

The development of prestige goods constituted the key process in our first transformation, one that occurred early in the period considered here (c. 1200 to 500 BC). This was followed by a period of revolutionary change in regional goods, especially utilitarian pottery, salt, and obsidian, from the latter Formative through the Classic Period (500 BC to AD 700). While both prestige goods and regional goods persisted through the remainder of the pre-Hispanic sequence, by the Late Postclassic (AD 1200 to 1520), world-system processes, especially as reflected in interregional production specializations, were more pronounced than in earlier periods, a product of growth in the volume of "bulk luxuries" such as green obsidian, fine salt, decorated cotton cloth and cacao. We summarize the great transformations next.

Prestige Goods Transformation

Though prestige goods are exchanged and consumed in the context of the political strategies of an elite, they had few uses in the social economics of ordinary life ("wealth finance" in the phraseology of Brumfiel and Earle 1987; cf. Peregrine 1992). The phases of greatest irregularity in rates of techno-logical change and social impact of the prestige goods occurred during the Early and Middle Formative Periods, when rapid change is evident in some pottery-making methods; in lapidary methods in semiprecious stone such as jade; and in cut iron cubes, mirrors, and compasses (Carlson 1975; Clark 1996; Pires-Ferreira 1975:chapter 3). While the suite of prestige goods changed in composition over subsequent periods, as a category they maintained symbolic and processual significance in the political realm, and their elite exclusiveness, over the whole pre-Hispanic sequence (e.g., Blanton and Feinman [1984], although that early paper failed to distinguish between prestige goods and bulk luxuries). Prestige goods saw their most luxuriant expression in the lowland Classic Period Maya states, where the cacao beverage became an important prestige good (McAnany 2004). New prestige goods, such as gold, silver, and bronze (e.g., Hosler 1988), were developed in later periods. By the Postclassic, metal items of personal adornment, jaguar-skins, crystal, jade, and turquoise, were all depicted as accoutrements for the leading political elite (Anawalt 1990:108), but, as with earlier prestige goods, they apparently had few or no significant systemic outcomes in agroecology, demography, market evolution, or ordinary household economies.

Regional Goods Transformation

The emergence of regional goods signifies the first of two impulses of revo-lutionary change in Mesoamerican home economics during the time span considered here. The regional goods transformation was initiated during the latter Formative and Classic Periods, in some cases establishing basic economic patterns that persist to this day (e.g., Blanton et al. 1999:131–132). Utilitarian pottery is the most sensitive barometer of regional goods evolution, although some salt, cloth, and obsidian products, of our limited list, can be included. By contrast with elite prestige goods, regional goods first emerged in response to the state formation, population growth, urbanism, and production intensifica-tion that occurred in regions such as the Basin of Mexico and the Valley of

Oaxaca during the latter Formative and Classic Periods. We call them regional goods because they were developed primarily in the context of regional-scale systems of tribute flows and periodic markets. Unlike the primarily elite-driven sociotechnic changes of the prestige goods, the development of regional goods reflects the intertwined processes of political and domestic restructuring that incorporated a vast number of ordinary households as both surplus producers and benefactors of growing political and economic systems expressed as state formation and regional market evolution (e.g., Blanton et al. 1999:chapter 4). Rather than bringing about exotic new technological processes or products, the development of regional goods was primarily a response to behavioral change in ordinary households, including foodways, labor allocation and work intensity, production specialization, and interhousehold exchange; standardization of specialist-produced utilitarian pottery types is one typical outcome (e.g., Blanton et al. 1999:chapter 4; cf. Rice 1981). Households in at least some areas benefited from the new regional economies, although the degree of benefit varied in time and space through the remainder of the pre-Hispanic sequence. The growing use of clothing and increased access to obsidian (a superior lithic material) corresponded with a shift to better housing such as the masonry apartment compounds of Teotihuacan (Millon 1973:56) and the shaped stone, mud brick, and plaster houses of the Valley of Oaxaca (Blanton et al. 1999:109).

Bulk Luxury Goods Transformation

Susan Kepecs (2003:130) coined the phrase "bulk luxury" from her research on the "gemlike white salt of Yucatán" that, despite its cost, was widely distributed over Mesoamerica during the Late Postclassic. The bulk luxury category includes other Late Postclassic goods, most notably decorated cotton cloth, green obsidian, cacao, and possibly some pottery types such as Mixteca-Puebla polychrome (Smith and Heath-Smith 1982). A small number of Classic Period goods, however, such as Thin Orange pottery (Kolb 1986) and, possibly, obsidian and cotton cloth, were among the first of this category. As costly but widely distributed goods consumed across social sectors, bulk luxuries form an imprecise category occupying a middle ground between the rare and exclusive preciosities of the prestige-goods systems and the regional bulk goods, circulating through regional-scale markets, that were available to many consumers (Smith and Berdan 2003:9). Caught in a middle ground between exclusivity and commonality, bulk luxuries were a source of cultural contestation in the Late Postclassic as the political elite attempted to uphold their exclusivity and efficacy in elite political transactions in the face of their ready availability for market purchase. For example, the Aztec ruler Motecuzoma attempted to restrict cotton clothing to an elite (Durán 1964:131; cf. p. 142).

Changes in the Classic and Postclassic Periods (especially the latter) in production technologies, in the organization of production, in labor intensity and allocation, in transport, in the institutional organization of international commodity flows, as well as in consumer preferences and strategies, figured into how bulk luxury goods came to have wide circulation and use across social sectors. Hence, bulk luxuries reflect the second of two impulses of revolutionary change in Mesoamerican home economics. Bulk luxury goods, while costly and often carried long distances, were in wider use by the Late Postclassic compared to the more restricted elite-dominated prestige goods (e.g., Smith 2003:123). Decorated cotton was the pre-eminent bulk luxury of this late period. Anawalt (1990:104) describes Aztec clothing as "resplendent," and not in reference to elite garments alone. In fact, she disagrees with the earlier claims that cotton clothing was restricted to the nobility, and argues that these claims probably reflect "a nostalgic colonial creed rather than a stringent pre-Hispanic reality" (Anawalt 2001:153; cf. 1990:104). As the volume of goods in international trade increased (Smith and Berdan 2003:7), the *tlameme* (professional burden carrier) emerged as a type of occupational specialization in Central Mexico (Hassig 1985), and large transport canoes that could carry up to 40 people were evidently a Postclassic development in the commercially active lowland zones (Kepecs 1999:104, 107). Highly commercialized regions in areas intermediate between the Maya kingdoms and the central and southern highlands, including Xicalango, Acalan, and the Gulf of Honduras, among other locations, were dotted with international trade centers that served as commercial nodes in the exchange of bulk luxury as well as prestige goods (Gasco and Berdan 2003).

Bulk luxury goods were central to the evolution of the Mesoamerican world-system, especially, of our list, cacao and cotton cloth, but also green obsidian and fine salt to some degree. For these goods, increased production and use had significant agroecological, social, and demographic outcomes, especially in production zones. Although these were not the only goods in international circulation, they alone precipitated regional production specializations on such a massive scale that we are able to speak of Mesoamerica as a locus of world-system evolution. The growth in use of bulk luxuries had profound outcomes across diverse social and geographical settings. They intensified interregional and intercultural divisions of labor, brought about demographic and agroecological changes, resulted in altered modes of labor mobilization, and stimulated the growth of secondary products industries to a degree that surpassed both prestige goods and regional goods. As such, the most important of our bulk luxury goods, fine salt, green obsidian, cacao, and cotton cloth, are the Mesoamerican analogs of wool, cotton, sugar, spices, and tea that figured so importantly in the growth of the modern world-system (Mintz 1985; Sahlins 1994; Wallerstein 1974).

OUR CONCLUDING THOUGHT: "LIVE AND LET DYE"

All the goods in our three categories were "systemic" in the sense of Wallerstein (1974:41–42) in that they were central to processes of sociocultural change and in the reproduction of social and economic systems. But, the impact of the bulk luxuries was greater than the other two across cultures and social classes. Why the Mesoamerican world of goods became so comparatively luxurious by the Late Postclassic is a question whose answer would require a consideration of many topics related to biotechnology and technology, labor intensification, household economy, transport, distribution, consumer preferences, and culture. Bulk luxuries can be traced back to the Classic Period, exemplified by Thin Orange pottery, the expansion of the cotton industries of central and southern Veracruz and parts of Morelos, and the export products of the Teotihuacan/Tepeapulco obsidian industries. Yet, even these notable developments appear minor compared to the expansive incorporation of these and other bulk luxuries into economy and society by the Late Postclassic. By the end of that period, a greater volume and diversity of costly goods were in use, more regions could be characterized as having undergone periphery incorporation into the world-system, and secondary industries such as those related to cloth dyeing were becoming more developed. Hence, if we place the beginning of world-system formation at, or just prior to, the beginning of the Classic Period (AD 200), then we conclude that its full development took well over 1,000 years, with most of the variation explained by a growth spurt during the Late Postclassic (after AD 1200).

It is not clear what kind of causal scenario might reasonably be proposed to explain the extended time frame and varied tempo of world-system development over more than 1,000 years. A hypothesis attributing change to the cumulative development of productive technologies, in particular, we think, would be highly subject to falsification. While technological improvements did accompany the growth of the Postclassic world-system, such as annual cotton (possibly), spinning bowls, ground striking platforms for obsidian core blanks, and large transport canoes, they all seem minor, consisting only of what amounts to small variations around established themes. At the same time, many long-established technologies remained largely unchanged, such as the back-strap loom, persistently the production instrument of choice in spite of a drastic increase in the volume of cotton cloth production. Metallurgy did flourish after about AD 1300, but its products served primarily symbolic functions, and metal use across the Mesoamerican world remained spotty and limited (Hosler 2003). Copper and bronze implements were just beginning to join the family of bulk luxuries in some areas by the end of the Postclassic (Smith 2003b:90). Labor—counted in terms of increased intensity, restructured time allocation, modes of mobilization, and production specialization—is more central to understanding Mesoamerican change than the accumulation of productive technologies. But changes in labor can only be understood in relation to changes in consumer behavior.

We suggest that in addition to the technological, agroecological, demographic, and social factors we have emphasized to this point, a more complete discussion of the growing world-system will need to address analytically the alteration over time of cultural codes that endowed goods with new or modified meanings. We situate the growing world-system within the framework of culture change from the minimalist, introverted aesthetic of natural goods at Teotihuacan to a flamboyant Aztec material culture that predicated value on a more overt solidification of human labor. The values expressed through the Teotihuacan culture of goods, including depersonalization, egalitarianism, and group-orientation, were all in decline by the Late Postclassic.

In proposing this research direction, it is not our intent to take a position of idealist determinism (in the manner of Sahlins 1976). The issues we address are far too complex to be reduced to any simplistic scheme that would espouse either materialist or idealist causation. But we would point to the possible causal salience of a persistent cultural pattern, found particularly in the Classic Period cultures of the Central Highlands (and possibly also Oaxaca), that operated to inhibit world-system evolution by restricting the forms and uses of bulk luxuries. This cultural pattern entailed an introverted consumer behavior that was most elaborately developed and widely adhered to during the central highlands Classic Period, especially at Teotihuacan and culturally related areas. We suggest that a propensity to socially and culturally restrict luxury consumption, especially in public venues, was one expression of Teotihuacan's highly developed corporate political economy (Blanton et al. 1996:9–10), and that this egalitarian ideology lay behind the development of an abstract and severe artistic style that minimized individualism through a pervasive cultural pattern that Pasztory (1992:288) terms "impersonal uniformity." As she puts it, Teotihuacan culture was based on "…a utopian view…in which the individual was de-emphasized for the sake of the group…" (Pasztory 1992:288).

The cultural code of impersonal uniformity influenced some of the goods discussed here. For example, while most Teotihuacan figurines and figural images are depicted clothed, the clothing styles portrayed are elegant and simple, rarely showing elaborate decoration (e.g., Pasztory 1997:Figures 10.9, 14.3) (Figure 10-1). Major figurine types imply simple modes of dress (Pasztory 1997:226–267), and although it is not clear to what degree these scenes are meant to depict everyday life, ordinary persons shown cavorting in mural scenes depicting the after life mostly wear minimal and simple clothing (e.g., Pasztory 1997:226, Figure 12. 4). Portrayals of the apical Teotihuacan elite, in murals showing the tassel-headdress officials, although masked and usually not

Figure 10-1. Figurine with wide-band headdress, early Classic Period, Teotihuacan. With permission of the Saint Louis Art Museum. Gift of Morton D. May.

named, do depict elaborately decorated clothing. But even here, as Anawalt points out (2001:152), rather than being foregrounded, decorated clothing is often largely covered by an abundance of feathers.

An exception to the simplicity of most Teotihuacan clothing is found in the so-called host figures. Small figurines placed inside host figures are found "smothered in clothes and headdresses" (Pasztory 1997:176), but are enveloped within a mostly unclothed host that, as hypothesized by Pasztory, served as a metaphor for the "body politic" (1997:173). Following her logic, host figures would be analogous to the introverted domestic architecture of the city's numerous masonry apartment compounds, which exhibit a "faceless" exterior but an often quite exuberant interior decoration (Cowgill 1997:137; Millon 1992:353).

We suggest that these various material systems signify a tension in Teotihuacan society in which any propensity toward public communication of wealth or control of labor was opposed by well-developed cultural norms emphasizing egalitarianism and depersonalization. We also suggest that this reticent consumer pattern explains the relative lateness in the growth of bulk luxuries and world-system evolution in Mesoamerica, and that the decline of the old Classic Period centers like Teotihuacan brought with it the unfolding of a new Mesoamerican world of goods. The Mesoamerica of the Postclassic was more commercialized based on what has been described as "...the increasing separation of governmental and commercial institutions" (Blanton et al. 1993:213). But, an additional factor to consider in explaining the transition was the relative decline in corporate governance, and we suggest its associated cultural code emphasizing depersonalization and egalitarianism that had their major expression at Classic Period Teotihuacan.

We will not go so far as to imply that with growing commercialization the old cultural code of the central highlands people was completely rejected. Instead, a relative but significant decline occurred in consumer reticence and depersonalization, but constrained by a canon reproduced through myth and moral disciplinary texts that depicted luxury as a symptom of degeneration. Native texts produced during the early Colonial Period, but reflecting the disciplines of shame and success promulgated during the Late Postclassic, may signify continuity in cultural sensibility. These texts contrast the positive outcomes engendered by a life of virtuous conduct, modesty, and thrift, with the personal doom that follows on a life of covetousness, self-indulgence, and pomposity (Sahagún 1961:Book 10; cf. Calnek 1990:83, commenting on the Codex Mendoza). Some Late Postclassic myths add weight to these moral disciplines. In one characteristic story, the Aztec ruler Motecuzoma Ilhuicamina is said to have sent 60 priests to discover the homeland of his people. When his contingent discovered the hill of Colhuacan, they were chastised by its priest for their inability to keep up with him as they ascended the mountain, saying, "You have become old, you have become tired because of the chocolate you drink and because of the foods you eat. They have harmed and weakened you. You have been spoiled by those mantles, feathers and riches that you wear and that you brought here. All of that has ruined you" (translated in Coe and Coe 1996:80).

Judging from the material record of the period, by the Late Postclassic the moral disciplines and mythic accounts do not appear to have carried much weight as guides to action. For example, in Calnek's (1976:300) description of city life in Late Postclassic Tenochtitlan, we find a situation unlike Teotihuacan's introverted domestic architecture: "Even commoners could achieve high rank through military service or the acquisition of great personal wealth...The architectural segregation of relatively small residential compounds permitted the public display of status markers—most commonly architectural ornamentation—to distinguish individual compounds from their immediate neighbors."

Depictions of Teotihuacan and Late Postclassic persons also invite comparison. Images of an Aztec elite from the Late Postclassic, albeit in some cases influenced by European norms, display little evidence of consumer reticence. The magnificent and very personalized images of the Texcocan dignitaries Nezahualpilli, Tocuepotzin, and Quauhtlatzacuilotl, in the Codex Ixtlilxochitl, for example, depict an elite, not masked, as were their Teotihuacan analogs, decked out in the full regalia of decorated cloth and gold and silver jewelry (Figures 10-2 through 4).

These finely decorated garments and jewelry signify value in part through their solidification of aesthetic labor (cf. Wengrow 2001), especially in the elaborately decorated and dyed cotton cloth. Labor is objectified in all material culture, of course, but in Teotihuacan culture, by contrast with the Aztec, the solidification of aesthetic labor is less evident in clothing and items of personal adornment. Instead, "material and form rather than decoration predominate in artistry" (Pasztory 1997:156), for example, in the regalia of the Teotihuacan elite, previously mentioned, that masked decorated cloth with feathers. Costly pottery also shows this pattern. Thin Orange is the main Classic Period ware found in Teotihuacan and related areas exemplifying our criteria for a bulk luxury (Kolb 1986). Thin Orange can be compared with its Late Postclassic bulk luxury analog, Mixteca-Puebla polychrome, but while Thin Orange was produced in simple, elegant forms, almost always lacking surface decoration, the famous Mixteca-Puebla pottery exhibits a riot of polychrome designs and elaborate vessel forms including serpent-headed supports and jar handles (cf. Caso, Bernal, and Acosta 1967:Figures 13–30; Pasztory 1997:150–154; Smith and Heath–Smith 1982).

Pasztory (1997:chapter 9) sums up the composition of Teotihuacan style as a "minimalist aesthetic" which was "more concerned with material and basic craftsmanship than with flamboyant form and imagery" (ibid:159). We propose that by the Late Postclassic, more so than in earlier periods, consumer preferences frequently entailed the consumption of valuable goods, including those representing a solidification of aesthetic labor, which were ideally suited to the encoding of social status. This development, we suggest, emerged hand in hand with the evolution of the world-system and the growth in volume of its abundance of bulk luxury goods.

We hope these final suggestions will stimulate further research by others more versed in the methods of cognitive archaeology. It is evident to us that any study of Mesoamerican goods that aims to be more analytically satisfying than what we have done here must find ways to better address the question of how goods come to be endowed with meanings—for commoners as well as an elite—that flow from their uses in social life.

Figure 10-2. A member of the Texcocan nobility, Quauhtlatzacuilotl. Codex Ixtlilxochitl, folio 107r. Provided by Akademische Druck-u. Verlagsanstalt, Austria, and reproduced with permission.

Figure 10-3. A member of the Texcocan nobility, Tocuepotzin. Codex Ixtlilxochitl, folio 105r. Provided by Akademische Druck-u. Verlagsanstalt, Austria, and reproduced with permission.

Figure 10-4. The Texcocan ruler Nezahualpilli. Codex Ixtlilxochitl, folio 108r. Provided by
Akademische Druck-u. Verlagsanstalt, Austria, and reproduced with permission.

Acknowledgments

Richard Blanton owes his start in archaeology to Jeffrey R. Parsons (and secondarily to James B. Griffin, then director of the Museum of Anthropology of the University of Michigan), and he is grateful for the stimulating graduate training he received at the Museum of Anthropology and in the field in the Basin of Mexico. I also have benefited from my long-standing association with my fellow settlement pattern researchers in the Valley of Oaxaca, Stephen Kowalewski, Gary Feinman, Linda Nicholas, and Laura Finsten, and the many younger colleagues who have followed us in Oaxaca, now totaling three generations of archaeologists devoted to settlement pattern research. Lane Fargher and Verenice Heredia Espinoza have not worked directly with Jeff, but both completed dissertation projects in Mexico inspired by the regional methods that he pioneered. We thank three anonymous reviewers and Stephen Kowalewski for comments on an earlier draft of the paper that helped improve it and the other chapters of this book, although we alone are responsible for any errors or omissions.

REFERENCES CITED

Adams, Robert Mc.C.
  2000   Accelerated Technological Change in Archaeology and Ancient History. In *Cultural Evolution: Contemporary Viewpoints*, edited by Gary M. Feinman and Linda Manzanilla, pp. 95–118. Kluwer Academic/Plenum Publishers, New York.

Algaze, Guillermo
  1993   *The Uruk World System: The Dynamics of Expansion of Early Mesopotamian Civilization.* University of Chicago Press, Chicago.

Anawalt, Patricia Rieff
  1990   A Comparative Analysis of the Costumes and Accoutrements of the Codex Mendoza. In *Codex Mendoza*, Vol. 1, edited by Frances F. Berdan and Patricia R. Anawalt, pp. 103–150. University of California Press, Berkeley.
  2001   Clothing. In *Archaeology of Ancient Mexico and Central America: An Encyclopedia*, edited by Susan Toby Evans and David L. Webster, pp. 152–159. Garland Publishing, New York.

Andrews, Anthony P., and Shirley B. Mock
  2002   New Perspectives on the Prehispanic Maya Salt Trade. In *Ancient Maya Political Economies*, edited by Marilyn Masson and David A. Freidel, pp. 307–334. AltaMira Press, Walnut Creek.

Appadurai, Arjun (editor)
  1986   *The Social Life of Things: Commodities in Cultural Perspective.* Cambridge University Press, Cambridge.

Arnold III, Philip J., Christopher A. Pool, Ronald R. Kneebone, and Robert S. Santley

2000   Intensive Ceramic Production and Classic Period Political Economy in the Sierra de las Tuxtlas, Veracruz, Mexico. *Ancient Mesoamerica* 4:175–191.

Balkansky, Andrew K., Gary M. Feinman, and Linda M. Nicholas

1997   Pottery Kilns of Ancient Ejutla, Oaxaca, Mexico. *Journal of Field Archaeology* 24:139–160.

Barlow, Robert H.

1949   *The Extent of the Empire of the Culhua Mexica*. Ibero Americana Vol. 28, University of California Press, Berkeley.

Berdan, Frances F.

1975   *Trade, Tribute, and Market in the Aztec Empire*. Ph.D. dissertation, University of Texas, Austin. University Microfilms, Ann Arbor.

1987   Cotton in Aztec Mexico: Production, Distribution, and Uses. *Mexican Studies/ Estudios Mexicanos* 3:235–262.

Berdan, Frances F., and Patricia Rieff Anawalt

1997   *The Essential Codex Mendoza*. University of California Press, Berkeley.

Bergmann, John F.

1969   The Distribution of Cacao Cultivation in Pre-Columbian America. *Annals of the Association of American Geographers* 59:85–96.

Blanton, Richard E.

1994   *Houses and Households*. Plenum, New York.

1996   The Basin of Mexico Market System and the Growth of Empire. In *Aztec Imperial Strategies*, by Frances F. Berdan, Richard E. Blanton, Elizabeth Hill Boone, Mary G. Hodge, Michael E. Smith, and Emily Umberger, pp. 47–84. Dumbarton Oaks Research Library and Collection, Washington, D.C.

Blanton, Richard E., and Gary M. Feinman

1984   The Mesoamerican World System. *American Anthropologist* 86: 673–682.

Blanton, Richard E., Gary M. Feinman, Stephen A. Kowalewski, and Linda M. Nicholas

1999   *Ancient Oaxaca*. Cambridge University Press, Cambridge.

Blanton, Richard E., Gary M. Feinman, Stephen A. Kowalewski, and Peter N. Peregrine

1996   A Dual-Processual Theory for the Evolution of Mesoamerican Civilization. *Current Anthropology* 37:1–14.

Blanton, Richard E., Stephen A. Kowalewski, Gary M. Feinman, and Laura M. Finsten

1993   *Ancient Mesoamerica: A Comparison of Change in Three Regions*, Second Edition. Cambridge University Press, Cambridge.

Blanton, Richard E., and Jeffrey R. Parsons

1971   Ceramic Markers Used for Period Designations. In *Prehistoric Settlement Patterns in the Texcoco Region, Mexico*. Memoirs No. 3, Museum of Anthropology, University of Michigan, Ann Arbor.

Brumfiel, Elizabeth M.
  1991   Weaving and Cooking: Women's Production in Aztec Mexico. In *Engendering Archaeology: Women and Prehistory*, edited by Joan M. Gero and Margaret W. Conkey, pp. 224–251. Basil Blackwell, Oxford.
Brumfiel, Elizabeth M., and Timothy K. Earle
  1987   Specialization, Exchange, and Complex Societies: An Introduction. In *Specialization, Exchange, and Complex Societies*, edited by Elizabeth M. Brumfiel and Timothy K Earle, pp. 1–9. Cambridge University Press, Cambridge.
Calnek, Edward E.
  1976   The Internal Structure of Tenochtitlan. In *The Valley of Mexico: Studies in Pre-Hispanic Ecology and Society*, edited by Eric R. Wolf, pp. 287–302. University of New Mexico Press, Albuquerque.
  1990   The Ethnographic Context of the Third Part of the Codex Mendoza. In *Codex Mendoza*, Vol. 1, edited by Frances F. Berdan and Patricia R. Anawalt, pp. 81–91. University of California Press, Berkeley.
Carlson, John B.
  1975   Lodestone Compass: Chinese or Olmec Primacy? *Science* 189:753–760.
Caso, Alfonso, Ignacio Bernal, and Jorge R. Acosta
  1967   *La Cerámica de Monte Albán*. Memorias del Instituto Nacional de Antropología e Historia 13, Mexico, D.F.
Castellón Huerta, Blas Román
  1998   Tecnología de producción y calidad de la sal en Zapotitlán Salinas, Puebla: Época prehispánica. In *La Sal en México II*, edited by J. Reyes, pp. 107–128. Universidad de Colima, Colima.
Charlton, Thomas H.
  1978   Teotihuacan, Tepeapulco, and Obsidian Exploitation. *Science* 200:1227–1236.
Charlton, Thomas H., and Michael W. Spence
  1982   Obsidian Exploitation and Civilization in the Basin of Mexico. In *Mining and Mining Techniques in Ancient Mesoamerica*, edited by Phil C. Weigand and Gretchen Gwynne, special issue, *Anthropology* 6:7–86. State University of New York, Stonybrook.
Chase-Dunn, Christopher, and Thomas D. Hall
  1997   *Rise and Demise: Comparing World Systems*. Westview Press, Boulder.
Chase-Dunn, Christopher, and Thomas D. Hall (editors)
  1991   *Core/Periphery Relations in Precapitalist Worlds*. Westview Press, Boulder.
Clark, John E.
  1985   Platforms, Bits, Punches and Vises; a Potpourri of Mesoamerican Blade Technology. *Lithic Technology* 14:1–15.
  1996   Craft Specialization and Olmec Civilization. In *Craft Specialization and Social Evolution: In Memory of V. Gordon Childe*, edited by Bernard Wailes, pp. 187–199. University Museum Symposium Series VI, University Museum of

Archaeology and Anthropology, University of Pennsylvania, Philadelphia.

Cobean, Robert H.

2002   *A World of Obsidian: The Mining and Trade of a Volcanic Glass in Ancient Mexico.* Arqueología de México. Instituto Nacional de Antroplogía e Historia/ University of Pittsburgh, Pittsburgh.

Coe, Sophie D., and Michael D. Coe

1996   *The True History of Chocolate.* Thames and Hudson, New York.

Cowgill, George L.

1997   State and Society at Teotihuacan, Mexico. *Annual Review of Anthropology* 26:129–161.

Crabtree, Don E.

1968   Mesoamerican Polyhedral Cores and Prismatic Blades. *American Antiquity* 33:446–478.

Díaz del Castillo, Bernal

1956   *The Discovery and Conquest of Mexico, 1517-1521.* Translated by A.P. Maudslay. Farrar, Straus, and Cudahy, New York.

Dillon, Brian D., Kevin O. Pope, and Michael W. Love

1988   An Ancient Extractive Industry: Maya Saltmaking at Salinas de los Nueve Cerros. *Journal of New World Archaeology* 7:37–58.

Donkin, R.A.

1977   *Spanish Red: An Ethnogeographical Study of Cochineal and the Opuntia Cactus.* Transactions of the American Philosophical Society, Vol. 67, Part 5, American Philosophical Society, Philadelphia.

Douglas, Mary, and Baron Isherwood

1979   *The World of Goods: Towards an Anthropology of Consumption.* W.W. Norton and Company, New York.

Durán, Diego

1964   *The Aztecs: The History of the Indies of New Spain.* Orion, New York.

Fargher, Lane F.

2004   *A Diachronic Analysis of the Valley of Oaxaca Economy from the Classic to Postclassic.* Ph.D. dissertation, University of Wisconsin. UMI Dissertation Services, Ann Arbor.

Feinman, Gary M.

1982   Patterns in Ceramic production and Distribution, Periods Early I Through V. In *Monte Albán's Hinterland, Part I: The Prehispanic Settlement Patterns of the Central and Southern Parts of the Valley of Oaxaca, Mexico,* by Richard E. Blanton, Stephen A. Kowalewski, Gary M. Feinman, and Jill Appel, pp. 181–206. Memoirs No. 15, Museum of Anthropology, University of Michigan, Ann Arbor.

1997   Macro-Scale Perspectives on Settlement and Production in Ancient Oaxaca. In *Economic Analysis Beyond the Local System,* edited by Richard E. Blanton, Peter N. Peregrine, Deborah Winslow, and Thomas D. Hall, pp. 13–42.

Monographs in Economic Anthropology No. 13, Society for Economic Anthropology, University Press of America, Lanham.

1999   Rethinking our Assumptions: Economic Specialization at the Household Scale in Ancient Ejutla, Oaxaca, Mexico. *In Pottery and People: A Dynamic Interaction*, edited by James M. Skibo and Gary M. Feinman, pp. 81–98. The University of Utah Press, Salt Lake City.

Feinman, Gary M., Richard E. Blanton, and Stephen A. Kowalewski

1984   Market System Development in the Prehispanic Valley of Oaxaca, Mexico. In *Trade and Exchange in Early Mesoamerica*, edited by Kenneth G. Hirth, pp. 157-178. University of New Mexico Press, Albuquerque.

Feinman, Gary M., Stephen A. Kowalewski, and Richard E. Blanton

1984   Modeling Ceramic Production and Organizational Change in the Pre-Hispanic Valley of Oaxaca, Mexico. In *The Many Dimensions of Pottery: Ceramics in Archaeology and Anthropology*, edited by S.E. van der Leeuw and A.C. Pritchard, pp. 295–333. Universiteit van Amsterdam, Amsterdam.

Feinman, Gary M., Stephen A. Kowalewski, Sherman Bunker, and Linda Nicholas

1992   Ceramic production and Distribution in Late Postclassic Oaxaca: Stylistic and Petrographic Perspectives. In *Ceramic Production and Distribution: An Integrated Approach*, edited by George J. Bey III and Christopher A. Pool, pp. 235–260. Westview Press, Boulder.

Feinman, Gary M., and Linda M. Nicholas

1992   Pre-Hispanic Interregional Interaction in Southern Mexico: The Valley of Oaxaca and the Ejutla Valley. *In Resources, Power, and Interregional Interaction*, edited by Edward Schortman and Patricia Urban, pp. 75–116. Plenum, New York.

Feldman, Lawrence H.

1978   Inside a Mexica Market. In *Mesoamerican Communication Routes and Cultural Contacts*, edited by Thomas A. Lee, Jr, and Carlos Navarrete, pp. 219–222. New World Archaeological Foundation, Brigham Young University, Provo, Utah.

Finsten, Laura

1996   Periphery and Frontier in Southern Mexico: The Mixtec Sierra in Highland Oaxaca. In *Pre-Columbian World Systems*, edited by Peter N. Peregrine and Gary M. Feinman, pp. 77–96. Prehistory Press, Madison, Wisconsin.

Flannery, Kent V., and Joyce Marcus

1994   *Early Formative Pottery of the Valley of Oaxaca, Mexico*. Memoirs No. 27, Museum of Anthropology, University of Michigan, Ann Arbor.

Frank, Andre Gunder, and Barry K. Gills (editors)

1993   *The World System: Five Hundred Years or Five Thousand?* Routledge, London.

Gasco, Janine

2003   Soconusco. In *The Postclassic Mesoamerican World*, edited by Michael E. Smith and Frances F. Berdan, pp. 282–296. The University of Utah Press, Salt Lake City.

Gasco, Janine, and Frances F. Berdan
  2003   International Trade Centers. In *The Postclassic Mesoamerican World*, edited by
          Michael E. Smith and Frances F. Berdan, pp. 109–116. The University of
          Utah Press, Salt Lake City.
Gregory, Chris A.
  1982   *Gifts and Commodities*. Academic Press, New York.
Hall, Barbara Ann
  1997   Spindle Whorls and Cotton Production at Middle Classic Matacapan and in
          the Gulf Lowlands. In *Olmec to Aztec: Settlement Patterns in the Ancient Gulf
          Lowlands*, edited by Barbara L. Stark and Philip J. Arnold III, pp. 115–135.
          The University of Arizona Press, Tucson.
Hassig, Ross
  1985   *Trade, Tribute, and Transportation: The Sixteenth Century Political Economy of the
          Valley of Mexico*. University of Oklahoma Press, Norman.
Heredia Espinoza, Verenice Y.
  2005   The Nature of Governance in Secondary Centers of the Classic Period,
          Mixteca Alta, Oaxaca, Mexico. Unpublished Ph.D. dissertation, Department
          of Sociology and Anthropology, Purdue University.
Hewitt, William P., Marcus C. Winter, and David A. Peterson
  1987   Salt Production at Hierve El Agua, Oaxaca. *American Antiquity* 52:799–816.
Hicks, Frederic
  1994   Cloth in the Political Economy of the Aztec State. In *Economies and Polities
          in the Aztec Realm*, edited by Mary Hodge and Michael Smith, pp. 349–376.
          State University of New York, Albany.
Hirth, Kenneth
  1980   *Eastern Morelos and Teotihuacan: A Settlement Survey*. Vanderbilt University
          Publications in Anthropology No. 25, Nashville.
Hirth, Kenneth, and Jorge Angulo Villaseñor
  1981   Early State Expansion in Central Mexico: Teotihuacan in Morelos. *Journal of
          Field Archaeology* 8:135–150.
Hosler, Dorothy
  1988   Ancient West Mexican Metallurgy: South and Central American Origins and
          West Mexican Transformations. *American Anthropologist* 90:832–855.
  2003   Metal Production. In *The Postclassic Mesoamerican World*, edited by Michael
          E. Smith and Frances F. Berdan, pp. 159–171. The University of Utah Press,
          Salt Lake City.
Kepecs, Susan M.
  1999   The Political Economy of Chikinchel, Yucatán, Mexico: A Diachronic
          Analysis from the Prehispanic Era through the Age of Spanish Administration.
          Unpublished Ph.D. dissertation, Department of Anthropology, University
          of Wisconsin, Madison.

2003   Salt Sources and Production. In *The Postclassic Mesoamerican World*, edited by Michael E. Smith and Frances F. Berdan, pp. 126–130. The University of Utah Press, Salt Lake City.

King, Mary Elizabeth
1979   The Prehistoric Textile Industry of Mesoamerica. In *The Junius B. Bird Pre-Columbian Textile Conference*, edited by Ann Pollard Rowe, Elizabeth P. Benson, and Anne-Louise Schaffer, pp. 265–278. The Textile Museum and Dumbarton Oaks, Washington, D.C.

Kirkby, Anne V.T.
1973   *The Use of Land and Water Resources in the Past and Present Valley of Oaxaca, Mexico*. Memoirs No. 5, Museum of Anthropology, The University of Michigan, Ann Arbor.

Kolb, Charles C.
1986   Commercial Aspects of Classic Teotihuacan Period 'Thin Orange' Wares. In *Research in Economic Anthropology*, Supplement 2, edited by Barry L. Isaac, pp. 155–206. JAI Press, Greenwich.

Kowalewski, Stephen A., Gary M. Feinman, Laura M. Finsten, Richard E. Blanton, and Linda M. Nicholas
1989   *Monte Albán's Hinterland, Part II: Prehispanic Settlement Patterns in Tlacolula, Etla, and Ocotlán, the Valley of Oaxaca, Mexico*. Memoirs No. 23, Museum of Anthropology, University of Michigan, Ann Arbor.

MacKinnon, J. Jefferson, and Susan M. Kepecs
1989   Prehispanic Saltmaking in Belize: New Evidence. *American Antiquity* 54:522–533.

MacNeish, Richard S., Antoinette Nelken-Terner, and Irmgard W. Johnson
1967   *The Prehistory of the Tehuacan Valley, Volume 2: Nonceramic Artifacts*. University of Texas Press, Austin.

McAnany, Patricia A.
2004   Appropriative Economies: Labor Obligations and Luxury Goods in Ancient Maya Societies. In *Archaeological Perspectives on Political Economies*, edited by Gary M. Feinman and Linda M. Nicholas, pp. 145–166. The University of Utah Press, Salt Lake City.

McAnany, Patricia A., Ben S. Thomas, Steven Morandi, Polly A. Peterson, and Eleanor Harrison
2002   Praise the Ajaw and Pass the Kakaw: Xibun Maya and the Political Economy of Cacao. In *Ancient Maya Political Economies*, edited by Marilyn A. Masson and David A. Freidel, pp. 123-139. Altamira Press, Walnut Creek.

McCracken, Grant
1988   *Culture and Consumption: New Approaches to the Symbolic Character of Consumer Goods and Activities*. Indiana University Press, Bloomington.

Millon, René

1955   *When Money Grew on Trees: A Study of Cacao in Ancient Mesoamerica*. Ph.D. dissertation, Columbia University. University Microfilms, Ann Arbor.

1973   *Urbanization at Teotihuacan, Mexico, Vol. 1, The Teotihuacan Map, Part 1: Text*. University of Texas Press, Austin.

1992   Teotihuacan Studies: From 1950 to 1990 and Beyond. In *Art, Ideology, and the City of Teotihuacan*, edited by Janet Katherine Berlo, pp. 339–419. Dumbarton Oaks Research Library and Collection, Washington, D.C.

Mintz, Sidney

1985   *Sweetness and Power: The Place of Sugar in Modern History*. Penguin Books, New York.

Moholy-Nagy, Hattula

2003   *The Artifacts of Tikal: Utilitarian Artifacts and Unworked Material*. Tikal Report No. 27 Part B, Museum of Archaeology and Anthropology, University of Pennsylvania, Philadelphia.

Neff, Hector

1989   Origins of Plumbate Pottery Production. In *Ancient Trade and Tribute: Economies of the Soconusco Region of Mesoamerica*, edited by Barbara Voorhies, pp. 175–193. University of Utah Press, Salt Lake City.

Nobel, Park S.

1994   *Remarkable Agaves and Cacti*. Oxford University Press, New York.

Parsons, Jeffrey R.

2001   *The Last Saltmakers of Nexquipayac, Mexico: An Archaeological Ethnography*, Anthropological Papers No. 92, Museum of Anthropology, University of Michigan, Ann Arbor.

Parsons, Jeffrey R., and Mary H. Parsons

1990   *Maguey Utilization in Highland Central Mexico*. Anthropological Papers No. 82, Museum of Anthropology, University of Michigan, Ann Arbor.

Pasztory, Esther

1992   Abstraction and the Rise of a Utopian State at Teotihuacan. In *Art, Ideology, and the City of Teotihuacan*, edited by Janet Catherine Berlo, pp. 281–320. Dumbarton Oaks Research Library and Collection, Washington D.C.

1997   *Teotihuacan: An Experiment in Living*. University of Oklahoma Press, Norman.

Peregrine, Peter N.

1992   *Mississippian Evolution: A World-System Perspective*. Prehistory Press, Madison.

Peregrine, Peter N., and Gary M. Feinman, editors

1996   *Pre-Columbian World Systems*. Prehistory Press, Madison.

Peterson, David A.

1976   *Ancient Commerce*. Ph.D. dissertation, State University of New York at Binghamton. University Microfilms, Ann Arbor.

Pires-Ferreira, Jane W.

1975   *Formative Mesoamerican Exchange Networks with Special Reference to the Valley of Oaxaca*. Memoirs No. 7, Museum of Anthropology, University of Michigan, Ann Arbor.

Rattray, Evelyn C.

1988   Un taller de cerámica anaranjada San Martín en Teotihuacan. In *Ensayos de alfarería prehispánica e histórica de Mesoamerica: Homenaje a Eduardo Noguera Auza*, edited by M. C. Serra Puche and C. Navarette, pp. 249–266. Instituto de Investigaciones Antropológicas, Universidad Nacional Autónoma de México, Mexico, D.F.

Rice, Prudence M.

1981   Evolution of Specialized Pottery Production: A Trial Model. *Current Anthropology* 22:219–240.

Sahagún, Fray Bernardino de

1961   *Florentine Codex: General History of the Things of New Spain, Book 10: The People*, translated by Charles Dibble and Arthur J.O. Anderson. The School of American Research and the University of Utah Press, Salt Lake City.

Sahlins, Marshall

1976   *Culture and Practical Reason*. The University of Chicago Press, Chicago.

1994   Cosmologies of Capitalism: The Trans-Pacific Sector of 'The World System.' In *Culture/Power/History: A Reader in Contemporary Social Theory*, edited by Nicholas Dirks, Geoff Eley, and Sherry Ortner, pp. 412–456. Princeton University Press, Princeton.

Saindon, Jacqueline

1977   Cotton Production and Exchange in Mexico 1427-1580. Master's thesis, Department of Anthropology, Hunter College, New York.

Santley, Robert

1983   Obsidian Trade and Teotihuacan Influence in Mesoamerica. In *Interdisciplinary Approaches to the Study of Highland-Lowland Interaction*, edited by Arthur Miller, pp. 69–123. Dumbarton Oaks Library and Collection, Washington, D.C.

1984   Obsidian Exchange, Economic Stratification, and the Evolution of Complex Society in the Basin of Mexico. In *Trade and Exchange in Early Mesoamerica*, edited by Kenneth G. Hirth, pp. 43–86. University of New Mexico Press, Albuquerque.

1989   Obsidian Working, Long-Distance Exchange, and the Teotihuacan Presence on the South Gulf Coast. In *Mesoamerica After the Decline of Teotihuacan, A. D. 700-900*, edited by Richard A. Diehl and Janet Catherine Berlo, pp. 131–152. Dumbarton Oaks Research Library and Collection, Washington, D.C.

Santley, Robert S., and Rani T. Alexander

1992   The Political Economy of Core-Periphery Systems. In *Resources, Power, and Interregional Interaction*, edited by Edward M. Schortman and Patricia A. Urban, pp. 23–50. Plenum Press, New York.

Santley, Robert S., Philip J. Arnold III, and Christopher A. Pool

1993   Craft Specialization, Refuse Disposal, and the Creation of Archaeological Records in Prehispanic Mesoamerica. In *Prehispanic Domestic Units in Western Mesoamerica*, edited by Robert S. Santley and Kenneth G. Hirth, pp. 37–66. CRC Press, Boca Raton, Florida.

Schneider, Jane

1977   Was There a Pre-capitalist World-System? *Peasant Studies* 6:20–29.

1978   Peacocks and Penguins: The Political Economy of European Cloth and Colors. *American Ethnologist* 5:413–448.

1987   The Anthropology of Cloth. *Annual Review of Anthropology* 16:409–448.

Schortman, Edward, and Patricia Urban (editors)

1992   *Resources, Power, and Interregional Interaction*. Plenum, New York.

Smith, Michael E.

2003a   Key Commodities. In *The Postclassic Mesoamerican World*, edited by Michael E. Smith and Frances F. Berdan, pp. 117–125. The University of Utah Press, Salt Lake City.

2003b   *The Aztecs*. 2nd ed. Blackwell, Oxford.

Smith, Michael E., and Frances F. Berdan

2003   Postclassic Mesoamerica. In *The Postclassic Mesoamerican World*, edited by Michael E. Smith and Frances F. Berdan, pp. 3–13. The University of Utah Press, Salt Lake City.

Smith, Michael E., and Frances F. Berdan (editors)

2003   *The Postclassic Mesoamerican World*. The University of Utah Press, Salt Lake City.

Smith, Michael, and Kenneth Hirth

1988   The Development of Cotton-Spinning Technology in Western Morelos. *Journal of Field Archaeology* 15:349–358.

Smith, Michael, and Cynthia M. Heath-Smith

1982   Waves of Influence in Postclassic Mesoamerica? A Critique of the Mixteca-Puebla Concept. *Anthropology* 4:15–50.

Spence, Michael W.

1967   The Obsidian Industry of Teotihuacan. *American Antiquity* 32:507–514.

1981   Obsidian Production and the State in Teotihuacan. *American Antiquity* 46:769–788.

1984   Craft Production and Polity in Early Teotihuacan. In *Trade and Exchange in Early Mesoamerica*, edited by Kenneth G. Hirth, pp. 87–114. University of New Mexico Press, Albuquerque.

1985   Specialized Production in Rural Aztec Society: Obsidian Workshops of the Teotihuacan Valley. In *Contributions to the Archaeology and Ethnohistory of Greater Mesoamerica*, edited by William J. Folan, pp. 76–125. Southern Illinois University Press, Carbondale.

Spence, Michael W., and Jeffrey R. Parsons
   1972   Prehispanic Obsidian Exploitation in Central Mexico: A Preliminary Synthesis. In *Miscellaneous Studies in Mexican Prehistory*, by Michael W. Spence, Jeffrey R. Parsons, and Mary Hrones Parsons, pp. 1–43. Anthropological Papers No. 45, Museum of Anthropology, University of Michigan, Ann Arbor.

Stark, Barbara
   1990   The Gulf Coast and the Central Highlands of Mexico: Alternative Models for Interaction. *Research in Economic Anthropology* 12:243–285.

Stark, Barbara, Lynette Heller, and Michael Ohnersorgen
   1998   People with Cloth: Mesoamerican Economic Change from the Perspective of Cotton in South-Central Veracruz. *Latin American Antiquity* 9:7–36.

Stein, Gil J.
   2002   From Passive Periphery to Active Agents: Emerging Perspectives in the Archaeology of Interregional Interaction. *American Anthropologist* 104:903–916.

Tolstoy, Paul
   1971   Utilitarian Artifacts of Central Mexico. In *Handbook of Middle American Indians, Vol. 10: Archaeology of Northern Mesoamerica, Part 1*, edited by Gordon F. Ekholm and Ignacio Bernal, pp. 270–96. University of Texas Press, Austin.

Wallerstein, Immanuel
   1974   *The Modern World-System: Capitalist Agriculture and the Origins of the European World-Economy in the Sixteenth Century*. Academic Press, New York.

Wallert, Arie
   1997   The Analysis of Dyestuffs on Historical Textiles from Mexico. In *The Unbroken Thread: Conserving the Textile Traditions of Oaxaca*, pp. 57–86. The Getty Conservation Institute, Los Angeles.

Wengrow, David
   2001   The Evolution of Simplicity: Aesthetic Labor and Social Change in the Neolithic Near East. *World Archaeology* 33:168–188.

Whitecotton, Joseph W.
   1992   Culture and Exchange in Postclassic Oaxaca: A World-System Perspective. In *Resources, Power, and Interregional Interaction*, edited by Edward M. Schortman and Patricia A. Urban, pp. 51–74. Plenum Press, New York.

Winter, Marcus, and William O. Payne
   1976   Hornos para cerámica hallados en Monte Albán. *Boletin del Instituto Nacional de Antropología e Historia* 16:37–40.

Woolf, Greg
   1990   World-Systems Analysis and the Roman Empire. *Journal of Roman Archaeology* 3:44-58.

Young, Allen M.
   1994   *The Chocolate Tree: A Natural History of Cacao*. Smithsonian Institution Press, Washington, D. C.

THE ACHIEVEMENTS OF AND PROSPECTS FOR SURVEY ARCHAEOLOGY

RICHARD E. BLANTON

Purdue University

"The most prolific and widely used means of generating new data in the field of archaeology is now survey…" (Renfrew 2003:313).

Full-coverage regional archaeological survey, derived from the method developed by Jeffrey Parsons and others in the Basin of Mexico, has been among the most important sources of new archaeological knowledge about pre-Hispanic Mesoamerica and is now finding acceptance in other world areas. The chapters in this book epitomize many reasons for its notable success. The research productivity of survey archaeology and its diffusion outward from the Basin of Mexico are attributable to several factors. For one, it is often a source of unanticipated findings leading us to new and productive research questions. Some of these are evident in this book and are highlighted below. Secondly, while the Basin of Mexico survey method had its origins in the surge of cultural materialist theory of the 1950s, 60s, and 70s, it has persisted as a consistent contributor of relevant data and new insights in the face of archaeology's rethinking of both its research agenda and its scientific epistemology. Finally, the availability of survey data has proven timely in light of the growing urgency concerning site conservation and preservation, by providing regional planners with rich inventories of regional cultural resources (e.g., Cherry 2003:155–159).

TOWARD A MORE HOLISTIC ANTHROPOLOGICAL ARCHAEOLOGY

In multiple ways, since its beginnings some 40 years ago, regional archaeological research based on full-coverage survey has transcended its original goals to find relevance in relation to research problems not anticipated by its founders. A primary impetus for the development of a regional survey method was to get "beyond the site" to address the population density and food production variables given causal priority in cultural materialist theories of sociocultural evolutionary change (e.g., Logan and Sanders 1976). But survey archaeology had traction beyond cultural materialist theory because what we found pushed us toward a more holistic and less materialist anthropological enterprise. As one example, the data resulting from survey could transcend resource and population variables to provide information pertinent to understanding behavioral regions and their changes. Hence, the goals of archaeological survey converged with those of other regionally-oriented disciplines including cultural geography and regional analysis in cultural anthropology (Skinner 1964; cf. Smith 1976). Regional analysis provided survey archaeology with an apposite vocabulary for multiscalar spatial organization, pushed its research agenda toward issues such as market system evolution and other aspects of central place development and rural-urban interactions, and provided a suite of spatial analytical methods such as the rank-size measures used in the chapter by Drennan and Peterson. And survey methods continue to progress. Geographical Positioning Systems allow for more efficiencies in data collection in the field. Managing very large regional data sets is facilitated, and more sophisticated multivariate spatial analyses are made possible by applying the methods of Geographical Information Systems to regional archaeological data (Aldenderfer and Maschner 1996; cf. Balkansky et al. 2000).

In addition to its ability to absorb a rich new vocabulary and methodology from regional analysis and GIS, in other ways, archaeological survey has exceeded its original goals because survey has resulted in unanticipated discoveries pointing us to new questions and lines of research. For example, full-coverage survey was developed largely to estimate regional population densities and to document the causal role of continuous population growth in social and subsistence change (Sanders et al. 1979:364). While full-coverage survey remains the single most important method for the reconstruction of long-term population histories of premodern periods (e.g., Kowalewski 2003), surveys discovered complex and variable population histories not anticipated by cultural materialists. For example, while cultural materialists predicted linear growth based primarily on a continuous surplus of births over deaths, surveys identified migration as a key demographic process that could be linked to important instances of social change including the early growth phases at Teotihuacan and Monte Albán (Blanton et al. 1982:41; Parsons 1968; cf. Blanton 2004a:214–215, 227). Research projects such as the one reported on in the Spence, White, Rattray, and Longstaffe chapter have developed out of these kinds of demographic insights. The study of boundary phenomena, not always well studied or properly theorized in archaeology (Lightfoot and Martinez 1995), got a boost from regional archaeological research, especially where surveys extending over thousands of square kilometers discovered boundaries and their changes over time (e.g. Balkansky et al. 2000; Finsten 1999). The discovery of boundaries within and between regional systems posed new questions about social processes on the margins and their possible roles in sociocultural change. Elizabeth Brumfiel's chapter, stimulated by findings of the Basin of Mexico survey, uses the regional data as a starting point to address boundary formation in relation to politics, exchange, and ethnogenesis during the Late Postclassic Period (cf. Kowalewski et al. 1983).

Reflecting its cultural materialist origins, food production and related technologies remain among the key analytical topics for archaeological survey research, but, again, survey data revealed other significant forms of rural and urban production, including the salt, fiber, and cloth highlighted in several chapters in this book. Jeffrey and Mary Parsons have been leaders in drawing attention to these diverse productive activities (J. Parsons 2001; Parsons and Parsons 1990; M. Parsons 1972, 1975). Susan Evans's chapter continues this line of research, addressing the consequences of maguey cultivation and maguey cloth production for gender relations in household economy. Similarly, Feinman and Nicholas's chapter addresses the economic significance of a xerophytic crop complex in more arid parts of the Valley of Oaxaca. The chapter by Blanton, Fargher, and Heredia Espinoza highlights the powerful transformative consequences for demography, agroecology, commerce, and world-system growth of changes in the production, distribution, and consumption of goods such as decorated cloth and cacao, which served primarily to encode social action with symbolic meaning. These chapters typify ways in which survey archaeology can contribute to an anthropologically holistic archaeology whose aims overlap with a broader social science literature that addresses the interplay of gender, household, market, polity, world-system, and culture in the evolution of social complexity.

REGIONAL SURVEYS AND SCIENTIFIC ARCHAEOLOGY

Archaeological research executed at multiple scales, including the regional scale, has contributed to change in archaeological theory and epistemology (e.g., Cherry 2003). Although regional survey method was not developed by cultural materialists with theory testing in mind, the rigorous methodology of full-coverage survey, originated after a lengthy process of trial and error as detailed in the chapter by Charlton and Nichols, provided data that allowed for a critical evaluation of cultural materialist theory (e.g., Blanton 2004b). Questions about the causal roles of population pressure and irrigation management followed quickly on the application of full-coverage survey method (e.g., Millon 1973:47–49; Nicholas 1989; cf. Adams 1965). As a result, the systematic survey method envisioned by the Basin of Mexico researchers has matured beyond serving a "cultural materialist way of knowing" (from Harris [1979:29]) to become an important contributor to a scientific archaeology epistemologically premised on the falsification of hypothesis and theory, the gold standard of contemporary scientific practice (e.g., Blanton 1990; Feinman and Nicholas 1988).

Regional survey also contributes to the development of scientific practice through its potential for comparative analysis (Alcock and Cherry 2004). While neoevolutionist theory brought cross-cultural comparison back into the anthropology of mid-twentieth century, its early practitioners (e.g., Service 1975) were limited by their sparse and largely qualitative comparative methods. Systematic, full-coverage survey method makes possible reliable and valid comparison across time periods, regions, cultures, and even whole civilizations, built on a foundation of data collected by archaeologists working in different regions but sharing both problem orientation and method (cf., Blanton 2004a; Cherry 2003:150). Jeffrey Parsons and other archaeologists not only developed an approach suitable for the study of regions, they also helped to promulgate it through their publications that describe its methods and merits (e.g., Fish and Kowaleski 1990). Carla Sinopoli's survey at Vijayanagara, described in her chapter, is one example of a research project that was inspired to apply regional survey method and its aims to local circumstances. While comparative research would benefit if we had many more systematic regional surveys in South Asia and elsewhere, already the results of this kind of work are impacting on theory by forcing us to rethink the rather structured, step-like deterministic evolutionary sequence of neoevolutionist theory. This kind of rethinking is evident in the results of the Upper Mantaro survey project completed by Jeffrey Parsons and in the ensuing multiscalar research described in Timothy Earle's chapter. From this work, we know that Tunanmarca polities were large (up to 20,000 people) but, unlike the prototypical chiefdoms of neoevolutionist theory, were comparatively lacking in "formal institutional order" or evidence of chiefly "ideological power." The chapter by Drennan and Peterson provides another view on chiefdom variability. Their comparison of chiefdoms in Inner Mongolia, the Valley of Oaxaca, and Colombia demonstrates cross-cultural differences in rates of change, patterns of population growth and density, degree of interhousehold production specialization, and degree of village-scale community development. They conclude that a perspective on chiefdoms that sees local communities (villages) as the necessary building blocks of more inclusive hierarchical organizations will not always apply, even in social formations approximately similar in scale and political complexity. These and other chapters in this book, all growing out of a methodology of regional archaeological survey shared across researchers and regions, challenge us to rethink what we mean by social complexity and how we think about its causes, and from this, we invigorate our discipline.

REFERENCES CITED

Adams, Robert Mc.C.
   1965   *Land Behind Baghdad: A History of Settlement on the Diyala Plains.* University of Chicago Press, Chicago.
Alcock, Susan E., and John F. Cherry (editors)
   2004   *Side-by-Side Survey: Comparative Regional Studies in the Mediterranean World.* Oxbow Books, Oxford.
Aldenderfer, Mark S., and Herbert D. G. Maschner (editors)
   1996   *Anthropology, Space, and Geographic Information Systems.* Oxford University Press, Oxford.
Balkansky, Andrew K., Stephen A. Kowalewski, Verónica Pérez Rodriguez, Thomas J. Pluckhahn, Charlotte A. Smith, Laura R. Stiver, Dmitri Beliaev, John F. Chamblee, Verenice Y. Heredia Espinoza, and Roberto Santos Pérez
   2000   Archaeological Survey in the Mixteca Alta of Oaxaca, Mexico. *Journal of Field Archaeology* 27:365–389.
Blanton, Richard E.
   1990   Theory and Practice in Mesoamerican Archaeology: A Comparison of Two Modes of Scientific Inquiry. In *Debating Oaxaca Archaeology,* edited by Joyce Marcus, pp. 1–16. Anthropological Papers No. 84, Museum of Anthropology, University of Michigan, Ann Arbor.
   2004a   A Comparative Perspective on Settlement Pattern and Population Change in Mesoamerican and Mediterranean Civilizations. In *Side-by-Side Survey: Comparative Regional Studies in the Mediterranean World,* edited by Susan E. Alcock and John F. Cherry, pp. 206–242. Oxbow Books, Oxford.
   2004b   Prologue to the Percheron Press Edition. In *Monte Albán: Settlement Patterns at the Ancient Zapotec Capital.* Reprinted by Percheron Press, Clinton Corners, New York.
Blanton, Richard E., Stephen Kowalewski, Gary M. Feinman, and Jill Appel
   1982   *Monte Albán's Hinterland, Part I: The Prehispanic Settlement Patterns of the Central and Southern Parts of the Valley of Oaxaca, Mexico.* Memoirs No. 15, Museum of Anthropology, University of Michigan, Ann Arbor.
Cherry, John F.
   2003   Archaeology Beyond the Site: Regional Survey and its Future. In *Theory and Practice in Mediterranean Archaeology: Old World and New World Perspectives,* edited by John K. Papadopoulas and Richard M. Leventhal, pp.137–159.

Cotsen Advanced Seminars 1, The Cotsen Institute of Archaeology, University of California, Los Angeles.

Feinman, Gary M., and Linda M. Nicholas

1988   Comment on William T. Sanders and Deborah L. Nichols, Ecological Theory and Cultural Evolution in the Valley of Oaxaca. *Current Anthropology* 29:55–57.

Finsten, Laura

1996   Frontier and Periphery in Southern Mexico: The Mixtec Sierra in Highland Oaxaca. In *Pre-Columbian World Systems*, edited by Peter N. Peregrine and Gary M. Feinman, pp. 77–95. Prehistory Press, Madison, Wisconsin.

Fish, Suzanne K., and Stephen A. Kowalewski (editors)

1989   *The Archaeology of Regions: A Case for Full-Coverage Survey.* Smithsonian Institution Press, Washington, D.C.

Harris, Marvin

1979   *Cultural Materialism: The Struggle for a Science of Culture.* Vintage Books, New York.

Kowalewski, Stephen A.

2003   Scale and the Explanation of Demographic Change: 3,500 Years in the Valley of Oaxaca. *American Anthropologist* 105:313–325.

Kowalewski, Stephen A., Richard E. Blanton, Gary M. Feinman, and Laura Finsten

1983   Boundaries, Scale, and Internal Organization. *Journal of Anthropological Archaeology* 2:32–56.

Lightfoot, Kent G., and Antoinette Martinez

1995   Frontiers and Boundaries in Archaeological Perspective. *Annual Review of Anthropology* 24:471–492.

Logan, Michael H., and William T. Sanders

1976   The Model. In *The Valley of Mexico: Studies in Pre-Hispanic Ecology and Society*, edited by Eric R. Wolf, pp. 31–58. University of New Mexico Press, Albuquerque.

Millon, René

1973   *Urbanization at Teotihuacan, Mexico, Vol. 1, The Teotihuacan Map, Part 1: Text.* University of Texas Press, Austin.

Nicholas, Linda M.

1989   Land Use in Prehispanic Oaxaca. In *Monte Albán's Hinterland, Part II: Prehispanic Settlement Patterns in Tlacolula, Etla, and Ocotlán, the Valley of Oaxaca, Mexico*, edited by Stephen A. Kowalewski, Gary M. Feinman, Laura Finsten, Richard E. Blanton, and Linda Nicholas, pp. 449–506. Memoirs No. 23, Museum of Anthropology, University of Michigan, Ann Arbor.

Parsons, Jeffrey R.

1968   Teotihuacan, Mexico, and its Impact on Regional Demography. *Science* 162:872–877.

2001   *The Last Saltmakers of Nexquipayac, Mexico: An Archaeological Ethnography.*
        Anthropological Papers No. 92, University of Michigan, Museum of
        Anthropology, Ann Arbor.

Parsons, Jeffrey R., and Mary H. Parsons

1990   *Maguey Utilization in Highland Central Mexico.* Anthropological Papers No.
        82, Museum of Anthropology, University of Michigan, Ann Arbor.

Parsons, Mary H.

1972   Spindle Whorls From the Teotihuacan Valley, Mexico. In *Miscellaneous Studies
        in Mexican Prehistory*, by Michael W. Spence, Jeffrey R. Parsons, and Mary
        Hrones Parsons, pp. 45–80. Anthropological Papers No. 45, Museum of
        Anthropology, University of Michigan, Ann Arbor.

1975   The Distribution of Late Postclassic Spindle Whorls in the Valley of Mexico.
        American Antiquity 40:207–215.

Renfrew, Colin

2003   Retrospect and Prospect: Mediterranean Archaeology in a New Millennium.
        In *Theory and Practice in Mediterranean Archaeology: Old World and New World
        Perspectives*, edited by John K. Papadopoulos and Richard M. Leventhal, pp.
        311–318. Cotsen Advanced Seminars 1, The Cotsen Institute of Archaeology,
        University of California, Los Angeles.

Sanders, William T., Jeffrey R. Parsons, and Robert S. Santley

1979   *The Basin of Mexico: Ecological Processes in the Evolution of a Civilization.*
        Academic Press, New York.

Service, Elman R.

1975   *Origins of the State and Civilization: The Process of Cultural Evolution.* W. W.
        Norton and Company, New York.

Skinner, G. William

1964   Marketing and Social Structure in Rural China, Part I. *Journal of Asian Studies*
        24:3–43.

Smith, Carol A. (editor)

1976   *Regional Analysis.* 2 Vols. Academic Press, New York.

Author Index

Subject Index